THE MAN WHO INVENTED AZTEC CRYSTAL SKULLS

THE MAN WHO INVENTED AZTEC CRYSTAL SKULLS

The Adventures of Eugène Boban

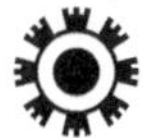

Jane MacLaren Walsh and Brett Topping

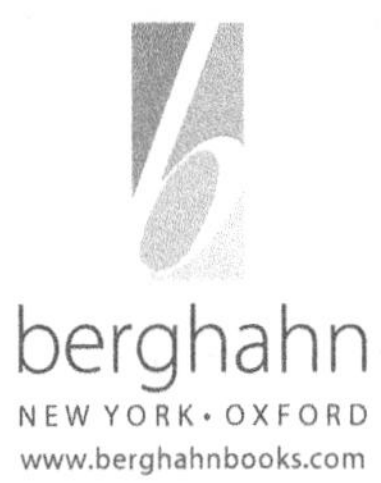

berghahn

NEW YORK · OXFORD
www.berghahnbooks.com

First published in 2019 by
Berghahn Books
www.berghahnbooks.com

Library of Congress Cataloging-in-Publication Data
Names: Walsh, Jane MacLaren, author. | Topping, Brett, 1947- author.
Title: The Man Who Invented Aztec Crystal Skulls: The Adventures of Eugène
  Boban / Jane MacLaren Walsh and Brett Topping.
Other titles: Adventures of Eugène Boban
Description: First edition. | New York: Berghahn Books, [2019] | Includes
  bibliographical references.
Identifiers: LCCN 2018047588 (print) | LCCN 2018048818 (ebook) | ISBN
  9781789200966 (ebook) | ISBN 9781789200959 (hardback: alk. paper)
Subjects: LCSH: Boban, Eugène. | Archaeologists--Biography. | Crystal
  skulls--History. | French--Mexico--Biography. |
  Mexico--Antiquities--Forgeries. | Swindlers and swindling--Biography. |
  Art dealers--Biography. | Archaeology--Latin America--Miscellanea. | Latin
  America--Antiquities--Collectors and collecting--History.
Classification: LCC CC115.B59 (ebook) | LCC CC115.B59 W35 2019 (print) | DDC
  930.1092 [B] --dc23
LC record available at https://lccn.loc.gov/2018047588

British Library Cataloguing in Publication Data
A catalogue record for this book is available from the British Library

ISBN 978-1-78920-095-9 hardback
ISBN 978-1-78920-478-0 paperback
ISBN 978-1-78920-096-6 ebook

Contents

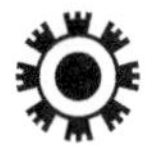

Illustrations

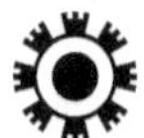

ACKNOWLEDGMENTS

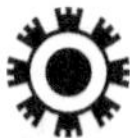

I am indebted to a long list of people who assisted and guided me during my research into the life and career of Eugène Boban. First and foremost, I am grateful to my coauthor and partner, Brett Topping, who organized and edited the book. She also provided much of the historical research relating to the California Gold Rush, France in the nineteenth century, the Siege of Paris, and the terrible events of the Paris Commune revolt. Her research yielded invaluable context for Boban's story. Her insights helped me better appreciate his achievements and idiosyncrasies.

When I began my research for an article about crystal skulls in museum collections and first encountered Eugène Boban's name, I was helped by two good friends, the late Robert von Kaupp and Randall Dean. They translated a number of Boban's letters and articles for me, as my reading comprehension of French was negligible at the time.

I have enjoyed the friendship, advice, and guidance of a great number of people whom I have met through this project, particularly in Washington, DC, New York, Mexico City, London, and Paris. Elizabeth Carmichael's wonderful letter about the British Museum's crystal skull led me to the trail of Eugène Boban. I am very grateful to her and Tony Kitzinger for their encouragement, kindness, and friendship. Many people in the British Museum have shared expertise and information. Margaret Sax's pioneering work dating Mesopotamian cylinder seals introduced me to the use of scanning electron microscopy in the study of tool marks. Ian Freestone, Andrew Rankin, and Nigel Meeks generously shared their expertise. Philippa Glanville, formerly of the Victoria and Albert Museum, and her husband, Gordon Glanville, have for many years offered stimulating conversation, encouragement, and possible sources of information.

During my first visit to Paris, Sally McLendon and her late husband, William Sturtevant, a Smithsonian colleague, introduced me to Marie-France Fauvet-Berthelot at the Musée de l'Homme. She allowed me to examine the Boban/Pinart papers and would later invite me to research Boban's artifact collection, in particular the French crystal skull. I have worked closely with her ever since and have always been grateful for her generosity and kindness. Marie-France introduced me to anthropologist Eric Taladoire from the Sorbonne, who shared his work on a contemporary of Boban's, Dr. Jean-Baptiste Fuzier. Christine Lorre, a conservator at the Musée d'archéologie nationale, provided me with photographs that Boban had sent to Gabriel Mortillet. She also told me that Mortillet's papers were at the Universität de Saarlandes in Germany. Wolfgang Muller from that university later provided me with pdf images of Boban's correspondence with Mortillet.

A close friend, the late Claude François Baudez, encouraged and advised me, introducing me to a number of important people in France. One of these was Pascal Riviale, who was at the Musée d'Orsay when we first met and is now with the Archives nationales de France in Paris. He has written about Boban's career and helped me access his correspondence in the Bibliothèque nationale. I am especially grateful to Pascal and his wife, Frédérique, for their enthusiasm and many kindnesses. Claude also put me in contact with other colleagues and friends in France, including the historian and archivist Nadia Prevost Urkidi. Nadia introduced me to Armelle Le-Goff and Christiane Demeulenaere-Douyère of the Archives nationales, and the three of them shared their work on the papers of Colonel Louis Toussaint Doutrelaine. In addition, Christiane provided information she located in public archives on the Boban family, including birth, marriage, and death records. I greatly appreciate her help.

Pascal Riviale later introduced me to Christine Besson, curator at the Musée Pincé in Angers, which holds a small collection donated by Boban in 1869. Christine gave me complete access to the collections and the accompanying archive. She also put me in contact with Sylvain Bertoldi, the director of the municipal archives in Angers. He provided information about Boban's great-grandparents, grandparents, and aunts, all of whom lived in Angers during the eighteenth and nineteenth centuries.

At the Musée du quai Branly I have enjoyed the assistance of a number of colleagues and friends. In particular Fabienne de Pierrebourg, Paz Nuñez Regueiro, Andre Delpuech, Christophe Moulherat, and many others. I have also been fortunate to consult with Thomas Calligaro and Yvan Coquinot of the Louvre's C2RMF (Centre de Recherche et de Restauration des Musées de France).

In New York I have used extensively the archives held by the Hispanic Society of America. John O'Neill, the society's curator of manuscripts and rare books, has been exceedingly kind and helpful, allowing me complete access to Eugène Boban's papers. I am also indebted to the society's director, Mitchell A. Codding, and to Sharon Lorenzo, who first informed me of the existence of these papers at the Hispanic Society.

My thanks to Leonardo López Luján, director of the Museo del Templo Mayor in Mexico City, and his wife, Laura Filloy, conservator at the Museo Nacional de Antropología. They assisted me in myriad ways when I first went to Paris to do research on Boban's artifact collection, and Laura helped me obtain permission to publish several images from Mexico.

In Mexico City, Leopoldo Batres's great-granddaughter, Elvira Pruneda, provided me with some of Batres's correspondence. We had a fascinating conversation about him in Teotihuacan's restaurant, La Gruta. Teresa Matabuena Peláez and Maria Eugenia Ponce Alcocer of the Universidad Iberoamericana assisted in locating papers in the Porfirio Díaz collection.

In Italy I have been helped by several people who provided information on crystal skulls, including Annamaria Ippolito, Barbara Nepote, Enrica Pagella, Paola Ruffino, and Paola Cordera. Martin Berger in the Research Center for Material Culture in Leiden and Gerard van Bussel in the Welt Museum in Vienna have also been of great assistance.

I am grateful to Norman Hammond of Cambridge University, Adam Sellen of the Universidad de Mérida, and Javier Urcid of Brandeis University for many broad-ranging discussions. Melissa Mead of the University of Rochester provided insights into the career of Henry Ward. I am particularly indebted to Kate Ralston of the Getty Research Library in Los Angeles for access to Boban's photo albums. Many thanks also to Jacob Wainwright Love, James Hardin, Mary Sykes Wiley, Marie-Christine Bonzom, Basile Baudez, and Brian Jordan for their comments and suggestions.

Having worked at the Smithsonian Institution in Washington for more than four decades, I have enjoyed the friendship and invaluable assistance of a large number of people. I want to thank James Diloreto, Deborah Hull-Walski, James Krakker, Paula Fleming, Bruno Frohlich, Dave Rosenthal, Scott Whittaker, Tim Rose, and David Hunt from the National Museum of Natural History. I would like to thank Maggie Dittemore and Leslie Overstreet from the Smithsonian Libraries, as well as Ellen Alers and Pamela Henson of the Smithsonian Institution Archives. Pat Nietfield, formerly the collections manager at the National Museum of the American Indian, was always helpful.

Authors' Note

As a self-educated man, Eugène Boban had an improvised style of writing French. He used accents and punctuation erratically, often misspelled words, and did not always employ the most sophisticated terms. In recording his French writings in our notes, we have maintained as far as possible his original style, including, in some cases, his mistakes. Since we were working mostly from handwritten material, we may inadvertently have introduced some mistakes of our own. We have endeavored, however, to smooth out his language in our translations.

Abbreviations

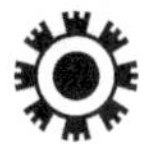

AD	Archives départementales
AGN	Archivo General de la Nación
AMM	Army Medical Museum
AMNH	American Museum of Natural History
AN	Archives nationales
BM	British Museum
BNF DMO	Bibliothèque nationale de France, Département des Manuscrits Occidentaux
CADN	Centre des Archives diplomatiques de Nantes
HSA	Hispanic Society of America
MNHN	Musée national d'histoire naturelle
MQB	Musée du quai Branly
NAA	National Anthropological Archives
SIA: RU	Smithsonian Institution Archives: Record Unit
UI CPD	Universidad iberoamericana, Mexico City, Colección Porfirio Díaz
USNM	United States National Museum

INTRODUCTION

On the Trail of Crystal Skulls

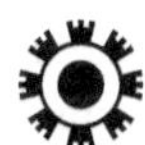

The human skull has been a source of fascination throughout history. The head is the most captivating feature of our anatomy, containing as it does the power center of the brain, which animates and regulates bodily functions and is the recording apparatus for all of our senses. The skull is a skeleton's most recognizable element. It is a symbol that has been used to convey such concepts as danger, mortality, conquest, forethought, and redemption.

The skull is multivalent in Christian iconography. At the foot of the cross, it represents all of humanity as personified by Adam. When shown in paintings of saints, it is a reminder of the brevity of life. Echoing this theme, sixteenth-century Dutch still lifes often feature skulls and insects nestled among exotic blooms and luxury items. Skulls were the most important element of memento mori, as a reminder of the need to be prepared for the afterlife. The skull and crossbones displayed by pirates was universally recognized as a threat of murder and mayhem.

In the Americas, the skull was an important feature of Aztec ceremonies in Mexico from the fourteenth to the sixteenth century. Captives and slaves who were sacrificed before the images of their gods had their hearts torn out, their bodies divided up for consumption, and their heads removed to be impaled and placed on skull racks. The Aztecs fashioned skulls out of stone to be architectural ornaments, carved images of deities wearing skulls on necklaces and belts, and occasionally painted them on pottery.

In the second half of the nineteenth century Aztec skulls carved from rock crystal appeared in museum collections on both sides of the Atlantic. They were much admired for the beauty of their translucent material and the evident skill with which they had been carved by ancient artisans using primitive stone tools. Increasing their exotic allure was the notion that they played some role in the bloody human sacrifices practiced by Aztec priests.

A rock crystal skull, sent through the US Postal Service, arrived at the Smithsonian Institution a number of years ago as an anonymous donation. The package had gone to the National Museum of American History. A handwritten note accompanying it said that it was an Aztec skull purchased in Mexico in 1960. The note also said that the skull had belonged to Porfirio Díaz, the dictator of Mexico from the late 1870s until 1910.

I entered the picture when Richard Ahlborn, a colleague at American History, called me. He knew I was the primary researcher on Mexican pre-Columbian archeology in the Smithsonian's Museum of Natural History. He asked me what I knew about crystal skulls, and I told him that the British Museum had a life-size crystal skull on exhibit which was said to be Aztec, as did the Musée de l'Homme in Paris, and that my own department in the National Museum of Natural History had once exhibited a small crystal skull as a fake. After a short discussion, he said, he wasn't sure what to do with it. "I'll take it!" I said, without giving it too much thought.

Richard delivered it the next day. It was surprisingly large, 10 inches in height—about the size of a football helmet—and heavy, weighing 31 pounds. It had been carved and hollowed out from milky white quartz. It had prominent teeth, deep eye sockets, and circular depressions at the temples. I asked for a cart to move it from the loading dock to my office. An archivist standing nearby jokingly warned, "Don't look it in the eye! It might be cursed."

Once I had gotten the skull upstairs, I examined it carefully. It was an impressive and interesting artifact, but did not look at all Aztec, or even pre-Columbian. It was much too big, the proportions were off, the teeth and circular depressions at the temples did not look right, and overall it seemed too rounded and polished. It went into a locked cabinet and I forgot about it for a while.

When a colleague asked me to write a book chapter about an unusual or problematic object in the Department of Anthropology's collection, the crystal skull came to mind. The Porfirio Díaz provenance was anecdotal, and the Aztec attribution seemed unlikely to me since no crystal skull had ever been found in an archeological excavation in Mexico. When the editors accepted my proposal, I began to concentrate my research on crystal skulls.

I first investigated the archival and published history of the two-inch crystal skull I knew about in the Smithsonian's collections. It came to the museum from Mexico in the nineteenth century as part of the Wilson Wilberforce Blake Collection, but it disappeared sometime in the 1970s after it was taken off exhibit. When Smithsonian geologist William Foshag examined this small skull in the 1950s, he determined that it had been carved and polished with modern lapidary equipment. Foshag had spent many years studying pre-Columbian carvings in jadeite and other hard stone and was extremely knowledgeable about carving and polishing techniques (Foshag 1957). He wrote on the catalog card that the skull was "definitely a fake, made on a lap wheel and polished with a wheel

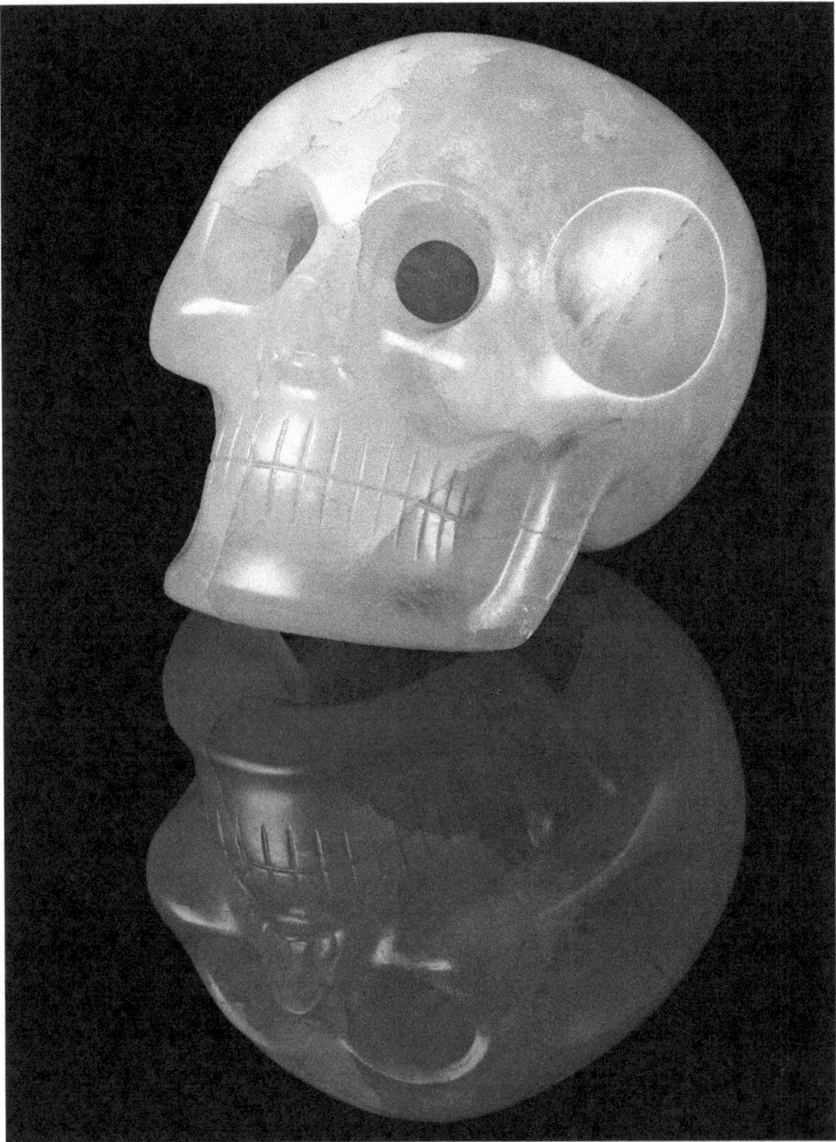

Figure 0.1 Smithsonian crystal skull. Photo by James Diloreto (National Museum of Natural History, Department of Anthropology, 562841).

buffer" (National Museum of Natural History, Department of Anthropology, cat. Card #98949 5/27/1952).

The collection accession file contained a sheaf of letters Blake had written to the Smithsonian curator, William Henry Holmes. Blake's letters were filled with journalistic details discussing archeological questions and general goings-on in Mexico City. One letter from 1886 passed on some juicy gossip about a "Frenchman named Boban," who had tried to sell a fake crystal skull to Mexico's Museo Nacional in partnership with Leopoldo Batres, the Mexican government's inspector of archeological monuments. This was the first time I encountered Boban's name.

I already knew that both the British Museum in London and the Musée de l'Homme in Paris had a large crystal skull in their collections, so I contacted Elizabeth Carmichael at the British Museum and Daniel Levine at the Musée de l'Homme requesting information about their skulls. Carmichael's response was full of interesting notes about the acquisition history of the British Museum crystal skulls—they had two—as well as comments on scientific studies performed on them since the 1960s. A copy of the original registration slip for the smaller skull indicated it might have been purchased in the 1860s, and the larger skull, which was the one I had known about, was purchased in November 1897 from Tiffany & Co. of New York, through George F. Kunz.

Daniel Levine's letter informed me that he believed the crystal skull was one of the most important artifacts in the museum's pre-Columbian holdings. A copy of the object's catalog card indicated that the skull was part of the Alphonse Pinart Collection, which had arrived in 1878, when the Musée d'Ethnographie du Trocadéro, France's national ethnographic museum and the Musée de l'Homme's predecessor, first opened to the public.

One fact stood out at this point in my research: all the crystal skulls I had identified in Europe's major museums seemed to have appeared within a thirty-year period, between the 1860s and the 1890s. This was true of the two Smithsonian crystal skulls as well. The small one from Blake was purchased in 1886 and the newly arrived, much larger skull would have surfaced during the same time period if it had, in fact, been part of the Porfirio Díaz Collection. Were they from a cache of ancient artifacts that someone had uncovered and slowly sold off or were they all fashioned by a nineteenth-century crystal carver who had some odd affinity for crania? I knew that at least one of them, the small Smithsonian skull examined by Foshag, had been carved with modern lapidary equipment, but what about the others? This trail was already becoming interesting.

Turning to the literature on crystal skulls, I consulted books, articles, and exhibition catalogs. The skulls were always described as amazing examples of pre-Columbian lapidary art, given that the carvers had worked only with stone tools. Rock crystal is quartz, a relatively hard stone—seven on the ten-point Mohs scale. It is extremely brittle, making it even more difficult to carve and prone to shattering when worked inexpertly.

William Foshag's assessment that the early Smithsonian skull had been carved with modern tools led me to consult published studies on faked pre-Columbian antiquities. One of the earliest scholarly investigations into the nature and problem of faked antiquities came from William Henry Holmes, a geologist, archeologist, and artist who served in numerous capacities at the Smithsonian Institution for more than six decades. In an 1886 article in the journal *Science*, he wrote about fake Mexican pre-Columbian artifacts that he believed were being sold in large quantities to the world's museums at the time.

Following in Holmes's footsteps, I focused my research on faked pre-Columbian artifacts, and soon found a 1982 compilation entitled *Falsifications and Misconstructions of Pre-Columbian Art*, published by Dumbarton Oaks Research Library and Collection in Washington, DC. The chapter "Three Aztec Masks of the God Xipe," written by Esther Pasztory, the noted art historian from Columbia University, provided an unexpected clue about the origins of the crystal skulls. One of the three stone masks she discussed, which she believed to be a fake, was part of the Alphonse Pinart Collection in the Musée de l'Homme. This was the same collection mentioned in Daniel Levine's letter about his museum's crystal skull. However, according to Pasztory, Pinart had not actually formed the collection himself—he had purchased it from a French antiquarian named Eugène Boban (Pasztory 1982: 94). The name immediately rang a bell, bringing to mind Blake's letter to Holmes naming Boban as an accomplice in the attempted sale of a fake crystal skull to Mexico's Museo Nacional (SIA 3/29/1886). Now it appeared that the crystal skull in France's foremost anthropological museum had originated with Boban! I would soon discover that the Pinart Collection contained a second, though much smaller, crystal skull, also purchased from Boban.

Another link between Boban and crystal skulls came from the catalog entry for the British Museum skull, which named George F. Kunz, a gemologist and vice president of Tiffany & Co., as the intermediary in this purchase. Also referenced on the catalog card was Kunz's book *Gems and Precious Stones*, published in 1890. In it he enumerated several artifacts in rock crystal then known to him. "Small skulls are in the Blake Collection at the United States National Museum [Smithsonian Institution], the Douglas Collection New York, The British Museum and the Trocadéro Museum. A large skull, now in the possession of George H. Sisson of New York, is very remarkable. . . . Little is known of its history and nothing of its origin. It was brought from Mexico by a Spanish Officer sometime before the French occupation of Mexico, and was sold to an English collector, at whose death it passed into the hands of E. Boban, of Paris, and then became the property of Mr. Sisson" (Kunz 1890: 284). Could the large crystal skull in the British Museum be the same one that had belonged to Sisson? If so, this meant that the London and Paris museums had gotten their crystal skulls from the same man, Eugène Boban. But how had the skull moved from Sisson to the British Museum's collection?

Delving deeper into Holmes's papers in the Smithsonian Institution Archives, I found an annotated sales catalog for an auction of Boban's ethnographic and archeological collection that took place in New York in December 1886. The catalog listed almost two thousand objects. Holmes had attended the auction and noted names and prices alongside most of the pre-Columbian artifacts, which were of particular interest to him. Some ceramic vessels, several of which he sketched, sold for between $5 and $10. A terra cotta group of three figurines, described as Maya Quiche gods, sold for $35, and a carved stone figure from Veracruz went for $46 (Leavitt 1886a: 22, 24, 27). Several small crystal skulls appear, and one of "natural size" is described.

According to Holmes's annotations, the natural-sized skull went for the highest price of anything in the catalog, being purchased for $950 by someone named Ellis. Further investigation revealed that a jeweler named J. L. Ellis had been a partner at Tiffany & Co., although he had retired from the firm by 1886 (Hannan 2008: 513). This meant that Tiffany's purchased this crystal skull at the Boban auction in New York City. In any case, as recorded by Kunz in his gem book, George H. Sisson, who made a fortune in mining ventures in Colorado and Arizona (Bancroft 1889: 734), owned the skull in 1890. In the mid-1890s Sisson either sold the skull back to Tiffany's or asked Kunz to sell it for him. The British Museum purchased it from Tiffany's, through Kunz, in 1897.

At this point almost all the crystal skulls I had identified—the large and small skulls at the Musée de l'Homme and the large skull at the British Museum—could be traced directly back to Eugène Boban. However, I still was unsure of their authenticity.

The opportunity to scientifically determine the authenticity of the skulls came from an unexpected source. As a result of my correspondence with the British Museum curator, Elizabeth Carmichael, an independent producer of documentaries contacted me, describing a television program about crystal skulls that he hoped to make for the BBC. Eventually this led us to plan a joint study of the crystal skulls in the British Museum, the Smithsonian Institution, the Musée de l'Homme, and possibly in a few private collections, filming the entire process.

Because we needed an example of carved rock crystal that we knew was definitively pre-Columbian as a basis of comparison with the skulls, I suggested that the documentary's producers contact the Instituto Nacional de Antropología e Historia (INAH) in Mexico City to request the loan of a rock crystal goblet that had been recovered from excavations at Monte Albán in Oaxaca, to use in the study. To my knowledge the goblet is the only large quartz or rock crystal object that has come from an archeological dig. It would give us an unquestionable example of pre-Columbian materials, procedures, and carving techniques to use as a yardstick for evaluating our array of crystal skulls.

After completing a couple days of filming at the Smithsonian, the production crew moved on to London to continue at the British Museum. Arriving at the Department of Scientific Research, located in an early nineteenth-century row house on Russell Square, I met with Elizabeth Carmichael and Margaret Sax, a specialist in prehistoric stone carving. She and her colleagues were poised to examine the two British Museum skulls and the large Smithsonian skull. Mexican archeologist Arturo Oliveros had brought the rock crystal goblet from Monte Albán. The goblet, insured for a million dollars, was placed on a long table in the center of the room next to the British Museum skulls and the Smithsonian skull, which dwarfed the other artifacts.

Margaret Sax had developed a method for studying tool marks left on carved stone from her work examining several thousand Mesopotamian cylinder seals dating from 3500 to 400 BC. First, she would look for residual tool marks on the seals under a light microscope. Then, to get a clearer view of the tool marks, she would take silicone molds of the incised areas of the seals and examine them using a high-powered scanning electron microscope (SEM). As the SEM beam scans the mold's surface, it generates an image of its topographical features. Sax was now prepared to try out her method on the crystal skulls in question.

Placing the super-sized Smithsonian skull under the light microscope was quite an undertaking. Sax had to stand on tiptoe to look through the lens, but within a short time she seemed certain about what she was seeing. Then she moved on to the two skulls in the British Museum's collections. Ultimately, after taking silicone molds and reviewing them under SEM, she determined that the two British Museum skulls and the Smithsonian skull had all been carved with rotary cutting tools. By analyzing the impressions of the tool marks replicated on the silicone molds, she could clearly demonstrate that all three crystal skulls had been carved and polished using modern technology. The remnant marks on the skulls did not resemble in the least those found on the pre-Columbian crystal goblet from Monte Albán. None of these skulls could possibly be Aztec.

The next task was to examine the crystal skulls Boban had sold to Alphonse Pinart. Since the Musée de l'Homme had refused to lend its skulls for the study, I flew to Paris, following our work at the British Museum, to at least have a close look at them. Although I thought that I had arranged to see them through my correspondence with Daniel Levine, upon my arrival at the Musée de l'Homme, I discovered that he had left for Mexico the previous day. Luckily mutual friends introduced me to Marie-France Fauvet-Berthelot, an archeologist who had worked at Copán in Honduras and at archeological sites in Mexico. She was then the museum's curator of pre-Columbian archeology. Fauvet-Berthelot directed me to the exhibit area, where I spent some time examining the larger crystal skull through its glass vitrine. She later showed me a small pamphlet entitled "Museo Científico," which advertised a private museum that Boban opened in Mexico City in the mid-1880s. The pamphlet's descriptions of the exhibit rooms included one where a crystal skull was on display. By then it had become clear to me that the entire crystal skull story revolved around Eugène Boban. But who was he?

In the early years of the twenty-first century, I read an article about Boban's career written by Pascal Riviale, a French historian who has focused on nineteenth-century archeological explorations in Latin America. His research gave me an entirely new perspective on Boban. According to Riviale, Boban corresponded with Max Uhle, a pioneer of Andean archeology and curator at the Royal Museum of Zoology, Anthropology and Archeology in Dresden, Germany; Enrico Giglioli, the director of the Royal Zoological Museum of Florence, Italy; Ernest T. Hamy, founding director of the Trocadéro; and many others—a veritable who's who of nineteenth-century museum curators. Up to that point I had no inkling that this man, whom I knew only through his association with crystal skulls, could have had business dealings with so many well-known European intellectuals, or that he sold artifacts to most of the important museums in Europe.

A few years later, Leonardo López Luján, a Mexican archeologist and friend, emailed me saying he was in Paris working with Marie-France Fauvet-Berthelot to create a catalog of the Musée de l'Homme's Aztec collection. He wondered what he should say about the crystal skulls. I decided the time was right to go to Paris to see what more I could learn about Boban through the collection he formed. Working with López Luján and Fauvet-Berthelot in the storage of the Musée de l'Homme during that time was enormously rewarding and enlightening. The Pinart/Boban collection was impressive, comprising some 2,400 artifacts. Seeing and handling it helped me appreciate Boban's broad expertise and inspired me to continue following his trail.

I later returned to Paris for further work on the collection and met with Pascal Riviale, who introduced me to Boban's correspondence at the Bibliothèque nationale. The library had five albums of letters sent to him over nearly four decades. Four albums have letters that he received from a variety of correspondents arranged in alphabetical order, while the fifth contains only letters from the French-Mexican industrialist Eugène Goupil arranged chronologically. Paging through the albums for the first time, I hoped at least to recognize the names of people and places, since my reading French was still quite limited.

The second album yielded several familiar names and even had letters written by the Smithsonian's William Henry Holmes. They were in English and were of great interest to me. A bit further on in the album I found several letters from George Kunz, including a note about retrieving a box for a skull—yet another confirmation that the British Museum skull originated with Boban.

After a few hours of reading through the albums, I had found quite a number of familiar Mexican, French, American, and German names. The letters provided a wealth of information about Boban, the business of archeology, and museum formation in the nineteenth century. Through his correspondence I learned much about his commercial activities—to whom he sold and with whom he traded, which museums purchased his artifacts, and how extensive his collections and knowledge were. However, only a few of these business letters yielded much information about the man himself.

The following year, thanks to Sharon Lorenzo, who was working on a dissertation on the famous Joseph Marius Alexis Aubin Collection of Mexican codices and painted manuscripts, I learned that there were fourteen boxes of Boban's personal papers at the Hispanic Society of America (HSA) in New York City. Arts patron and connoisseur Archer Huntington, who founded the society, had purchased the collection from a German bookseller in 1910. Boban had organized the papers in leather-bound boxes with gold embossed titles "Collection Boban," with individual headings such as "Mexican Antiquities," "Mexican Manuscripts," "Weapons and utensils," "Mexican civilization, indigenous literature," and "Myths and monuments." Reading through the thousands of pages in Boban's own hand has done much to fill out the picture of his collecting and dealing. Each box is packed with a welter of information, including copies of published articles, newspaper clippings, notes about artifacts, and personal reminiscences of his life, written on the back of business receipts and other scraps of paper. This trove of information has provided a few more details about the man and his life's trajectory living and working in France, the Unites States, and Mexico.

I found a kindred spirit in Boban. His writings in the Hispanic Society reveal a man who was passionate about collecting ancient artifacts and illuminating their meaning. His recollections of his idyllic life in Mexico struck a chord with me. I, too, spent much of my youth in Mexico City, studying and traveling throughout the country, falling in love with the land and the people. There is a saying that once the dust of Mexico has settled on your heart, you will never be happy in another place. Boban's life and career seem to corroborate that sentiment. Our shared love and appreciation of Mexico and its ancient cultures has generated an ongoing interest in discovering more about this intriguing and enigmatic man.

I

Caveat Emptor

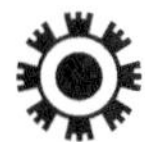

The nineteenth century was the Wild West of archeological and ethnographic collecting, fueled by the increasing ease of travel to remote places and a growing interest in ancient cultures. It was also a watershed in museum history and collections acquisition. Newly opened national museums in Europe and the Americas had public money to spend, museum collections to amass, and vitrines to fill. The goal was to acquire as many artifacts as possible from the greatest number of places in the least amount of time. Curators busily purchased objects from dealers, private collectors, and agents who lived among native peoples in far-flung places. They also frequently traded objects that were plentiful in their museum collections for others they judged to be rare.

The increased demand gave "a considerable money value to antiquities," in the words of the Smithsonian's curator of aboriginal pottery, William Henry Holmes. The added value of the artifacts, combined with the relative dearth of knowledge about archeology and ethnography at the time, led to "attempts, on the part of dishonest persons, to supply the market by fraudulent means" (Holmes 1886: 170). Worries about the prevalence of misattributed or faked artifacts gave rise to the expert—an individual with enough knowledge in a specific field to evaluate and authenticate objects entering private and museum collections. Still, tourist art and outright fakes became ever more pervasive.

Onto this scene came a minor figure destined to make major contributions to the field of pre-Columbian studies: Eugène Boban. This young Frenchman threw himself wholeheartedly into the chaotic world of collecting, trading, and dealing. He excavated and gathered artifacts, helped museums build collections, and became a recognized authority in Mexican archeology whose opinions were sought after by curators and collectors in Europe and the Americas. He also occasionally passed off fake objects as genuine, thereby confusing museum history for over a century.

Boban went so far as to invent a class of archeological artifact—the Aztec rock crystal skull. They were not copies or fake artifacts, since the Aztecs did not carve crystal skulls, as he was well aware. The skulls were beautiful and interesting objects, acquired through purchase or trade, for which he deliberately created a false identity.

Boban was able to sell "Aztec crystal skulls" because most people knew very little about pre-Columbian Mexican archeology, while he knew a lot. Despite coming from a family of tailors, seamstresses, artisans, and laundresses, he had educated himself about ancient Mexican cultures, their language, customs, and documented history, and later began selling artifacts he had excavated himself. He spent decades becoming a recognized archeologist, collector and dealer, whose expertise in pre-Columbian studies was unquestioned. Added to all of this he had a magnetic personality, which combined fearlessness, charm, supreme confidence, and bravura. Nonetheless, he risked his reputation and livelihood in passing off these artifacts as genuine. In fact, more than once, he came close to being undone by these beautiful, mysterious objects.

Capturing light in their morbid details, the skulls astounded museum curators and visitors alike, since, according to Boban, they had been laboriously fashioned with primitive stone tools. They were also exceedingly rare. Fewer than a dozen could be found in the world during the last quarter of the nineteenth century. In 1897 the British Museum paid $950 or £220, a great deal of money at that time for the largest of these artifacts. The Musée d'Ethnographie du Trocadéro in Paris had already been exhibiting two of its crystal skulls for nearly twenty years.

By the end of a life of prodigious work and research, Boban had amassed and sold important collections of pre-Columbian artifacts that were displayed in major museums in Europe and the United States. His colleagues considered him a better educator than some of the famous professors at the Sorbonne. He was known in some circles for his erudite, two-volume catalog of pre-Columbian painted manuscripts. His papers entered the collections of the Bibliothèque nationale in Paris and the Hispanic Society of America in New York. Yet his contributions to pre-Columbian scholarship were soon largely forgotten.

As luck would have it, his story has come to light through his connection with crystal skulls, an occurrence he seems almost to have anticipated. In the last decade of his life, he chose to highlight this lucrative sideline. In fact, he seems to have bragged about it when Charles Inman Barnard, the *New York Tribune*'s Paris correspondent, interviewed him for a newspaper article about the problem of faked artifacts that appeared on 20 August 1900. "Numbers of so-called rock crystal pre-Columbian skulls have been so adroitly made as almost to defy detection, and have been palmed off as genuine upon the experts of some of the principal museums of Europe," asserted Boban, whom Barnard describes as a most trustworthy source (Barnard 1900).

Boban's remarks are cynical on several counts. In essence he is undercutting the knowledge and sophistication of the curators at the British Museum and the Trocadéro. This statement is doubly sardonic because he himself "palmed off" the skulls on colleagues who bought them trusting in his guarantee that they were authentic. Surprisingly, all of these "so-called rock crystal pre-Columbian skulls" continued to be exhibited as impressive examples of ancient technology for the next hundred years.

The story of how Boban came from humble circumstances to become a world-renowned expert in the field of pre-Columbian studies is one of inspiring self-invention. It is filled with almost unbelievable achievements, various mysteries, some contradictions, and a few large gaps. His journey from recognition to anonymity and later rediscovery through his connection with crystal skulls is also a cautionary tale of how little we control our legacies. No matter what legitimate contributions we make, we may ultimately be remembered for what we did on our worst day. Research has revealed a nuanced history of a complex human being who dared greatly and accomplished much.

Boban Family History

Eugène André Boban Duvergé was born in Paris on 10 March 1834. The surname Boban, which he and some family members used occasionally with Duvergé or Duverger, does not seem particularly French, and caused some ongoing confusion among even his close friends and colleagues as to its spelling. It may have its origins in Croatia, where Boban is a rather common surname, associated with the village of Bobanova Draga in what is now Bosnia Herzegovina (Bellamy 2003). This said, his paternal ancestors had lived in France since before the 1740s.

The first family members recorded in France were his great-great-grandparents, René Boban, a master cloth maker specializing in serge, and his wife, Marie Houdu, who lived in Sablé-sur-Sarthe, between Le Mans and Angers. For several generations the family continued to live in and around Angers, moving back and forth to Paris as their economic circumstances dictated.

Eugène's grandfather, André Michel Boban Duvergé, was a tailor, like his father and grandfather before him. He married three times. His first wife was Marie Renée Hémon, a seamstress. She died in 1805, leaving him to raise their infant son, also named André.

Two years later, at the age of twenty-nine, André Michel married Marguerite Victoire Licoys, the 21-year-old daughter of a day laborer, who was also a seamstress. She died in 1810, leaving him with a two-year-old son named René Victor

Boban dit [called] Duvergé, born in Angers on 4 May 1808. He was Eugène Boban's father.

In 1815 André Michel, now thirty-seven and a widower for a second time, married Henriette Chardon. Her parents were listed as property owners in the marriage document, so, presumably, she came from a prosperous family. Within the next ten years André Michel and Henriette had three daughters: Françoise Henriette, called Fanny, born in 1816 in Angers; Henriette, born in 1823 in Paris; and Victorine, born in 1825, also in Paris. Eugène Boban's aunts Fanny and Henriette would play a significant role throughout his life.

As the birth location of two of his daughters' attests, André Michel and his third wife went to Paris in the early 1820s in search of business opportunities. The family lived at 35, rue des Boucheries in Saint Germain, quite close to the church of Saint-Germain-des-Prés on the left bank. The abbey and cloisters of this church had been one of the wealthiest in France, but during the French Revolution they were nearly destroyed by an explosion and fire. In the nineteenth century the area around the surviving church became somewhat less fashionable than it had been in the eighteenth century.[1]

For reasons of his own, Eugène's father, René Victor, used only the surname Boban, unlike other immediate family members, and was the first to pursue a profession outside the textile trades. He followed his father to Paris and became a *gainier*—a craftsman who produced chests, boxes, jewel boxes, scabbards, and other leather-covered luxury items. Gainiers often dyed the hides they used and occasionally gilded and embossed them with specialized tools. Their products were intended for the wealthier classes. In March 1830, when he was twenty-one, René Victor married Laurence Michelle Simon, a laundress who was nineteen. The couple lived in Paris at 3, rue Cardinale, a block away from André Michel's house, near the church of Saint-Germain-des-Prés.

René Victor and Laurence Michelle Boban eventually had five children. The eldest, Rose Louise, was born in 1831; Eugène André in 1834; and Marie Françoise in 1836. These three were born at rue Cardinale. Julie Félicité, the fourth child, was born around the corner at 1, rue Childebert, in 1838. The youngest, Charlotte Heloise, was born in 1841 in Montrouge, a working-class suburb of Paris, later the 14th arrondissement.

René Victor and his family seem to have fallen squarely into the stratum of French society known as the petit bourgeoisie, a broad denomination that, as historian Gordon Wright notes, "included the mass of little independents of city, town, and village—small enterprisers, shopkeepers, artisans, clerks, schoolmasters, petit employees of the state." As though speaking about this family directly, he adds, "Some of them inherited an old family tradition of shop keeping or craftsmanship" (Wright 1987: 166).

The Bobans lived in rented flats mostly in the Saint-Germain-des-Prés district, until the early 1880s. That their standard of living was relatively modest is indicated by the address of one of the buildings in which they resided, 22, rue des Grands Augustins, constructed in the 1670s.[2] The apartment shared by the seven members of the family consisted of two small rooms with a fireplace and a small kitchen alcove. Several other artisans were living and perhaps working at the same address. The other tenants may have been involved in the gainier trade as well, since they are listed as upholsterers, staplers, and leather guilders.[3] It seems as though the family was struggling to get by, as were many Parisian artisans and tradespeople of the day.

The history of the Boban Duvergé family in Angers and Paris is illustrative of the economic and social developments of the nineteenth century in France. Following the debacle of the Napoleonic Era, the country was slow to industrialize, falling well behind European rivals such as Germany and England. However, textile production was one area that did experience industrial growth of sorts, although the majority of textile manufacturers were small businesses. According to the economist Armand Audiganne, in 1847 only 318 workshops in the department of the Seine, which included Paris, used mechanical power or employed more than twenty workers. Of the 29,216 clothing and shoe producers in Paris in 1847–48, 18,930 (65 percent) consisted of a proprietor and a single worker or a proprietor working alone (Price 1972: 6–7).

Aside from the slow pace of industrialization in France, another indication of stagnation in economic and social development was the lack of upward mobility in most of the country. At mid-century, the one exception was Paris, although the majority of individuals who were able to enhance their prospects in the capital had moved there from less advantageous circumstances in the provinces, like the Boban Duvergés.

For the first decade and a half after Eugène Boban's birth, the Orleanist king Louis Philippe ruled France. Uninterested in the pomp and formality that had been hallmarks of previous generations of nobles, he was sometimes called the "Citizen King" or more derogatorily the "Grocer King" (Horne 2006: 251). After 1840, he and his ministers, particularly former historian François Guizot, who became foreign minister and later prime minister, helped expand French business through protective tariffs and low taxes, government deregulation and large expenditures in public works. Like many conservatives today, Guizot firmly believed that France was a country of equal opportunity and that those who failed to get rich and acquire the privileges of the rich had only their own limitations to blame (Wright 1987: 118, 154).

Boban would have finished his primary schooling at about the age of twelve in 1846. There is no record that he went on to receive a secondary education, so he probably assisted his father as a gainier at that stage, learning the trade as an apprentice.

From 1845 onward France had experienced extremely poor harvests, partly caused by a potato blight that had begun spreading across Europe. The situation was extremely difficult for the poorer classes, who saw prices of their two staple foods—wheat and potatoes—rise dramatically at the same time, with other food products in short supply. The weakness in the farming sector soon rippled throughout the French economy. In 1847 alone 4,672 businesses failed in France, compared with 2,618 in 1840, which had not been a good year either (Price 1972: 84).

Support for Louis Philippe's government had eroded among many classes in France by the beginning of 1848, a year that was to experience revolution and chaos across Europe (Wright 1987: 125–26). Parisian students and workers took to the streets, clashing with the police on 22 February 1848. Called upon to restore order, the National Guard proved disloyal to Louis Philippe, and the clashes turned into all-out rioting. The following day the king attempted to calm matters by firing Guizot, who had become hugely unpopular.

The news of Guizot's dismissal inspired a public demonstration of thanks in front of the minister's former office. Unfortunately, what started as a celebration ended in tragedy.

> A column of students and artisans, unarmed, but singing 'Mourir pour la patrie,' came down the boulevards; at the same instant a gun was heard, and the 14th Regiment of the Line leveled their muskets and fired. The scene that followed was awful. Thousands of men, women, children, shrieking, bawling, raving, were seen flying in all directions, while sixty-two men, women, and lads, belonging to every class of society, lay weltering in their blood upon the pavement. (St. John 1848: 167–68)

After this the situation in Paris was beyond Louis Philippe's control, and he abdicated in favor of his grandson. (Wright 1987: 126–27).

The citizens of Paris then declared a Second Republic (the first having been established during the French Revolution) and appointed a temporary government. At first it seemed that a new era of universal accord and understanding had dawned (Price 1972: 95–96). Despite this apparent harmony, the economy worsened bringing about even greater unemployment.

On 15 May the National Assembly came under attack as thousands of armed workers convened on its chambers demanding reform. On 21 June the situation got out of control when the Assembly issued a decree restricting membership in the National Workshops, which had provided some financial support for unemployed workers. The announcement was like a spark to tinder. Barricades immediately appeared all over Paris, and for the next five days skirmishes and pitched battles occurred across the city between working-class Parisians and the government's soldiers. By the time the fighting ended, 900 soldiers along with 1,500 citizens, and perhaps as many as 3,000, lay dead (Knapton 1971: 392; Wright 1987: 134).

The fiercest battles took place around the enormous barricades near Place de la Bastille and Faubourg Saint-Antoine, immortalized by Victor Hugo in *Les*

Misérables—across the Seine and some distance from the Boban family household. There also was intense fighting just across the river from them in the 3rd and 4th arrondissements, and the Left Bank and Latin Quarter up the street (Price 1972: 170). Living day-to-day in Paris during the June Days of 1848 had to have been frightening and disturbing for the family as for so many others. Eugène was only fourteen at the time, and the violence and killings must have affected him deeply. As order was restored in the weeks and months that followed, some 12,000 to 15,000 people were arrested, with about a third being deported to the French colony of Algeria (Wright 1987: 134; Knapton 1971: 392).

The bloody conflict of June 1848 was to have long-term repercussions for France's prospects for peaceful reform and social progress. As British historian Roger Price notes:

> The June days clearly revealed how far men's attitudes had changed since the first relatively harmonious days of the Republic. They indicated the insufficiency of political reform, even that of granting universal male suffrage, as a means of giving satisfaction to the poor. They indicated the desperation with which those who had a vested interest under the *status quo* would defend this. Above all they indicated the shape of things to come by revealing this basic split in society and convincing many that differences between social groups could only be resolved by conflict. French society and its politics were for long to bear the mark of the hatreds generated by the insurrection of June 1848, and its brutal suppression. (Price 1972: 155)

The economic impact of the revolution of 1848, which grew out of the disenchantment and frustration of the working class unable to make a living wage, was devastating. The business class refused to invest capital in their operations, and "no real signs of recovery would be seen until 1851" (Traugott 1988: 22). Unemployment would continue to rise for the next few years, and workers would continue to be exploited by subcontractors and the growth of piecework, which was particularly prevalent in the textile industry.

With France in an economic tailspin at the end of 1848, the news that gold had been discovered in California at the beginning of the year came as a thunderclap of good news. The French had already begun developing a keen interest in the American West, due partly to the reports from John C. Frémont's exploratory expeditions of the West and California throughout the 1840s, which had become available in translation. France considered Frémont a native son because of his French-Canadian ancestry, taking to heart his expansionist view that the American West was a land full of opportunity and adventure. Once gold was discovered, the bookstalls of Paris displayed more and more information about California—sailors' reminiscences, accounts from Frenchmen living in California, articles taken from American publications—all of which added heat to the gold fever (Brands 2002: 94).

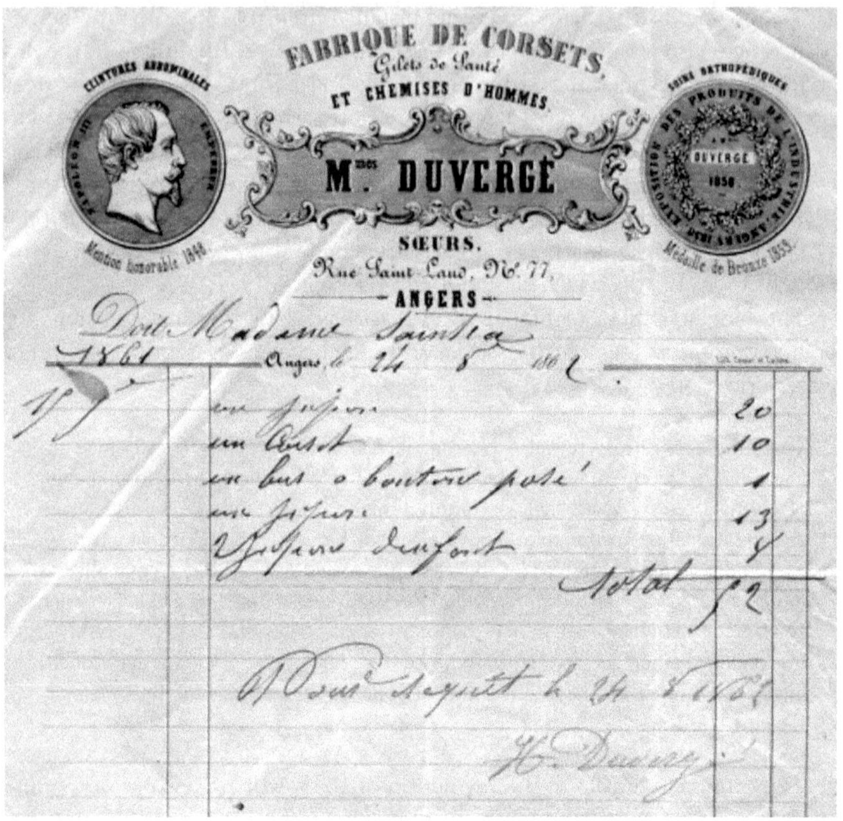

Figure 1.1   Duvergé sisters' invoice (courtesy of Sylvain Bertoldi, Archives municipales d'Angers, 1 Num. 15).

According to an 1851 census, Boban's grandfather, who had dropped the Boban surname and was known as André Michel Duvergé, had left Paris to return to Angers with his wife and two of their daughters, Fanny and Henriette. The youngest daughter, Victorine, may have stayed in Paris or perhaps had died, since she is no longer listed in census records in either Angers or Paris. André Michel, then seventy-two, is described as supported by the labor of "his children"[4]—his daughters, by then thirty-five and twenty-eight, who were corset makers or *corsetières*. René Victor's younger half-sisters had followed the Boban Duvergé tradition to become successful in the textile industry, ultimately owning an award-winning business in Angers that manufactured corsets, "gilets de santé," which may have been special vests or a type of undergarment, and men's shirts.

Boban's grandfather, André Michel, died in October 1851, but his third wife, Henriette Chardon, and his daughters continued to reside in Angers at least until the early 1860s. Their business seems to have prospered. Fanny married a blacksmith just a few months before her father's death, and they had a domestic as a member of their household. Their names last appear in the Angers census in 1861.[5]

In 1852, Louis Napoleon, the nephew of Napoleon Bonaparte, declared himself Emperor Napoleon III in a bloodless coup d'état that ended the Second Republic. One of his first enterprises was to design the modernization of Paris in collaboration with Georges-Eugène Haussmann, a civil servant and city planner who was prefect of the Seine region. Napoleon III and Haussmann envisioned the complete transformation of the capital into a safer city with better housing, sanitation, and more open communities. Additionally, they designed tree-lined boulevards too wide for the barricades that had figured so prominently in 1848, which would also provide easy access for the police and the military. There was a growing feeling in the country that the capital's insurgents needed to be controlled. Eight times since 1827 Parisians had brought life and commerce to a standstill by erecting their infamous barricades, and this needed to be stopped (Merriman 2014: xiv).

In August 1853, the Bobans' eldest daughter, Rose Louise, was married. The family was still living in two rooms at 22, rue des Grands Augustins in the 6th arrondissement, only a few blocks from their original home at rue Cardinale. Rose Louise's husband, André Martial Backès, was a gainier like her father, and may have worked with him.[6]

Eugène André Boban was nineteen when his older sister was married in the St. Sulpice church. If he had completed his schooling around the age of twelve, he would have already been working with his father for about seven years. Prior to the education reforms of the late 1880s in France, school ended for most boys after they had made their first communion (Prost 1968: 100–2). In 1852 the baccalauréat ès lettres and the baccalauréat ès sciences were created. One had to be sixteen years old to have the right to take this examination, which, if one passed, gave access to university or advanced studies. Boban's name does not appear in the records of the baccalauréat tests for those years, however (Pascal Riviale, pers. comm.).

Notes

1. AN, F/7/10843/B, demandes de résidence à Paris, dossier Boban.

2. Information on addresses was provided by Christiane Demeulenaere-Douyère of the Archives nationales in Paris.

3. AD Paris, D.1P4/505: 22, rue des Grands Augustins, Cadastral revision of 1852.

4. "Vivant du travail de ses enfants."

5. All information about the Boban family in Angers, France, was provided by Sylvain Bertoldi from census records in the Angers archives.

6. Rose Louise's marriage certificate is available online through various sites, including the Paris public records, ancestry.com, and so forth.

2

BETWEEN OLD WORLD AND NEW

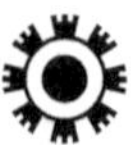

Exhibiting a courage and zest for adventure that would characterize him through-out his life, soon after his sister's wedding, Eugène Boban decided to look for work far away. His great-grandfather and grandfather had moved from Angers to Paris seeking employment, but the capital apparently held little opportunity for him at this stage. His sights were set on California.

His father, René Victor, joined him in this great adventure, leaving his wife, Laurence Michelle and three young daughters on their own. Marie was eighteen years old, Julie was fifteen, and the youngest, Charlotte, was twelve. It could not have been easy for their mother, a 42-year-old unemployed laundress with four mouths to feed. She may have received some assistance from her eldest daughter, Rose Louise, and her son-in-law, the gainier. Her husband's half-sisters may have helped as well. However, later events indicate that the departure of the two males of the Boban family had a devastating effect on the women left behind.

In notes now in the collections of the Hispanic Society of America in New York, written in his own hand, the younger Boban briefly describes this momen-tous journey—not the setting out or the voyage itself, but rather the destination (HSA: B2240 Box I, folder III). Despite the fact that there are some fourteen boxes of handwritten notes, correspondence, and unpublished manuscripts in the Hispanic Society's collection, they contain very little about his personal life or his family, and only a few pages about his sojourn in California. Given the timing of the journey, he was undoubtedly seeking his fortune. Additionally, and perhaps more important, Eugène was less than a year short of the age when he would almost certainly have been drafted into the French army.[1]

How he traveled to California is not known, although there were a vari-ety of possible methods. One could sail across the Atlantic and then cross the North American continent. Other options were to sail around the horn of South

America or to sail to Veracruz, Mexico, cross the Isthmus of Tehuantepec and then board a ship to San Francisco. Yet another route was to sail to Nicaragua, disembark and travel overland to the Pacific Ocean and then take a ship north to the gold fields.

None of these would have been an easy journey, as noted by historian H. W. Brands. "California was about as far from the centers of Western civilization as a land could be. The sea voyage around South America from New York or Liverpool or Le Havre required five or six months, depending on the conditions off Cape Horn, which could terrify the most hardened unbeliever to prayer" (Brands 2002: 25–26).

The "shortcut" route developed in the late 1840s, which took less time if one was lucky, was no easier. Harris Newmark, a European traveler, left for California at just about the same time as Boban. He sailed from Liverpool on 10 July 1853 and arrived in New York some six weeks later. From New York he sailed to Nicaragua, continuing up the San Juan River to Lake Nicaragua. The next leg of the journey was long and arduous, particularly crossing the narrow strip of jungle between Lake Nicaragua and the Pacific Ocean. Crossing the isthmus had never been easy, but as Spain's oversight dwindled through the early decades of the nineteenth century, it became more and more dangerous as "outlaws, freebooters, adventurers, and other undesirables flocked to this crossroads of two continents and two oceans and made merry havoc" (Brands 2002: 74).

By the time Harris Newmark sailed into the harbor at San Francisco, more than three months had elapsed since he had embarked in Liverpool, even though he had successfully taken the "shortcut" to California. No land routes existed from San Francisco to Los Angeles, so after arriving at the larger port it was necessary to take a smaller ship for a four-day voyage to this more southern boomtown (Newmark 1916: 16).

Aside from the question of which route Eugène Boban took to America is that of how he paid for his passage, which could have cost a thousand francs or more, a considerable amount of money, particularly for someone of Boban's station (Brands 2002: 95). And the passage was just the beginning of the potential expenses. As he may have learned by reading journalist Étienne Derbec's letters from San Francisco and the California gold fields, published in the popular *Journal de Débats* in 1850, "Those emigrants who plan to come to California must prepare themselves, for without doing so, many regrets await them when they arrive here without money and without help. . . . It is necessary that they know that from San Francisco to the first mines it is not less than 60 to 80 leagues, and that it is necessary to have a well filled pocket to make the trip" (Derbec 1964: 79). Derbec goes on to say that double-decked steamboats ply the waters between San Francisco and the interior of the state, but that the fares range from $30 to $60. At a conversion rate of five to one—which had become the standard for all foreign currency—that represented a cost of 150 to 300 francs. Added to that considerable expense was the cost of transporting any baggage, for which travelers were charged $2 (or 10 francs) for a 14-ounce pound (Derbec 1964: 83).

Given the manner in which the Boban family pulled together in later years, taking care of and supporting each other as much as possible, it is likely that they pooled their resources for the funds necessary for Boban's California adventure. Numerous other publications available at the time offered differing opinions and advice to miners about what they should bring to the gold fields. Aside from proper tools, several pamphlets suggested bringing things they could sell, like clothing, shoes, etc., since these were hard to come by and brought enormously inflated prices. It may be that aside from money to help transport their nephew to America, his aunts, the Duvergé sisters, also provided him with men's shirts from their small factory, which would have brought a considerable sum in San Francisco and the other California Gold Rush boomtowns.

Despite the perils and expenses of the journey to get there, by 1853, California had become a haven for French adventurers and gold seekers. France was the first country to establish a foreign presence in the California territory after Alta California declared independence from Mexico in 1848. This diplomatic gesture occurred in 1852, a short time after Louis Napoleon became Emperor Napoleon III. His purpose was to create a toehold for a potential new colony in North America since Spain's influence over the area was dwindling and the United States' claims had yet to be fully established. He also had an eye to developing a new market for French goods as an incentive to the country's struggling economy (Derbec 1964: 19).

There were some twenty thousand French immigrants in the new territory, many of them fleeing the political upheavals of 1848 and the subsequent economic depression. It was customary for each new arrival to go to his country's consulate in San Francisco for assistance—emergency cash, a place to stay, and eventually, if one was lucky, help in setting up mining claims. "By 1853, a French envoy estimated that twenty-five percent of Californians were foreigners, and, of these, a third were French" (Chalmers 1998: 20).[2]

Although many place names in California—French Camp, French Bay, French Corral, Les Fourcades, and others—attest to French presence in the gold fields, they were not the most popular or convivial group working in the area. "It was said that if ten Frenchmen should get together, they would be quarreling and insulting one another within five minutes. They lived in groups together, but they lived the life of France as far as possible; they did not become citizens of the United States, for they considered the Americans a savage and ignorant people. They did not learn English; they glorified French" (Chalmers 1998: 24–25). Possibly to drive them away, the authorities tried to impose a $20 per month license fee on the unpopular foreign miners, which nearly started an all-out riot. The French consuls in California, Patrice Dillon and Jules Lombard, had to go to the mines to restore order (Derbec 1964: 24–25).

From his own notes and later accomplishments, it appears that Boban did not associate with or think so highly of the other Europeans in the area, preferring the company of the Spanish-speaking population and native groups. "I lived in California for 4 years, beginning in 1853 and for two of those years all I did was travel the country in all directions; this wandering life among the Indians allowed me to study their customs" (HSA: B2240, Box 1, Folder III).[3] He seems to have been an unusually empathetic observer of the circumstances and customs of California's indigenous people. He wrote with some sadness and shock about the impact of the "violent European immigrants" and the disastrous effect they had on the land and lives of the native peoples.

Traveling up the Sacramento River, he met native Californians all along the way. The California Indians, he wrote, were

nomads and hunters, who ordinarily live in small groups (Rancherias), they choose always to build their rancherias on a hilltop with a view that stretches into the distance and located near extensive river valleys so that water is easily accessible. Their huts or shelters are made with tree branches (chamisos) stuck into the ground and joined at the other end in the shape of a bell, the base is circular, and in the center is a small fire that is kept going night and day. They all sleep pell mell, with their feet toward the fire. The Indians never make large fires for a number of reasons: lack of firewood because of deforestation, a desire not to frighten off game, and to avoid providing a target for their enemies. (HSA: B2240, Box 1, Folder III)[4]

He lived for a while in Los Angeles, which was a boomtown during the Gold Rush, filled with foreign fortune seekers, many of them violent, prone to strong drink and generally out of control. The "violent European immigrants" lynched Mexicans and brutally hunted and killed native peoples by setting fire to the many stands of trees. They "hunted them, burned their beautiful forests and disturbed the earth," writes Boban. He later commented, "Certainly nothing is stranger than seeing a man, claiming to be civilized, take such great pleasure in burning and destroying everything, and if the Indians had the word 'savage' in their language, how often they should have applied it to those Europeans" (HSA: B2240, Box 1, Folder III).[5]

Other observers, both contemporary participants and later historians, echoed Boban's concerns about the treatment of the original inhabitants of California. Peter H. Burnett, governor of California from 1849 to 1851, expressed the view that, "a war of extermination will continue to be waged between the two races until the Indian becomes extinct" (Heizer and Almquist 1971: 26). Unfortunately, Burnett's prediction proved all too accurate. According to some sources, California's native population plummeted between 1848 and 1860 from about 150,000 to about 30,000 (Heizer and Almquist 1971: 26).

The arrival of European and American settlers affected every aspect of the Indians' lives and ruined their environment. As Edward Castillo, an historian and member of the Cahuilla tribe, wrote in a later history of California Indians, the violent immigrants exhibited a total disregard for the native inhabitants, and enthusiastically participated in "the destruction of the natural environment in their frenzy to exploit the land." Their ceaseless violent devastation "struck a mortal blow to the Indians' sacred relationship with nature" (Castillo 1978: 108).

Although he was minimally educated and came from a completely different culture, Boban exhibited an unusual openness and sophistication about the native people he met. He wrote about them with tenderness and admiration, detailing their customs and daily subsistence practices. "The Indians live by hunting and fishing. One day I was watching one of them fishing along the Sacramento and I tried to figure out what sort of bait he had at the end of his line. I saw him bend down and take some flesh from his heel and attach it to the line. Indians have very cracked heels. The bait was excellent, the fish seemed to find it tasty, and the fishing was successful" (HSA: B2240, Box 1, Folder III).[6]

The young explorer (*voyageur* in French) seems also quite sympathetic to the plight of native women. In another passage Boban recalled, "On a day of hunting—the Indian man leaves before daybreak and upon return he throws all the game on the ground in front of his wife, who is in charge of preparing everything, because she has the worst part of the share."[7] He commented on native hygiene as well. "The hunter goes off to bathe in the temascalli, a sort of steam bath like that used among the Aztecs and today also among the modern Mexicans as well, and leaving the steam bath, the California Indian jumps into the freezing water. I have always thought the Indian owes the freshness of his skin to that sort of bath" (HSA: B2240, Box 1, Folder III).[8]

Boban was a keen observer, noticing and recording a variety of different customs. He was always eager to try new experiences. "I was also present at a particular hunt undertaken by Indian women. This was at a place where there were very many grasshoppers—the women set fire to the grass and picked up the grasshoppers in their baskets. The grasshoppers were already half grilled, and they ate them with great gusto. The taste reminded me of shrimp" (HSA: B2240, Box 1, Folder III).[9]

Somewhere along the Sacramento River, the young traveler witnessed a funeral that touched him deeply.

The ceremony made a profound impression on me. One of the brothers of the dead man set fire to the funeral pyre and stirred the fire with the end of a branch so that the cadaver was completely consumed—during that time all the relatives and others danced around the fire. His poor mother was overwhelmed by despair. I saw her bend down and pick up one of her son's vertebrae, which was still on fire, and put it in her mouth. The scene is still before my eyes. I will never forget it. When everything was reduced to ashes, the chief's widow disposed of all her ornaments and rolled around in the burnt ashes of her husband. Then the ashes were picked up and placed in a terra cotta vessel and then put into the ground. (HSA: B2240, Box 1, Folder III)[10]

He also described his sadness about the cause of this young man's death.

> I arrived in this region the day before the death of this chief, a young man of 25 years at most, who was big and strong. He procured eau de vie [liquor], I really don't know how, because it was far away from any village, and he was drunk for 15 days in succession, and finally succumbed to an attack of delirium tremens. All the remedies having failed, about ten Indian women formed a magnetic chain, which did not keep him from dying. I don't know if alcohol is good for anything in Europe, but I can affirm that it is the veritable and principal cause of making the Indian race of America brutish and the principal cause of their destruction. (HSA: B2240, Box 1, Folder III)[11]

By 1856, the California Gold Rush was over, and most people had not struck it rich. The violence continued, however, with one French consul describing the country as giving "the most revolting examples of disorders and crimes. Every day the newspapers mention murders and frightful assassinations" (Nasatir 1945: 116).

It is unknown how profitable this period was for Boban financially, but the young adventurer certainly had acquired valuable knowledge about the native peoples of California. He apparently had also acquired a working knowledge of Spanish. In 1850 the northern part of California became part of the United States, with Baja California still a part of Mexico. In both Californias, however, the predominant language continued to be Spanish.

Probably by late 1856, Boban began making his way south toward Mexico City, perhaps stopping for a while in the northern part of Baja California, where he again wrote about the native peoples' habits that he observed, in particular their fishing practices and pearl-diving enterprises. In an unpublished manuscript about the natural resources of Mexico, which he compiled in the early 1890s, he wrote about Baja California pearls. "Forty years ago in Los Angeles, where we lived at that time, we often saw people from California and from Sonora who came to offer pearls, which they brought from the coast of Baja California" (HSA: B2253, Box 14).[12] Boban often writes these memoirs in the first person singular, although in many instances he crosses out the "I" and writes "we." It is unclear whether he does this out of a sense of modesty or is actually talking about traveling companions—his father or someone else.

Boban continues writing about the pearl industry quoting from a French-published source "Notes Statistiques sur la Basse Californie" by Édouard

Guillemin about the quality of pearls from La Paz, at the southern end of Baja California. He wrote that they have a "very nice finish, and that black pearls are unusual; the pink pearl, a local variety, is even more rare" (HSA: B2253, Box 14).[13]

In the nineteenth century pearls were an extremely valuable commodity in Mexico. In a publication about the industry, the gemologist George Kunz, who was vice president of Tiffany & Co., quoted from an 1859 report that by 1857 (the year Boban left California), 95,000 tons of oysters had been removed from the Sea of Cortés, between Baja California and the mainland of Mexico. The Baja California pearl yield was "2770 pounds of pearls, worth $5,540,000 (Kunz and Stevenson 1908: 246).

Whether he sailed from California to Acapulco or traveled south overland, Boban arrived in Mexico City in the spring of 1857. The city was the capital of the still struggling republic, which after gaining independence from Spain had recently lost California—a significant portion of its territory—to the United States. The country had developed a liberal constitution in 1857 but was about to enter three years of civil war before the constitution would be ratified and Benito Juárez declared president.

"Eugenio" Boban's first *carta de seguridad*, a sort of visa, dated 1 April 1857, is in the Archivo General de la Nación (AGN) in Mexico City. The document states "For the term of a year [the bearer] may live and travel in the territory of the Republic observing the regulations of 1 May 1828" (AGN: Movimiento Marítima, Vol. 201, Exp. 135, foja 24). The security letter lacks the usual descriptive information such as height, weight, hair color, complexion, and so forth; although presumably the original document that Boban would have carried was complete in those details. The young man is listed as being twenty-two years old, although he was actually twenty-three. Interestingly, there are a variety of documents relating to Boban that give conflicting information about his age. This is also true of the census data documenting his family in Angers and Paris. The security letter may be the first of many indications that Boban had a habit of losing years, perhaps out of vanity.

After wandering for four years through California, his arrival in Mexico City would mark the beginning of a new life and career. He had traveled thousands of miles from Paris. He had learned to live with many nationalities, some prone to violence in search of gold. Yet he seems to have come to the realization that the New World offered great riches, despite its hardships.

He brought with him to Mexico an appreciation for the struggles of native peoples, who had taught him many things about their lives and customs. Boban also brought a basic knowledge of Spanish, which would provide considerable aid in reinventing himself as a student and dealer of all things Mexican.

Notes

1. French conscription laws decreed that all twenty-year-old males undertake military service (Baker 2001: 194).

2. After Napoleon III's coup in 1851, disenchanted revolutionaries emigrated, many free of charge, under the auspices of a huge lottery supervised by the Prefect of Paris.

3. J'ai habité la Californie pendant 4 années, à partir de 1853 et pendant deux de ces années je n'ai fait que parcourir le pays en tous sens; cette vie errante au milieu des Indiens m'a permis d'étudier leurs moeurs. (Our transcriptions are, as far as possible, accurate to the original with regard to spelling, grammar, or missing words. In many cases we are working with handwritten material, which is sometimes hard to decipher. Some of the errors in grammar and punctuation are Boban's, and some may be ours.)

4. Les Indiens, nomads et chasseurs, vivent ordinairement en petits groups (Rancherias); ils choisissent toujours pour établir leur rancherias un mamelon d'ou la vue s'etend au loin, et situé à proximité des grands ravins afin d'avoir facilement de l'eau. Leurs cases ou abris sont formées avec des branches d'arbres (chamisos) fichées en terre et réunies à l'autre extrémité en forme de cloche; la base en est circulaire; au centre se trouve un petit feu qui dure nuit et jour. Ils se couchent tous pêle-mêle, les pieds vers le feu. Les Indiens ne font jamais de grands feux pour plusieurs raisons: le manque de bois, par suite du déboisement, le désir de ne pas effrayer le gibier et celui de ne point offrir un point de mire à leurs ennemis.

5. Qui leur donnerent la chasse, brulerent leurs belles forêts et bouleversérent le sol. Certes rien n'est plus étrange que de voir l'homme qui se prétend civilisé, prendre un si grand plaisir à tout brûler et à tout détruire, et si les Indiens ont dans leur langue le mot "sauvage" que de fois ils ont pu l'appliquer avec raison aux Européens.

6. Les Indiens vivent de chasse et de pêche. Un jour que je regardais l'un d'eux pêcher sur les bords du Sacramento et que je cherchais inutilement à me rendre compte du genre d'appât dont il se servait pour amorcer sa ligne, je le vis se baisser et arracher de son talon des fragments de peau (l'Indien a souvent les talons fendilles); l'appât était excellent, le poisson en paraissait très friand et la pêche était fructueuse.

7. Les jours de chasse l'Indien part bien avant le jour, a son retour il jette le gibier sur le sol devant sa femme qui est chargée de tout faire, car elle est la plus mal partagée.

8. Puis il va se baigner au Temascalli, sorte de bain de vapeur en usage chez les Azteques et aujourd'hui encore chez les Mexicains modernes; au sortir du bain de vapeur l'Indien Californien va se jeter dans l'eau glacée, puis se reposer; j'ai toujours cree que la race indienne devait la fraicheur de sa peau à cette sorte de bains.

9. J'ai assisté aussi à une singuliére chasse faite par les femmes indiennes; celles ci dans les lieux ou il y avait beaucoup de sauterelles, mettaient le feu à l'herbe et ramassaient dans leurs corras les sauterelles à moitié grillées, elles les mangent de très bon coeur. Cela me rappelait les crevettes.

10. J'ai assisté une fois aux funérailles d'un grand Chef et cette cérémonie a fait chez moi une profonde impression. Un des frères du défunt mit le feu au bûcher et attisait le feu à l'aide d'une perche afin que le cadavre fut bien réduit en cendres, pendant que tous les parents et assistants dansaient ensemble autour du foyer. Sa pauvre mère fut prise d'un accès de désespoir; je la vis se baisser et porter à sa bouche une des vertebres enflammées de son fils; cette scène est encore devant mes yeux et je ne l'oublierai jamais. Quand tout fut réduit en cendres, la veuve du chef se depouilla de tous ses ornements et se roula sur la cendre brûlante de son mari; puis les cendres recueillies dans un vase en terre cuite furent enfouies en terre.

11. J'étais arrivé dans le pays la veille de la mort de ce Chef; c'était un jeune homme de 25 ans au plus, grand et fort. Il s'était procuré, je ne sais trop comment, car on était loin de toute ville, quelques bouteilles d'eau de vie, pendant 15 jours de suite il s'était enivré et avait fini par succomber à une

attaque de delirium tremens; tous les remèdes ayant échaué, une dixaine d'Indiens forma la chaîne magnétique, ce qui ne l'empêcha point de mourir; c'était une victime de l'alcool. Je ne sais si l'alcool fait du bien en Europe, mais je puis affirmer qu'il est la véritable et principale cause de l'abrutissement et de la destruction de la race indienne en Amérique.

12. Une autre contrée . . . La Basse Californie, fournissait aussi, et fournit même encore actuellement des perles fines. Nous avons vu il y a une quarantaine d'années a Los Angeles que nous habitions a cette epoque venir souvent des Californiens, des Sonoriens, nous offrant des perles qu'ils apportaient, des cotes de la basse Californie.

13. Les perles de la Paz ont un tres-bel orient. Les perles noires sont peu communes; la perle rose, variete locale, y est plus rare encore.

3

Mexico

Ancient to Modern

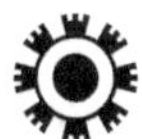

Mexico is a country immersed in its ancient history, despite the concerted efforts of its European conquerors to obliterate the past. In subjugating these new lands, the Spaniards destroyed the architectural monuments they initially admired and went on to exploit the people who had created them.

At first astounded by the beauty and majesty of Tenochtitlán, the Aztec capital, the Spanish conquistadors compared it to imaginary castles of chivalric romances. Bernal Díaz del Castillo, a soldier in Hernán Cortés's army, wrote appreciatively about the Spaniards' first view of Moctezuma's capital.

> During the morning we arrived at a broad Causeway and continued our march towards Iztapalapa, and when we saw so many cities and villages built in the water, and other great towns on dry land and that straight and level causeway going towards Mexico, we were amazed and said that it was like the enchantments they tell of in the legend of Amadís, on account of the great towers and cues and buildings rising from the water, and all built of masonry. And some of our soldiers even asked whether the things that we saw were not a dream. (Díaz 1956: 190–91)

The architectural and artistic remnants of the precontact cultures continued to fascinate and repel the Spaniards exploring the New World throughout the nearly three centuries of colonial rule, extending from 1521 until the beginning of Mexico's War of Independence in 1810. The conquistadors were horrified by the human sacrifices performed by the Aztecs. Hernán Cortés's first letter to the Spanish crown described this practice as a "most horrid and abominable custom." Providing more details, he adds,

> Whenever they wish to ask something of the idols, in order that their plea may find more acceptance, they take many girls and boys and even adults, and in the pres-

ence of the idols they open their chests while they are still alive and take out their hearts and entrails and burn them before the idols, offering the smoke as sacrifice. Some of us have seen this, and they say it is the most terrible and frightful thing they have ever witnessed. (Pagden and Elliott 1986: 35)

Human sacrifice and other customs considered pagan by the Spaniards and the Catholic Church engendered a debate in Spain about what to do with the native peoples of the conquered lands. Finally, it was decided to undertake the conversion of the Indians to the Catholic faith, and to send priests to accomplish this task. The first to arrive in Mexico—a group of twelve, like the apostles—landed in 1524.

As they Christianized Mexico, baptizing hundreds of thousands, the priests were supported by the Spanish conquistadors and recent settlers. These Spaniards received grants of land still occupied by the villages and towns of native Mexicans. The expectation was that the Indians would continue to work the land and pay tribute to the new landowners in exchange for their education in Christianity. Essentially Spain took over Aztec tribute lists, and the Indian population continued to pay tithes to their overlords.

Later the Spanish Catholic church would establish an office of the Inquisition in Mexico to deal with the natives' ongoing attachment to their old gods. That Holy Office conducted trials against those it considered idolatrous heretics. Anyone accused who did not confess voluntarily to the charges was tortured and sometimes burnt alive at the stake. Ironically, the Spaniards did not consider such public executions a "most horrid and abominable custom."

The chilling rituals of the sixteenth century on both sides of the cultural divide eventually receded in memory as Spain colonized Mexico. North Americans and Europeans had little idea of what occurred during the several hundred years after the Conquest since they were denied access. Spain effectively closed the country to anyone other than Spaniards. A result of Mexico's isolation from the rest of the world was that Spain had free rein to hide and even obliterate the country's pre-Hispanic accomplishments, in particular its architectural monuments and written history.

From the fall of the Aztec Empire in 1521 until approximately 1670, the Spaniards systematically destroyed and buried all the precontact monuments that they could find, as part of their project of Christianizing Mexico (Bernal 1980: 36). In 1531 the bishop of Mexico, Juan de Zumárraga, wrote to his Franciscan brethren, "We are much busied with great and constant labor to convert the infidel . . . five hundred temples razed to the ground, and above twenty thousand idols of the devils they worshipped smashed and burned" (García Icazbalceta 1881: 311; Bernal 1980: 36). Clearly Zumárraga thought that the old and new religions could not coexist peacefully. One had to be destroyed before the other could truly take hold.

In pursuit of Spain's goal of Christianizing Mexico, Bishop Diego de Landa of the Yucatán became a zealous destroyer of Maya ritual books—the codices that elucidated Maya history, religion, and science. Despite the fact that Spaniards kept meticulous records of their activities, it remains unclear how many of these invaluable cultural documents he succeeded in burning, whether tens, hundreds, or even thousands. Some scholars have compared the resulting loss of knowledge to that caused by the accidental burning of the library of Alexandria in 48 BC, fifteen hundred years earlier. However, Diego de Landa "simultaneously scoured the Yucatecan peninsula looking for stelae from which to draw the history of the ancient kingdom of Mayapan" (Cañizares-Esguerra 2001: 67), clear evidence of the polarized feelings of repulsion and attraction the Spaniards had toward Mexicans and their history. Paradoxically the alphabet that Bishop de Landa constructed would eventually be used by twentieth-century Russian linguist Yuri Knorozov to finally decipher Maya glyphs.

In the early years of the Conquest countless carved monoliths in the Aztec capital of Tenochtitlan, modern-day Mexico City, were broken up for use in building Spanish churches and palaces, or simply buried facedown and hidden away from the populace. Aztec pyramids and temples were covered over and employed as foundations for colonial buildings. Spanish clergy and secular administrators apparently believed in the adage "out of sight out of mind," and continued to bury clues to pre-Columbian Mexican history until the turn of the nineteenth century. Their principal fear was that the pagan images would continue to be venerated by native peoples, who, in fact, did find ways to keep their ancient beliefs and customs alive.

The destructive animosity towards the country's pre-Hispanic past began to fade in the last third of the seventeenth century, according to archeologist and historian Ignacio Bernal's influential *History of Mexican Archaeology*. At that point Mexican scholars such as Carlos de Sigüenza y Góngora first became interested in the country's archeology and history. A Jesuit scientist, historian, and cartographer, Sigüenza carried out some of the first archeological excavations at the ruins of Teotihuacan, attempting to determine whether the great pyramid contained a tomb within its purported hollow core. He also collected manuscripts and books about the Indians of New Spain.

Part of Sigüenza's library came from his friend and colleague Juan de Alva Ixtlilxóchitl, the son of Fernando de Alva Cortés Ixtlilxóchitl. Father and son were direct descendants of the ruling family of Texcoco, one of the states closely allied with the Aztecs. Juan inherited his father's writings and invaluable collection of early painted codices that depicted the lives, customs, and beliefs of Mexico's indigenous cultures. These and other painted manuscripts became the focus of increasing interest among European scholars in the succeeding centuries (Bernal 1980: 51).

Sigüenza's library and archive first inspired and later entrapped the Italian nobleman Lorenzo Boturini Benaducci, who arrived in Mexico in 1736 hoping to research the history of the apparition of the Virgin of Guadalupe at Tepeyac, north of Mexico City. When he learned of Sigüenza's incomparable collection, he decided to acquire or copy as many painted manuscripts as he could. Unfortunately, he ran afoul of the viceroy in Mexico City, who disapproved of his Virgin of Guadalupe project and of his study of pre-Hispanic Mexican texts. Boturini was accused of entering the country without permission, jailed, and deported to Spain eight years after his arrival in Mexico. The viceroy confiscated and ultimately dispersed Boturini's library and manuscripts—the Ixtlilxóchitl documents as well as many others—but the knowledge of their existence continued to entice scholars of Mexico's pre-Columbian past.

As the eighteenth century progressed, scholarly pursuits opened up to a broader segment of the populace. Previously most who made their names in the study of antiquity came from the nobility or the clergy. Ironically, as Adam Sellen has pointed out, some of the earliest collectors of pre-Columbian objects were priests, who had been previously tasked with destroying them (2015: 40–41).

However, with the advent of the egalitarian principles associated with the Enlightenment, the ranks of those researching the ancient world began to expand, soon opening up to tradesmen's sons, like the art historian Pierre-François Hugues (self-styled Baron d'Hancarville) and the influential archeologist Johann Joachim Winckelmann. The careers of these scholars and others like them underscore the power that the thirst for knowledge would hold during the eighteenth and nineteenth centuries. "Intellectual brilliance such as theirs, combined with a lust for social self-improvement, was to be a driving force of Enlightenment culture" (Jenkins 2003: 168).

Although access to knowledge was more egalitarian during the eighteenth century, European opinions and views of other cultures often reflected hierarchical, patronizing, and decidedly ethnocentric thinking. The pronouncements made by Europeans about pre-Columbian Mexican history in particular were demeaning and antagonistic, prompting Mexican scholars to react with anger and defensiveness. Jesuit scholars were particularly active in defending Mexico's indigenous heritage, even after 1767, when they were expelled from the country by order of King Charles III. Writing from Bologna, Italy, Francisco Javier Clavigero "indignantly denied the charge of Indian inferiority" presented by Enlightenment writers in Europe (Keen 1971: 300). Another indication that Mexican scholars had begun to reframe the narrative of their country's precontact history is the work of the Jesuit Pedro José Márquez. In 1804 he wrote about the recent archeological finds by José Antonio Alzate, who had excavated at the sites of El Tajín in Veracruz and Xochicalco in Morelos. This was the first extensive treatise on Mexican archeology to be published in Europe.

In 1790 workers discovered an eleven-foot sculpture of the Aztec mother goddess Coatlicue in Mexico City's central plaza, the Zócalo, which they were re-grading and paving with cobblestones. A few months later they uncovered the twenty-four-ton Aztec Calendar Stone, also called the Sun Stone, lying face down sixteen inches below the plaza's surface (León y Gama 1792; López Luján 2009). The chronicler Fray Diego Durán described the Calendar Stone as being located, early in the sixteenth century, on the southeast corner of the central plaza, where the daily market was held. Then, Fray Alonso de Montúfar, archbishop of Mexico from 1551 until 1572, ordered the stone buried because he believed it caused violent criminal activity in the area (Durán 1994: 100).

The Spaniards had so successfully obliterated the remnants of precontact cultures over more than 250 years that the grandeur and craftsmanship of the Calendar Stone and Coatlicue carvings were a complete revelation. The discovery offered a surprising window into Mexican antiquity, causing scholars to worry that the enormous works would meet the same fate that other pagan monuments had before them—destruction or burial.

The Calendar Stone was soon mounted on the western wall of the cathedral, piquing the curiosity of scientists and interested bystanders. The Coatlicue monolith was moved to the patio of the Real y Pontificia Universidad de México (Royal and Pontifical University of Mexico), where it prompted a greater range of responses. The figure incorporates many of the features of Aztec iconography and ritual that the Spaniards found so repellant. Her face is composed of two serpent heads. She is dressed in a skirt of intertwined snakes and wears a necklace of human hands and hearts, from which hangs a skull. However, the image of the mother of all Aztec deities was so powerfully evocative to the Indians of Mexico City, even after nearly three centuries, that they laid flowers in front of her. The Catholic Church began to suspect that pagan rituals were being carried out around the monolith, so very soon after the statue's discovery the administrators of the Pontifical University ordered that the goddess be reinterred.

Hard on the heels of the discovery of the monoliths in the Zócalo of Mexico City came attempts to illustrate the newly rediscovered Mexican archeological monuments and artifacts. Of particular note is the work of Guillermo Dupaix, a native of the duchy of Luxembourg, who was a captain in the dragoon regiment of Mexico. He began a journey of discovery and documentation in 1791, shortly after landing at Veracruz. He examined ruined archeological monuments around Mexico City, describing them and depicting them in pen-and-ink drawings, continuing over a period of more than a dozen years. Initially concentrating on pre-Hispanic monuments located mostly around the city, he eventually ventured much further afield. Later descriptions and drawings recorded the largest and most important pyramidal structures of Teotihuacan: the elaborate bas reliefs of the Feathered Serpent pyramid (Quetzalcoatl) at Xochicalco, about 75 miles southwest of Mexico City; the ancient monuments of Mitla and Tlacolula in

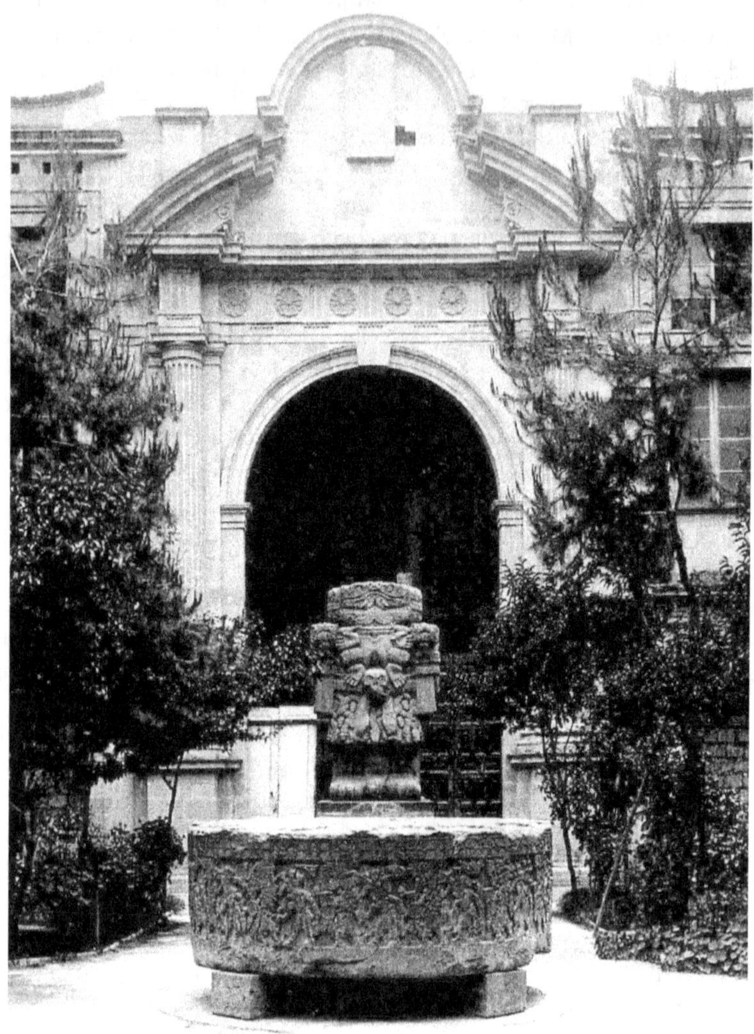

Figure 3.1 Coatlicue monolith just behind the Tizoc stone in the patio of the Museo Nacional de México. Photo by William Henry Jackson (Smithsonian Institution, National Anthropological Archives).

Oaxaca; and the amazingly intricate pyramid of El Tajín in Veracruz (López Luján 2015: 45).

His accomplishments brought him considerable renown, later eliciting an invitation from the King of Spain to lead the first Royal Antiquary Expedition. In the first decade of the nineteenth century Charles IV of Spain commissioned

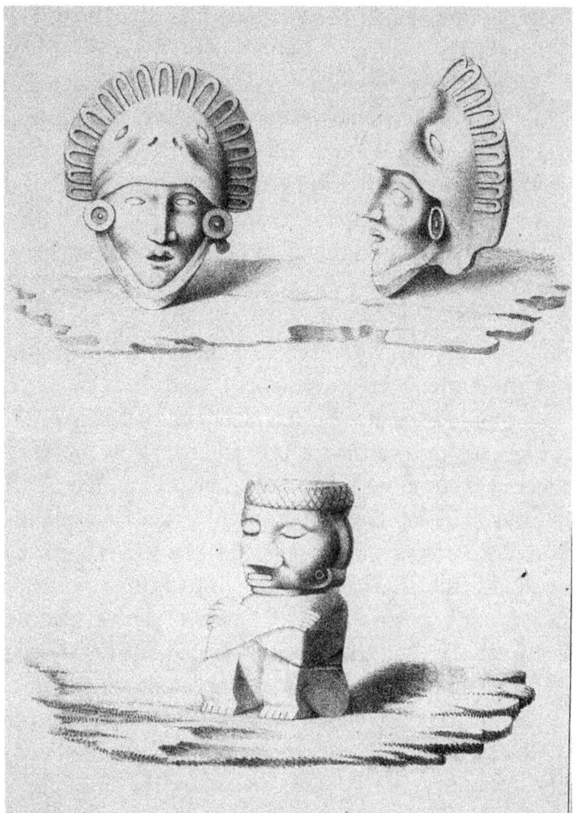

Figure 3.2   Artifacts from Oaxaca drawn by José Luciano Castañeda (Smithsonian Libraries).

Dupaix and artist José Luciano Castañeda to "investigate the ancient monuments of the realm" (Kingsborough 1831: vol. 4, 209). On the third expedition in 1807, Dupaix and Castañeda spent several months in Palenque in Chiapas, where they made a thorough examination and study of the ruins. His report and drawings were to be sent to Spain, "but the outbreak of the Mexican revolution [War of Independence] frustrated this design and they remained during those troublous times in the custody of Castañeda, who deposited them in the museum of the city of Mexico" (Rau 1879: 9).

At the turn of the nineteenth century Alexander von Humboldt, a Prussian naturalist and explorer, arrived in the country. He was one of the few early scientists not from Spain to be allowed to travel freely in Mexico. He wrote extensively about his journey, describing the landscape, the geology, the flora, the fauna, and the monuments he saw, along with the customs of the people—all new and exotic topics to the rest of the world. Interested in ancient monuments, he prevailed upon the authorities to unearth the statue of Coatlicue in 1803, more than a decade after it had been reburied, so that he could study it and document its features. The published account of his research in Mexico, *Vues des cordillères et monuments des peuples indigènes de L'Amérique*, had a profound impact on European and North American readers. As American historian Benjamin Keen notes in *Aztec Images in Western Thought*, "Not only did it greatly increase European interest in Aztec civilization but it raised the study of the subject to a higher scientific level" (Keen 1971: 336). It was the first authoritative writing about Mexico in the Enlightenment tradition, and Europeans immediately became eager to know more about this country that had been closed to them for so long.

The resurgence of interest in the pre-Columbian past, partially the result of the discovery of the buried Aztec monuments and the Dupaix reports, culminated in the founding of Mexico's Museo Nacional in 1825. This engendered a national effort to gather more artifacts. It would be a slow process since, then as now, most collectors were more interested in acquiring objects than in selling or giving them away. The museum occupied an upper floor of the building that housed the Real y Pontificia Universidad de México—the first university in North America, founded in 1551. The museum had three departments: antiquities, natural history, and industrial products, with displays intended principally to inform and inspire scholars and the university's students (Acevedo 1995: 179).

In the year of the museum's founding, an important collection of Aztec stone carvings and other artifacts was removed from Mexico and exported to France by a French collector named Latour Allard. He had purchased the artifacts from Castañeda. As it happened, Tomás Murphy, the first officer of Mexico's first embassy in Europe, located in London, heard about the removal and proposed sale of the artifacts by Latour Allard and registered vehement objections. He asserted that the collection was not the private property of Castañeda but belonged to the Mexican people. Murphy's protests had little effect, however, and the collection was sold to the Louvre in 1849 (Fauvet-Berthelot, López Luján, and Guimarães 2007:104–26; Sellen 2015: 70–72).

During the first half of the nineteenth century a number of European artists became interested in Mexican archeology, among them Bavarian-born Maximilien Franck, who arrived in Mexico in 1827 (Franck 1831: 283). He spent two years in the country, enjoying the hospitality of Joel Poinsett, the first United States ambassador to the newly independent republic (Franck 1831: 128). During his stay Franck sketched pre-Columbian artifacts housed in the Museo Nacional and in several important private collections in Mexico City. He completed eighty-one large folio drawings of artifacts, more than half of them illustrating some 360 individual objects then in the collections of the Museo Nacional.[1]

In addition to documenting the Museo Nacional's holdings, Franck illustrated objects in the private collections of the Count of Peñasco; José Luciano

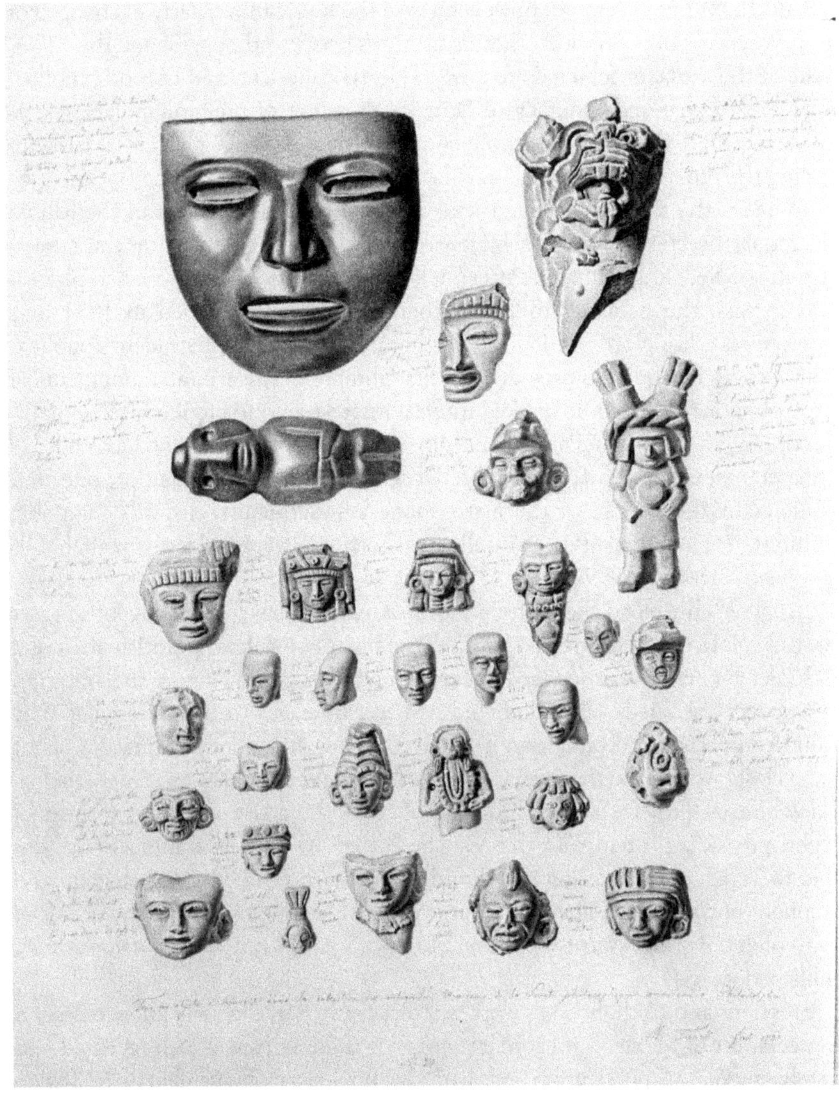

Figure 3.3   Stone mask and ceramic figurines in the Poinsett Collection drawn by Maximilien Franck (courtesy of the British Museum, London, AM2006, Drg. 128, pg. 21).

Castañeda, who apparently still considered the government's collection his own; the Marquis de Silva Nevada; and Poinsett. The images are extremely accurate, making the artifacts easily identifiable today. Franck meticulously gave measurements when important or noted that the illustration was life-size.

The Franck drawings were the first to accurately record the scale and existence of most of these extraordinary objects. Many of the artifacts ultimately became part of the Museo Nacional; however, since the museum regularly exchanged or sold objects to collectors and other institutions between the 1850s and the 1870s, some of the artifacts depicted are now in North American and European collections. The range and accuracy of Franck's drawings of pre-Columbian objects in Mexico's private and public collections in the late 1820s provides a basis for tracing the provenance of certain artifacts later acquired by Eugène Boban.

In 1828, the same year Franck was documenting the artifacts in the Museo Nacional, the French priest abbé Henri Barradère discovered Castañeda's drawings in the fledgling museum. After "delicate negotiations" he obtained permission to take the drawings to Paris, where they were published in 1834 in a "sumptuous edition" (Keen 1971: 313). For most of Europe, Barradère's publication of these illustrations provided the first glimpse of the art and monuments of pre-Columbian Mexico. It sparked intense interest among French intellectuals.[2] According to historian Paul N. Edison, "French scholars likened Barradère's *Antiquités mexicaines* to a second discovery and conquest of America, one that would right the wrongs of the first conquest by exhuming a dead, but noble civilization. Huge expanses of intellectual territory were suddenly available to European science" (1999: 64).

In 1839 John Lloyd Stephens, a North American lawyer and adventurer, set out to explore southern Mexico and the Yucatan peninsula; the British artist and architect Frederick Catherwood accompanied him. Following in the tradition of Dupaix, Castañeda, and Humboldt, they were eager to illustrate what they found to educate and enlighten a public thirsting for more information about these "lost" worlds. To that end Catherwood had brought along a camera lucida, a device that projects a ghostly image of what the artist sees onto a sheet of paper, producing a template that can be traced. With this equipment he was able to depict with amazing detail and accuracy the ruined cities that he and Stephens encountered. Their explorations were chronicled in a highly successful two-volume work, *Incidents of Travel in Central America, Chiapas, and Yucatan*, published in 1841.

Stephens and Catherwood's work was a watershed in the early knowledge and appreciation of Mexico's precontact past. For the first time a well received and widely circulated publication extolled the majestic achievements of Mexico and Central America's pre-Columbian inhabitants. Catherwood's meticulous drawings of buildings and sculptures contrasted greatly with most of what had gone before, providing a richness of detail and accuracy of scale that superseded many of the distortions prevalent in earlier renderings. Additionally, Stephens rejected the diffusionist notions then prevalent among many Europeans, who saw Egyptian and Asian influence throughout pre-Columbian art and architecture. In their publications Stephens and Catherwood clearly stated their opinion that the creators of the ruined cities and temples they had documented were none other than the ancestors of the present-day inhabitants of the region. This opened a new era in the study of pre-Columbian Mexican history. Their descriptions of ruined cities in Chiapas, the Yucatan, and Central America would entice many generations of archeologists, artists, and adventurers to follow in their footsteps.

Although the North American lawyer and the British artist had advanced ideas about the meanings and origins of what they saw, they behaved in the same rapacious way that others later did—helping themselves to what they wanted. Stephens himself pointed out the ease with which he had purchased not only ancient artifacts, but also entire archeological sites, over which he felt he held all rights. "The reader is perhaps curious to know how old cities sell in Central America . . . I paid 50 dollars for Copan. There never was any difficulty about price. I offered that sum, for which Don Jose Maria thought me only a fool" (1841: 128). Copan is one of the largest and most important Maya sites in Central America and has been almost continuously studied since Stephens purchased it. At the time many people did not appreciate the importance and value of the ruins and artifacts on their property. Stephens had dreams of moving all the important monuments and sculpture from Copan to museums in the United States, but fortunately never managed to accomplish this. Stephens and Catherwood's purchases and publications were to have unintended consequences. There soon developed a strong trade in looted artifacts. Then as demand outpaced supply, more and more fake artifacts appeared on the scene.

By mid-century Europeans and North Americans were completely in the thrall of Mexico's ancient cultures. In 1850 the Louvre's curator Adrien de Longpérier convinced the director of the museum to expand the Louvre's collections to include the pre-Columbian civilizations of the Americas. At his urging the museum purchased and exhibited for the first time a collection of ancient American artifacts.

Eugène Boban owned a manuscript copy of Longpérier's catalog of the exhibition (Leavitt 1886b: 150). The catalog presented countless sculptures in "basalt, jasper, granite, and jade" as well as numerous "terra cotta figures," including animal and human depictions. There were necklaces, bracelets, and plaques made from a wide range of materials, such as jade, agate, obsidian, and crystal. Household objects included mirrors, needles, and weights (Longpérier 1850). In the years to come Boban would search for and collect many of these same artifact types.

By the middle of the nineteenth century, scholars in Mexico, Europe, and North America had built a solid foundation of knowledge about Mexico's precontact cultures. Public and private collections were being formed at an unprecedented rate. Scholarly investigation had opened up to people of all backgrounds and classes, and there was a growing business in the sale of ancient artifacts. The increased demand for such objects engendered a corresponding increase in the manufacture of "ancient" artifacts. The stage was set for a man of Eugène Boban's diverse interests and talents to succeed in this stimulating and promising New World.

Notes

1. Eighty-one plates, measuring 21–22 in. by 17 in., accompanied by a twenty-six-page catalog in French, are in the British Museum in the Anthropology Library and Research Center (Am2006-Drg128-208-Fra.).

2. Castañeda's drawings in the Royal and Pontifical University later became part of the collections of the Museo Nacional (Fernández 1988:109). According to Charles Rau, curator of the Department of Antiquities at the Smithsonian Institution, copies of these drawings were purchased by Latour Allard, a French collector, who sold his own pre-Columbian collection to the Louvre. These copies were recopied by Augustine Aglio and published in 1830, some two years earlier than the Barradère edition, by Lord Kingsborough (Rau 1879: 9).

4

MEXICO AT MID-CENTURY

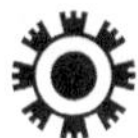

In the spring of 1857, after four years exploring California, Eugène Boban started a new life in Mexico City. His entry into the country is documented by his first visa, which is dated 1 April of that year (AGN, Movimiento Marítima, Vol. 201, Exp. 135, f. 24). The last of these archived letters is dated 22 February 1859. Perhaps regulations for foreign visitors changed in 1860, or the documents for subsequent years were lost as a result of the country's political turmoil. Whatever the case, we know for certain that Boban lived in Mexico City for more than a decade—until 1869.

Now known simply as Eugenio Boban, he arrived in Mexico City at a time when the newly reformed republic provided boundless opportunity for a young French émigré. The country had struggled to achieve a relatively peaceful business and political climate at mid-century but would continue to cope with the effects of Spain's long colonization and other nations' encroachments for decades to come.

By the middle of the nineteenth century the capital was an urban center bustling with more than 200,000 inhabitants—about half the size of Paris at that time (Ciudad de México 1976: 778). The metropolis was surrounded by numerous small towns and villages, all nestled within the magnificent Valley of Mexico, encircled by high mountains and snow-peaked volcanoes.

When the Spanish conquistadors first saw the Aztec capital of Tenochtitlan, in 1519, the valley was covered by a series of fresh- and saltwater lakes. The streets and walkways were crisscrossed by canals and surrounded by floating gardens. The high plateau sheltered by the mountains provided a near-perfect climate, and the valley brimmed with flowers, wildlife, and possibility.

Much of Mexico City's natural beauty remained in the 1850s. The Spanish colonial city built atop Tenochtitlan made use of the canals that the Aztecs had constructed for traversing their floating domain, and many of these ancient waterways could still be seen when Boban arrived. So, too, could the stone aqueducts that the conquerors had built to bring fresh water down from the hills of Chapultepec. And, of course, the valley's majestic volcanoes—Popocatépetl (Smoking Mountain) and Iztaccihuatl (White Woman)—and their related peaks were a constant presence on the horizon.

Along the Calzada de la Viga, now a high-speed motorway, there were then four graceful stands of enormous trees bordering a broad canal, which meandered among the streets of the city. Accounts from the nineteenth century describe afternoon and early evening *paseos* (processions) of horse-drawn coaches and horseback riders parading along these avenues throughout the seasons, particularly Easter season, which was just about the time of year Boban first entered the city. The Viga Canal connected the center of the city with the outlying *chinampas*, or floating gardens. At dawn the canals were filled with barges and canoes overflowing with fruit, vegetables, and flowers, a floating Mexican market (Calderón 1970: 167).

Frances Calderón de la Barca, the Scottish wife of a Spanish diplomat who lived in Mexico in the 1840s, ten years before Boban's arrival, described the principal features of the city and its splendors while looking down from Chapultepec castle.

> The whole valley of Mexico lies stretched out as in a map; the city itself, with its innumerable churches and convents; the two great aqueducts which cross the plain; the avenues of elms and poplars which lead to the city; the villages, lakes, and plains, which surround it . . . the whole landscape, as viewed from this height, is one of nearly unparalleled beauty. (1970: 116)

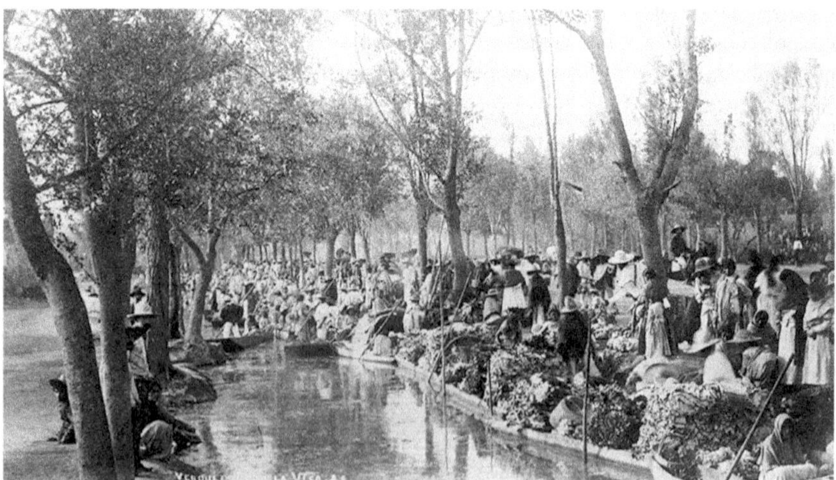

Figure 4.1 The vegetable market on canoes along the Viga Canal, ca. 1860 (Smithsonian Institution Archives, Nelson-Goldman Collection, RU 7364).

Not only were the ancient waterways still evident at mid-century, so were some of the astounding archeological features of the Aztec past. The description of the capital in 1850 by Alexander Clark Forbes, writing under the name A. Barrister, captures the sense of multilayered history available to visitors.

> In the heart of the city is the Grand Square (Plaza Mayor) [or Zócalo], perhaps as large as Lincoln's Inn Fields. On one side of this stands the Cathedral, on another the Palace. . . . The Cathedral is a large handsome church, standing upon exactly the same spot as stood the chief temple (*Teocalli*) of the Astecs [*sic*] before the conquest. Into one side of it is built an enormous circular stone, about twelve feet in diameter, covered with hieroglyphics, and purported to be a perpetual calendar used by the original occupants of the city. Its ancient name is *Kellenda* [*sic*], and it is popularly called Montezuma's watch. (Barrister 1851: 66)

He is actually describing the Aztec Calendar Stone, which had been mounted on the wall of the sixteenth-century cathedral in the center of the main square after its rediscovery in 1790.

Despite the natural beauty of the capital, the years preceding Boban's arrival in Mexico in 1857 were anything but serene. The country had been in an almost continuous state of unrest or war since its independence. After finally securing its freedom from the Spanish crown in 1823, Mexico was ruled briefly by Agustín de Iturbide, a self-declared emperor. Iturbide was replaced after two years by President Guadalupe Victoria and executed a year later when he tried to return to power. Following President Victoria, General Antonio López de Santa Anna, a hero to the Mexican army, would be elevated to the presidency through various means, numerous times between 1833 and 1855 (Kandell 1988).

The battle of the Alamo and Mexico's subsequent loss of Texas, which Santa Anna had signed away in 1836 in exchange for his own liberty, initiated a particularly intense period of conflict. Mexico declared war on the United States when it admitted Texas to the union in 1845. In retaliation, the United States declared war on Mexico in 1846 and invaded the country in 1847. Santa Anna, who had been living in Cuba after his loss of Texas, "tendered his services to the Mexican government for an end to his exile; at the same time, he offered the United States most of Mexico's territories north of the Rio Grande in exchange for a payment of 30 million and Washington's aid in recovering the presidency" (Kandell 1988: 322).

Santa Anna lost Mexico City to the invading American general, Zachary Taylor. Despite having the much larger army at his disposal, he surrendered to US troops, once again, in 1848. The Treaty of Guadalupe Hidalgo, which ended the Mexican-American War, forced Mexico to cede the territories of California and New Mexico and most of the American Southwest. The inept but politically savvy Santa Anna went into exile again, only to be called back to the Mexican presidency in 1853 for an eleventh term.

At this point, Benito Juárez, a Zapotec Indian lawyer who had been elected governor of Oaxaca, went into exile in the United States to protest the corruption of Santa Anna's government. In 1855 Santa Anna resigned his office for the last time, and Juárez returned from New Orleans to become one of the leaders of the Liberal Party. The years that followed, known as the War of Reform, saw constant, bloody battles between liberals and conservatives, resulting in anarchy throughout the country. As the journalist and author Jonathan Kandell notes, "In the capital itself, during the early 1850s, troops were out of control and pillaged shops and houses at will" (1988: 323). Finally, in January 1861, more than fifty years after Mexico had begun to shake off the yoke of Spanish colonialism, Juárez, the country's first native Mexican leader, took office as president.

Boban's early years in Mexico must have been terrifying at times, since they spanned the War of Reform between 1858 and 1861. Pitched battles occurred regularly between armies supporting the Liberal cause, who sought to overthrow the economic and political power of the Catholic Church, and the conservative forces who supported the clergy. The situation bore similarities to what he had experienced in his youth in Paris—times of political upheaval, danger, and bloodshed.

In numerous drafts of his unpublished memoirs, Boban wrote that he lived and worked in Mexico City for two decades, sometimes saying that it was a quarter-century, which would mean he had arrived in the country sometime in the 1840s or early 1850s, since he returned to France in 1869. In addition to changing his age with some regularity, he seems to have exaggerated the amount of time he spent in Mexico. His own writings attest that he went to California in 1853, traveling throughout the region for four years. This itinerary fits perfectly with the visa issued in Mexico City in April 1857. This means that, in reality, he spent some sixteen years away from Paris, including four years in California and twelve years in Mexico. It could be said, however, that he lived in Mexico *during* two decades, i.e., in the 1850s and 1860s.

Boban's later notes indicate that his father, René Victor, lived in Mexico with him, although it is not known when he arrived. He may have preceded his son or accompanied him from California; however, there is no visa in his name in the Archivo General de la Nación. What is known is that by 1862, René Victor was back in Paris, since he is listed as a witness on the birth certificate of his granddaughter, Jeanne Laurence, the child of his eldest daughter, Rose Louise, and her husband Andre Martial Backès.[1] One of Eugène's younger sisters, Marie, had had a daughter out of wedlock two years earlier, and was living apart from her mother at the time. It may be that this event had some influence on the senior Boban's decision to return to Paris, since it appears that by this time both Marie and her younger sister Julie were living by themselves, some distance from the family apartment.

In Mexico City, however, according to a directory of businesses in the capital in 1865, Eugène Boban owned a *fábrica de cajas de cartón*—a factory that manufactured cardboard boxes. René Victor's profession as gainier, making sheaths and chests or boxes out of leather and other luxury materials, seems to have been translated in the New World into the newer medium of cardboard, which is listed as a commercial product in England in 1858 (Simmonds 1858). The factory was located on a block-long street named Callejón del Espíritu Santo (Alleyway of the Holy Spirit) in a fashionable Mexico City neighborhood that was an important shopping district. This was one of several public roads and passageways named after the church that had formerly occupied the site. This address was where Boban had established an antiquities shop as well.

A traveler's guide to Mexico published in 1858 vividly described the many attractions of this section of the city, which seems to have been home to many French expatriates.

> The streets are so straight that many of them frame vistas to far away trees in the countryside and the mountains of the broad valley . . . along the streets are beautiful houses brightly-painted . . . elegant Mexican ladies depart in the morning to the churches to fulfill their devotions. . . . The Indian sellers in their blue wool garments, the water carriers with their own original outfits, the ranchers with their harnessed and saddled horses . . . all contribute to a pleasant aspect of novelty. In the shops on Plateros street [a few blocks from Boban's shop] stores of luxury goods and the latest French fashions are displayed in beautiful glass cases to tempt the appetite of the elegant ladies. They also admire the French dressmaker shops for their remarkable good taste. Hairdressers are found on the same street . . . which also are French owned. (Arróniz 1991: 40–41)

Within blocks of the cardboard factory were French doctors, pharmacists, educators, photographers, booksellers, and other French-owned businesses catering to the expatriate community. At Callejón del Espíritu Santo no. 2 there was a hardware store owned by F. A. Lohse and sons, who sold sewing machines; Henri Escabasse sold French clothing at the corner of Espíritu Santo and Tercera Calle de Plateros; a Mr. Linet sold tin and iron beds at Callejón del Espírito Santo no. 14; and the Delanoes' shop (also known as Maison Delanoe Frères) sold paper, writing material, and blank books at the corner of Refugio and Calle del Espíritu Santo (Maillefert 1992: 225–29). The French enclave was not far from the fashionable Alameda Park and just three blocks from the Zócalo.

Almost as soon as he arrived in Mexico City, Boban began to study Mexican history and archeology and to acquire artifacts through surface collecting, as indicated in his unpublished memoirs and the record he jotted down in his field notes. These endeavors were facilitated by his ability to speak Spanish, which he learned in California and on his travels south. Early on he seems to have visited the Museo Nacional, which was then housed in the Real y Pontificia

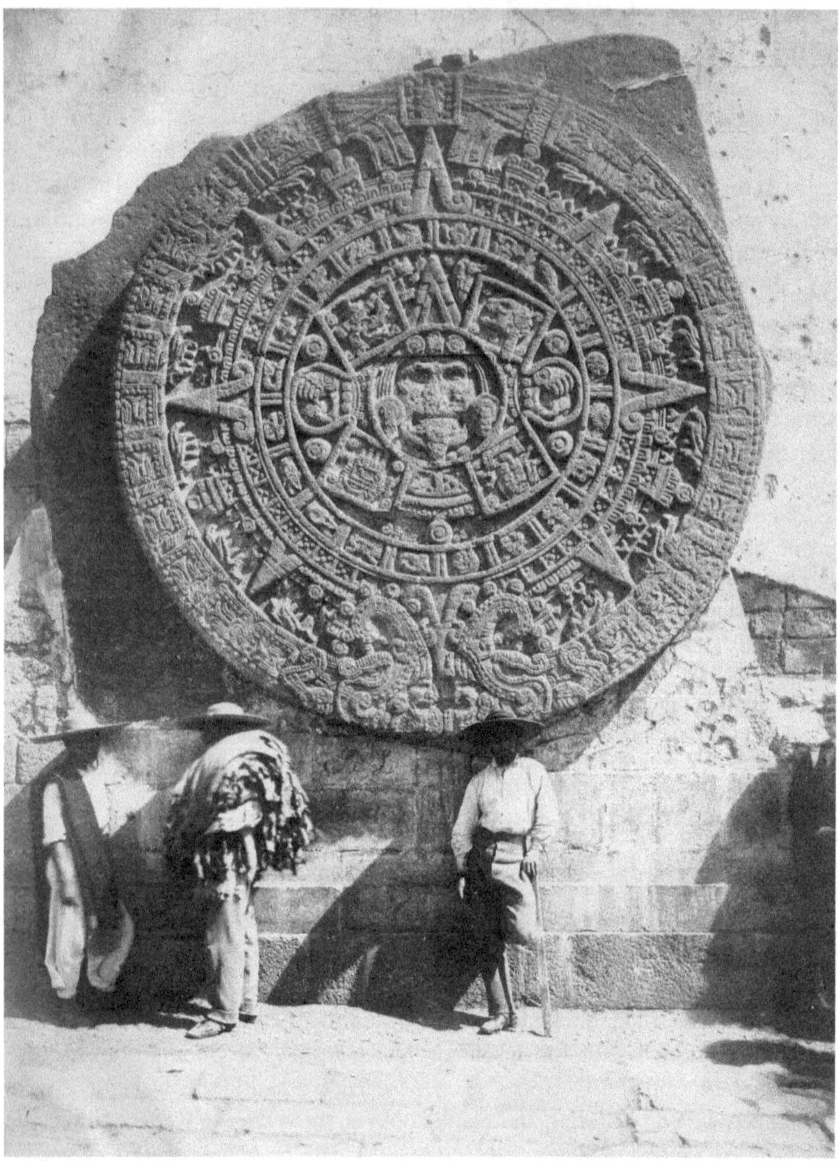

Figure 4.2 Aztec Calendar or Sun Stone on the western wall of Mexico City's cathedral, ca. 1860 (courtesy of Hispanic Society of America, New York).

Universidad. There he admired the exhibits and examined the artifact types, comparing them with the objects he himself was collecting.

Many fanciful ideas about pre-Columbian Mexico were passed around for the consumption of tourists in the nineteenth century. Some of them seem to have originated with the staff of the museum itself. Frances Calderón de la Barca provides a dramatic description of what she learned during her first visit to the Museo Nacional.

> We are told that five thousand priests chanted night and day in the Great Temple, to the honour and in the service of the monstrous idols who were anointed thrice a day with the most precious perfumes. . . . We afterwards saw the Stone of Sacrifices [the Tizoc stone], now in the courtyard of the university, with a hollow in the middle, in which the victim was laid, while six priests, dressed in red, their heads adorned with plumes of green feathers (they must have looked like macaws) held him down while the chief priest cut open his breast, threw his heart at the feet of the idol, and afterwards put it into his mouth with a golden spoon. (1970: 102, 105)

The circular Tizoc stone, which is almost a yard thick and three yards wide, was another of the Aztec monuments discovered beneath the Zócalo in 1790, and it was prominently displayed at the museum. Some scholars called it the gladiator stone because they believed warriors battled each other on top of it, with the loser becoming a sacrificial victim. The stone actually commemorates and glorifies battles waged under the rule of Tizoc, the seventh emperor of the Aztecs, who ruled from 1481 to 1486.

Boban wanted to make a serious study of Mexico's prehistory and began educating himself in all aspects of the country's ancient past. He assiduously read most of the Spanish authors who chronicled the discovery and conquest, including the historian Francisco de Gómara and the Franciscan ethnographers Bernardino de Sahagún and Juan de Torquemada. He also consulted later writers like the Jesuit scholar Francisco Javier Clavigero, the Mexican astronomer Antonio León y Gama, and the historian and collector José Ramírez (HSA B2044, Box V). He refers to all of them in his writings and in the catalogs he prepared for his own collections and those of others. He began to learn Nahuatl, the language of the Aztecs, which was still spoken by most of the native people of Mexico City and its environs. Boban's fascination with the history and artifacts of ancient Mexican civilizations melded seamlessly with burgeoning interest in the native cultural history expressed by increasing numbers of Europeans, North Americans, and Mexicans by mid-century.

In the nineteenth century, Paris was known not only for the luxurious lifestyle of many of its richer inhabitants, but also for its sophisticated intellectual climate that had grown out of the Enlightenment. The city's inhabitants were aflame with interest in the world and its myriad cultures. Boban would refer to his own "natural Parisian curiosity" when describing his enthusiasm for the history and archeology of Mexico. His travels through California, where he first studied the ways of native peoples and learned Spanish, facilitated his investigations, as did his later study of Nahuatl. His early efforts to educate himself about Mexico's past sparked, in turn, a desire to learn even more.

It is likely that his father, René Victor, oversaw the management of the cardboard factory for the first few years—the time during which he remained in Mexico City. This allowed Eugène the freedom to travel the country collecting pre-Columbian artifacts from surface finds and later carrying out excavations with the help of native laborers. In the 1850s and 1860s there still was evidence of many centuries of the pre-Columbian and colonial past all around Mexico City. To this day it is difficult to dig anywhere in Mexico without finding remnants of its ancient inhabitants. A profusion of obsidian blades, spindle whorls, and potsherds can still be gathered from the surface or just below.

While Boban was educating himself about Mexico's past and gathering a collection of archeological materials, the War of Reform raged throughout the country. The Catholic Church was the principal financial backer of the conservatives battling Benito Juárez's liberals. To defray some of the costs of the civil war, the clergy sold off gold and silver ornaments, candelabra, and gems, hoping that their side would win and the Church would be able to retain its extensive holdings of land, buildings, and treasure. Many years later Boban recounted a story told to him by "an old Israelite jeweler from Bordeaux" who had lived in Mexico for thirty years.[2] The jeweler said that he had participated in the removal of precious stones and pearls from numerous churches at the request of the clergy and had replaced them with imitation jewels that he had brought from Europe. He added that this was done without the government's knowledge (HSA: B2253, Box XIV). Boban would not have been involved in activities to support the Church's political ambitions. He became a Mason while in Mexico, a decidedly anti-Catholic fraternity, which actively supported the Liberal Party. It is possible however, that he may have profited from the sales in light of later events.

Notwithstanding the efforts of the Church and its supporters, however, the liberals won the day in 1861. Eugène Boban only rarely mentions events and activities occurring during the War of Reform years. In his later recollections of life in the capital, all was idyllic in his rose-colored memory, as he hunted and excavated, befriending native peoples and learning their language to record their history.

In 1856 Ignacio Comonfort, then president of Mexico, instituted the Lerdo Law, which restricted the privileges of the Church, declared all citizens equal, and brought about the confiscation of the Mexican Catholic Church properties. Benito Juárez, who had resisted American incursions into Mexico and was dedicated to reforming the country's treatment of its indigenous population, was finally elected president in 1861. He proved to be extremely fair-minded with his military opponents but was rather less charitable with the clergy. The Church represented the most powerful opponent to the liberal cause. After the protracted wars to gain independence from Spain, it was the Church that retained much of the property, money, and power that had once belonged to the Spanish crown. Juárez was intent on stripping it of its riches and, even more important, its power once and for all.

One of Juárez's first acts as president was to demolish many of the earliest colonial structures in Mexico City, principally convents and monasteries, particularly those in the neighborhood where Boban lived. As one author noted, the reformists appeared to confuse ideology with architecture. Perhaps the destruction of monuments to colonial power represented a form of retribution. The Spanish conquerors had destroyed the temples and idols of the indigenous people, and now in the mid-nineteenth century, the president of Mexico, a Zapotec Indian, laid siege to the Christian temples that had been built atop the Aztec structures.

In addition to exiling five bishops who had sided with the conservatives, Juárez forbade priests and nuns from wearing vestments outside their churches. He sought to limit the Church's power by restricting clerical privileges, in particular the authority of the Church courts. This move was exceedingly unpopular with the clergy.

The Lerdo Law called for the expropriation of numerous Church properties, but little had taken place during the War of Reform. Eventually, under Juárez, countless churches, monasteries, and convents were torn down, and their contents sold to the highest bidders. These actions put Juárez's government on a collision path with the traditional ruling classes of Mexico—the Spanish monarchists and the Catholic clergy—both intent on protecting their wealth and power.

Guillermo Tovar de Teresa, the Mexican historian, published in 1992 a two-volume chronicle of the destruction of Mexico's religious and colonial properties that began in 1861 and went on for several years. It is a grim record of the country's lost patrimony, including countless sixteenth- and seventeenth-century edifices. One of the incidents Tovar describes is the dismantling of the main altar in the church of Tlatelolco. The Spaniards began construction in 1536. The sacred edifice was filled with superb paintings, most of which were taken down and used as firewood. A few of the paintings were saved and taken for protection to the Academia San Carlos, the first art academy and museum in the Americas, for protection.

The great church and monastery of San Francisco, just around the corner from Boban's factory and antiquities shop, was entirely dismantled, its art and gilded choir removed to make room for the stabling of cavalry horses. The monastery was eventually torn down (Tovar 1992: vol. II, 27).

The convent and monastery of the church of Santo Domingo, some three blocks from the cathedral in the Zócalo, were also demolished, revealing numerous burials of priests and nuns in the process. Their corpses appeared to be mummified because of the conditions in which they had been interred.

All told, more than forty religious structures in Mexico City—nearly half of the eighty-four the Spanish had built to promote Catholic worship in the city—were razed. As a result, some of the most important colonial buildings in the capital simply disappeared. The demolition experts worked overtime, employing axes, picks, and ropes to pull down altars and walls, while gathering up relics, paintings, crucifixes, and statues of saints. The objects retrieved amidst the destruction were sold, purportedly to help finance the government and further reforms, but the financial aspects of the project were largely a hoax. As Tovar notes, "The sale of Church property was a comedy played out between shrewd dealers and money launderers, a dramatic case of fraud, the state giving huge advantages to the purchasers. Most of the little cash that was obtained was spent on the salaries of workers, who carried out the task of reducing eloquent examples of our colonial art to dust and debris" (Tovar 1992: vol. I, 14).

W. H. Bullock, the son of the British impresario who created shows of exotic artifacts and unusual people to enthrall the London public, toured Mexico in 1864 overseeing some of his father's land investments and looking for new opportunities to make money. He corroborated how little financial gain Juárez achieved from the confiscation of Mexican Catholic church properties. "So hard-pressed for ready money was the Government of Juárez at this period—the beginning of the year 1861—that the sites of the ruined churches—sometimes including the sacred edifice itself—were sold for the most trifling sums" (Bullock 1866: 82).

Not everyone was able or willing to benefit from the government's fire sale of religious objects, however. The supporters of the conservative party feared that they would be excommunicated if they tried to purchase any of the religious art. That meant that there was a trove of art available at unbelievably low prices to those who were not bothered by their consciences or beliefs. As Bullock notes, foreigners "were willing to pocket their scruples and invest in it. In this way, many Frenchmen and Belgians, and some English, realized considerable fortunes" (Bullock 1866: 82–83). Boban appears to have taken full advantage of this volatile and uncertain situation, and, in so doing, amassed a rather large collection of religious objects and colonial artifacts.

The destruction of colonial religious structures and the sale of their contents would have a long-term impact on the composition of Boban's collections and the number of religious objects he would eventually offer for sale—perhaps even including some of the crystal skulls. However, when he first arrived in the country his focus was ancient Mexican cultures and people. He became a devoted archeologist and began cataloguing the artifacts and human remains he recovered from his early digs in 1857, his first year in Mexico. His notes provide details about his excavations of burials and temple mounds in a variety of neighborhoods in and around the capital and in the smaller surrounding towns.

His collecting activities were informed by those of the early archeologists and adventurers who had explored the ancient sites for the previous half century and were facilitated by Mexico's dawning "neo-technological era," characterized by new modes of transportation. Mexico City was one of the first urban centers in Latin America to inaugurate a steam railroad line, which began transporting travelers throughout the city and its adjoining suburbs as early as 1852. *Diligencias*, or stagecoaches, provided a relatively secure, though somewhat less comfortable, method of travel. One might also traverse the city by horse-drawn tram pulled along iron rails (Podgorny 2008: 579). When all else failed, there was always a horse, a mule, or one's own feet. Even Paris was not as well equipped with public transportation as Mexico City in the mid-nineteenth-century (Morrison 2003).

The sites Boban excavated were scattered far and wide in the Valley of Mexico, but their locations in some cases can be linked to the expanding tramlines and steam railways. His excavation catalog, now in the Hispanic Society of America in New York, includes notes written on slips of paper on digs he conducted in Chalco, about fifteen miles to the east of Mexico City, in 1857; San Angel to the south, near the railroad station, in 1860; and to the west of Lake Texcoco, in Azcapotzalco, in 1858 and 1860. In Azcapotzalco he uncovered many funerary *ollas* (large ceramic vessels) buried in the grounds or patios of the ancient ruins, along with stone amulets, which he called *yollotli* (HSA: B2245, Box VI). According to a modern Nahuatl dictionary, this word means heart or seed, but it may be what native workmen told him such pieces were called.

His excavation catalog also has information about locating human remains. "During the year 1858, we began to explore the ancient capital of the Acolhua or Chichimec, in the remains of the great site [Texcutzingo], which is now the village of Texcoco. . . . We found a series of mounds, one of which contained a mummy" (HSA: B2245, Box VI).[3] Finding skeletal material and associated grave goods would be a constant interest for Boban throughout his archeological career. The Aztec emperor Netzahualcoyotl originally created Texcutzingo, located some twenty miles northeast of the center of Mexico City, during the fifteenth century. He envisioned it as an imperial garden filled with plants gathered from throughout Mexico, with baths and pools carved into the mountain on which it was located. Today it is an impressive archeological site frequented by tourists.

Boban's description of a bit of fun he had with some Texcoco natives captures something of his youthful bravado, along with the social formalities of the period. Some local people had told him about a deep cave where an Englishman had disappeared. They cautioned him, however, that he was much too young to face the dangers of *el abismo* (the abyss). Nonetheless, he was determined to see what was down below and could not be dissuaded by the possible dangers. "After much procrastination and especially with the aid of that universal lever, a few pesetas, we descended into the cave," he later wrote.

Once Boban had been lowered down to the entrance, his courage and impishness led him on.

> I entered the famous *Cueva* by myself, where the entrance was hidden by vegetation, and discovered inside a small opening about a dozen meters long, leading to a precipitous vertical drop . . . but nothing unusual, some animal bones, foxes, and birds of prey, and every so often I would hear my guides shouting to me 'Señor, it's been a long time, and you haven't answered our calls. Are you dead?' and a host of questions like that. I took some malicious pleasure in my silence. After carefully examining the place, I left my card there. (HSA: B2246, Box VII)[4]

It is revealing (and endearing) that Boban left only his calling card to document his visit, perhaps to let future explorers know that he had been there first, when many of his contemporaries carved their names on archeological monuments after removing portions for their own collections.

Boban made the rounds of Mexico City's neighborhoods and suburbs throughout the late 1850s and early 1860s. In 1859 he dug to the southwest of Coyoacán near Popotla. He excavated small mounds and burials in the areas to the north of the city center around Tlatelolco, Zahuatlán, and Tlalnepantla. To the south he explored Tlahuac, Iztapalapa, Tlalpan, and Xochimilco near the floating gardens. Journeying to the west, he worked around Tacuba, Azcapotzalco, and the hills of Chapultepec. All these places are now part of metropolitan Mexico City, but at the time they were still separate towns and villages whose inhabitants spoke Nahuatl. Even given the greater ease of travel in Mexico in the mid-nineteenth-century, the number and extent of field trips he took in pursuit of artifacts is remarkable. One can imagine many days spent journeying to the far reaches of the Valley of Mexico and many nights spent sleeping under the stars or in the houses of his Indian friends and helpers.

Of his excavations in Tepito, which like the suburb of Tlatelolco is now part of the metropolis, he wrote that some of the artifacts he found there came from the burials of warriors, because they included *tentetl*, the Nahuatl word for "military insignia [lip plugs] of obsidian." To explain this reasoning further, he added, "The ornaments of the lower ranks, [are] made of terra cotta." Boban's awareness of the hierarchy of materials allowed for personal adornment by the Aztecs comes from Bernardino de Sahagún, the sixteenth-century Franciscan ethnographer, to whom he often makes reference. Controlling who was allowed to use which adornments enabled the Aztecs to maintain rigid class distinctions. Boban's understanding of this indicates a close reading of early Spanish chronicles to inform his archeological investigations. He also recorded finding at Tepito many bronze and copper objects, such as needles, little axes, and bells (HSA: B2245, Box VI).

Presumably, Boban learned Nahuatl from his encounters with local people and his excavation work in outlying villages. His dig catalog almost always includes a translation of the Nahuatl or Otomí place name of the site or region where he excavated and gives a short description of the culture he presumes crafted the artifacts discovered. He also includes the original native terms for what he had found.

For instance, in 1857 he was working near Chalco at the southeastern edge of the capital, where he unearthed a human cranium that, he noted, was accompanied by a beautiful piece of obsidian, along with a sacrificial knife. Writing at a much later date, he explained that the sacrificial knives were made from flint and that, "These fine flint and obsidian blades in the shape of a bay leaf are very similar to those known to Professor Gabriel de Mortillet as Solutrean. In Mexico we call them *tecpatl*, or sacrificial knife blades used to open the chest and tear out the heart of victims." *Tecpatl* means flint knife in Nahuatl (HSA: B2243, Box IV).[5]

In his memoirs he recalled that he and a crew of Indian adobe makers from Chalco found several of the tecpatl that would later become part of the Trocadéro collections. The day after his first finds of a piece of obsidian and a flint double-edged blade with two pointed ends, he returned to the area. "I found two other large tecpatls. My joy was so great, but only those who excavate will understand the pleasure that I felt."[6] He thought he could not leave the four beautiful artifacts because they might be stolen, so his solution to the problem was to sleep in the field clutching his finds to his chest—further evidence of the passion he brought to his archeological endeavors (HSA: B2243, Box IV).

In other notes he proposed that this particular burial dated to the tenth century, and that "Chalco, according to Clavigero, means the place of fine stones." Continuing with his description of the objects he found there, he writes, "The skull, #2010, was found in a burial, with a very beautiful stone chest covered with hieroglyphs. Assuredly it belonged to a great dignitary of the country" (HSA: B2245, Box VI). The discovery of this carved stone box and burial, during his first year in Mexico City, must have greatly inspired his later collecting since they were such significant finds. The box figures prominently in later photographs of his collection.

At first Boban carried out considerable digging and surface collecting throughout the Central Valley, an area now containing the enormous metropolis of Mexico City. He also worked in parts of the states of Mexico, Hidalgo, Tlaxcala, and Puebla. Then in the early 1860s he began visiting San Juan Teotihuacan in the state of Mexico. The impressive archeological site of the ruined metropolis is located at the northeastern end of the Central Valley, some twenty-five miles from Mexico City. He described the ruins as "very rich in fragments of the ancient inhabitants, especially in their tombs, and there are a great number of them. But, unfortunately, after the arrival of the conquerors, all of this ruin has been plundered for its treasures" (HSA: B2245, Box VI).

Despite the quantity of artifacts that had already been removed throughout the previous centuries, he made a significant collection of his own from the ruined city. He may have purchased these artifacts from *campesinos* or farmers in the surrounding area, although it is possible that some of the obsidian and

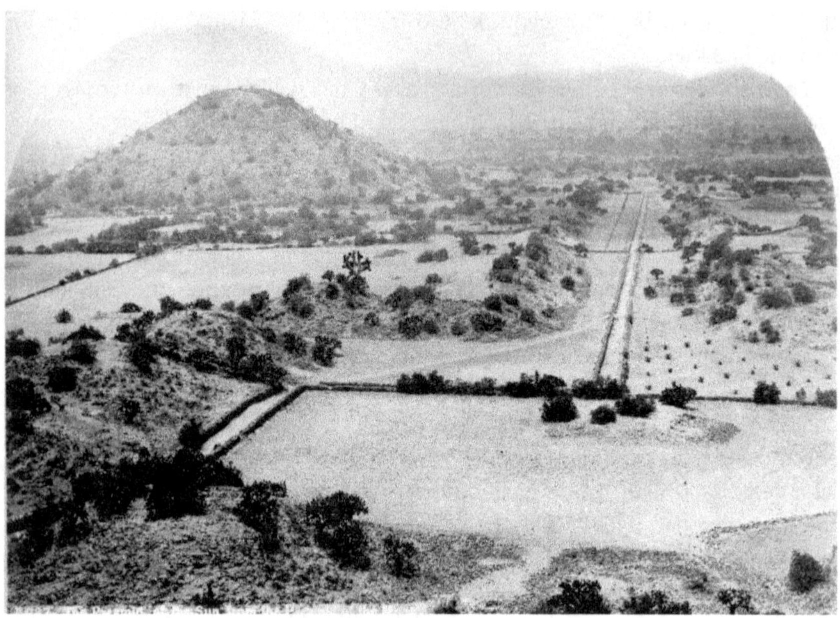

Figure 4.3   View of Teotihuacan archeological site showing the Pyramid of the Sun. Photo by William Henry Jackson (Smithsonian Institution, National Anthropological Archives).

figurine fragments came from his own surface collecting. The large Teotihuacan-style stone faces in his collection seem to have come from excavations he undertook in Azcapotzalco, however (Hamy 1884: 143). There are no extant field notes regarding Boban's work at Teotihuacan during this time to give proper provenience to these objects. The references in the catalogs of his collection say only that they come from San Juan Teotihuacan, a designation that includes the site and the nearby town.

Boban is meticulous about including as much information as possible about each of his finds, often referencing supporting data provided by early Spanish chroniclers. Including such extensive explanatory notes about individual artifacts was unusual for a collector at that time, or really almost any time. Frequently, collectors make little effort to record the source of an object, let alone details about its name within the culture of origin, its use, significance, and so forth. Clearly, from the beginning, the young amateur archeologist was intent on becoming a scholar of pre-Columbian Mexico.

Boban owned more than one copy of Clavigero's *Historia antigua de México*, published in 1780 (Leavitt 1886b: 120). The Jesuit historian was the first to outline a chronology of pre-Columbian Mexican cultures, which Boban adopted and followed assiduously. Judging from the number he assigned to the skull from Chalco, he had already amassed some two thousand artifacts during his first year of residence, although, presumably, a large proportion of these numbered items would have been fragments of figurines and pottery.

Just as he had in California, Boban writes with great fondness and empathy for the native people, with whom he worked regularly and came to know intimately. He sympathized with them for the hard lives they led, despite all the changes that had taken place in Mexico over three hundred years. As he reported in one of his biographical notes, "An old Indian, who lived in the village of Culhuacan, for whose son I was the godfather, told me with a resigned air mixed with some sadness, 'No, my little compadre [a term of endearment used by parents to address the godfather of one of their children], apart from the [end to human] sacrifices, we aren't much better off since the arrival of the Spaniards'" (HSA: B2243, Box IV).[7] It is easy to see why Mexican Indians might have felt that little about their lives had improved since the Conquest. They had paid tribute to the Aztecs and other conquering tribes over the centuries and would continue to do so with the Spaniards. Their only protection came from the friars, to whom they also paid a tithe in work and agricultural products. Overall, they labored ceaselessly but continued to inhabit the lowest rung of Mexico's cultural and economic ladder.

Clearly Boban had a special relationship with his Indian compadre, since the role of godfather would only be given to a close and trusted friend. Boban thought highly of the native Mexicans with whom he worked and associated. "The Indian race," Boban wrote, "is by far the better part of the population of Mexico, by a good measure" (HSA: B2240, Box I). Being as private and discreet as he was, he does not clarify his reasons for saying this, and he seldom indicates that his interactions with Mexican creoles and mestizos were unpleasant or unproductive; however, he always describes the Indians in the most respectful and admiring terms.

Boban also became interested in Mexico's natural history. He kept a handwritten notebook detailing the flora and fauna of the country containing approximately 150 pages replete with information on amphibians, birds, butterflies, and reptiles in addition to trees, agave, corn, chilies, tomatoes, and other plants. Every entry begins with French, Spanish, and Nahuatl words for the subject, which is then discussed at length (HSA: B2247, Box VIII; Natural History).

In his observations, Boban strove to make clarifying links and connections. In another unpublished manuscript in the Hispanic Society of America's Boban Collection, he wrote that hummingbirds were called *huitzitzilin* in Nahuatl, and that despite their diminutive size, they could be quite aggressive and warlike when threatened. Demonstrating his keen interest in understanding precontact Mexican cultures, he goes on to say, "Probably ancient Mexicans noticed this [defensive aggression against much larger birds], and it is why the name of the god of war is Huitzilopochtli, the left-handed hummingbird warrior" (HSA: B2247, Box VIII, Natural History).

He wrote at considerable length about the habits and behaviors of the hummingbirds that he had personally observed.

> After residing in Mexico close to a quarter of a century we lived with those little winged phoenixes and raised them, . . . They disappear, that is certain, but like our European swallows, they migrate to warmer regions, probably not for fear of cold, but because the small insects, the mosquitos that are their food, disappear, forcing them to migrate. Hummingbirds behave in the same way when certain flowers or types of flowers disappear, and for that, a few hours will suffice for them to cross the chain of high mountains surrounding the Mexican plateau. Immediately south they are in warm lands with new flowers full of small insects. . . . Then they are like swallows returning with the season, . . . Suddenly they appear in the city gardens and in the houses and around flowerpots in patios and on windowsills. . . . They are preserved best in spacious sunlit rooms with flowers, especially cooked honey, since sugar water gives them diarrhea very quickly. We have kept them alive for many months. We were quite fond of them, and my father often brought them wildflowers. Those charming little creatures would surround him and perch on his spectacles. (HSA: B2247, Box VIII, Natural History)[8]

Ornithology was an important ancillary interest. Boban hunted and trapped birds and had them mounted, or may have learned to mount them himself through the many collecting manuals available at the time. Birds were incredibly plentiful in the central valley in the nineteenth century, even as late as 1892, when the American naturalist Edward Nelson described what he saw in the principal market of Mexico City. "At the market of the Merced southeast of the main plaza, by the border of the canal and in the midst of the poorer quarter of the town, surrounded by hundreds of pulque shops with gaudily ornamented fronts and interiors, there is a great gathering place of Indians of Aztec descent from the valley, who bring in here wild ducks by the thousands from the marshy lakes of the valley" (Nelson: SI Archives RU 7634).

In yet another memoir, Boban boasted of having kept numerous rattlesnakes in his collection, which were caught and sold to him by Indians. He kept some alive and preserved others in alcohol. His notes refer to the cult of the snake, perhaps referencing Quetzalcoatl, the feathered serpent, saying that it had deep roots in Mexico. He also believed the Indians had great sympathy for snakes. One of his pet snakes, Lili, enjoyed entertaining, and sometimes frightening, visiting friends with her noisy rattling.

The country was a paradise for him, a veritable Garden of Eden, and the younger Boban created his own commercial enterprise by selling and trading objects and specimens that were simply free for the taking. The 1865 business directory for Mexico City contains an advertisement for his shop, which offers for sale: "Collections of birds from Mexico, typical crafts of the country, ceramic vessels and objects, paintings, weapons, Chinese porcelains, and Aztec antiquities" (Maillefert 1992: 231). This establishment ultimately would propel him into prominence and renown among both foreign and Mexican clientele, generating considerable financial success. In the early days, however, he was simply enjoying life. "My twenty-year residence in this country was for me all digging and fiestas, all of which gives me great pleasure to remember. My good Indians, so peaceful, and with our work, I believe that a kind of kinship brought us together" (HSA: B2244, Box V).

Other memories glowed even brighter. "We were very happy in Mexico during that time, and not much inclined to return to Europe. We were in a very good position, dividing our leisure time between the hunt and the digs, and every day we brought back something new, something never seen before" (HSA: B2244, Box V).[9]

In reminiscences of his life in Mexico, Boban presents himself as a fearless, knowledgeable explorer who is discerning in his research. In his telling of his exploration of the abyss he seems ready and able to increase the drama of his exploits for the benefit of his audience and enjoys himself while doing so. These characteristics remain constant throughout his career. He continues to be an active investigator in a broad range of fields. He pursues knowledge tirelessly, becoming an expert on pre-Columbian antiquities and other subjects. A battery of international scholars comes to respect his erudition. Yet throughout his career, he expands time and distance, exaggerates his discoveries, and enhances and even misrepresents the importance and quality of his collections. He does this, possibly to increase the perceived value of the objects he sells, possibly to promote his own sense of self-worth, but most likely for both reasons.

Notes

1. Archives.paris.fr.com record #371, naissance [births], 3 March 1862, Paris, 1st arrondissement.

2. Me contait un vieil Israelite Bordelais établi bijoutier-orfevre a Mexico, mort tres vieux et cela depuis plus de trente ans. Je puis vous l'assurer me disait il sur la fin de sa vie c'est moi qui ait fait venir ces pierre fausse d'europe, et qui dit demontés les autres pour les faire vendre a petit a petit sur l'ordre des autorites ecclésiastiques, mais en cachette du gouvernement surtout.

3. Dans le courant de l'année 1858, nous entre d'explorer l'ancienne capital des Acolhuas ou chichimeque. Ce qui reste de cette grand cité aujourd'hui le village de Texcoco, et ses environs. Se trouve une série de collines l'une d'elle momie Texcutzingo.

4. Je pénêtra donc seul dans la fameuse cueva dont l'entrée était enpartie cachée par la végétation c'était une petite galerie percée horizontalement sur le flau de la montagne. D'un dizaine de metres de long, aboutissant à une sorte de précipice vertical, irregulier dont la profondeur ne dépassait . . .—mais rien d'anormal . . . puis quelques squelettes, d'animaux, renards, et oiseaux de proie, a chaque instants j'entendrais mes guides qui me criaient Señor, hace tanto tiempo, que le ha sucedido que no nos conteste. Etes-vous mort, et une foule de questions du même genre. Je me faisait un malin plaisir de garder le silence. Après avoir bien examine l'endroit, j'avais laisse mon carte.

5. Ces belles lames en silex et en obsidienne affectant la forme de sa feuille de laurier (connue en Europe et classé par le Prof. Gabriel de Mortillet, pour celles trouvier en France surtout qui on dureste beaucoup d'analogie, il les a nomée lames solutriennes). Au Mexique on les connais sous le

nom de tecpatl, ou lames de couteau de sacrifice pour ouvrir la poitrine des victimes et leur arracher la coeur.

6. Le même jour après avoir remuer bien de la terre j'ai retrouvé moi même deux autres superbes tecpatl ma joie était grande et seul ceux qui ont pratique des fouilles pour tout comprender le plaisir qui j'en éprouvais.

7. No, compadrito, aparte los sacrificios, no hemos mejorado mucho con la llegada de los españoles.

8. Ayant habité le mexique pres d'un ¼ de siècle nous avons suivés ces petit Fénix de la gente ailée nous en avons elevés, . . . Ils disparaissent cela est certain, mais comme nos hirondelles en Europe, qui émigrent vers des contrées plus douces, non sans doute par crainte du froid, mais parce que les petits insects, les moustiques qui forme leur nourriture disparaissent, se cachent; c'est ce qui les force a émigrés. Le colibris se conduit de la même manière quand les fleurs disparaissent ou au moin certaines classes de celui-ci, et pour cela quelques heures lui suffises il n'a qu'a traverser la chaine des hautes montagnes qui entoure le plateau de Mexico, vers le sud, et immédiatement il est en terre chaude ou de nouvelles fleurs contenant aussi des petits insects. . . . Puis comme les hirondelles ils reviennent a la saison, . . . On les voit alors apparaître en volant dans les jardin de la ville et jusque dans les maisons et autours des pots de fleurs placés dans les vestibules et sur les fénêtres. . . . On les conserves mieux dans des chambres spacieuses au soleil avec des fleurs et surtout du miel cuit, car l'eau sucrée leur donne la diarrhée au bout de fort peu de temps. Nous en avons gardés vivants plusieurs mois. On ils sont assez familiers, mon père leur apportait des fleurs des champs ces charmantes petites bêtes l'entourerait et plusieurs variantes le posées sur les bords de ses lunettes.

9. A cette époque fort peu disposé a revenir en Europe, nous [étions] très heureux au Mexique [dans] une très bonne position, partagean nos loisir entre la chasse et les fouilles, qui nous rapportait toujour quelque chose d'inconnue.

5

THE EMPEROR'S ANTIQUARIAN
A Collection Takes Shape

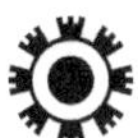

Moving on from appropriating and selling church property to raise money, in 1861, President Juárez took steps to suspend interest payments on loans from European powers. The holders of that foreign debt were not at all happy about this decision and pressed their governments to take action, with surprising results. Later that year England, France, and Spain signed the Treaty of London. As the historian William Spence Robertson explains, with this treaty, these governments "undertook to press vigorously the claims of their citizens against Mexico which aggregated untold millions of dollars" (Robertson 1940: 167). They were, in effect, signing an agreement to force Mexico to pay what it owed its creditors.

These nations were encouraged to interfere in Mexico's economic policies by groups in the country who were still loyal to Spain's monarchy, including, not surprisingly, the Catholic Church. As journalist Jonathan Kandell writes in *La Capital*, "The Mexican Church and its allies encouraged the [European] intervention and sought to broaden their scope into a full-fledged invasion that would replace Juárez with a foreign ruler, who would support their conservative program. Defeat in the civil war had led the Mexican clergy and conservatives to openly advocate monarchism as a solution to the country's ills" (Kandell 1988: 334). In essence, the conservatives preferred to have a foreign ruler who served their interests than to accept their democratically elected president.

Then without much warning, Spanish troops invaded Veracruz from Cuba in December 1861. The British and French invaded a few months later, in early 1862. England and Spain soon recalled their armies. France, however, then governed by the impetuous and ill-fated Emperor Napoleon III, chose to leave its troops in place.

The French suffered an initial defeat at the Battle of Puebla on 5 May 1862, a date called simply Cinco de Mayo and now commemorated by colorful celebrations in Mexico and the United States. They then retreated to the port of Veracruz and held it for several months. Their commander, General François Achille Bazaine, who had fought bravely in Algeria, the Crimea, and Italy, eventually defeated the Mexicans, despite their early victories. Juárez fled Mexico City, heading north with his cabinet on the last day of May 1863; he never left Mexican territory, however.

This invasion of a sovereign nation, which has since become known by the euphemism the "French Intervention" in Mexico, lasted from 1862 to 1867. It was an undisguised attempt by the French government to extend its influence to North America by establishing a monarchy in Mexico, supported by the Mexican conservative party and backed by the French army. The United States was in the midst of its own civil war and could do little to help Mexico, aside from Abraham Lincoln's steadfast refusal to recognize any government other than that of Benito Juárez. After the French captured Mexico City in 1863, Napoleon III installed Maximilian von Habsburg, the younger brother of Emperor Franz Joseph of Austria, as emperor of Mexico. This takeover was accomplished with the full agreement and collaboration of Mexico's conservative party and the Catholic Church.

As a Habsburg, Maximilian was related to the Spanish kings, who had conquered and ruled Mexico from the sixteenth to the nineteenth century. The conservatives and the church saw him as the answer to the problems created by Juárez and the Reform Movement; the monarchists had achieved their long-held dream of returning royalty to Mexico.

The French intellectual community that had become so captivated by the books and artifacts documenting Mexico's precontact civilizations during the previous decades sought to capitalize on the opportunity handed them by the armed invasion of the country. Immediately after Emperor Maximilian took the throne, the French government established the Commission Scientifique du Mexique to study the occupied territories. Just as his uncle Napoleon I had taken scholars to Egypt with his invading armies in 1798, Napoleon III sent his own scientists, linguists, and historians to learn about Mexico and collect artifacts and specimens for research and exhibition in France.

Victor Duruy, a historian and reformer of French public education, assembled the commission and outlined its goals in February 1864. According to historian Paul N. Edison, from Duruy's standpoint, the commission "was intended to simultaneously advance scientific knowledge, civilize Mexico, and bring commercial profits to both nations. Evoking the memory of the 'colony of scholars' who accompanied 'the bravest soldiers in the world' in Egypt, [Duruy] said that Napoleon III wanted to do in Mexico 'what was done on the banks of the Nile'" (Edison 1999: 201–2). The commission consisted of four committees: one to research the natural and medical sciences; another to explore the physical and chemical sciences; a third for history, linguistics, and archeology; and a final committee to study the political economy.

The history, linguistics, and archeology committee included some of the most famous French scholars of the period, among them the former diplomats Baron Gros and Léonce Angrand, in addition to Adrien de Longpérier, curator at the Louvre. There were two renowned architects, Eugène Emmanuel Viollet-Leduc and César Daly. The two most highly regarded experts in pre-Columbian manuscripts, Charles Étienne Brasseur de Bourbourg and Joseph Marius Alexis Aubin, both of whom were scholars of pre-Columbian cultures and had collected in Mexico for many years, also joined the commission (*Archives de la Commission Scientifique du Mexique*, vol. 1, 1865: 12–13). As odd as it may seem, with the exception of Brasseur, none of these men actually traveled to Mexico during the tenure of the Commission Scientifique du Mexique, being content to oversee its activities from the other side of the Atlantic.

As the Commission Scientifique was being organized in Paris, General Bazaine, who remained as commander of French forces in Mexico, formed a second commission to provide more hands-on assistance. The Commission Scientifique, Littéraire et Artistique du Mexique was comprised of some two hundred Mexican and French scientists and army officers residing in the country. Bazaine appointed Col. Louis Toussaint Simon Doutrelaine to oversee this group. The Paris-based commission also chose Doutrelaine to oversee French voyageurs journeying to Mexico and act as an intermediary with Mexican authorities (Edison 1999: 204–5).

For a man of Boban's ambition and temperament, the French Intervention presented a golden opportunity to bring his collection to the attention of a much wider audience. Within a short time, he became friendly with leaders of the occupying forces and showed them his extensive archeological and natural history specimens, in addition to the books and manuscripts he had amassed. In October 1863, a few months before being named chief of the Commission Scientifique, Littéraire et Artistique, Col. Doutrelaine, then commander of the French army's engineering corps, wrote a long letter referencing Eugène Boban to Marshal Vaillant, who presided over the physical and chemical sciences committee of the Parisian Commission. "There is an industrialist here, who has a remarkable collection. A Frenchman, who has travelled throughout Mexico, the Yucatan, Sonora, and California and was even a bit married in Chiapas" (Le Goff and Prévost-Urkidi 2011: 63). The 29-year-old "industrialist" seems to have made quite an impression on the head of the Mexican division of the Commission Scientifique.

Recognizing that Boban's materials represented an unusually comprehensive collection that had taken years to assemble, Doutrelaine evidently thought that it would be more efficient for the French government to purchase it than to have the Commission Scientifique attempt to replicate it. He understood that it was of paramount importance to document the objects in the collection through catalog notes and illustrations, so he assigned one of his draftsmen from the engineering corps to begin drawing the archeological specimens.

Doutrelaine's letter to Marshal Vaillant continues,

He would give his collection to the Museum at a cost of 20,000 francs, very discreet, he alleges. I told him that the first thing he must do, in support of his offer, is to make an inventory of its parts, categorical and analytical, with descriptive details and historical and archeological information. He has begun and asked me to promise to send his work when he is finished. I promised, but he has several months before completing it. The collection, which I think quite valuable indeed, is a mess (Le Goff and Prévost-Urkidi 2011: 63).[1]

It is noteworthy that at this early date, Doutrelaine is already acting as an intermediary for the potential sale of Boban's collection to the "Museum," presumably the Louvre. His description of Boban's having been a "little bit married" to a woman from Chiapas is an indication of how close the two men had become. In fact, in his later writings, Boban refers to him as "mon ami, M. Doutrelaine" (HSA: B2244, Box V—Preface).

The two men were soon working together overseeing the discovery and excavation of archeological artifacts uncovered when Doutrelaine's engineering corps began constructing earthen fortifications intended to protect the French army from attack. Their working relationship seems to have been that Boban provided the necessary expertise to recognize what should be saved, and in exchange many of the objects uncovered became part of his collection. The colonel's reports provide details of artifacts recovered from digs carried out in Metlatoluca, a site near Huauhchinango in Veracruz, and another on the hill of Las Palmas, west of Mexico City. In March 1866 he announced in the official reports of the Commission Scientifique du Mexique, "the sending of several drawings of antiquities from the Boban collection," adding that he planned to transport the objects themselves later via the French expeditionary corps (*Archives de la Commission Scientifique du Mexique, vol. 2*, 1865: 360; Riviale 1999: 329; Riviale 2001: 353).

By this time Eugène Boban was also becoming known to Emperor Maximilian and his circle, who had arrived in Mexico in 1864. His initial introduction may have caused some awkwardness, however, since he was being investigated as an apparent draft dodger for having left France without reporting for duty with the "class" of 1854. There are two documents, written in March and September of 1864, which discuss the problem of French expatriates in Mexico, who are referred to as *insoumis*, meaning they had failed to answer their draft calls when they reached the age of twenty. Boban is specifically mentioned in both of them; however, he was apparently forgiven his failure to join the army, probably as a result of his association with and assistance to the Commission Scientifique and the intervention of Col. Doutrelaine (CADN, Mexico [legation] rating: 432PO/1/337: File No. 1427).

In 1865 Emperor Maximilian himself became Boban's patron, visiting his shop on at least one occasion and admiring his collections of Mexican antiquities. The abbé Lanusse, a French priest attached to the court, described the young emperor as an artist and a man who loved beautiful things, taking note of the fact that he made the merchant in a small business of the capital very happy with a visit to his shop to view his collection of antiquities (Riviale 2011: 454).

Maximilian purchased items from Boban in June 1866, as recorded on a bill of sale. The items the emperor bought were not pre-Columbian artifacts, but rather three Chinese porcelain vases. These may have actually been a type of pottery from Puebla, which was made to imitate Chinese porcelain. Whatever the case, as with many government bureaucracies, it took nearly five months for Boban to receive payment. He signed a receipt for the payment of forty piasters, some two hundred francs, in November of the same year (AGN Segundo Imperio, Vol. 6, exp. 38b). Always a master of self-promotion, Boban began adding "Antiquarian to His Majesty the Emperor" on his business cards.

No record of a transaction between Boban and the Emperor involving Mexican pre-Columbian artifacts has been located, but it is certainly possible that some of the Mexican antiquities Maximilian sent home to his Austrian castle Miramar near Trieste were purchased at Boban's store. Many of the archeological artifacts sent from Mexico eventually became part of the Museum für Völkerkunde in Vienna, Austria, including stone faces and figures from Teotihuacan from Emperor Maximilian's personal collection and that of his director of the Natural History Museum, Dominik Bilimek (Gerard Van Bussell, pers. comm.; Rose and Walsh 2016).

Aside from Doutrelaine and Boban's officially sanctioned excavations, there was a great deal of freelance digging of pre-Columbian artifacts—what would now be considered looting—carried out during the French Intervention. The same sort of activities had taken place during the US invasion almost two decades earlier. Many years after the fact, Boban recalled an incident in Mexico City that demonstrates the expertise in early Mexican cultures he had already acquired and the freewheeling nature of the digs that were being carried out. He said it happened around 1865.

Someone who remains nameless, a Mr. X, as Boban described him, had gathered a group of foreigners. "French, Germans, and Austrians, who had come with Maximilian—the group provided the funds necessary to excavate a site in Santiago Tlatelolco, a suburb of Mexico City, where they sought to discover the great gold chariot of Moctecuhzoma" (HSA: B2246, Box VII; *antiquites*). This spelling has now become the accepted scholarly transposition of the Aztec emperor's name. Boban's use of it was more than a century ahead of its time and must represent his accurate recording of what he heard from his Nahuatl-speaking assistants.

Boban attempted to dissuade the adventurers from this fool's errand, as he saw it, since, certainly, the Aztec emperor would not have had a chariot, lacking horses to pull it. As he pointed out, native Mexican royalty had been carried around in palanquins on the shoulders of slaves. He evidently enjoyed providing details of what happened during the dig that took place despite his protests. "In the first layers the enthusiastic diggers found some idols and weapons, fragments of obsidian, vases, and ceramic pots, but then it was all mud and much water." After all, the city was built on a lake, as he noted (HSA: B2246, Box VII; *antiquites*).

Boban had his fun with the foreign diplomats' dig, although in the end he seems to have been the recipient of most of the ceramics, obsidian points, and scrapers they uncovered. Needless to say, no trace of a chariot was found. The seasoned antiquarian enjoyed both the looted artifacts and a good laugh at the expense of the gullible diggers.

Taking advantage of his advisory position to the Commission Scientifique, he excavated, and/or collected artifacts at Mesquitic in the northern Mexican state of San Luis Potosí and in Durango in 1865. In Zahuatlán, he excavated small mounds, located about a mile from Tlalnepantla, north of Azcapotzalco, now part of Mexico City, where he noted in his dig catalog that there were "many mounds and burials, which had excited the interest of Maximilian." According to Boban's notes, the emperor sent a team of diggers, and the remains of more than one hundred burials were subsequently sent to Mexico City. The antiquarian profited greatly from these organized excavations, as he matter-of-factly states: "They sent only the bones and skulls [to Paris], and the pottery, vases, and terra cotta idols became part of our collection" (HSA: B2245, Box VI).

The bones and skulls were the particular interest of several important French scientists of the era, notably Paul Broca and Armand de Quatrefages. In the mid-nineteenth century, French anthropology principally encompassed the study of human skeletal remains. There was much less interest in the material culture of past eras, which as we have seen greatly benefitted Boban's ability to increase his collection of artifacts.

In July 1865 Col. Doutrelaine was commanding a large force working to build earthen terraces to fortify the hill of Las Palmas, which dominated the route between Mexico City and Toluca. While the terracing and other major earth works were in progress under the supervision of French soldiers, they discovered countless fragments of figurines and pottery, in addition to human remains. Col. Doutrelaine invited Boban to participate in the excavations, to provide an expert's advice on the importance of the items found in the area. The manpower provided by Doutrelaine's forces offered a rare opportunity for Boban to oversee extensive excavations. He had carried out his previous digs either by himself or with a few Indian helpers. The excavations revealed a series of burials, vessels, stone figures, and fragments of ceramic figurines. In his notes Boban commented, "the officers dug to a great depth due to the persistence and quantity of the artifacts they were finding" (HSA: B2245, Box VI).

Once again the skulls from the burials were sent to Paris and the vessels, figurines, and flint and obsidian points were added to Boban's collection. The antiquarian took special note of these excavations, writing about discovering the remnants of mammoth bones and teeth from a much earlier period, the Archaic (3500–2000 BC), along with obsidian and flint lance points within the same context (HSA: B2245, Box VI). The artifacts and human remains recovered indicate that it was an early prehistoric site whose inhabitants settled just west of the center of Mexico City, on the hills overlooking the lakes. All the ceramic figurines and vessel fragments, which are now in the Musée du quai Branly, are representative of the earliest formative period in Mexico, sometimes called the Early Preclassic (2000–200 BC). Several of the skulls recovered from the digs at Las Palmas had been artificially deformed (Hamy 1884: plate 8). According to some sources, the earliest practice of cranial deformation found in Mexico, a type known as the Tabular Erect, began around 1400 BC (Evans and Webster 2001: 181). The Las Palmas skulls exhibited this type of deliberate cranial deformity, further underscoring that this material represents an important early find.

By the mid-1860s Boban was the owner of a well-known antiquities business on the Callejón del Espíritu Santo, which was listed in the *Directorio del Comercio del Imperio Mexicano* (Directory of Commerce in the Mexican Empire). A selection of his collection of pre-Columbian artifacts from his shop can be seen in a photograph in which he is standing commandingly in front of his treasures (see Figure 5.1, pg. 66).

He is a young man in his early thirties, dressed in a frock coat over long dark-colored trousers. He wears a white shirt with cravat and appears to have a chain around his neck, perhaps for attaching spectacles. He seems supremely confident, staring intently and directly into the camera with a serious expression. His full mustache is waxed at the ends. Judging from the size of several of the artifacts, Boban is about five feet seven or eight inches tall.

Although many of the several hundred objects are difficult to make out, the photograph rewards close scrutiny since the pieces exhibited are unusual and varied. There are numerous terra cotta figurines and stamps arranged atop a shelf just behind his head. This shelf anchors long chords of stone beads and ceramic spindle whorls or *malacates* strung together. These were quite common in nineteenth-century collections and are still found with some frequency in cultivated fields and archeological sites throughout Mexico. At least three masks are attached to the top shelf, two of which are classic Teotihuacan-style stone faces.

The second shelf has other ceramic and stone objects, only a few of which are visible because of the positioning of Boban's body. However, prominently displayed to the right of the antiquarian's cocked elbow is a stone statue of the Aztec water goddess, now identified as Chalchiuhtlicue-Chicomecóatl (López Luján and Fauvet-Berthelot 2005: 63). He collected the figure at Mexicaltzingo, near Iztapalapa, now part of the Federal District of Mexico City. He described

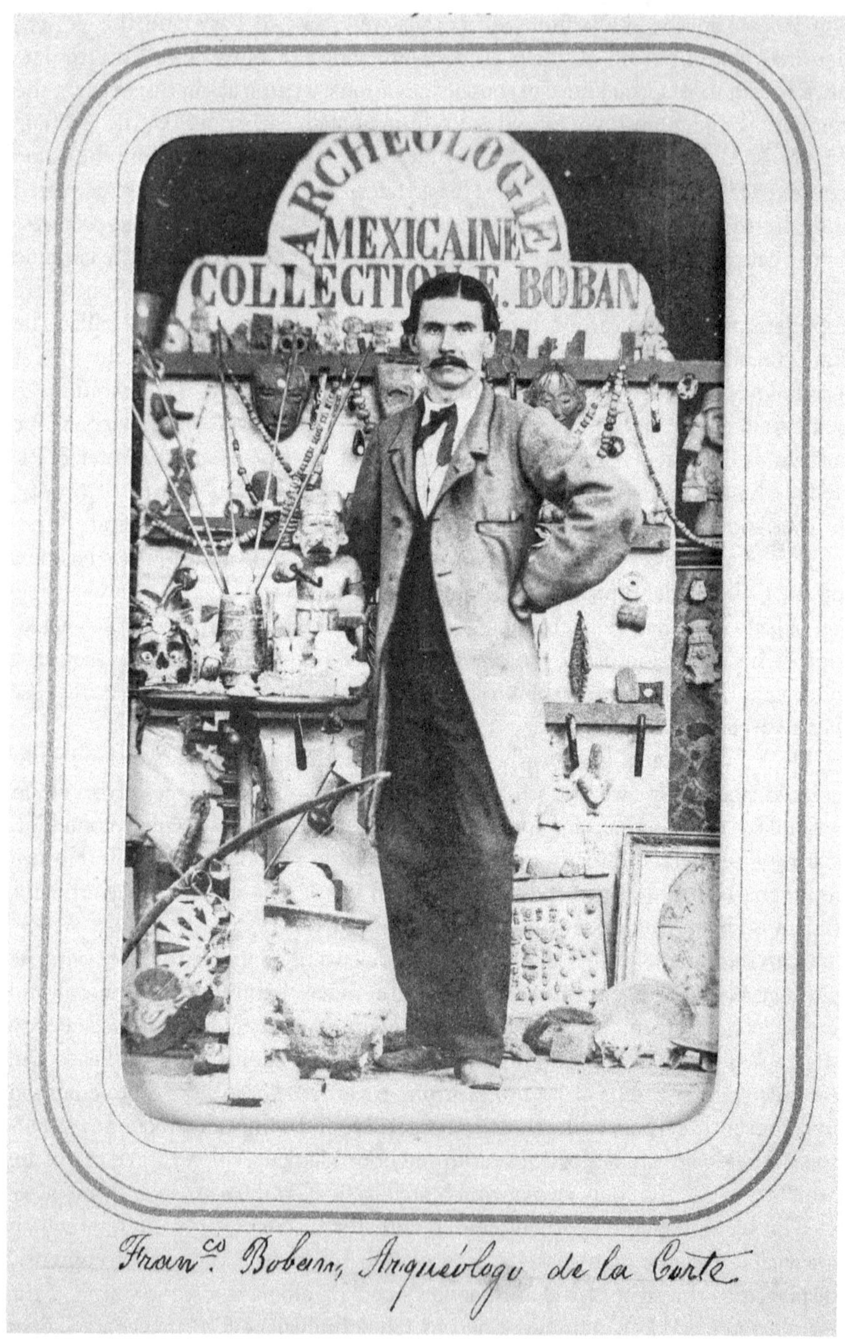

Figure 5.1 Eugène Boban, carte de visite (courtesy of Museo Nacional de Historia, Chapultepec Castle, Mexico City).

the statue as an Indian priestess, whom he identified as Centeotl, the "goddess of the harvest" (Reichlen 1962: 1075).

The bottom shelf holds a decorated human skull at the far left, which appears to have shell and obsidian inlaid eyes and is crowned by an arrangement of feathers. This almost certainly was not the way the skull was found, but more likely a reconstruction of Boban's. The skull is next to a beautiful cylindrical ceramic vessel that appears to be Mixteca-Puebla polychrome ware, described in his later catalog as being from Oaxaca. On this shelf just to the left of Boban is a carved stone figure of the deity Ehécatl-Quetzalcoatl, or the feathered serpent in his guise as the wind god (López Luján and Fauvet-Berthelot 2005: 77) with what appears to be a pipe inserted in its closed fist. Boban described this figure in his catalog as a warrior that he called Teyoachiuani, collected in the Valley of Mexico (Reichlen 1962: 1945).

Obsidian blades and scrapers are attached to the front edges of the shelves, and a variety of ceramic vessels and fragments, stone figures, and ceramic figurines hang here and there. Obsidian implements are ubiquitous in the Valley of Mexico and can routinely be found on or close to the surface in and around cultivated fields. A framed group of Teotihuacan terra cotta figurine heads and fragments sits on the floor on the right, next to Boban's left leg, with a few pieces of Aztec pottery placed in front. On the far right is what would become known as the "Boban calendar wheel," which is also framed. The calendar wheel was published by Col. Doutrelaine in the Commission Scientifique volumes, and illustrated by a facsimile, presumably made under Boban's direction. The illustration provided more detail than could be easily seen on the original manuscript, which was faded and torn. This calendrical manuscript is certainly one of Boban's most important artifacts since there were very few painted manuscripts still available when he began forming his collection.

Arranged on the floor to the left of Boban is at least one other framed group, displaying an arrangement of stone arrowheads and spearpoints. Such items are also found throughout the Valley of Mexico, on or close to the surface. Here they are artistically displayed in a manner quite common in the nineteenth century.

Interestingly, his collection of pre-Columbian artifacts includes some pieces that he may have collected in California, such as the bow and arrows on the lower left. In close proximity to the bow and arrows is a nineteenth-century Mexican version of an Aztec war club (*macuahuitl*)—a wooden bat with obsidian scrapers inserted into both sides.

The piece shown here (Figure 5.2) is nearly identical to the one in the Boban photograph, which is now in the collection of the Musée du quai Branly. This macuahuitl is in the Smithsonian Institution from another nineteenth-century collection. It is one of a group of pre-Columbian artifacts gathered by Father Agustín Fischer, the confessor and private secretary to Emperor Maximilian.

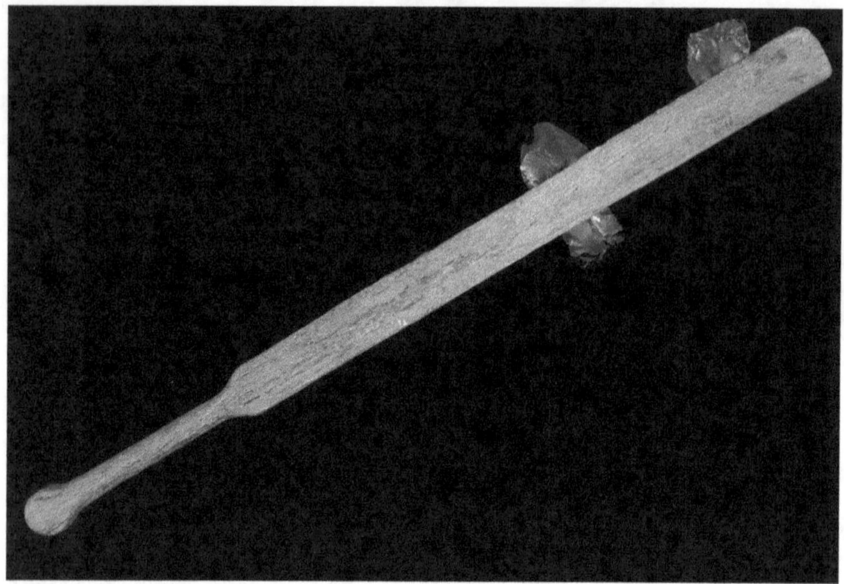

Figure 5.2 Boban's version of the Aztec macuahuitl (Smithsonian Institution, National Museum of Natural History, Blake Collection, 99009).

Father Fischer sold his collection to Wilson Wilberforce Blake, who then sold it to the Smithsonian. Blake is the collector who warned William Henry Holmes to be wary of Eugène Boban.

Father Fischer evidently knew Boban, since his calling card is in the antiquarian's files (BNF DMO n.a.f. 21479: item 547). The priest, an avid collector of pre-Columbian artifacts and a renowned bibliophile, possessed an important library of rare books. He died in Mexico in 1887. It may be that Father Fischer purchased the club from Boban, or perhaps they both obtained one from the same artisan in Mexico City.

These rather ungainly clubs were supposed to be replicas of the Aztec weapon depicted in pre-Columbian codices. However, they are not accurate reproductions since they incorporate obsidian implements used for scraping hides placed perpendicular to the shaft instead of thin razor-sharp obsidian blades embedded along both edges. Actual macuahuitls were capable of decapitating humans, and in some cases even horses. Boban wrote in the catalog of his collection that the club was based on one that had been found in a tomb in Tlatelolco. That part of Mexico City was notorious for the production of fakes during the nineteenth century. Only one macuahuitl is known from preconquest times, and it was held in the Real Armería de Madrid (Royal Armory of Madrid) until 1884, when it was destroyed in a fire. A drawing of this artifact bears no resemblance to Boban's reproduction (Jubinal 1846; Hassig 1992).

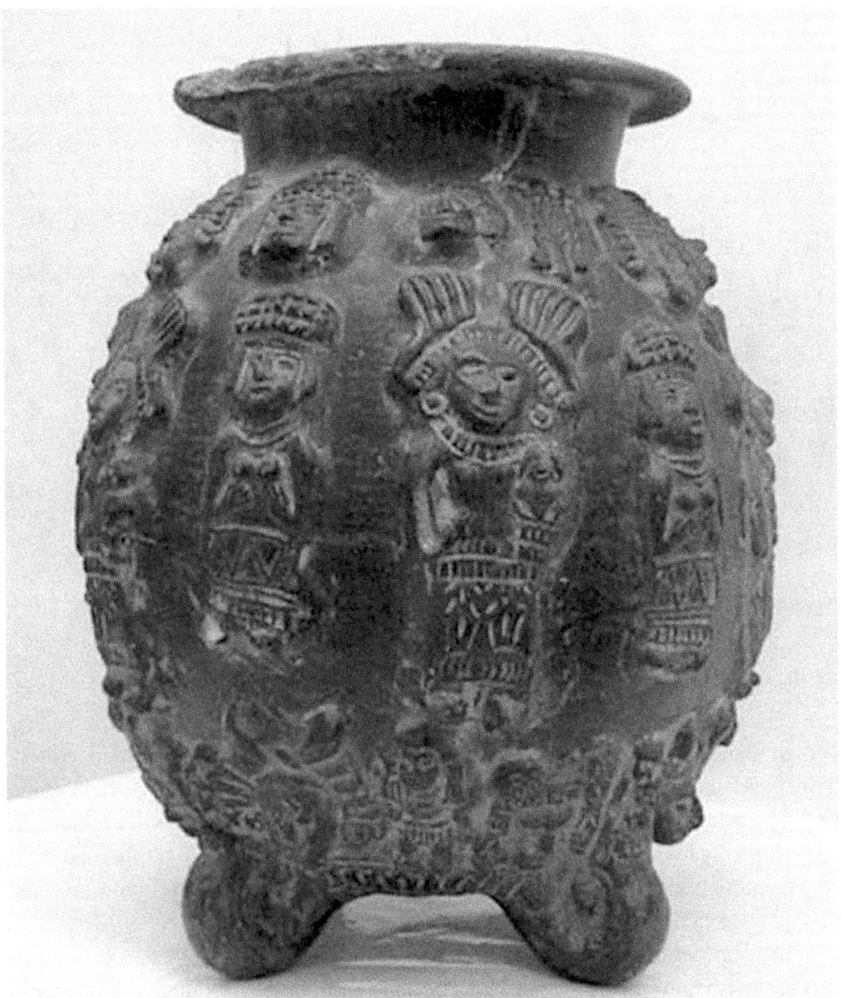

Figure 5.3 Blackware fake in Smithsonian collections (National Museum of Natural History, Department of Anthropology).

The macuahuitl is next to another obvious fake—the ceramic vessel almost touching his right foot. It is an excellent example of the fake blackware pots covered with embedded faces and figurines of contrived deities that flooded museum collections in the nineteenth century, before curators and collectors knew much about what constituted authentic pre-Columbian artifacts. Boban or another member of the Commission Scientifique would have purchased it in Mexico City, or perhaps near Teotihuacan, where there were several manufacturers of these wares.

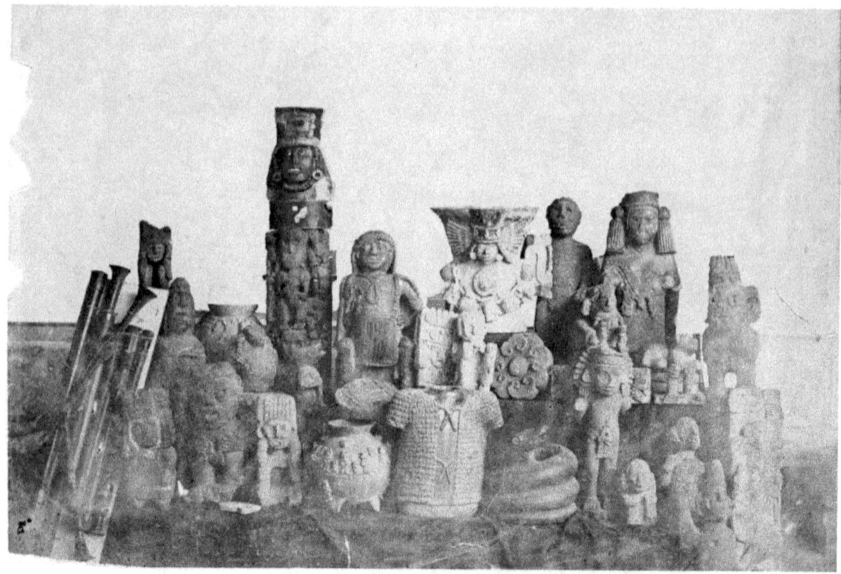

Figure 5.4 Museo Nacional Collection, 1865 (courtesy of Getty Research Collections, 2002.R.10).

Blackware ceramic vessels were in wide circulation by the second half of the century, and can be found today in nearly every museum collection of any size in Europe and the United States, unless the collection has been culled. The Smithsonian has many examples of this type of pottery, all of which came into its collections between the 1850s and 1880s. They were even exhibited in the Museo Nacional in Mexico and are documented by photographs taken by the Commission Scientifique and kept by Eugène Boban in an album entitled *Antiquités Américaines* (Getty #2002.R10, box 2).

This photograph (Figure 5.4), taken when the Museo Nacional's collection was moved from the university to the National Palace around 1865, clearly demonstrates that the museum held numerous examples of nineteenth-century fakes at that time (Getty Research Collection; Walsh 2010b).

Despite the few problematic pieces, Boban's selection of objects for this photograph is representative of a number of important pre-Columbian cultures in Mexico, and clearly shows that he has gathered artifacts from throughout the central valley and quite a distance beyond. The photograph of him dates to 1866 or early 1867, before Col. Doutrelaine shipped the archeological collection to Paris for Commission Scientifique displays at the Exposition Universelle of 1867.

Boban's enthusiasm and his desire to share all of the wonderful things he had found in Mexico is evidenced by a letter written by Col. Doutrelaine to the Commission Scientifique in September 1866. In it he says that Boban had not

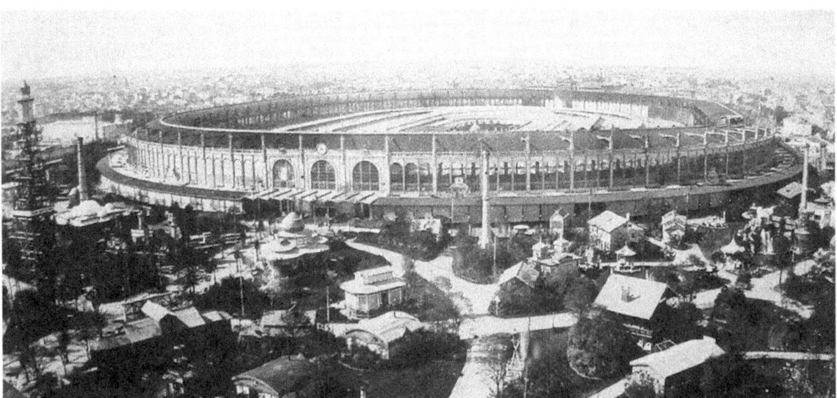

Figure 5.5   Exposition Universelle Paris, 1867 (Smithsonian Libraries).

only lent his pre-Columbian collection, but had also packed all the crates by himself and at his own expense. In addition, he offered to send to the Exposition Universelle a range of other ethnographic material, including wax and terra cotta figurines, Puebla pottery, and Mexican mosaic featherwork. In the area of natural history, Doutrelaine adds that "Boban has in his collection something like 150 jars of reptiles, fish, mollusks, amphibians, arachnids, etc., etc., preserved in alcohol that he has collected in Mexico. I know from M. Boucard, that there are a number of rare and even some unknown species. If the Commission wants this collection to be sent, the owner is ready to give it to me" (Le Goff and Prévost-Urkidi 2011: 392–4).[2] Luckily, as it turned out, only the archeological collection went to Paris, and not everything in his shop.

The exhibition of Boban's collection in the Exposition Universelle of 1867 was an important event in the antiquarian's life, and certainly a great honor. It was the largest world's fair ever seen in Europe, occupying more than one hundred acres on the Champs de Mars near where the Eiffel Tower stands today. Some 42,237 exhibitors filled the central pavilion, an enormous glass-and-ironwork building described as a "Titanic creation of modern metallurgy." Surrounding this colossus were more than a hundred other structures (Sala 1868: 20).

The major nations of the world displayed their recent advancements and noteworthy features in the main pavilion. Among the contributions from the United States were a medical field service—the very latest in military medicine, developed during the Civil War—and a rocking chair. Britain showed off its massive locomotives, along with an amazing new metal, aluminium. More ominously, Germany displayed the largest gun ever seen—weighing fifty tons and capable of firing a 1,000-pound shell. Adding to the liveliness of the exposition were kiosks, stalls, and cultural displays featuring people from all over the world dressed in colorful costumes.

Russians wandered about with their little steppe ponies among Yakut and Kirghiz *yurts*; while Mexicans in gay ponchos ogled a reconstruction of the Roman catacombs, pigtailed Chinese wandered serenely round a replica of the Green Mosque of Bursa [in Turkey]. Bosomy maidens from Bavaria dispensed beer to morose Andalusians, who in turn were wooed by Arab coffee-vendors, with their raucously insistent calls and magnificent robes. (Horne 2007: 4–6)

To make the best impression possible with his exotic objects, at the urging of Col. Doutrelaine, Boban carefully composed a long and detailed catalog of the artifacts sent to Paris. It is now in the archives of the Musée du quai Branly. Because he was so drawn to the scholarship about pre-Columbian cultures and wanted so much to share it, he attempted to present as much as he could about the artifacts he had assembled, giving long descriptions of groups of objects and individual pieces, the culture and time periods to which he believed they belonged, along with his own ideas about their iconography and artistic styles.

The Exposition Universelle of 1867 opened with great fanfare on the first day of April. Unfortunately, the opening festivities were to be Napoleon III's last hurrah, establishing the high-water mark of the Second Empire. With the French forces fighting an increasingly unpopular, losing battle in Mexico, Col. Doutrelaine and the rest of the occupation forces had left the country and returned to Paris before the Exposition Universelle opened. They abandoned Maximilian, who had refused to abdicate, some say on the advice and urging of Father Agustín Fischer (McAllen 2014: 319–20).

Two months after the opening, a young Pole attempted to assassinate Russia's Tsar while he was visiting the Exposition, derailing the accord that Napoleon III had hoped to establish with Russia (Horne 2007: 12). Then came the shocking news that the Emperor Maximilian, who had been left to his own devices when the French army was evacuated from Mexico in 1866, had been shot by a firing squad on 19 June by order of President Benito Juárez.

Although the Exposition was an enormous success overall, with more than 15 million visitors exclaiming over its wonderful displays of artistic and technical innovations (Horne 2007: 13), Maximilian's execution cast a pall on the exhibits presented by the Commission Scientifique du Mexique. Boban's hopes that fame and fortune would flow from his extensive and intriguing display of Mexico's wonders were dashed, at least temporarily.

In the face of the disappointing outcome of France's activities in Mexico, Col. Doutrelaine remained an enthusiastic supporter of the young antiquarian and his collections. He soon attempted to convince Adrien de Longpérier, then curator at the Louvre, to purchase Boban's pre-Columbian artifacts. He had been a member of the Commission Scientifique, but had never visited Mexico during this period, and would not have known Boban personally.

In October 1867 Col. Doutrelaine wrote to his friend Boban, saying, "I saw your sister recently, who gave me your good news. She also told me you were regularly receiving letters from France, which I almost could not believe. . . . I hasten to take her assurances to end my too long silence and write to you." He goes on to say that the Louvre's curator, Adrien de Longpérier, declined to purchase the collection. The asking price was then 50,000 francs ($10,000), quite an increase from the original figure of 20,000 francs quoted by Col. Doutrelaine in an earlier letter about the collection (BNF DMO n.a.f 21477: item 93). In fact, the new price may not have been at all realistic, considering that the entire budget for all four committees of the Commission Scientifique du Mexique had been no more than 200,000 francs just a few years earlier (*Archives de la Commission Scientifique du Mexique*, vol. 2. 1867: 185).

The colonel tries to encourage the antiquarian by saying that they need to accept the situation as it is—presumably referring to the French public's antipathy toward anything Mexican at that moment. There is nothing to be done, he concludes, except to wait for better times (BNF DMO n.a.f. 21477: item 93). All in all, this letter must have offered rather cold comfort to Boban, despite its expressions of friendship and concern.

Although mail was being delivered between Mexico and France, some members of Maximilian's court who had been left behind when the army departed did experience a backlash. A few of them were imprisoned, among them Father Agustín Fischer and Felix Eloin, the Emperor's Chef du Cabinet Civil (Blumberg 1971: 135). They were freed within months of the French departure, however, and subsequently returned home. Napoleon III's adventure, which led to the emperor's execution, took a far greater toll on Mexico. The French army had killed some 50,000 people, and what remained was a country with "a stunted economy left in total disarray; and a yearning for order over political liberties that would test a shaky electoral system in the years ahead" (Kandell 1988: 351–52).

Boban makes no mention of suffering repercussions for his work with the Second Empire, although certainly he would have lost many of his most valued customers with the departure of the French and the death of the emperor. There is an odd parallel between this experience and that of his great-grandfather Michel, a tailor in Angers. Boban lost business when Mexico repulsed its foreign invaders in 1867, and his great-grandfather had lost his clientele after the evacuation of the British riding academy from Angers during the French Revolution some eighty years earlier. A notable distinction between the two situations is that the two men had different reserves following their debacles. By the late 1860s Eugène Boban had made a number of acquaintances and important connections in French military and scientific circles. He could count on numerous Mexican colleagues and friends. His great-grandfather had not been so fortunate when his clients departed and he was forced to move to Paris in search of employment.

Even though daily life appeared to proceed relatively unchanged, instability plagued the Mexican capital. According to a variety of newspaper accounts, the first item of business once the French had departed was to reestablish the federal government in Mexico City. That government then had to deal with the remnants of the French empire and their conservative allies. Establishing a new balance of power seems to have been conducted in a fairly evenhanded way. Despite the fact that several attempts on President Juárez's life occurred in the months following the French departure, at the end of 1867 the English-language newspaper, *The Two Republics*, would compliment the government on its "remarkable degree of liberality and forbearance towards foreigners" (Two Republics, 21 December 1867). President Juárez tried to implement forward-thinking programs for public education and hoped to attract foreign investment with plans to build a railway system to serve the whole of Mexico. But economic progress proved slow after the trauma of the French Intervention.

Another problem faced by the Juárez government was a rising crime rate, including a rash of kidnappings. "The country is plagued with a curse that cries every day for cure," reported another issue of *The Two Republics* at the end of 1867. "We mean the outrageous *plagios* [kidnappings], details of which are appalling and provoking by turns. A wealthy hacendado is decoyed from his farm, and kidnapped to the mountains, where he is tortured daily, till a ransom of five or ten thousand dollars is procured from his friends" (Two Republics, 4 December 1867). The kidnappers, known as *plagiarios*, had been dealt with harshly during Maximilian's rule, receiving a mandatory death sentence once arrested. They suffered the same fate under Juárez; however, despite the threat of capital punishment, they operated everywhere in the republic. They were the bane of Mexico City residents, preying upon anyone who appeared prosperous enough to afford a ransom payment.

Boban was a man caught between two worlds. The country in which he had spent over a decade educating himself about pre-Columbian cultures, exploring ancient ruins, amassing artifacts and building up his business as an antiquarian was not as appealing as it had been, with the Juárez government struggling to set up a stable administration and reduce a growing level of crime and violence. French citizens were trying to come to terms with the costly and embarrassing setback of Napoleon III's failed attempt at empire building in the New World and were no longer captivated by all things Mexican. The impressive collection of pre-Columbian artifacts that Boban had worked so hard to assemble and catalog was now sitting on the other side of the Atlantic, beyond his immediate control and apparently unappreciated. Contrary to his friend Col. Doutrelaine's conviction that the passage of time would make the objects more attractive to potential buyers, time seemed to be having the opposite effect.

In April 1869 Major Charles Loysel wrote Boban a newsy letter from home. The two had met while Loysel had been aide-de-camp to Emperor Maximilian,

and they must have become close friends, since Boban mentions him with fondness several times in his memoirs. According to one of Boban's stories, one day,
while visiting the antiquities shop, Lili, his pet snake, who was out of its cage,
startled the major as he came through the front door (HSA B 2247, Box VIII).
In the letter Loysel says that the collection sent to Paris had been delivered to
Boban's sister Marie and was being cared for by their mother. He reports that
he visited Madame Boban and found her in excellent health, but that she had
been unable to sell his *bibelots* (knickknacks). Loysel, recognizing that he is in
the classic bind of being caught between a friend and his dissatisfied parent,
concludes with some friendly advice and a glimpse at his diplomatic skills. "You
should in any case return sometime soon to take care of your business. For me it is
my greatest desire to see you succeed as you deserve, so I told her that she should
let you judge the appropriateness of returning in such a time and manner that
you are rewarded for all your efforts" (BNF DMO n.a.f. 21478, item #204). It is
hard to imagine the discomfort his parents must have experienced storing crates
of artifacts in their tiny two-room flat.

As luck would have it, Loysel's letter arrived in Mexico after Boban had
already left for Paris, having concluded that it was time to take on the task
himself of selling his collection. He was not the only foreign businessman to
pull up stakes in the capital in the early spring of 1869. The March 3rd edition
of *The Two Republics*, bemoaning the dismal economic situation, reported that
there were "more than 30 merchants and manufacturers, foreigners established
in Mexico, who are making preparations to leave early next month. The greater
part of those gentlemen will not return; the others leave only a small portion of
their capital invested in the various enterprises in which they are engaged" (Two
Republics, 3 March 1869).

The 35-year-old antiquarian Eugène Boban had met with disappointment in
his ambition to sell his extensive and valuable archeological collection to the
Louvre, the most important museum in France. Yet he would not be deterred
from the course he had set: to profit from his experiences in Mexico. He was
about to renew a campaign to make his mark in Europe.

Notes

1. Il y a ici un industriel qui en a une collection remarquable: un Français, qui a couru le
Mexique, du Yucatán à la Sonora et à la Californie et qui s'est même un peu marié au Chiapas. Il
voudrait céder cela au Musée, au prix de 20,000 francs, très discret, prétend-il. Je lui ai dit que la
première chose qu'il ait à faire, à l'appui de son offre, était de dresser un inventaire de ses pièces,
catégorique et analytique, avec détails descriptifs et renseignements historiques et archéologiques.
Il s'est mis à l'oeuvre et m'a prié de lui promettre que je vous enverrai son travail quand il l'aurait
terminé. J'ai promis, mais il en a pour plusieurs mois avant d'en finir. La collection, que je crois assez
précieuse d'ailleurs, est un véritable fouillis.

2. M. Boban possède dans son cabinet quelque chose comme 150 bocaux où sont conservés dans l'alcool des reptiles, des poissons, des mollusques, des amphibies, des arachnides, etc., etc., qu'il a recueillis au Mexique. Je sais, par M. Boucard, qu'il y a dans le nombre, quelques espèces rares et même quelques espèces inconnues. Si la Commission désire que cette collection soit envoyée, son propriétaire est tout prêt à me la remettre.

6

Confronting a Different Paris

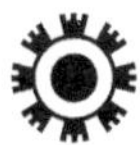

Eugène Boban returned to Paris in 1869 after an absence of sixteen years—twelve of them spent studying, excavating, and collecting in Mexico. Through no fault of his own, the previous few years had not gone as he had anticipated. The extensive collection of Mexican pre-Columbian artifacts that he had meticulously assembled and had hoped would bring acclaim at the Exposition Universelle of 1867 had proven to be a painful reminder to the public of how badly Napoleon III's plans for an empire in Mexico had misfired. The Louvre had refused to purchase these important objects, and for nearly two years they had been overcrowding his parents' small apartment. Despite his love for Mexico and pleasure in living there, he had been forced to return to France to try to sell his collection himself—"take care of his business," as his friend Charles Loysel had recommended. He undoubtedly felt keen disappointment in the lack of appreciation for his collection, along with some resentment about the French Intervention in Mexico, which had ultimately forced him and many others to abandon their adopted country.

Some of the resentment toward France's actions shared by friends living in the Mexican capital is palpable in a letter sent on 5 March 1869 to Boban in Veracruz. It is from Juan Francisco Fénélon, a medical doctor who was born in Oaxaca of a French father and Mexican mother (Pérez Siller and Skerritt 2010: 357). Fénélon is listed in the Mexican Imperial directory as having a residence and office at Coliseo Viejo no. 10, around the corner from Boban's shop (Maillefert 1992: 290). Apparently, the doctor was a progressive, who did not think highly of those in charge of the French government. He says to his friend, "You are at the edge of the great ocean, separating us from our dear France. Let us not speak ill of them, they are not as bad as the Señores Plagiarios" (BNF DMO n.a.f. 21477: item 167).[1]

Characterizing the government of Louis Napoleon as being not as bad as the kidnappers extorting money from unlucky people in Mexico is faint praise indeed; however, it reflects the attitude of many thoughtful people toward the excesses and iniquities of the Second Empire, which had overseen the installation of electric lighting, the building of railways, and other advances in France, along with a 45 percent increase in the cost of living. This was offset only partially by a 30 percent rise in average daily wages. In Paris the rents of the lower classes had doubled. Workers were spending 30 percent of their earnings on rent and almost all the remainder of their income on food. By the early 1860s half the Parisian population was nearly destitute and contending with employment and living conditions that were even worse than the appalling conditions Charles Dickens was recording in London (Horne 2007: 25). Thus, the backdrop to the Second Empire's "swaggering vulgarity, with plenty of gold trimmings" (Christiansen 1996: 18) was extreme poverty and misery.

In closing his letter to Boban, Fénélon added, "Courage, happy sailing, good health and preposterous sales! Flood France with your curiosities and squeeze out of them all their vile metal in exchange, that which our tyrants use so badly" (BNF DMO n.a.f 21477: item 167).[2]

Doctor Fénélon's letter contains a disquieting note about Boban's wife, whom he had apparently left in Mexico City. "Your wife is well, [but] she is exhausted from her fright with a case of vomiting, of which we will speak no further. She has instructed me to say that she is fine" (BNF DMO n.a.f 21477, item 167).[3] There are numerous references in newspaper reports and elsewhere to epidemics of *el vómito* in Mexico during these years, but it is unclear what Fénélon was referring to, although one description identifies it as yellow fever (Bullock 1866: 12). Many news items report that it was often fatal. Unfortunately, Boban tended to exaggerate some aspects of his working life while revealing little of his personal life, so there is virtually nothing known about this woman—not even her name. Having to leave her behind in Mexico must have been another cause of disappointment and concern for him, however.

In the years since Boban had left the capital, the city of Paris in 1869 had been completely transformed. Gone were the medieval streets running "higgledy-piggledy" in all directions, the clusters of ancient buildings that had been part of Parisian life since the days of Henri IV; gone were the intimate neighborhoods where workers lived alongside artisans, small merchants, and members of the nobility. In place of all this was the Paris of today—a cosmopolitan city of wide, straight boulevards down which traffic flows to the hubs of commerce and transportation; a city that appears to have been planned and built all at once, with tasteful but relatively nondescript buildings rising to a uniform height along its thoroughfares; a city filled with light and the modern conveniences—sewage and water systems, well-run transportation networks—whose poorer citizens are relegated to its outlying suburbs.

This complete makeover had been the vision of Napoleon III, working with Baron Georges-Eugène Haussmann, the emperor's supporter since 1848 and his prefect of the Seine from 1853 (the year Boban left Paris) to 1870 (the year after he returned). To accomplish the complete transformation of the city in a little over fifteen years, Haussmann oversaw the destruction of 100,000 apartments and 20,000 buildings, with the resulting displacement of some 20 to 30 percent of the city's inhabitants to nearby neighborhoods and the inner suburbs (Merriman 2014: xv). During this massive urban renewal project, Haussmann quadrupled the length of the city's sewers, doubled the number of water pipes, added fifty-two miles of roads and increased the average width of boulevards and large streets from twenty-five feet to between sixty-five and one hundred feet (Christiansen 1996: 100).

All of this had a cost. The government provided huge assistance for the redevelopment of Paris and for the country's industrial growth, as did newly formed financial institutions, such as the Crédit Foncier and Crédit Mobilier (Knapton 1971: 402). But the cost was not merely financial. The city had been flattened and homogenized. Despite the many advantages of the new Paris in 1869, it no longer had the same quality of mystery and surprise that had made a walk through its neighborhoods so enticing to the city's authors, artists, and cultured visitors for centuries. With one grand boulevard looking much like the next, it was no longer the Paris of Diderot, Voltaire, or Baudelaire. The changes had a cost in the animosity felt by the dispossessed. The fact that many could no longer afford the increased rents of the inner arrondissements resulted in what Alistair Horne calls "a kind of resentful apartheid." It created a volatile situation in which poor workers were segregated to outlying neighborhoods like Belleville and Ménilmontant, which became hotbeds of dissatisfaction and left-leaning politics (Horne 2007: 26).

Having adjusted as well as he could to the newly transformed Paris that greeted him in the spring of 1869, Eugène Boban promptly set to work launching himself as an authority on precontact Mexican cultures and an antiquarian specializing in pre-Columbian artifacts. He seems to have wasted little time getting the boxes of artifacts out of his parents' apartment. In October 1869, within just a few months of his return, he had already opened a shop at 35, rue du Sommerard, in a building that is still standing, although much renovated. It is across the street from the Musée de Cluny, France's national museum of medieval art and artifacts.

His business was a few blocks southwest of his family's home at 22, rue Grands Augustins. He rented it for 1,200 francs a year, while taking up residence in a modest apartment a few blocks west on rue Saint Jacques. Paris's property records describe the rental as a fourth-floor walkup in the rear court of the building. It was a divided room with fireplace for which he paid 350 francs per year rent (AD Paris, D.1P4/1102, Cadastral revision 1862; Christiane Demeulenaere,

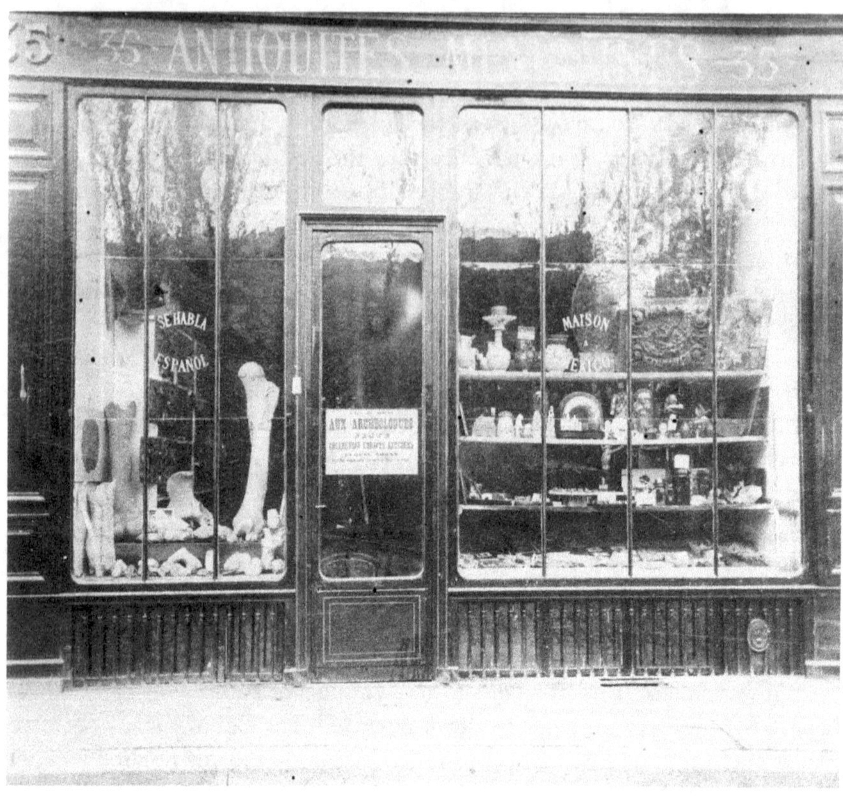

Figure 6.1 Boban's shop at 35, rue du Sommerard in the 5th arrondissement (courtesy of Hispanic Society of America, New York).

pers. comm.). Boban seems to have lived modestly for most of his career, and was exceedingly frugal, judging from his notes, made on the backs of every imaginable scrap of used paper he could find.

In the Sommerard shop Boban assembled all of his painstakingly gathered archeological and ethnographic collections, colonial artifacts, human skulls, mammoth bones (which added a rather dramatic touch to the window display), religious objects, paintings, books, and manuscripts. He did not rely exclusively on window and shop displays to attract potential buyers but took advantage of what was then still a relatively new technology—the photograph printed on paper, first perfected a few decades earlier. He made numerous "group portraits" of his merchandise and used them to advertise his wares. These photographs reside today in a number of museums and institutions in Europe and the United States.

The photographs of the interior of the shop demonstrate that Boban was one of the "shrewd dealers" described by the Mexican historian and art collector

Guillermo Tovar, who profited from the destruction of the convents, monasteries, and churches carried out by Benito Juárez's reform government. One arrangement shows numerous religious oil paintings, several depictions of the Virgin Mary, crucifixes of different sizes, images of saints, and what might be reliquaries principally on the upper shelves. They are displayed among stuffed iguanas, armadillos, the saws of sawfish or carpenter sharks, saddles, spurs, and stirrups. On the lower shelf are numerous books, some of which appear to be quite old. Another photograph of Boban's shop shows many more religious paintings, saddles, and riding accouterments, ornately carved chests, a carved head of Christ with a crown of thorns, and plaster-cast heads of native Mexicans. In mid-nineteenth-century France, such a collection would have attracted and amazed visitors. Everything was displayed in accordance with then-current ideas about how to present artifacts, known to the French as *bibelots*. They were to be taken completely out of context and admired exclusively for their decorative value.

As Elizabeth Emery and Laura Morowitz, experts in modern languages and art history, note, the emerging bourgeoisie of the nineteenth century was fascinated with the "bibelot (knick knack, curio or other collector's piece)." These items were sought-after less for their inherent artistic or cultural qualities than for their decorative function and current popular value as commodities. "While each category of object had unique characteristics and value, each was united in its logic of display, which was dependent on the capitalist market." This new valuation was facilitated by the rampant decontextualization that was taking place across the board. The objects had been removed or "migrated" from their "original settings (often churches, palaces or monasteries) to another (the antique shop, museum or living room) shedding their original function and intention along the way" (Emery and Morowitz 2004: 286).

Another means Boban used to introduce and advertise his collection was to share examples of the pieces it contained. In the fall of 1869 he selected some of his Mexican pre-Columbian artifacts to donate to the Musée Pincé, a museum of antiquities in Angers, his father and grandfather's birthplace. His aunts Fanny and Henriette Duvergé might have influenced his decision to make this donation, since they had been residents of Angers until about ten years earlier, running a successful business there. Their connection to their nephew appears to have been quite close. In later years they shared their business acumen when taking over his Paris shop whenever he was away.

To elucidate the donated collection of fifty artifacts to the Musée Pincé, Boban included a handwritten list, with notes about each object. Among the pieces he presented were the skull of an Aztec that he had found in a dig in Tlatelolco in 1857, casts of other skulls and heads, and a fragment of a mammoth tooth (perhaps found during the Las Palmas excavation). He also gave the museum several ceramic pieces, including an Aztec tripod vessel and spindle

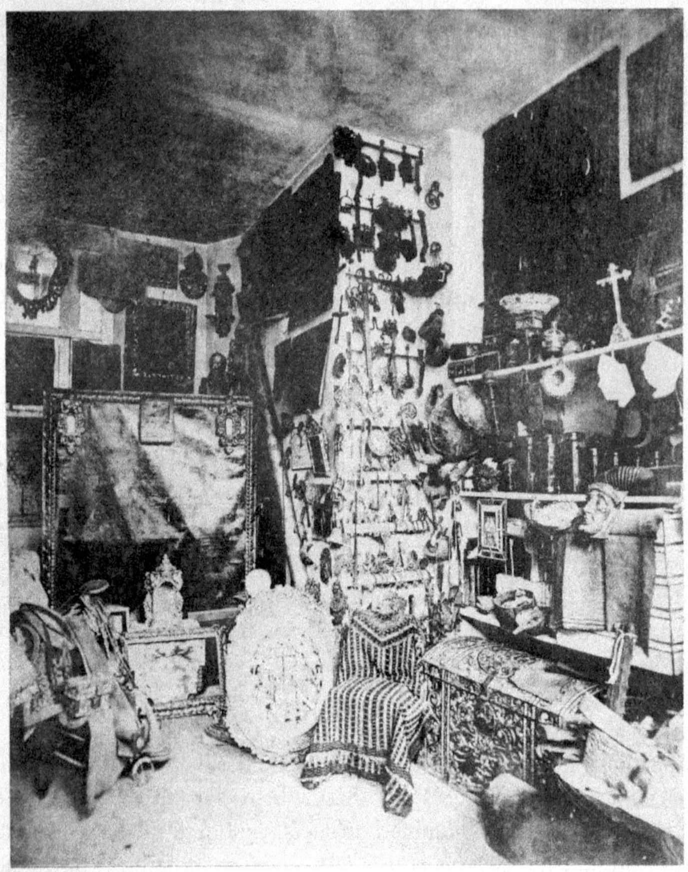

Figures 6.2a–b   Publicity photographs of the rue du Sommerard shop (courtesy of Hispanic Society of America, New York).

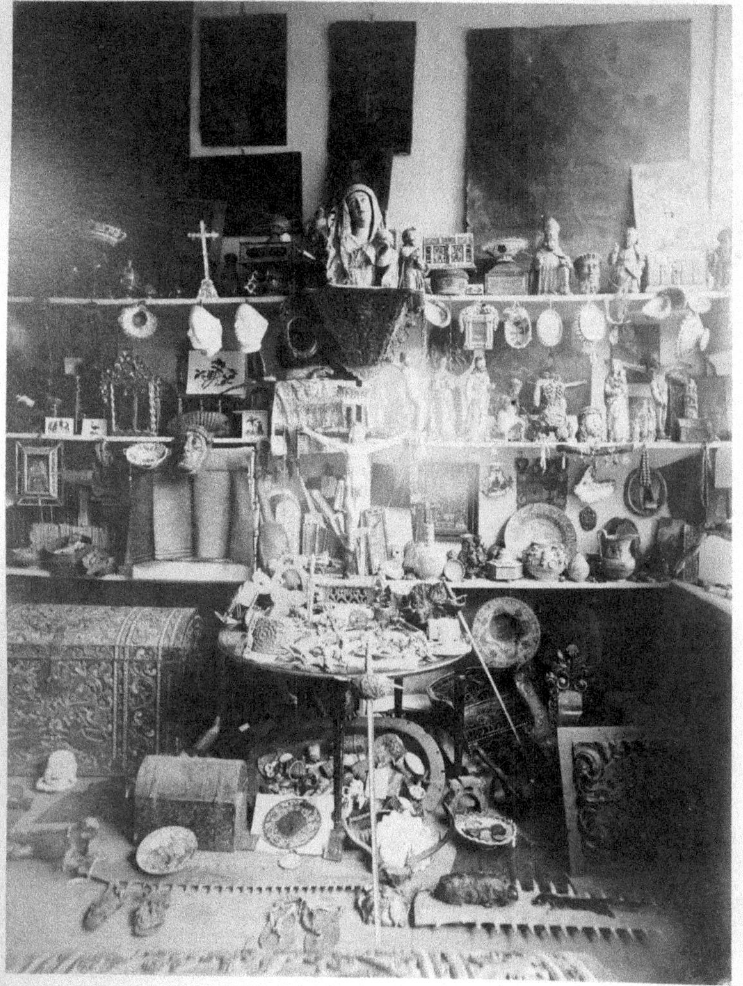
Objets d'Arts & Curiosités Mexicaines
EUGÉNE BOBAN DUVERGÉ
PARIS
35, Rue Du Sommerard
PHOT. BERTRAND
MEXICO
7 Callejon del Espiritu Santo
34, R. DAUPHINE, PARIS.
8032

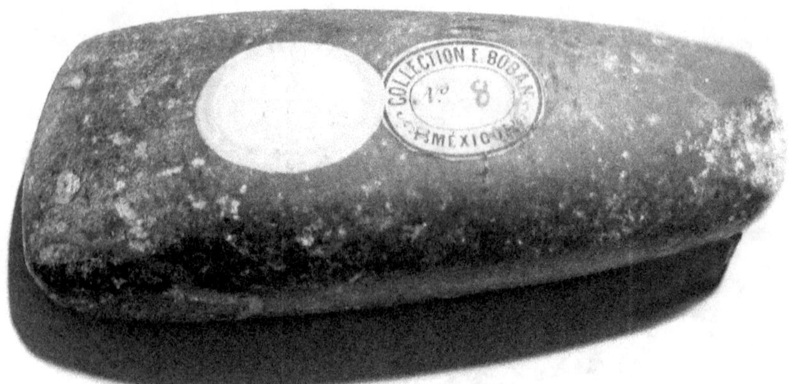

Figure 6.3   Stone ax from Boban's collection in the Musée Pincé (courtesy of Musées d'Angers).

whorls, some obsidian points, flakes and cores, and an agate amulet. The variety and scope of the collection make it an interesting early set, something of a starter kit for understanding Mexican archeology. Along with the list and description of the objects in the donation, Boban presented two business cards—one from his shop in Mexico City and the other from his new Paris establishment. The fact that he presented the card with his Mexican business address could mean that he had someone running the shop in his absence, perhaps his wife, and that he intended to return to Mexico as soon as he could.

Boban soon began exhibiting portions of his collection at fairs and at the meetings of scientific societies. In 1870 he exhibited archeological artifacts and indigenous costumes from Mexico and Guatemala at the Union Centrale des Beaux-Arts, receiving a bronze medal from the Société d'Ethnographie for the display (BNF DMO n.a.f. 21477: item 133).

Unfortunately, he could not have picked a worse time to return home and try to establish himself in the French capital. The political situation in France just over a year after his arrival must have reminded him of his early days in Mexico when the War of Reform was raging all around him, only much worse. The trouble began in the summer of 1870, when Prussia's ruthless and politically astute Prime Minister, Otto von Bismarck—the Machiavelli of the nineteenth century and architect of the modern German state—and Napoleon III disagreed about whether Prince Leopold, a member of Prussia's royal Hohenzollern line, should be allowed to become King of Spain. The prospect of having his country surrounded by Prussian interests made the French ruler uneasy (Merriman 2014: 1). The back story was that Bismarck wanted to lure Napoleon III into a confrontation because Prussia had been building up its war capacity for decades and he felt the time was right to challenge France's position in Europe.

Napoleon III took the bait and declared war on Prussia on 19 July 1870, and later left the Château de Saint-Cloud to lead his army in person, exhibiting one of his many strengths that were ultimately to prove to be flaws—exaggerated courage. He appears to have felt that since he shared the name of Napoleon Bonaparte, his country's greatest general, he had inherited Napoleon I's military genius.

That the Franco-Prussian war was going to be a disaster for France became clear after just a few weeks. Within eighteen days Prussia and its allies from south Germany had amassed nearly 1,200,000 troops on the border (Horne 2006: 270–71), while France, fighting alone, was struggling to mobilize a third of that number (Knapton 1971: 425). This was partly due to the fact that, during decades of military buildup, Prussia had taken over and modernized the country's public and private rail system with a view to its future mobilization needs. By 1870 the Prussian army could move personnel and materiel rapidly on double tracks to wherever the military command thought they would be needed, while in France the army was single-tracking its transports in one direction at a time (Merriman, 2014: 3). When French troops eventually arrived at the front, chaos reigned—supplies of food and weaponry often were nonexistent, brigades and commanders were not where they were supposed to be, many of the soldiers were untrained and unmotivated and such essentials as topographical maps were in short supply. By early September Napoleon's army was surrounded in the fortress town of Sedan, not far from the Belgian border. When efforts to break through the Prussian lines proved futile, the emperor and 100,000 troops surrendered on 2 September (Merriman 2014: 4–7).

News of the surrender in Sedan caused an immediate response in Paris. With the imprisonment of Napoleon III and the Second Empire at an end, Parisian crowds surrounded the legislative palace and demanded a new government, one that would be responsive to the people's needs. On 4 September the Third Republic was declared under leaders who were determined by the crowds' acclamations (Merriman 2014: 9). Banding together behind the city's peripheral ring of fortifications, the citizens of Paris vowed to continue their resistance to the Prussians, despite the capitulation of much of the rest of the country. They were encouraged in their hope that the city could hold out and somehow save France by the fact that 100,000 conscripted reservists of the Garde mobile were bivouacked in Paris, along with 300,000 members of the Garde nationale, the civilian militia established in 1789 (Christiansen 1996: 172–73). On 19 September 1870 the Prussian army began laying siege to Paris.

A month later, on 15 October, General François Achille Bazaine, who had withdrawn French troops from Mexico just a few years earlier following the failure of Maximilian's mission, unexpectedly surrendered an army of 155,000 men at Metz, a city in northeastern France. The citizens of Paris were irate at what they perceived to be the latest treachery of the country's military leaders, which virtually guaranteed that Paris would remain besieged and that the country would buckle before the Prussian onslaught (Merriman 2014: 12). In fact, the Siege of Paris would last until 28 January 1871—a total of 131 days, during which the city was bombarded by Prussian artillery for twenty-four days (Christiansen 1996: 264).

Many Parisians fled, settling in towns in the countryside. For those who remained, the fall and winter of 1870–71 became increasingly hellish as the capital was simultaneously blocked off from the rest of the country and fired upon by the Prussian army. Artillery shells rained down in all parts of town. The weather became intensely cold, and little fuel was available, particularly for the lower classes. Trees along the Avenue des Champs-Élysées, and indeed along all the beautiful wide boulevards so recently created by Baron Haussmann, were cut down and used for fuel. Food became increasingly scarce. Ordinary Parisians resorted to eating dogs, cats, and rats; those who could afford it ate horsemeat. The animals in the zoo were consumed. As the months passed, many Parisians, particularly women and children, died of exposure, malnutrition, and diseases that prey upon the weak. By the end of the siege, the weekly death counts in the city of just under 2 million people had risen from 1,266 to 4,444 (Horne 2007: 67, 221).

When Boban returned to Paris, one of his first influential contacts was an American named Joseph Karrick Riggs. A member of the prominent Riggs banking family of Washington, DC, he had become a doctor during the American Civil War and had moved to Paris in 1866. During the Siege of Paris, he founded the American Ambulance service, along with Thomas Evans, who had been the dentist to the imperial family and had helped Empress Eugénie flee the country when Napoleon III was captured (Christiansen 1996: 193). Their intention was to address some of the physical suffering of the city's residents.

In letters to his wife, who had moved to the safety of London with their young son, Riggs described the privations of life even for the upper class in Paris at the time. "We are all getting thin upon horsemeat . . . we had cat, rat, wolf and camel from the Jarden des Plantes, the last the best" he writes on the day after Christmas (Library of Congress, Manuscript Division, Riggs Family, box 125, 26, December 1870). Though he tells his wife not to worry about him, he provides many details, which must have caused her anxiety. "The roar of cannon is almost incessant, day and night, and we are so used to it that it no longer attracts special notice. Many civilians have been killed and wounded" (Library of Congress, Manuscript Division, Riggs Family, box 125, 16 January 1871). In fact, the daily newspapers were filled with chilling stories of "a little girl sliced in two on her way home; six women killed in a queue outside a shop; ten children blown to pieces at their boarding school in the rue Oudinot" (Christiansen 1996: 254–55). All of these events were foreshadowing the horrors to be visited on civilians throughout the twentieth century.

On 28 January France's Government of National Defense arrived at an initial peace agreement with the Prussians, ending the siege. The terms of the truce eventually agreed upon would in no way mollify the long-suffering citizens of the capital, however. They were draconian and humiliating—the imposition of crippling war reparations, the annexation of France's major industrial and mining regions of Alsace and Lorraine, in addition to the proclamation of a German Empire under Kaiser Wilhelm I at the Château de Versailles, a symbol of French sovereignty, style, and luxury for two hundred years. Historian Alistair Horne calls the terms, "One of the harshest peace settlements ever imposed by one European state upon another" (Horne 2007: 14–15).

In the early spring Adolphe Thiers, a former minister and acclaimed historian who had been appointed president by the Assemblée nationale on 17 February, began systematic actions to quell the independence of Paris. In an attempt to seize the city from those who had protected it, 20,000 troops tried to disarm Paris on the morning of 18 March by appropriating hundreds of cannons in Montmartre, Belleville, and other workers' arrondissements. The effort was badly coordinated and unsuccessful. Ten days later, on 28 March, Parisians declared the beginning of a new form of government: the Commune, a government by and for workers themselves.

The Paris Commune was organized as a community of citizens all entitled to their own opinions and encouraged to pursue their own actions. No leader emerged with the ambition or strength to impose his will on the shifting events and force through a plan of action, so anarchy and political chaos were the order of the day. Businessmen, government officials, and members of the social and cultural elite were appalled by the specter of lower-class workers—whom they often described as raging animals—assuming control of the government and the economy. Thiers's administration increased its efforts to bring a stop to what he viewed as madness by using the reconstituted French army, numbering 130,000 troops, to overwhelm Paris and rid the city of what he considered lower-class scum. As more and more of the forts surrounding the city fell to the invading French army, workers sought to protect themselves against the attack on the heart of Paris that each day became more likely. Their tactic was the same one that had served them for generations—building enormous barricades across the city's boulevards and intersections.

The terrible end of the Paris Commune started on 21 May 1871, when the French army began flooding into the city, meeting little resistance except for the heroic, ultimately futile, efforts of men, women, and children fighting from the barricades. The army slaughtered as it went, executing Parisians by the thousands. The killings and reprisals continued the week of 21 through 28 May, dubbed *la Semaine Sanglante* (the Bloody Week), and well beyond. It is estimated that during that week in May at least 20,000 Parisians were summarily killed by army troops (Horne 2006: 287). Hundreds were shot after they had surrendered;

thousands more were taken to the Lobau barracks, the Luxembourg Gardens, Père Lachaise Cemetery, and other locations and executed by machine-gun fire. No one in any part of town could have remained unaware of what was going on. Certainly not Eugène Boban. In fact, many died on the doorstep of his shop. "When the fighting ended in the Latin Quarter, twenty bodies lay on the rue Sommerard; more were scattered above the intersection of the boulevard Saint-Michel" (Merriman 2014: 178). A young boy who was trying to hide was chased down and shot dead outside the Musée de Cluny, across the street from Boban's shop. Others were killed even more deliberately. "On the rue Cardinal Lemoine, soldiers roused from bed Eugène André, a mathematician and professor known for his opposition to the Empire. He had not served in the Commune and refused a position in education offered him. André, who ignored advice to hide, was shot immediately" (Merriman 2014: 178).

Although Boban likely remained in the capital throughout the siege and the rise and fall of the Paris Commune, since his family lived there and they did not have an obvious alternative residence, his papers curiously contain almost no documentation of these momentous events. The only reference to the defeat of the French army by Germany in 1870 is a newspaper clipping dated 14 October of that year. The article is about the burning of the St. Cloud palace, which, according to the writer, took just six hours to be transformed into a pile of smoking ruins. The account blames the German army, which had occupied the palace where Napoleon III had once held court, although it was French artillery aimed at the German emplacements that actually set the building ablaze. Boban wrote a note on the clipping that the Germans had coldly burned the palace out of hatred for the French. This sort of revenge, he continues, had been taken by too many people, and from such events, sadly, one could get a good idea of the state of civilization (HSA: B2253, Box XIV).

His papers in the Bibliothèque nationale contain a certificate awarded by the Department of Public Works, stamped République Française, for his help with putting out fires during the bombardment. The undated certificate indicates that he was an adjunct district inspector for the 5th arrondissement (BNF DMO n.a.f. 21476: item 523). It is somewhat surprising that he chose to keep this award, given the climate of reprisals that followed the defeat of the Paris Commune, along with the denunciations that fueled them. Anyone seen to have had a connection to the Commune—just speaking a Parisian argot or having remained in the city—was subject to execution or deportation. The reprisals were aided by people's desire to settle grudges. It is estimated that the police received nearly 380,000 denunciations, most of them unsigned, between 22 May and 13 June 1871 (Merriman 2014: 233).

Boban's tactic for surviving the horrors of the Siege of Paris and the Commune seems to have been to keep his head down and continue with business as usual as far as he could—an approach he possibly had perfected during the tumultuous years in Mexico. As his correspondence shows, he carried on with his commercial activities throughout 1870 and 1871, despite the incessant bombing, lack of food, and general mayhem that surrounded him.

Notes

1. Je vous remets a'incluse la lettre dont je vous ai parlé. Je vous felicite d'avoir bien commencé votre voyage—vous voici bientôt au bord du grand océan, qui nous sépare de notre chère France. N'en parlons point mal, il est encore moins Canaille que Mmrs les plagiarios.

2. Courage, bon voyage, bonne santé et ventes abracadabrantes! Inondez la France de vos curiosités et soutirez lui en echange beaucoup de ce vilain metal, que nos tyrans emploient si mal.

3. Votre dame va bien, elle est exténue de sa frayeur, avec un vomitif, n'en parlons plus, elle me charge de vous dire qu'elle est très bien.

7

Marketing a Collection

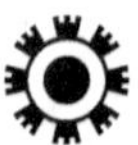

During the early 1870s, with the French public's interest in Mexican antiquities waning, Boban's enthusiasm for breaking developments in archeology led him to explore the findings of the French paleontologist Édouard Lartet and the wealthy English banker Henry Christy. During the previous decade the two men had revolutionized the study of early humans in Europe with their discoveries of Cro-Magnon artifacts and human remains in the caves of the Perigord region of southern France. This led to the earliest publication on the portable art of Stone Age hunters and gatherers, "Cavernes du Périgord" (Lartet and Christy 1864). In addition, they explored the rock shelter La Madeleine in the Dordogne valley, which was later dated to around 17,000 to 12,000 years ago.

One of Boban's first connections with Christy and Lartet's work may have come through William Bragge, F.S.A. (Fellow of the Society of Antiquaries), a dealer and collector from Sheffield, England, to whom Boban sent books and manuscripts in the spring of 1870. Bragge had previously written that he would be glad to have any examples of manuscripts and books to show to prospective buyers. The book dealer had told Boban that Augustus Wollaston Franks of the British Museum was one of his clients.

Franks, the curator of British and medieval antiquities, was an important potential contact for Boban. But being in charge of the museum's medieval antiquities was not the only thing that made him interesting. He was also chief curator of the Christy Collection, bequeathed to the British Museum in 1865, along with an endowment with which to maintain it. It encompassed more than 10,000 objects, including prehistoric stone tools from Europe, Asia, and Africa, and ethnographic artifacts from the Americas, Asia, Polynesia, New Zealand, and Melanesia. Boban was soon corresponding directly with Franks at the British Museum, possibly thanks to his connection to Bragge (BNF DMO n.a.f. 21477: item 240).

Bragge wrote again in September 1871, just a few months after the slaughter of Communards, informing Boban that he would soon be visiting his shop, and was hoping to look at his collection of tobacco pipes (BNF DMO n.a.f. 21476: item 385–86). Their relationship led to some profitable sales for Boban. In 1880 Bragge published *Bibliotheca Nicotiana,* which details his quite extraordinary array of smoking implements. Among them are eighteen Aztec ceramic tobacco pipes and fragments that he purchased from Boban. Some of these he describes as having come "from the private collection of the late Emperor Maximilian" (Bragge 1880: 153). Like many dealers, Boban was always ready to associate his objects with important individuals.

Looking to expand his collection beyond Mexico and Central America, Boban corresponded in July of 1871 with Philippe Lalande of Brive-la-Gaillard, one of the discoverers of cave shelters with archeological remains in Corrèze, France. He had a large collection of Cro-Magnon and Neanderthal artifacts. Lalande wrote, sending Boban his compliments on the remarkable series of photographs of his collection, and eagerly inquired about the possibility of trading European prehistoric artifacts and even furniture for Mexican archeological objects. Lalande eventually purchased quite a number of Mexican stone axes and other pre-Columbian pieces from Boban.

The trades with Lalande were just the beginning in a long series of deals with European collectors. Having dipped his toes into the stream of French prehistoric artifacts available at the time, Boban began to exchange notes with Théodore Baudon of Mouy, France, who wrote in August 1872 saying that his son had informed him that Boban possessed a large quantity of objects from Mexico. Baudon added that he was the possessor of a unique collection from a prehistoric site in Mouy, which he was willing to trade with Boban for Mexican flint and obsidian artifacts (BNF DMO n.a.f. 21476: item104).

Aside from selling archeological objects, a tactic Boban used to gain income from his collection and to participate in the sharing of knowledge about pre-Columbian subjects was to create casts of his more important pieces. He sold casts of his own artifacts and acquired casts of objects that he admired from other collections, which he also exhibited and sold. Making casts was a common practice in the nineteenth century, providing a method of sharing artifacts in private and public collections.

The Smithsonian Institution has many casts of objects that it acquired in the nineteenth and early twentieth century. Capturing rare or even one-of-a-kind artifacts, they include several from Boban's Mexican collection. The most notable of these is a cast of the Quetzalcoatl sculpture currently on exhibit in the Louvre's Pavillon de Sessions on loan from the Musée du quai Branly. Although it is an artifact from one of Boban's earliest collections, the Smithsonian obtained a cast of it from the Detroit Museum of Art in 1917. A laboratory in the Smithsonian's Museum of Natural History then fabricated three identical copies from the Detroit cast, which had been lent for that express purpose. A note on the catalog card states erroneously "the original of this carving is in the Museo Nacional in Mexico City, Mexico."

Another early important European contact was François Lenoir, an amateur collector of archeological artifacts and a close friend of Edouard Lartet's (Harvey 1997: 118). Lenoir, who corresponded with Boban for many years, wrote in 1871 that he could get objects from a dig in Bruniquel, a prehistoric site that contained Neanderthal artifacts. Apparently, none of these early prehistorians had qualms about selling or trading their finds, considering them to be their personal property to be used to build up and broaden their own collections. Their activities mirrored those of many nineteenth-century museum curators. Lenoir added that Boban need have no fear of any problems or claims on the objects, since his friend Peccadeau de l'Isle, who dug at Bruniquel, was happy to work with Boban (BNF DMO n.a.f. 21478: item 152). Both Lartet and Peccadeau de l'Isle had exhibited prehistoric artifacts from France at the 1867 Exposition Universelle, where they may have seen Boban's Mexican pre-Columbian artifacts for the first time (SI 1869: 408).

In 1872 Boban sold sixty-seven casts made from Edouard Lartet and Henry Christy's collection of prehistoric stone tools from the Perigord region for 167.50 francs. He had obtained the casts sometime in 1870 with the consent of Lartet, the Christy family, and Christy's curator, Augustus Wollaston Franks. Christy died in 1865 (3/8/1870: BNF DMO n.a.f. 21478: item 55). During the 1870s Boban advertised in English that his shop was "the only establishment authorized to sell moldings from the collection of Lartet and Christy" (BNF DMO n.a.f. 21479: item 264). The 1872 collection of sixty-seven casts went to the Laboratoire d'Anthropologie de l'École Practique, which was then under the direction of the famous French physician, anatomist, and physical anthropologist Paul Broca (BNF DMO n.a.f. 21476: item 393).

Boban, who was always thinking of new ways to advertise his collection, continually expanded his contacts in various scientific and academic fields, with whom he exchanged and sold artifacts. They, in turn, opened avenues for further sales and exchanges with other academics and collectors. Despite his growing network, however, he still was having no luck selling his pre-Columbian Mexican collection.

In May 1873 he received another letter from Dr. François Fénélon, his friend in Mexico City. There may have been a more regular correspondence between them, but only two letters have survived. Dr. Fénélon begins by asking Boban's forgiveness for delivering such bad news, but, that he feels it his duty from a distance "to tell you your wife has a grave infection of the tongue and I fear a prompt end despite the care we have given her."[1] He closes by saying, somewhat obliquely, "It would be well to take care about seeing to your interests in Mexico" (BNF DMO n.a.f. 21476: item 168).[2] Whether Fénélon was referring to familial or financial "interests" or both is not known. Notwithstanding this bad news, there is no evidence that Boban returned to Mexico during these years. In fact, his own writing suggests that he did not. Considering that Paris had been in turmoil for two of the four years since his return and with his Mexican archeological collection still unsold, he would hardly have had the funds to pay for a return trip.

Sadly, almost nothing is known of his relationship with the woman to whom Fénélon refers. She likely was Mexican, perhaps Maya, since Col. Doutrelaine wrote that she was from Chiapas. There is perhaps one clue about her in one of Boban's Nahuatl notebooks, where he recorded the date Wednesday, 15 October 1873 and the name Dolores Eulalia García (HSA: Box XII). There is also a cryptic and almost illegible notation about her being at the house of M. Bazaine and something about thirty centimes. Nothing else is added, but hers is the only name in the notebook. Although the date cited was five months after Dr. Fénélon's dire prediction, Dolores may have been the name of the wife he left behind and 15 October the day she died.

Boban seems to have gone on with business as usual, apparently his preferred method of coping with violent or tragic events in his life. Always keen to learn more himself and share what he knew, Boban attended meetings and congresses, and became a member of several French academic societies. This helped him expand his understanding of archeology and anthropology, exhibit his collections, and make new contacts. Then as now, these groups were instrumental in the democratization of access to information. As historian Elizabeth A. Williams notes, "In the nineteenth century, the Société savant was a ubiquitous form of organization in French intellectual, commercial, and social life. Bourgeois in character and devoted to specialized pursuits, learned societies replaced the aristocratic academies of science and letters that had dominated the intellectual landscape of the eighteenth century" (Williams 1985a: 332).

Boban had been interested in being part of these organizations from an early date. Just after returning to Paris in 1869 he became a member of the Société d'ethnographie, which had been established in 1859 by a group of linguists headed by the orientalist Léon de Rosny (BNF DMO n.a.f 21479: item 188). The society was formed partially to challenge the ideas of the Société d'anthropologie, founded by Paul Broca, which they viewed as being concerned with "anatomically based anthropology" (Williams 1985a: 334). That is to say, Broca's group was more interested in the physical anthropology of humans than in their cultural development.

While the purposes of these two societies may have been somewhat divergent, Boban was a member in good standing of both, regularly corresponding with Rosny and Broca. He also joined the Société Américaine de France, a group formed to study the ancient history of the New World, which Édouard Madier de Montjau had revived in 1873. Madier de Montjau personally invited Boban to become one of some ninety members of the society in 1874. Since one of the Société Americaine's goals was to publish grammars and dictionaries of American indigenous languages, a principal focus of the group was to make broadly available the famous collection of Mexican pre-Columbian and postcontact painted manuscripts amassed earlier in the century by Joseph Marius Alexis Aubin.

The Société Americaine's first great accomplishment, however, was "when it convened Americanists from around the globe to the provincial city of Nancy" in 1875 (Edison 1999: 296). This was the first international Americanist meeting ever held, and the list of those attending contained an impressive group of scholars. Among them was Eugène Boban. He gave a paper on Mexican antiquities and exhibited casts of his collection, demonstrating that he had already become a recognized member of this intellectual community.

Publications resulting from this first "Americanists" meeting noted that several "members of the Society who sponsored it have furnished from their own collections the elements of a truly interesting exhibition, and which during four days has not ceased to attract men of science and the curious." The writer continued with a very favorable mention of Boban's contribution to the displays. "A collection of casts representing the heads of fired clay idols found in the area around Vera Cruz. One notices in the casts a particular artificial deformation of the skull and a kind of false beard which was attached to the chin of the noble Mexicans and which recalls the goatees of certain Egyptian divinities." (Congrés International des Américanistes 1875: 21–22). Boban later donated the casts of these interesting objects to the new Musée anthropologique de Nancy.

In addition to exhibiting casts of pieces from his collection at the first Americanist conference, Boban displayed actual obsidian knives, points, scrapers, cores, and a "macuahuitl"—his reproduction of the Aztec war club. He also exhibited several enormous Spanish stirrups and spurs, which he said had belonged to the sixteenth-century conquistadors (Boban 1877: 22).

Perhaps one of Boban's most influential contacts was Gabriel de Mortillet, the renowned prehistorian who developed a chronological classification of humanity's earliest cultural development. This connection may have come through Boban's work with Lenoir and Lartet, since Mortillet based some of his chronology on the findings that Henry Christy and Edouard Lartet had made at La Madeleine cave.

Their relationship may have begun in 1872, when Boban had advertised his collection in a publication called *Indicateur de L'archéologue et du Collectionneur*, edited by Gabriel de Mortillet and Amédée Caix de Saint-Aymour. There he went into considerable detail listing and describing the extent of pre-Columbian material in his shop. The description of objects continues for several pages, and the assemblage is characterized as "surely one of the richest and most complete collections, the product of twenty years' research in most of the provinces of

Mexico from the shores of the Pacific Ocean to the Yucatan" (Mortillet and Caix de Saint-Aymour 1872: 174–75). His connection to both Mortillet and Caix de Saint-Aymour seems to have spurred another method for widening his audience: publishing articles in the journals of the scientific societies he had joined. Many of these academic publications compiled the papers presented at meetings, while others offered articles that the editors felt expanded the knowledge base of their subscribing members.

A handwritten proposal from Boban dated 10 November 1874 is among Mortillet's papers at the University of Saarsland in Germany. "I beg to acknowledge receipt of your letter of the 10th instant. The price of my Mexican collection is 35,000 francs."[3] Boban also kept a copy of this proposal to Mortillet in his personal papers, although, significantly, he used the rest of the paper to jot down notes about gold mining for a work on the natural history of Mexico (HSA: B2242, Box III, Folder I). Thus, several years after the Louvre rejected his offer to sell his collection for 50,000 francs ($10,000)—the equivalent of at least two hundred and fifty thousand dollars today—he proposed to sell Mortillet the same artifacts for 35,000 francs ($7,000). That sale was not finalized.

In 1875 the *Archives de la Société Americaine de France* published the text of an original Nahuatl manuscript from Boban's collection with a commentary by the president of the society, Edouard Madier de Montjau (1875: 269–75). Boban published a note in the same issue about Aztec lip plugs or *tentetl*, in which he stated that rock crystal labrets were the distinctive mark of members of the royal court. Presumably he is referring to what the sixteenth-century Franciscan historian and ethnographer Fray Bernardino de Sahagún wrote about the items rulers wore when they danced. Sahagún describes one ruler bedecked in "a long, white labret of clear crystal, shot through with blue cotinga feathers, in a gold setting, which he inserted in his lower lip" (Anderson and Dibble 1954: 27). The antiquarian's rock crystal labrets were of a much simpler variety.

In the same year, Boban published four other articles reporting on archeological material in his possession. These appeared in the first volume of a journal called *Le Musée Archéologique*, edited by the ethnologist Léon de Cessac and published by Amédée Caix de Saint-Aymour. The first article, under the general heading of *Antiquités Mexicaines*, is "Terres cuites, reproduisant des Déformations craniennes" (Terra cottas showing some cranial deformations). The article begins by noting the popular fascination with two "Aztec children" with strangely formed heads, who were exhibited in Paris during the 1850s. He goes on to say that, rather than being representatives of an ancient race as advertised, they were microcephalic—they had undersized skulls, as well as undersized bodies. Boban then moves on to a discussion of intentional cranial deformation. All of this is a buildup for his presentation in the article, for the first time, of a series of Remojadas-style figurine heads from his collection. In writing about them, he pays particular attention to their artificially deformed skulls.

Remojadas refers to a pre-Columbian culture and artistic style, particularly known for hollow ceramic figurines dating from 100 BC to around 800 AD characterized by beautiful, broadly smiling faces. Noting that the heads had been found recently in Estanzuela, some forty leagues from Veracruz, Boban gives generous and admiring credit to the man who uncovered the artifacts, the casts of which he had exhibited at the Americanist meeting in Nancy. "I am obliged to my friend, Mr. J. M. Melgar, knowledgeable Mexican archeologist, who excavates the necropolises and ruins of his country with praiseworthy zeal and devotion" (Boban 1876a: 47).[4] Melgar had been excavating for many years and had assisted the French occupation forces. In the archives of the Commission Scientifique, Col. Doutrelaine describes him as an amateur archeologist living in Veracruz (*Archives de la Commission Scientifique du Mexique* 1867b: 111).[5]

Boban's article is quite scholarly. He presents his collection of ceramic heads as rare and unknown even in Mexico (which was true at the time), and discusses the nature of their cranial deformation, which creates what he describes as a shield shape by broadening their faces. In conclusion he offers two hypotheses: the first, that the ceramic heads have astronomical significance because of the symbols depicted on their head coverings; the second, that they are not related to the Maya of Palenque, which some people had thought, but are rather the artistic production of a separate people.

Boban is well versed in his subject and clearly an independent thinker, capable of synthesizing a lot of information. While the meaning and function of the smiling faced figurines is still debated, he is correct in his assessment that the culture from which they originated was not related to the Maya. In addition, he seems particularly sensitive to the objects' artistic details. While the symbols depicted on the head coverings may or may not be astronomical, they are clearly important and had cultural significance.

A second article, "Le macuahuitl ou massue des anciens Mexicains" (The Macuahuitl or mace of the ancient Mexicans) begins with the brassy statement: "The following work may shock many accepted ideas. I know it is not always prudent to stray off the beaten path" (Boban 1876c: 147).[6] But, Boban writes, he has decided to solve a problem that he has mulled over for twenty years. He then challenges his colleagues in archeology to "read this note in the same spirit that dictated it to me, namely the love of the truth, without bias" (Boban 1876c: 147).[7]

Boban goes on to describe the reproduction of the wooden war club with embedded obsidian scrapers as the principal weapon used by the Aztecs, relating it to the saw of a sawfish, like those seen in the photograph of his shop. He notes that he has found the remnants of many sawfish in his digs and that he thinks the club was made to imitate them. He includes his own version of how the macuahuitl was constructed, claiming that it is based on the only archeologically recovered weapon, which was then in the Museo Nacional, and on drawings in postcontact codices.

A third short article is entitled "Emmanchement de haches Mexicaines," about the hafting of pre-Columbian stone axes. In it Boban employs various drawings from codices to explicate how the axes were made and suggests the possibility of making a comparative study of the hafting of European stone tools but says he will leave that up to the specialists to judge whether such a study is worthwhile.

The last article, published in the *Musée Archéologique*, "Grelots d'or trouvés dans un Tombeau Zapoteco" (Gold bells found in a Zapotec tomb), is an interesting description of two pre-Columbian gold-wire bells. Boban describes having seen them while working with the Commission Scientifique, although they did not form part of the official French collection. After the fall of Maximilian's empire in Mexico, the bells found their way to the United States and were purchased by a private collector in Washington, DC.

The 1876 article describes a gentleman named Joseph Karrick Riggs, a wealthy American, who had visited Boban's store in Paris. This is the same Joseph Riggs who cofounded the American Ambulance Service and provided so much aid to Parisians during the Prussian siege of 1870. According to the article, while examining pre-Columbian artifacts in Boban's shop, Riggs started up a conversation about some gold bells he had purchased from a Washington jeweler. "My memory went back immediately to the Franco bells presented to the emperor Maximilian," writes Boban, "and taking out an album of drawings, which I had carefully kept, I convinced him that these bells were the same" (Boban 1876b: 144–45).[8] Riggs must have been extremely impressed that Boban had illustrations at hand of the very objects he had described.

The drawings Boban mentions in this article, some of which are reproduced in it, are now in the Hispanic Society's collection. They were originally made in Mexico by order of Col. Doutrelaine, who sent them, or copies of them, to Paris before the 1867 exhibition. A French soldier in the engineer corps named Jean Amatus Klein (Riviale 2011: 454), who was under Doutrelaine's command, executed these accurate drawings of Boban's artifacts and other objects from Mexico in pencil and ink, with occasional watercolor enhancement. Boban appears to have kept, or later received, the original illustrations, drawn on yellowed tracing paper and wrinkled by the watercolor details. For many of the depictions Klein simply traced the outline of the actual object, thus creating life-size images.

According to Boban, once unearthed, the bells passed through the hands of the village priest to a Mr. Franco, who brought them to Mexico City to present as a gift to the Emperor Maximilian, who "was a great lover of art objects" (Boban 1876b: 143). Franco allowed drawings to be made under the direction of Col. Doutrelaine, and Boban mentioned seeing the bells on various occasions in the emperor's offices.

Boban includes numerous references to early chronicles and painted Mexican manuscripts in this article, which is also quite scholarly. He compares the Riggs bell with several depictions found in the Mexican Manuscript #3, also known as the Telleriano-Remensis codex, in the *Fonds Mexicaines* (Mexican holdings) of the Bibliothèque nationale in Paris. He also includes a long description from the library's catalog written by the well-known ethnographer, archeologist, and collector Charles Étienne Brasseur de Bourbourg, to back up his assertions.

These four papers demonstrate Boban's ability to expound upon the history of collecting, to share his knowledge about pre-Columbian cultures, and to write accurately and scientifically about the material in his possession (Boban 1876a; 1876b; 1876c). In each of them he makes use of painted Mexican manuscripts in the collections of the Bibliothèque nationale to illustrate the points he is making and is not at all timid about putting forth his theories or suggesting new areas of research. Although some of his views are incorrect, the papers demonstrate a broad knowledge of the field and a high intellectual standard. The fact that he is able to publish four different articles in the journal indicates that he was highly regarded by French anthropologists and prehistorians.

The history of Boban's involvement with the two golden bells said to have come from a Zapotec tomb near Mitla, Oaxaca, is illustrative of what was to become the antiquarian's modus operandi for many years—writing articles about objects he wished to sell or had already sold, using his scholarship as a form of advertisement. After Riggs walked into Boban's shop in 1871 and saw the illustrations of the bells he owned, he was apparently charmed by the antiquarian and became an active supporter. He wrote him saying he would be pleased to send his artifact catalog and photos to friends in the United States, who, he thought, might purchase the collection for the recently opened museum in New York's Central Park, presumably the Metropolitan Museum of Art (BNF DMO n.a.f. 2149: item 109). Subsequent letters from Riggs report on a variety of prospective contacts he was making for Boban, including Samuel Avery and Roland Knoedler, both important New York art dealers (BNF DMO n.a.f. 21479: item 106).

Riggs acted as a go-between for Boban and the eventual purchaser of one of the gold bells that he owned. He had purchased them from a Washington jeweler named Henry Howard, who claimed to have gotten them from a woman who had received them as a gift from the Empress Charlotte, Maximilian's wife, after her departure from Mexico.

Early in 1875 Riggs arranged a meeting between Boban and two prospective buyers, the well-to-do young Frenchman Alphonse Pinart and Count Serge Stroganoff, "aide de camp of His Majesty the emperor of Russia" (Boban 1876b: 147). Stroganoff was enormously wealthy, having inherited family riches made in the extraction and distribution of salt. He was a bon vivant and collector par excellence, who had more than enough money to indulge his every whim. When he died in 1923, he left a fortune to his wife and sister, in addition to "a palace in Rome, art treasures in Berlin, and bank accounts in England and America valued at $4,000,000 as well as property in France" according to a *Boston Globe* article (21 July 1935).

In the end, the count purchased the larger bell for 5,000 francs and paid Boban a commission of 250 francs, or 5 percent for his efforts (BNF DMO n.a.f. 21479: item 309). It is not unreasonable to assume that the article published in *Le Musée Archéologique* subsequent to the sale was intended to be an advertisement for the antiquarian's connoisseurship, not to mention his entrepreneurial finesse. The other articles showcased objects he had in his own collections— ceramic heads, Aztec war clubs, and stone axes—that were still available for sale. Stroganoff's bell entered the collections of the Hermitage in St Petersburg from the Stroganoff Palace in 1926 (Matos 1990: 230–31). The smaller bell apparently remained with Joseph Riggs.

The Stroganoff bell is shown below in the original Klein drawing from Boban's collection in the Hispanic Society and a recent photograph. The Metropolitan Museum of Art exhibited it in 1990. According to the Metropolitan's exhibition catalog, it represents an Aztec eagle warrior (Matos 1990: 229–31). In the *Musée Archéologique* article Boban writes that the larger bell is a depiction of the god Huitzilopochtli, the Aztec war god with hummingbird attributes. He goes on to say that the bells had been found by an Indian near the ancient palace of Mitla in Oaxaca, and were, therefore, more likely Mixtec.

The other prospective customer Riggs introduced to Boban as a potential buyer for the gold bells was the linguist, ethnologist, and collector Alphonse Pinart, who at the age of twenty-one had come into a small fortune, an inheritance from his father (Parmenter 1966: 11). Although not interested in the bells, Pinart subsequently purchased Boban's entire collection of pre-Columbian artifacts, which then included all of the objects exhibited in 1867 at the Exposition Universelle plus numerous additional artifacts that Boban had brought with him from his shop in Mexico in 1869. A few years prior to the sale, the 1872 article in *Indicateur de l'archéologue* described the collection as containing 2,025 cataloged pieces (Mortillet and Caix de Saint-Aymour 1872: 174).

This long-awaited happy outcome ultimately was marred by the fact that Pinart had already nearly bankrupted himself to purchase the extensive library of the abbé Brasseur de Bourbourg. He intended to publish some of Brasseur's manuscripts, which had long been one of the stated goals of the Société Americaine. Impressively, despite the fact that he was only twenty-three at the time, Pinart had already published more than a dozen articles on ethnographic and linguistic subjects, including a paper he had delivered at the maiden Americanist conference in Nancy (Parmenter 1966: 7–16).

At this juncture Pinart also had plans for a joint ethnographic research trip to the Americas with Léon de Cessac, editor of the *Musée Archéologique*, for which

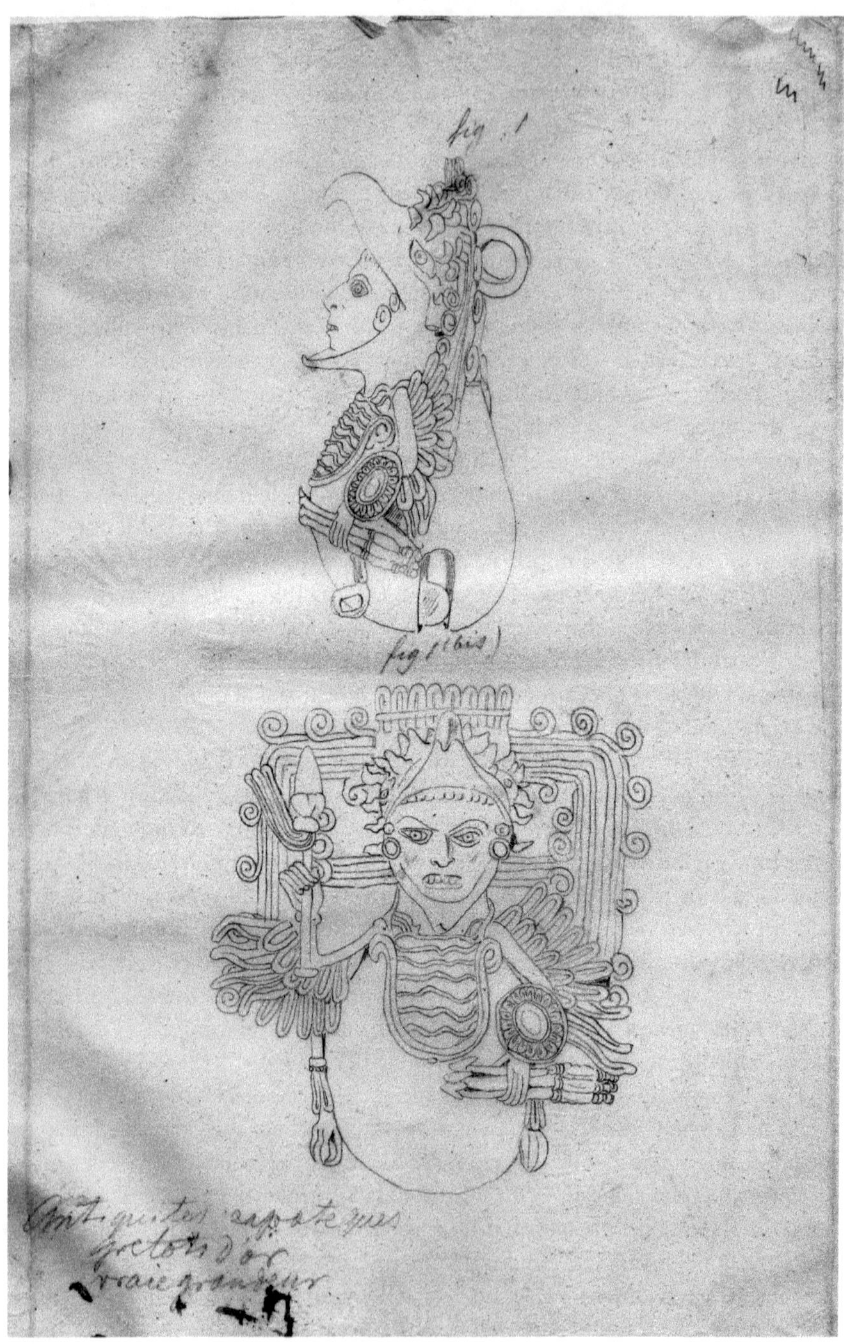

Figure 7.1a   Drawing of gold bell in Hispanic Society Collection (courtesy of Hispanic Society of America, New York).

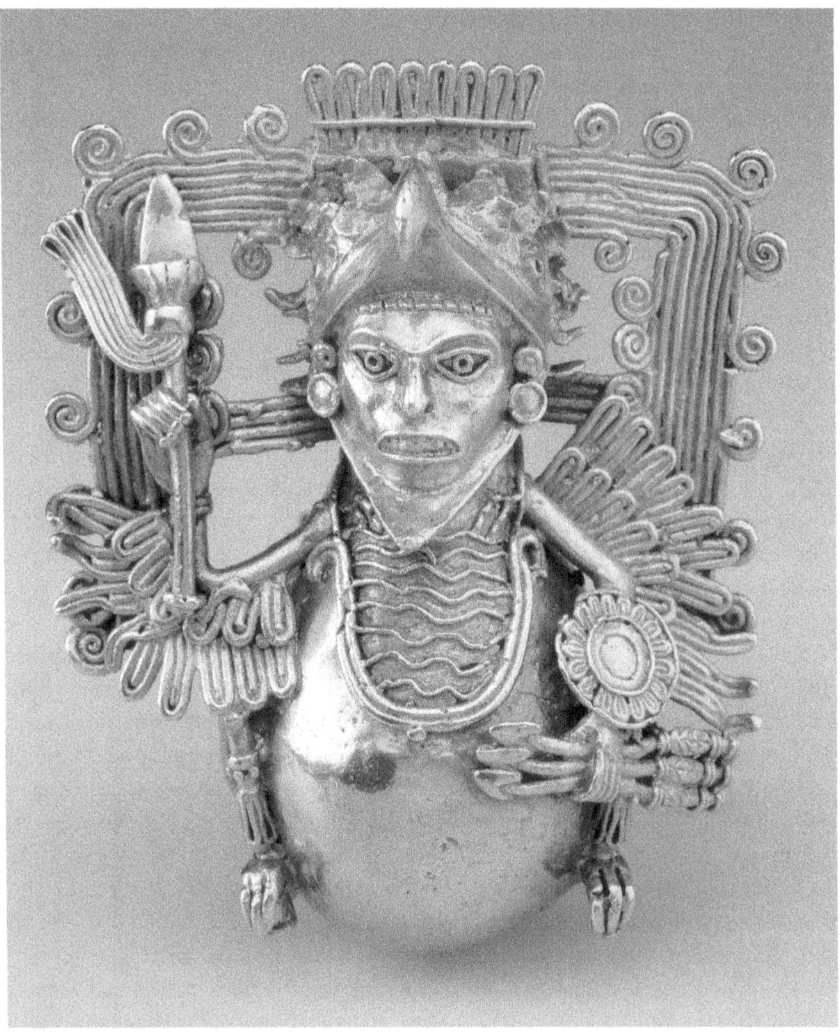

Figure 7.1b Photo of bell from The State Hermitage Museum, St. Petersburg. Photograph © The State Hermitage Museum. Photo by Vladimir Terebenin.

he had agreed to pay all expenses for himself and Cessac, in spite of the fact that he lacked funding. Fortunately, for him, however, he was able to arrange full financial support—to the tune of 25,000 francs per year from the French government—in a deal that involved donating to the nation the entire Boban pre-Columbian collection, now known as the Alphonse Pinart Collection, in exchange for the funds (Parmenter 1966: 21). The total of 125,000 francs was to support "a five-year mission to the Southwest of the United States, Mexico, the Antilles, Central America, and the Andean regions of South America"

(Reichlen and Heizer 1963, quoted in Parmenter 1966: 21). The Ministère de l'Instruction Publique sponsored the enterprise, although the planned research would be temporarily sidetracked when Pinart sailed to Oceania without informing Cessac, who had gone on alone to California to begin his field research (Parmenter 1966: 20).

Boban formally sold his Mexican collection in April 1875, when Pinart wrote that the affair, presumably the sale, had been concluded (BNF DMO n.a.f. 21478: item 556). The antiquarian would then face a long, difficult time getting paid. In a note jotted down on the back of a receipt for some stone axes, Boban listed "Pinart's bill dates: 31 July 1877; 31 December 1877; July 1878; December 1878" (HSA: B2243, Box IV). Apparently, he was still trying to collect the remainder of what Pinart owed him in six-month installments, but the first date on the list is already more than two years after the sale.

Alphonse Pinart returned to Paris, stopping at Easter Island en route early in 1878. He delivered several papers on his Pacific exploration and was appointed Commissioner for the Paris Exposition Universelle (Parmenter 1966: 21). There he exhibited nearly all of Boban's pre-Columbian artifacts as the Pinart Collection, when Boban had still not been paid in full.

In May 1878 Pinart wrote Boban saying that he did not know whether he had time to stop by the shop before he left for America but wanted to reassure him. "I will make every effort to settle with you before the end of the year" (BNF DMO n.a.f. 21478: item 564). Despite the fact that Pinart had inherited a good deal of money, he had spent it and more by 1878, mostly purchasing Brasseur de Bourbourg's library. In this note to Boban, he is using an age-old approach to creditors: painting rosy scenarios while avoiding any direct contact. In fact, Boban was still trying to get paid more than a year later.

Writing his mother from San Francisco in July 1879, Léon de Cessac, who had his own difficulties with Pinart, mentioned that someone in the French consulate had notified him that M. Boban had written asking whether Alphonse Pinart owned any property in California. The antiquarian wanted the French consul to seize anything belonging to the ethnographer; since after four and a half years Pinart still owed him 12,000 francs (pers. comm. Sally McLendon). This was a bold attempt to bring Pinart's lack of financial accountability into the court of public opinion. What percentage of the entire purchase price of the collection this represents is not known, but the gambit seems to have worked. Pinart did eventually settle the debt, either in cash, or a combination of cash, books, and Pinart's own artifact collection.

Years later Boban would remember this first important sale with some sadness, perhaps because it had come too late to finance his own return trip to the Americas and a chance to see his wife in Mexico again. As he recalls in his unpublished memoirs, "In 1875, this collection, which had been much enlarged by objects we had brought from our shop in Mexico, was acquired by a person, a voyageur, in charge of a mission to America, and given by him to the Musée d'Ethnographie of the Trocadéro, where it is to this day under his name" (HSA: B2244, Box V).[9] Continuing, he noted, "Due to a reverse of fortune, the voyageur [Boban never actually mentions Pinart's name] could not pay the agreed-upon price" (HSA: B2244, Box V). [10]

The antiquarian's efforts spent amassing a collection, researching, and cataloguing it over almost twenty years were nearly erased by the formerly wealthy Pinart, who treated Boban with some disdain and a good deal of misrepresentation. Despite this, Boban added, he never lost faith and, finally, the debt was paid in full. If it had not been, he felt he would have been well within his rights to request that the Trocadéro remove Pinart's name and replace it with his own. Perhaps writing for posterity, for the "Preface" of his unpublished autobiography, Boban glosses over his four- to five-year struggle to receive payment, and never mentions his attempt to have the French consul seize Pinart's property.

Notes

1. Je crois accomplir un devoir en vous disant que votre dame a une affliction grave de la langue que je crois une fin prompte malgré les soins que nous pourrons lui prodiguer.

2. Il vous convendra sans dout de prendre des précautions pour les intérêts que vous avez ici.

3. Jai l'honneur de vous accuser reception de votre lettre du 10 courant. Le prix de ma Collection Mexicaine est de trente-cinq-mille 35,000 f.

4. Je les dois à l'obligeance de mon ami M. J.-M. Melgar, savant archéologue mexicain, qui fouille avec un zèle et un dévouement dignes d'éloges les nécropoles et les ruines de son pays.

5. Don Jose-Maria Melgar, habitant de Vera-Cruz, est, si-non un archéologue, du moins un amateur, un *aficionado* d'archéologie.

6. Le travail qui suit choquera sans doute bien des idées reçues. Je sais qu'il n'est pas toujours prudent de s'égarer hors des sentiers battus.

7. Et je suis persuadé que mes collègues en archéologie voudront bien accueillir cette note dans la même espirit qui me l'a dictée, à savoir l'amour de le vérité, sans parti pris.

8. Mes souvenirs se reportèrent immédiatement sur les grelots de M. Franco, offerts à l'empereur Maximilien ... et tirant d'un album un croquis que j'avais eu soin de conserver, j'achevai de le convaincre que ses grelots étaient bien les mêmes que ceux dont je lui racontai l'histoire.

9. Bref. En 1875 cette collection notablement augmenter por des objets que nous avions reçu de notre maison de Mexico fut acquise par une personne un voyageur chargé d'une mission en Amérique et donné par elle au Musée d'Ethnographie du Trocadéro, ou elles sont actuellement exposes a son nom.

10. Depuis cette epoque un revers de fortune a empeché notre acheteur de nous solder integralement le prix convenue.

8

A PREMIER COLLECTION

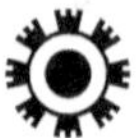

The collection that Pinart purchased from Boban formed the foundation of the Musée d'Ethnographie du Trocadéro's pre-Columbian holdings. Associated with the artifact collection, now housed in the Musée du quai Branly, is Eugène Boban's original handwritten catalog describing the 2,025 artifacts, along with a typescript version completed by Henry Reichlen in 1962.[1] The catalog resulted from Col. Doutrelaine's insistence that Boban make some order out of his important but messy collection and provide more information "both categorical and analytical" about the individual pieces. It is clear that the young antiquarian knew how to follow a mentor's advice since he produced a catalog of almost unprecedented detail.

The pre-Columbian Mexican artifacts exhibited at the Exposition Universelle were depicted in some 130 drawings that Col. Doutrelaine sent to the Commission Scientifique in Paris. They can be seen in photographs Boban commissioned when the objects were displayed in his shop, which he used to interest potential buyers prior to Pinart's purchase of the collection. The photographs now can be found in museum archives in Europe and the United States.[2] In addition to a set of photographs, the Hispanic Society of America's collections contain the 130 drawings of his pre-Columbian Mexican artifacts produced by Jean Amatus Klein.

The catalog of the collection opens with the antiquarian's statement of his purpose in writing it and the methods he used in compiling it. "It is not our intention to interpret the iconography of the divinities of the ancient Mexicans; that task would be beyond our abilities; we wish to give only notes, some details useful to know, that, after living in that country for twenty years, is information that we ourselves gathered from our daily interactions with the descendants of those Indians" (Reichlen 1962: 1).[3] It is interesting that Boban asserts that much

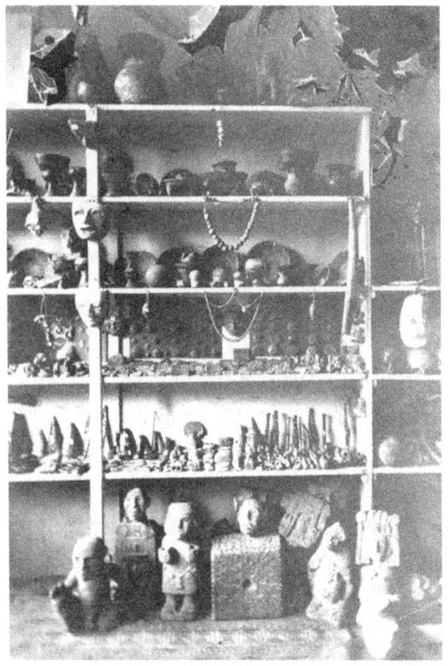
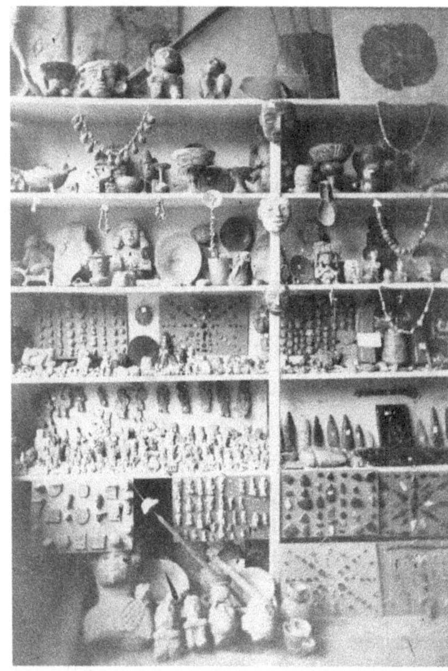
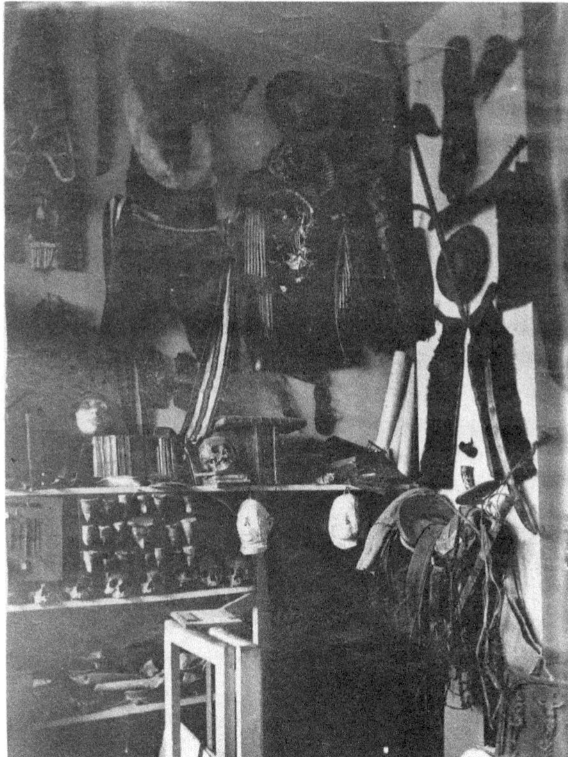

Figures 8.1a–c Publicity photographs of Boban's pre-Columbian collection in Paris (courtesy of Hispanic Society of America, New York).

of the information he is sharing about his artifacts was gathered from conversations with Mexican Indians in their own language, Nahuatl. In other words, it is original research, which he backs up with many references to scholarly publications. Boban follows the claim that he did not know enough to interpret the Mexican pantheon with a long description of some two thousand Mexican deities. The principal ones he lists are Huitzilopochtli (Hummingbird on the Left) and Tezcatlipoca (Smoking Mirror). "Their idols were placed on the highest part of the temple on two altars made of stone" (Reichlen 1962: 2).[4]

Boban's notion that there were two thousand deities reflects a nineteenth-century misunderstanding of the Aztec pantheon, which included gods in both male and female forms and in a variety of different manifestations. It is odd that he fails to mention Tlaloc (the Rain god) and Quetzalcoatl (Feathered Serpent), both of whom were principal gods in the Aztec religion.

He continues with a discussion of the physical representations of the deities, saying that they were often "covered with mother-of-pearl and precious stones in great numbers, encrusted with pieces of gold . . . turquoise mosaics and emeralds" (Reichlen 1962: 2).[5] He references this section to page 237 of the first volume of Francisco López de Gómara's *Historia de las Indias y de la conquista de Mexico.* Although López de Gómara published this work in 1552, the assertions it contains about indigenous religion and customs sometimes are inaccurate because, unlike Boban, the author never consulted any native sources in compiling his study. A later Franciscan historian, Juan de Torquemada, criticized López de Gómara's history on this point (Cañizares-Esguerra 2001: 85). In fact, although pre-Columbian artisans did inlay the eyes and teeth of deities with such materials as mother-of-pearl and pyrite to enhance their realism and used turquoise mosaics to enrich some images, the principal form of embellishment they employed was a thin coat of plaster, onto which they applied brightly colored pigments. The use of pearls, precious stones, gold, and emeralds more accurately describes the work of European artisans. However, despite some of the distortions Boban derived from López de Gómara and other early writers, for the most part, he seems to be on the right track in his own understanding of pre-Columbian cultures.

Boban then points out an important and rare feature of his catalog. "We give the provenance of the objects found in our excavations; we think it necessary to note that for the provenance of some objects, we must take into account the state of almost continuous war which existed in the country" (Reichlen 1962: 1).[6] He is not speaking here of the wars that he himself lived through while in Mexico—the War of Reform, the French invasion, and later the defeat of Maximilian—as one might expect, but rather what he took to be the constant warfare between pre-Columbian city-states and diverse cultural groups. Because of this view, when he found artifacts he considered foreign to the region in which he was working, he took them to have been looted pieces or war booty.

Boban is writing here generally about all of Mesoamerican cultures. "These wars led, as elsewhere, to ruin and plunder for the benefit of the victors. They took weapons, ornaments, small Penates [household deities] called *tepitoton* in Nahuatl; ultimately, all that was transportable was in continuous motion. For example, in excavations we were able to accomplish in the Valley of Mexico, we often encountered objects, small idols, [etc.] which were definitely from the country of the Zapotecs or Tzapotlan, which is located in the department of Oajaca, more than 100 miles away. If we also take into account what happened as a result of exchanges and gifts or presentations, we can explain the confusion and displacement of antiquities" (Reichlen 1962: 1).[7]

Boban's thinking on this subject of the dispersal of artifacts was well ahead of his day. Certainly, from the earliest European contact, it was clear that the Aztec empire was built on war and the tribute gathered from conquered regions. However, for several centuries most scholars assumed that the Aztecs were the exception—that other pre-Columbian cultures were more involved with recording time and understanding the celestial panorama than with conquest. Then came the unsettling discoveries of the twentieth and twenty-first centuries. The military swagger and chilling treatment of prisoners depicted so vividly in the murals of Bonampak and the deciphering of glyphs at Chichén Itzá and other sites demonstrate that warfare was a constant occupation for the Maya as well. Recent discoveries at Teotihuacan indicate that even this early, influential site ended in fire and pillage. Thus, war and conquest undoubtedly played a central role in the distribution of sacred and ritual objects among different pre-Columbian groups, just as Boban asserted.

Boban demonstrates his broadly scientific approach to cataloguing his collection by thanking Augustin Damour, who helped him with the mineralogical identification of numerous pieces in his collection. Damour was a highly respected mineralogist, who invented the term *jadeite* to distinguish New World and Burmese jade from Chinese nephrite. It is not known how Boban established this connection so early in his career, although it may be that Damour was associated with the Commission Scientifique and, in that capacity, offered to identify the minerals in the collection. However the connection began, it is a testimony to Boban's ability to make and maintain professional contacts and friendships among those in the highest intellectual circles.

Augustin Damour's scientific stature and importance can hardly be overstated. He was a decorated member of the Académie française who enjoyed an international reputation. Yet, he trusted Boban's knowledge and advice about his own collecting activities, requesting his guidance on several occasions. They were colleagues from early days and seemed to have remained friends until Damour's death at the age of ninety-four in 1902, when Boban attended his funeral.

In Boban's listing of his objects, he places some of the most important ones in the first few pages. The first item is the famous Boban calendar wheel, a manuscript on paper made from agave cactus fibers, that can be seen at the bottom right of the first photograph of the collection. The provenance he gives for the calendar is Texcoco in the Valley of Mexico. In 1866 Col. Doutrelaine published a fold-out, color facsimile of the calendar in the *Archives de la Commission Scientifique du Mexique* (1867, vol. 3: 120–33). In the text Doutrelaine explains the glyphs and deciphers the writing on the calendar with the help of a Mexican interpreter who was able to read the Nahuatl script.

The original manuscript is now in the collection of the John Carter Brown Library at Brown University. Unfortunately, the passage of time has not been kind to it. As noted in the online digitized presentation of this artifact, because of its deterioration, "the reproduction that was made in 1866 shows much greater detail than the original." Describing some of the Boban calendar wheel's other features, the site continues, "The names of the months are written in Nahuatl; the months are given different symbols than are usually present on other calendars" (JCB Library, #30891–1).

Boban wrote in his catalog that he believed the manuscript to be pre-Columbian, with the Nahuatl descriptions being added after the Conquest. Perhaps he is referring to the outer circle with the calendrical glyphs, since the center contains images of people from a later time, such as Hernán Cortés. The John Carter Brown library has dated the painted manuscript to ca. 1530, just nine years after the Spanish conquest.

Boban's catalog gives additional information about this important object. "In the middle of this manuscript, top and right side, there is a character whose head is half erased and is named Antonio Pimentel. This person is probably the same as that Antonio Pimentel, Lord of Texcoco, grandson of Neçahualpilli, whom Father Torquemada describes as a scholar and a distinguished man" (Reichlen 1962: 3).[8] Pimentel was the son of Ixtlilxóchitl, the last king of Texcoco. It was Fernando de Alva Ixtlilxóchitl, his grandson, who formed the first collection of painted manuscripts, later given to the famous writer and historian Carlos de Sigüenza y Góngora.

It is a tribute to Boban's assiduous collecting and broad knowledge of Mexican prehistory that he was able to acquire this calendrical manuscript. Painted manuscripts from the pre- and postcontact years were exceedingly rare, since most of them were burned by the zealous Catholic clergy. The fact that he made it the first entry in the catalog of his collection indicates that he knew it was an outstanding piece and wanted to showcase it.

It is not clear how or from whom Boban obtained the manuscript, nor how it was separated from his original collection, which he sold to Pinart, particularly since it is listed in the Trocadéro catalog.[9] According to the librarian at the John Carter Brown Library, it was acquired in 1950 through an autograph dealer named Forest H. Sweet in Battle Creek, Michigan. Sweet said the calendar came from the C. F. Gunther Collection, and that Gunther had told him it was

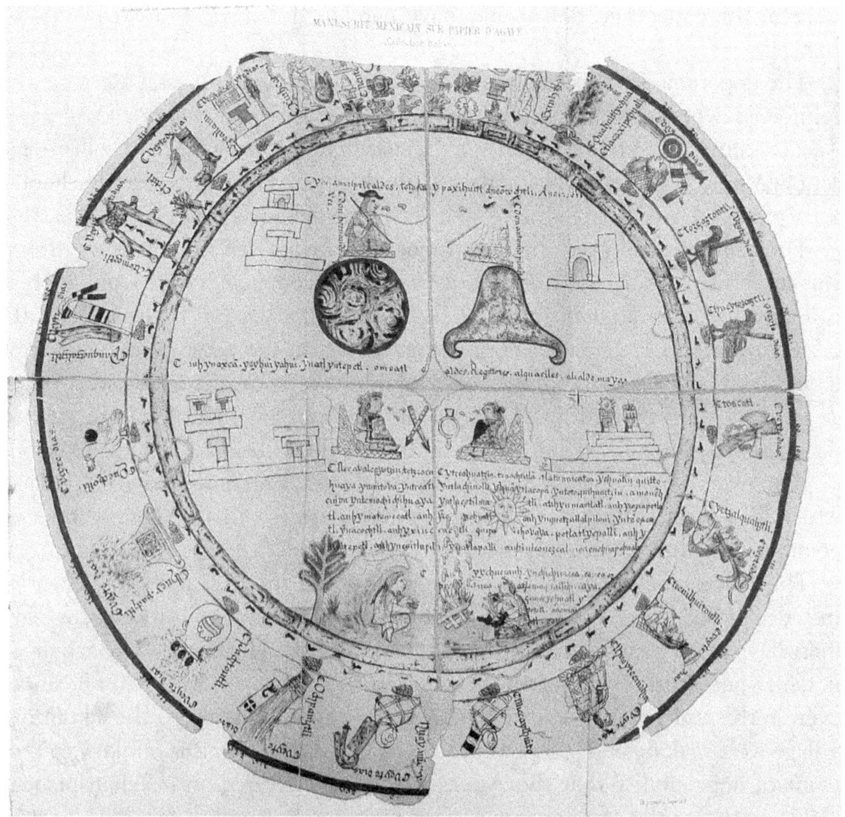

Figure 8.2   Reproduction of the Boban Calendar Wheel published in 1866 in the *Archives de la Commission Scientifique du Mexique* (Smithsonian Libraries).

"released by the Chicago Historical Society to me, and sold to you." Gunther, a confectioner in Chicago, was an established collector (Kim Nusco, archivist, pers. comm. 2010). The mystery remains of how it ended up in the Chicago Historical Society.

The second item cataloged is a beautiful ceramic whistling vessel made from a type of pottery called thin orange. It is a double-chambered pot in the shape of a monkey that emits a whistle when liquid passes from one chamber to the other. Boban describes it as a sacrificial vessel used for blood libations. It is a fine example of a type of light, durable ceramic ware that was an important trade item from Teotihuacan. He gives the provenance as San Martín Texmelucan, a town in Puebla at the eastern base of the volcano Popocatépetl. This piece was probably manufactured in the environs of Tepexi, Puebla—a center of thin orange ware production—which is not too far from San Martín Texmelucan. This piece is again quite rare, and important. Since it is the only example of thin orange ware in the collection, Boban may have purchased it instead of excavating it himself.

The importance of this beautiful thin orange ware monkey vessel was recently reinforced when it was included in the Musée du quai Branly's exhibition *Teotihuacán, Cité des Dieux*. Nearly all the artifacts displayed were from collections sent by Mexico's Instituto Nacional de Anthropología e Historia, with only a handful of pieces selected from European and American museums (Solís 2009: 348).

The third artifact is an obsidian plaque that Boban describes as being "from the environs of Teotihuacan. . . . It is certainly a commemorative stone with a calendrical date of a great historical event that took place in the year 4 Acatl, corresponding to 1327 of our era." Commenting on the date, he writes, "This date can probably be found in the Mexican work *Descripción histórica y cronológica de las dos Piedras* by Antonio León y Gama" (Reichlen 1962: 5).[10] This seems disingenuous, since he would have known that Tenochtitlan's Templo Mayor, or main pyramid, was first constructed by the Aztecs sometime after 1325, a date which had been published by numerous historians, so that 1327 might have commemorated an extremely important event indeed.

The placement of the plaque as number three in the catalog is an early instance of Boban's elevating what is certainly a nineteenth-century fake, one he must have, or at least should have, recognized as such. The fact that he acquired it somewhere in the vicinity of Teotihuacan should have tipped him off, since even in the mid-1800s it was well known that obsidian carvers in the adjoining village were making and selling countless fakes. In addition, it is unlikely to the point of impossibility that the Aztecs would have created an obsidian plaque commemorating the construction of their main pyramid and then buried it forty miles away at Teotihuacan, a site abandoned seven hundred years before they had arrived in the Valley of Mexico.

The tenth item on the list is an iron pyrite mirror that Boban says is from the Valley of Mexico (see Figure 8.3). It is 2.5 inches in diameter and pierced from side to side by a hole. On the convex side is a bas-relief representing an Aztec figure holding a shield and an *atlatl* (spear thrower) with a rattlesnake depicted as a hieroglyph above his head. Describing this item, Boban writes, "According to the legend about this object, it was very precious and belonged to Itzcoatl, 4th king in the Valley of Mexico. [It depicts] Tezcatlipoca, the god of providence, the soul of the world, the creator of the sky and earth, the lord of all things" (Reichlen 1962: 9–10).[11] Leonardo López Luján, director of the Museo del Templo Mayor, and Marie-France Fauvet-Berthelot, former curator of the American archeology collections of the Musée de l'Homme, more recently have identified the image as that of the deity Ehécatl-Quetzalcóatl or Feathered Serpent, in the guise of the wind god (2005: 79).

Boban writes that this precious article might have belonged to the fourth king of the Aztecs, although he characterizes many artifacts as having belonged

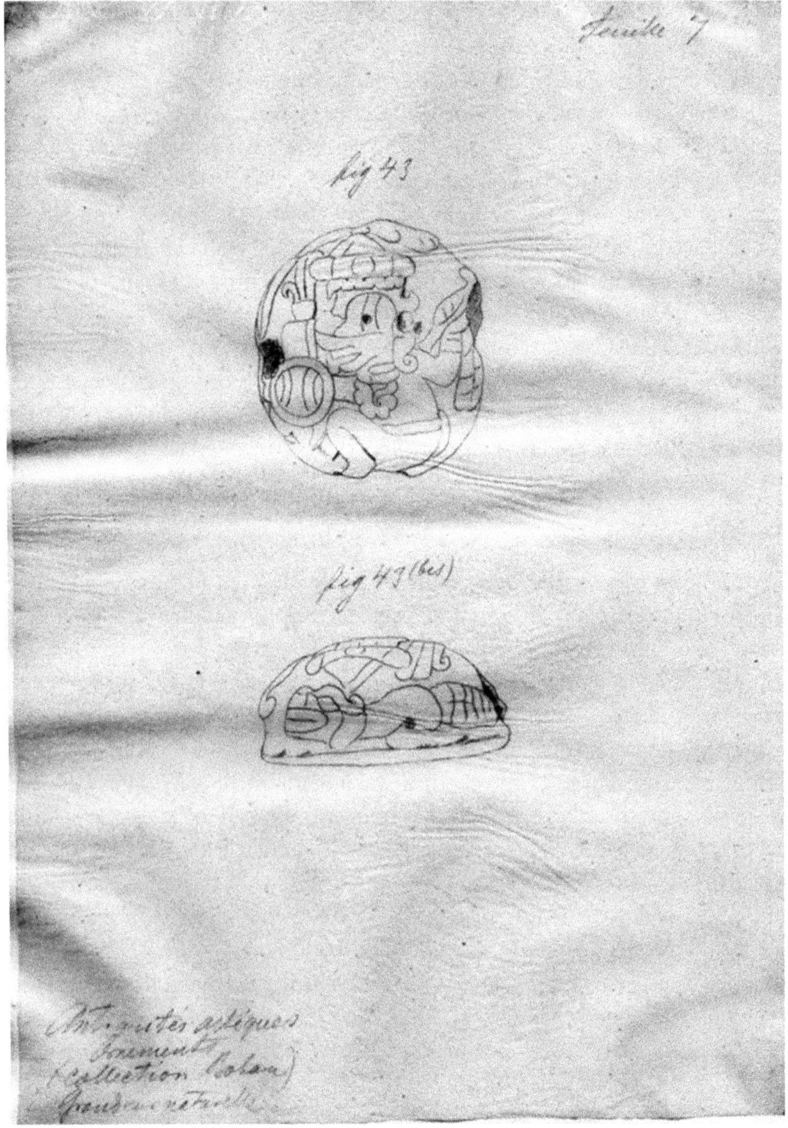

Figure 8.3   Drawing of pyrite mirror by Jean Amatus Klein, 1865 (courtesy of Hispanic Society of America, New York).

to royalty, particularly those in his collection fashioned from hard stone, rock crystal, or metal. The drawing of this piece in the Hispanic Society collection is life-size. It is shown here slightly reduced.

Maximilien Franck first illustrated this rare and important piece in 1828 or 1829, when it was part of collections of the Museo Nacional in Mexico City. His drawing includes the notation that it is an ornament carved in pyrite that chiefs wore around their necks (Am2006-Drg128-208-Fra). His supposition is presumably derived from the fact that it is drilled horizontally.

It is difficult to know how many artifacts in Boban's collection came directly from the Museo Nacional, but dozens of significant works may have originated there. For instance, among his pieces were several that had originally formed part of the Count of Peñasco's collection, much of which the Museo Nacional had purchased after his death in 1845. Others can be shown to have been in the Museo Nacional in the late 1820s, as documented in Franck's drawings (Am2006-Drg128-208-Fra).

Museums were just forming in the nineteenth century, and they routinely traded objects to fill gaps in specific collections or to broaden the scope of their holdings. All types of artifacts moved from museum to museum, and sometimes to private collectors. Adding to this, Mexico went through so many changes of government and governing policy during much of the nineteenth century that it is difficult to know why or when the Museo Nacional traded or sold off pieces from its collections, or whether attractive objects were simply appropriated from time to time by powerful or well-connected individuals.

Boban follows certain groups of objects listed in his catalog with long discussions of their cultural affiliations, the implications of the artifact types, and the particular ceremonies and deities with which they were associated, supplying bibliographic references to back up his statements. For example, he gives short treatises on human sacrifice, which, he writes, involved a variety of methods. Cutting open the chest of the victims was common, he says, although "some were drowned in the lake, others died of hunger walled up in caves or were buried alive, others were killed by gladiator sacrifice" (Reichlen 1962: 6).[12] He goes on to describe priests who assisted in the sacrificial rituals, what they wore, and the type of flint knives they carried to cut out the hearts of the victims. "Sometimes the priest would put the heart into the mouth of the idol with a sort of golden spoon; sometimes too he rubbed the lips of the idol and the cornice of the entrance to the temple with the victim's blood" (Reichlen 1962: 7).[13] His vivid depiction of the presentation of the sacrificed heart on a golden spoon is reminiscent of what Frances Calderón de la Barca recounted that she had been told during her visit to the museum at the Real y Pontificia Universidad de México in the 1840s.

He then lists a series of stone masks, some of which he uncovered in digs near Azcapotzalco, northeast of Mexico City. According to Boban's notes, the Aztecs had the habit of putting a mask on their idols during times when their emperors were sick, and he thought it likely that the majority of the masks were individual portraits. He wrote that "idols carved from stone were used in temples and in houses, and could be found at the corners of streets, along roads and in the forest." In fact, he was confident that their number was nearly infinite. Referencing Bishop Juan de Zumárraga he adds, "The first archbishop wrote that the Franciscans had destroyed 20,000 idols in the space of eight years. But this number is nothing when compared with what is still found in Mexico City alone" (Reichlen 1962: 18).[14] Thus, Boban underscores his view that the Spaniards were unsuccessful in their efforts to eliminate the iconography associated with pre-Columbian religions.

In these descriptions Boban marshals quite a bit of knowledge and sound reasoning, although some of his information is no longer accepted as accurate. For instance, the stone masks he found are not now thought to be images of sick rulers. Some archeologists in the past have thought that they may have been attached to funerary bundles, although there is currently no evidence to support this. Recent research suggests that the masks may have been displayed as part of altars in houses and temples, and that they were common throughout the city of Teotihuacan and elsewhere in Mesoamerica, which does in fact echo Boban's description of their use (Walsh and Rose 2014; Rose and Walsh 2016).

The catalog has a linguistic dimension as well. As Boban explains, "We have added to almost all the catalog numbers the translation of the objects described into Nahuatl or Aztec. This translation was made [using] the best linguists following the sixteenth century, Molina, Avila, Rincon, Betancourt, etc." (Reichlen 1962: 2).[15] It also includes long detailed descriptions of the Mesoamerican ball game, different types of weaving, ceramic seals or stamps, and other topics related to pre-Columbian cultures. He correctly theorizes that the ceramic stamps were used by the Aztecs to decorate the skin of humans, like tattoos, rather than to ornament pottery, as was then believed.

He does not go into great detail discussing the Mesoamerican pantheon, as he initially indicated, focusing almost exclusively on Huitzilopochtli (Hummingbird on the Left), the god of war, and Tezcatlipoca (Lord of the Night Sky), whose name means smoking mirror. He discusses Teteoinan, the mother goddess, also known as Coatlicue, and only incidentally does he mention the rain god, Tlaloc. His more detailed descriptions indicate that he thought that the attributes now associated with the rain god were those of Tezcatlipoca (Smoking Mirror). He believed that the goggle-like elements present in all depictions of Tlaloc were actually smoking mirrors (HSA: B2246, Box VII). He insisted, however, that the goggle elements should not be confused with eyeglasses or spectacles. "Several people have said that eyeglasses were in use among ancient Mexicans. In this they have misinterpreted the first historians. It is true that Gómara said the Aztec Tezcatlipoca wore *anteojos* [eyeglasses], which they translated using the word *lunette*. The author meant that the Mexicans put eyes on the masks that were meant for this god. Those eyes were gleaming mirrors (they used iron pyrite for these)—meaning with these eyes Tezcatlipoca could see all" (Reichlen 1962: 72–3).[16]

These statements are essentially erroneous and create some confusion about which images he believed related to the rain god, Tlaloc. Apparently, his self-education left some gaps, although it must be said that there was a great deal of confusion about the deities of ancient Mexico during the nineteenth century. In fact, the identities of pre-Columbian gods and goddesses are constantly being reinterpreted to this day.

In another section of the catalog, Boban explains the method of napping obsidian blades from cores, expressing his belief that the remnant cores were then reused to make ear spools and amulets. The insight of this opinion was verified recently by the work of Cynthia Charlton and her colleagues excavating the site of Otumba, near Teotihuacan. There they found broken obsidian cores and flakes that the early inhabitants were refashioning into ear spools, lip plugs, and other ornaments (1993). Judging from a number of fake amulets and small figurines in the Smithsonian Institution and other large museum collections, all clearly refashioned from obsidian cores, it seems that reworking remnant cores might have been a popular nineteenth-century activity as well, augmenting the recycling of these materials that took place in pre-Columbian times.

Throughout the catalog, Boban quotes liberally and authoritatively from Francisco López de Gómara, the historian of the Conquest; the sixteenth-century Franciscan friar Bernardino de Sahagún, ethnographer of the Aztecs; and Juan de Torquemada, another sixteenth-century Franciscan chronicler and historian. He also references eighteenth- and nineteenth-century writers, such as Francisco Javier Clavigero, Antonio de León y Gama, and José Fernando Ramírez. Considering that Boban had little formal education, his erudition in the field of Mexican prehistory is astounding. This helps explain how he was able to make so many connections with scholars of the highest reputation in the field.

Despite his reverence for the historians and chroniclers of the past centuries, Boban was not afraid to disagree with them and promote his own interpretation of an artifact. His ideas about the Aztec war club are a case in point. "The formidable *Macuahuitl*, corrupted to *Macana* by the Spaniards after the conquest—was said to be able to cut the head off of a horse, and of a human. It was composed of a large baton of wood, hard and weighty, with very sharp obsidian blades embedded along the sides. . . . Clavigero gives a minute description of the weapon" (Reichlen 1962: 68).[17] Although he cites Francisco Clavigero's description, Boban makes a point of contradicting his assertion that thin obsidian blades were embedded along the edge of the weapon. Nineteenth century European prehistorians thought the large obsidian implements Boban used in his model Aztec club were actually scrapers used for cleaning hides; he thought they, too, were mistaken. "It is impossible that pieces so thin and fragile could also be used for the construction of the Macuahuitl. The blades of this weapon were large and of the form seen in the model" he writes confidently (Reichlen 1962: 68).[18]

His vision of the weapon is explained in the facing drawing, which accompanied the collection he sent to the museum in Angers. It can also be seen in

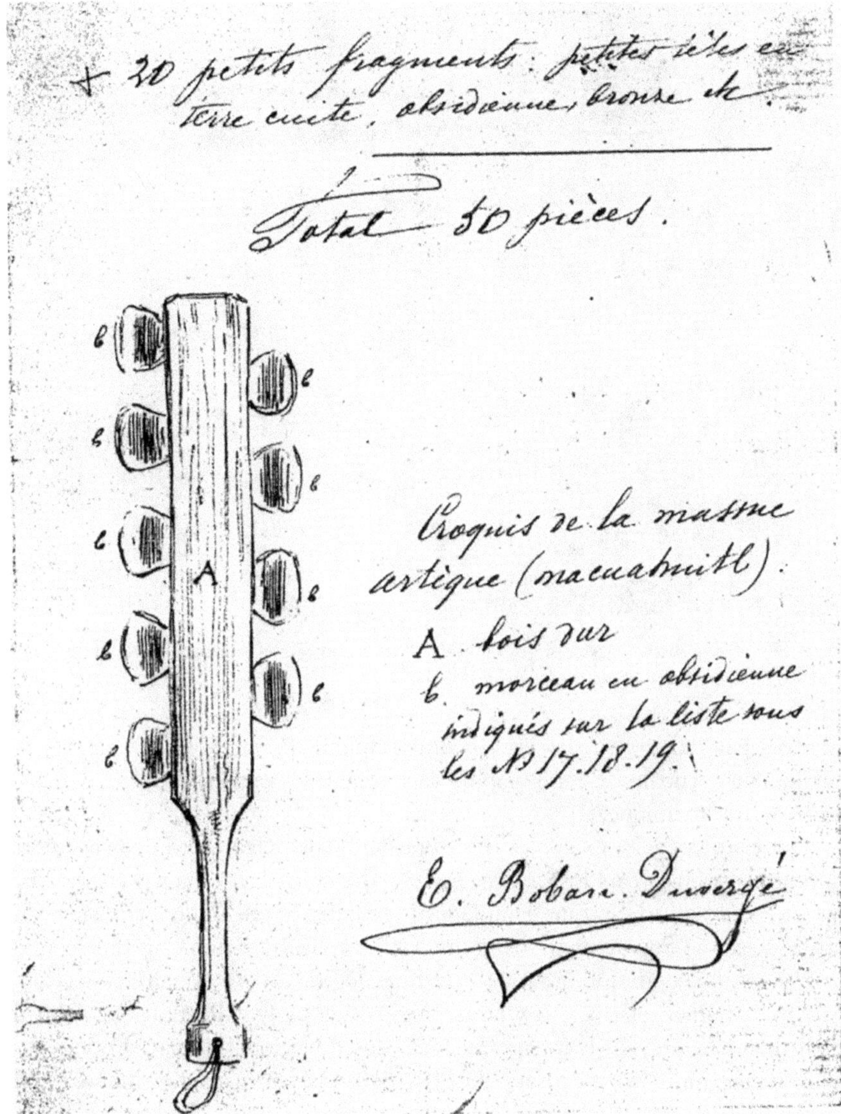

Figure 8.4   Drawing of Boban's concept of the Aztec macuahuitl (courtesy of Musée Pincé, Angers).

his 1876 article in the *Musée Archéologique*. In reality the obsidian projections depicted *are* scrapers and could never have functioned efficiently to decapitate anyone or any horse. The actual weapon looked like the one depicted in the hands of an Aztec jaguar warrior, who is brandishing the club after having taken off an enemy's head. The image is part of a highly unusual mural of pre-Hispanic

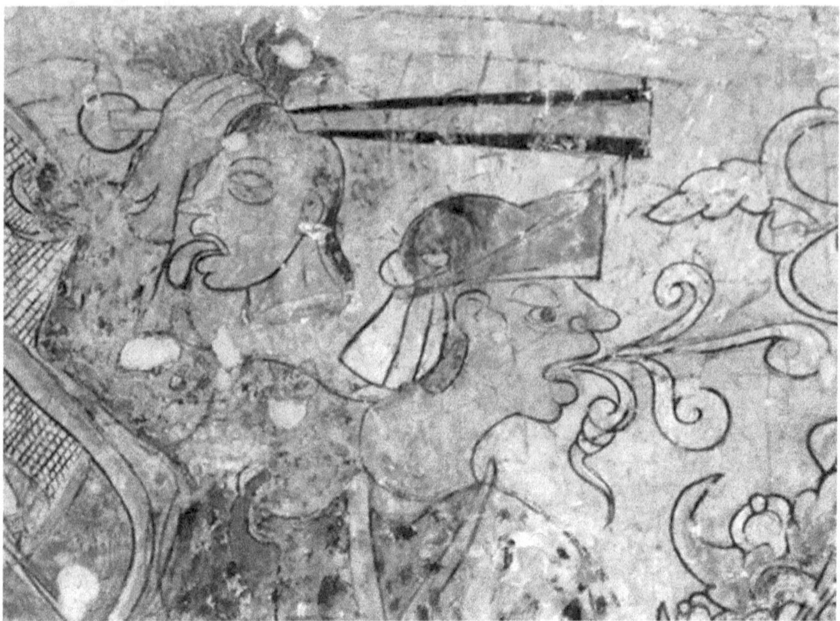

Figure 8.5   Mural showing jaguar warrior in the church of San Miguel Arcangel in Ixmiquilpan, Hidalgo, Mexico (detail of internet scan by author).

warriors painted in the sixteenth-century church of San Miguel Arcangel in Ixmiquilpan, Hidalgo. These graphic representations of Aztec and Otomi life and warfare are unique.

These are just a few examples of the outstanding artifacts that Boban acquired during his twelve years in Mexico. In fact, the collection he amassed was the largest, most varied, and most important grouping of pre-Columbian Mexican artifacts seen in Europe up to that point. Other collections from this time period lack the same depth and are not as well cataloged. Unlike Boban's collection, which contained relatively few fakes, many other early collections are riddled with them. As previously mentioned, the Museo Nacional displayed numerous fakes in the nineteenth century, and the Smithsonian Institution housed and displayed a variety of fake pre-Columbian objects from the Blake and Mayer collections, to name just a few.

Obviously Boban had taken seriously Col. Doutrelaine's advice about inventorying his collection. The catalog is a tour de force, presenting an immense amount of information and knowledge. In many instances his understanding of the importance and use of particular artifacts is considerably ahead of his time. Not only did he comprehend that ceramic seals were used to decorate skin and that obsidian cores were recycled as lip plugs and ear spools, he also rejected the nineteenth-century interpretation that stone yokes were used in human sacrifice.

As he noted, there were no descriptions of such use in any chronicle. These yokes are now associated with the Mesoamerican ball game.

While many collectors in the nineteenth century acquired their artifacts exclusively by purchase, Boban's collection is unique for its time because it represents artifacts that he gathered himself—through excavation, trade, purchase, or appropriation. The accompanying catalog he composed is a testimony to his love of archeology and his well-researched understanding of pre-Columbian cultures. All in all, amassing and cataloging the collection was an extraordinary feat.

Notes

1. A note introducing the catalog indicates that it is a "typed copy of the manuscript catalog of the collection of Mexican archeology of E. Boban," which, along with four photographs showing the pieces in the collection, was deposited in the museum's library. Reichlen also wrote that the original collection was "part of the Commission Scientifique's exhibit first in Paris in 1867, and it was later purchased by M. Alphonse Pinart, and was eventually donated to the Musée d'Ethnographie du Trocadéro in 1878" (Reichlen 1962: 1).

2. The Musée du quai Branly, Musée d'archéologie nationale in Saint-Germain-en-Laye, the Hispanic Society of America in New York, Yale University Library, and the Getty Research Institute in Los Angeles.

3. Nous n'avons point la prétention d'entreprendre l'Iconographie des Divinités des anciens Mexicains; cette tâche serait bien au-dessus de nos forces; nous ne voulons donner que des notes, quelques détails utiles à connaître, qu'une habitation de vingt années dans ces contrées nous a mis à même de recueillir dans nos relations journalières avec les descendants de ces Indiens.

4. Leurs Idoles étaient placées à la partie la plus élevée du temple sur les deux autels qui étaient en pierre.

5. Elles étaient couvertes de nacre et de pierres précieuses en très grand nombre, de pièces en or encastrées . . . en mosaique de turquoises, [et] d'émeraudes.

6. Nous indiquerons aussi la provenance des objets trouvés dans nos fouilles; nous croyons nécessaire de faire remarquer que pour la provenance de certains objets il faut tenir compte de l'état de guerre presque continuel dans lequel vivait le pays.

7. Ces guerres amenaient, comme partout ailleurs, la ruine et le pillage au profit des vainqueurs. Ils emportaient les armes, les ornements, les petits pénates nommés tepitoton, enfin tout ce qui était transportable; de là un déplacement continuel. Ainsi, par exemple, dans les fouilles que nous avons été à même de faire dans la Vallée de Mexico, nous avons plus d'une fois rencontré des objets, petites idoles, etc. etc., qui sont pour nous très certainement de provenance zapotèque. Or, le pays des Zapotèques ou Tzapotlan est situé dans le département de Oajaca, c'est-à-dire à plus de 100 lieues de distance.

8. Au milieu de ce manuscrit, en haut et à droite, il y a un personnage dont la tête est à moitié effacée et qui porte le nom de Antonio Pimentel. Ce personnage est probablement le même que cet Antonio Pimentel, Seigneur de Texcuco, petit-fils de Neçahualpilli, dont le P. Torquemada a parlé dans son ouvrage (Voir 2ème partie. L. XIV, p. 544) comme d'un savant et d'un homme distingué.

9. John Glass, who for many years was the Library of Congress's expert in Mexican manuscripts, described the calendar wheel's provenance as "Ex-Boban, Pinart, D.F. Gunther and Chicago Historical Society collections," indicating that it was perhaps Alphonse Pinart who sold it to Gunther (Glass 1975a: 96).

10. Environs de San Juan—Teotihuacan. . . . C'est certainement une pierre commémorative de la date d'un grand évènment historique qui dut avoir lieu l'an 4 d'Acatl. Comme époque cette pierre correspond à la date 1327 de notre ère. On pourra, probablement, retrouver cette date en consultant l'ouvrage mexicain intitulé: "Descripcion historica y chronologica de los Dos Piedras por Don Antonio de Leon y Gama."

11. D'après la légende cet objet serait très précieux car il aurait appartenu à Itzcoatl 4ème roi de Mexico. Tezcatlipoca El Dios de la Providencia el Alma del Mundo el Criador del Cielo y de la tierra y el Señor de toda las Cosas.

12. Mais quelques unes étaient noyées dans le lac, d'autres mouraient de faim enfermées dans les cavernes où l'on enterrait les morts; d'autres enfin dans le sacrifice gladiateur.

13. Si l'Idole était gigantesque et creuse, il introduisait parfois le coeur dans la bouche de l'idole avec une espèce de cuillère en or; quelquefois aussi il frottait avec le sang de la victime les lèvres de l'Idole et la corniche de l'entrée du temple.

14. Les Idoles ou représentations des divinités adorées dans les temples, les maisons, au coin des rues, sur les chemins, et dans les bois, étaient en nombre infini. Le premier évêque de Mexico assurait que les religieux franciscains avaient brisé, dans l'espace de 8 ans, plus de 20,000 idoles. Mais ce nombre n'est rien si on le compare avec ce qu'il s'en trouvait à Mexico seulement.

15. Nous avons joint à presque tous les numéros de ce catalogue la traduction en langue Nahuatl ou Aztèque des objets décrits. Cette traduction a été faite d'après les meilleurs linguistes du XVI siècle: Molina, Avila, Rincon, Bétancourt, etc. etc.

16. Plusieurs personnes ont dit que les lunettes étaient en usage chez les anciens mexicains, elles ont mal interprêté les premiers historiens. Il est vrai que Gomara a dit que les Aztèques mettaient des "anteojos" au dieu Tezcatlipoca, ce que l'on a traduit par le mot lunette. L'auteur voulait dire que les Mexicains mettaient des yeux au masque qui était destiné à ce dieu, que ces yeux étaient des miroirs reluisants (la matière employée étant de la pyrite de fer); Tezcatlipoca, à l'aide de ces yeux ne devait rien ignorer et tout voir.

17. Le formidable Macahuitl, par corruption Macana, appelé par les Espagnols épée et avec lequel, disent les témoins de la conquête, "on tranchait la tête d'un cheval jusqu'à la racine (a cercen)" et l'on coupait un homme par le milieu du corps, se composait d'un gros bâton de bois dur et pesant, sur les coins duquel étaient incrustées des lames d'obsidienne très affilées de 4 à 5 cent. de largeur sur 5 à 6 de longueur, comme le montre la figure. Clavigero donne une minutieuse description de cette arme.

18. Il est impossible que des pièces aussi minces et aussi fragiles pussent servir pour la construction du Macahuitl. Les lames de cette arme étaient grosses et de la forme que l'on voit dans la figure.

9

Narratives of Provenance

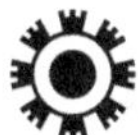

While the quality and significance of many of the objects in Boban's collection are clearly evident, the life and activities of their collector are still somewhat shrouded in mystery. A detailed look at the paths through which objects came into the collection, both what Boban himself says and doesn't say and what the historical record reveals, not only animates his field catalog or digging diary, but also sheds light on the variety of approaches and sources he used in building the collection, as well as the excellence of his collecting eye. The provenance of the objects he amassed reveals the friendships and contacts he made and the wide range of roles he adeptly inhabited and exploited to further his professional career. He was an archeologist, a teacher, a buyer, a seller, and a trader of antiquities, a friend who received gifts of antiquities, and a well-connected member of the French community, who was able to take advantage of the opportunities provided by the arrival of Maximilian and his court.

From close examination of the information Boban provides in his catalog, or the lack thereof, it is apparent that the majority of the objects he dug up himself consisted of figurine fragments, spindle whorls, pottery, and a few larger stone pieces, along with numerous human skulls. These artifacts are recorded with a specific provenance, whether a more central section of Mexico City, a suburb of the capital, or a nearby town.

It is not clear where Boban obtained his most important and best-known stone sculptures, usually the favorites of museum curators. However, it seems unlikely that he excavated them. Considering their inexact provenance, he probably purchased them or traded other pieces for them. Some artifacts were first in the Museo Nacional's collections, and he may have acquired them through his connection with the Commission Scientifique. The most common location of origin given for the Museo Nacional pieces is "Valley of Mexico,"

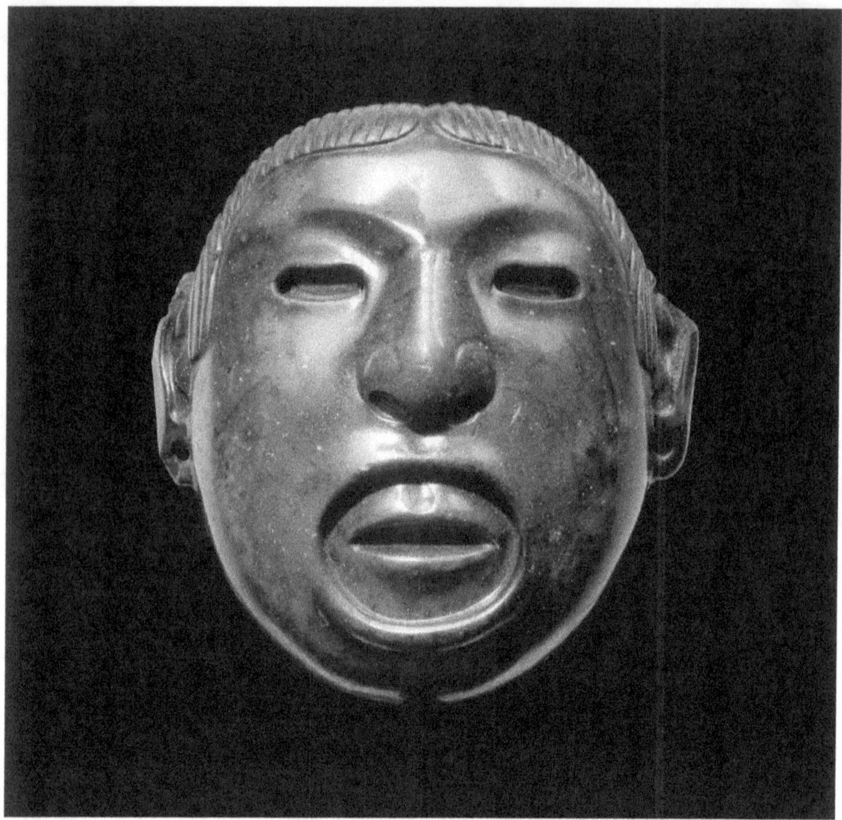

Figure 9.1a   Xipe Totec mask displayed in the Pavillon de Sessions, Louvre (courtesy of Musée du quai Branly, Paris).

an area of some 600 square miles. This uninformative provenance indicates a superficial knowledge of how and where the object was found. Whatever means he used to obtain them, he exhibited an excellent eye in selecting them, since they are all exceptional pieces.

One important artifact from the Museo Nacional, a mask Boban collected in the 1860s, does have a specific provenance, the state of Oaxaca. It was depicted much earlier in a drawing by Maximilien Franck made in 1829 and in another by Jean Frédéric Waldeck a few years later (Baudez 1993: 59). Both artists greatly admired the piece.

Franck executed his drawing of the mask when it was in the collection of José Mariano Sánchez y Mora, also known as the Count of Peñasco. This was one of the better known and more admired collections in Mexico City at the time. Brantz Mayer, the secretary of the US legation in Mexico in the 1840s, wrote about Sánchez y Mora's collection in his book *Mexico as It Was and as It*

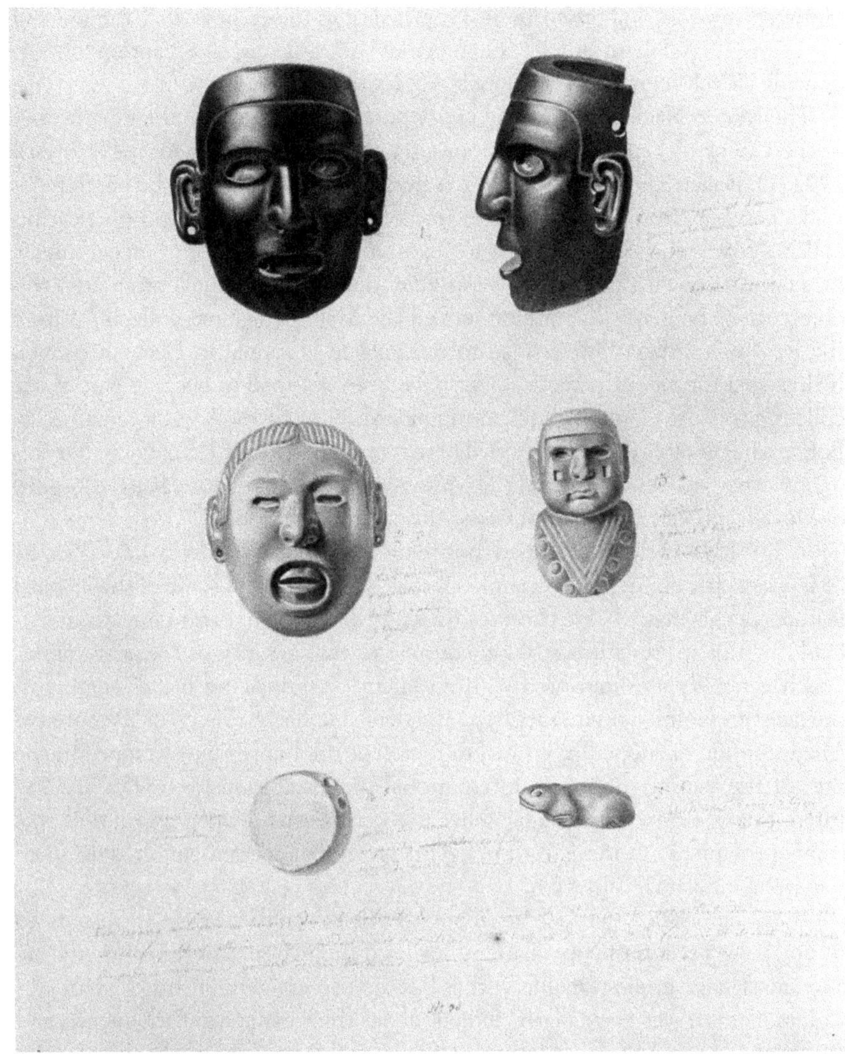

Figure 9.1b Maximilien Franck drawing of Xipe Totec mask (courtesy of the British Museum, London, AM2006, Drg. 128, pg. 30).

Is (1847), and Frances Calderón de la Barca noted in her book *Life in Mexico* (1843) that the count had his own private museum, which he later opened to the public (Adam Sellen, pers. comm.).

Franck's drawings of the artifacts in the Count of Peñasco's collection underscore that the count owned numerous extraordinary objects, many of which are now prized possessions of the Museo Nacional and other museums in Europe and the United States. Franck does not indicate that the mask came from Oaxaca.

He was, however, impressed by it. "It is amazing to see how well the ancient Mexicans carved hard stone," he remarked in a descriptive caption on the drawing (BM Maximilian [sic] Franck AM2006, Drg 128, pg. 30).[1]

The Museo Nacional in Mexico City purchased this mask, along with most of the Count of Peñasco's collection, after the Count's death in 1845 (Museo 1992: 1). Boban must have obtained it from the museum, either by purchase or trade, between 1857 and 1867—the year he arrived in Mexico and the year his collection was shipped to France for exhibition. It is possible that because of his connection with the Commission Scientifique, he simply appropriated this object when Emperor Maximilian moved the Museo Nacional collections from the Real y Pontificia Universidad to the Palacio Nacional in December 1865. If this were the case, the mask might have been destined to become part of the collections of the Commission Scientifique exhibited in 1867, but it remained in Boban's hands after the exhibition. There is no indication in his catalog that this or any other artifact came from the Museo Nacional, simply the evasive "Valley of Mexico" provenance in most cases, although not this one.

In an 1875 article published posthumously in the *Archives de la Société Américaine*, the eminent historian Lucien de Rosny captures some of the unusual features of this mask. "One observes the expression of calm and of death in this mask; by this it presents a striking contrast to the majority of Mexican masks, which generally are imprinted with an energetic, grimacing life. It represents the face of a Colhua virgin, sacrificed and deified under the name of 'Teteoinan.' The intention of the sculptor [was] to represent the human face wrapped in the skin of the victim" (Congrès International des Américanistes 1875: 308–9).[2] Interestingly, Rosny adds the fact that the Louvre then owned a beautiful wax copy of the piece, an ironic turn of events given that the museum had declined to purchase Boban's collection.

There has been some debate about the mask's authenticity. It appears to be an Aztec version of Xipe Totec (Our Lord the Flayed One), but its stylistic anomalies make it questionable. Esther Pasztory, an eminent art historian of pre-Columbian art, was particularly dubious about the treatment of the mouth and the parted, striated hair, which are similar to the carving on masks she believes to be fakes (Pasztory 1982: 80–83). A study of the tool marks conducted by myself on the piece has proven inconclusive. It may be an ancient carving that has been "improved upon" in more modern times, or it may be entirely genuine (López Luján and Fauvet-Berthelot 2005: 180–83).

Several other exceptional stone objects in the Pinart/Boban collection can be directly tied to the Museo Nacional, including a fine example of a large sandstone Huastec sculpture of a naked young man with his hands in fists. It is typical of the Huastec culture from the north coast of Veracruz, well known for depictions of nude young men and women. This particular image is included in the Maximilien Franck drawings now in the British Museum, confirming its

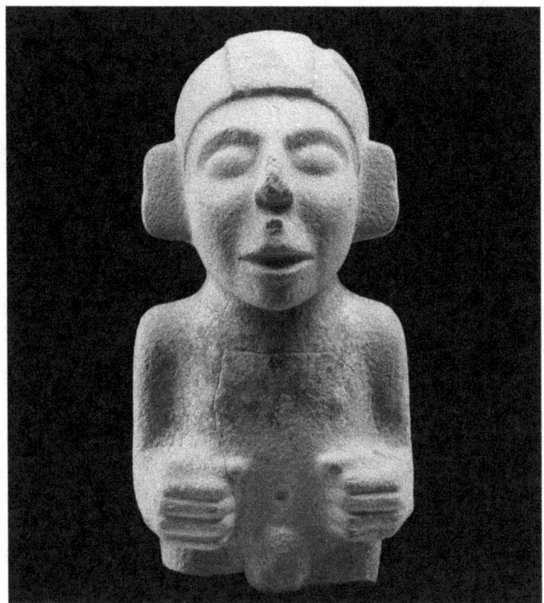

Figure 9.2a　Huastec sculpture in Musée du quai Branly (courtesy of Musée du quai Branly, Paris).

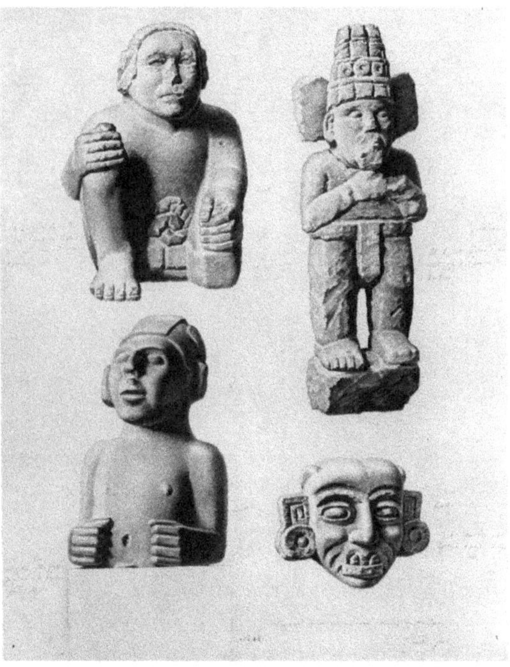

Figure 9.2b　The same figure as drawn by Maximilien Franck in 1829, when it was in the Museo Nacional (courtesy of the British Museum, London, AM2006, Drg 128, pg. 42).

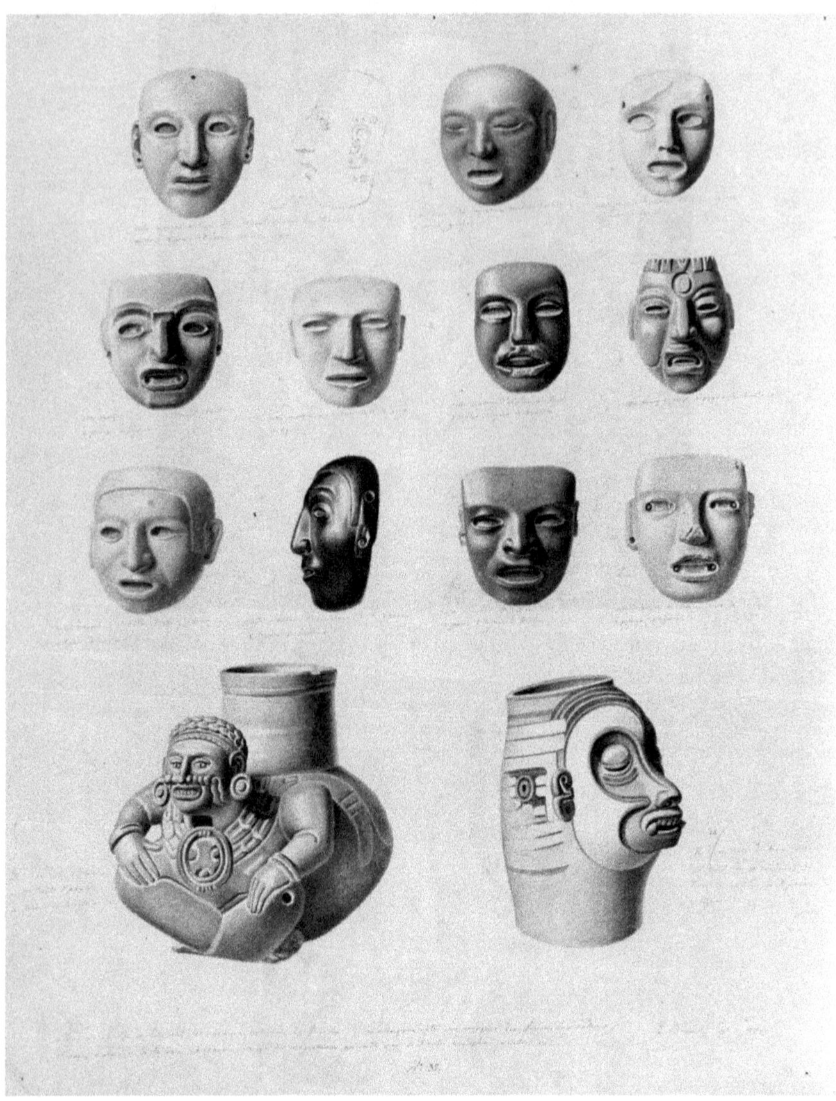

Figure 9.3a   Drawing of carved stone faces and ceramic vessels by Maximilien Franck, 1829 (courtesy of the British Museum, London, AM2006, Drg. 128, pg. 35).

provenance from the Museo Nacional. The Franck drawing has a small piece of paper affixed to the illustration over the lower part of the carving, presumably added at some later date to cover the statue's genitalia. Oddly, the stone sculpture is described by Boban in his catalog as being from the Yucatán, indicating that Boban was unfamiliar with Huastec sculpture, but recognized that it was not Aztec or Toltec.

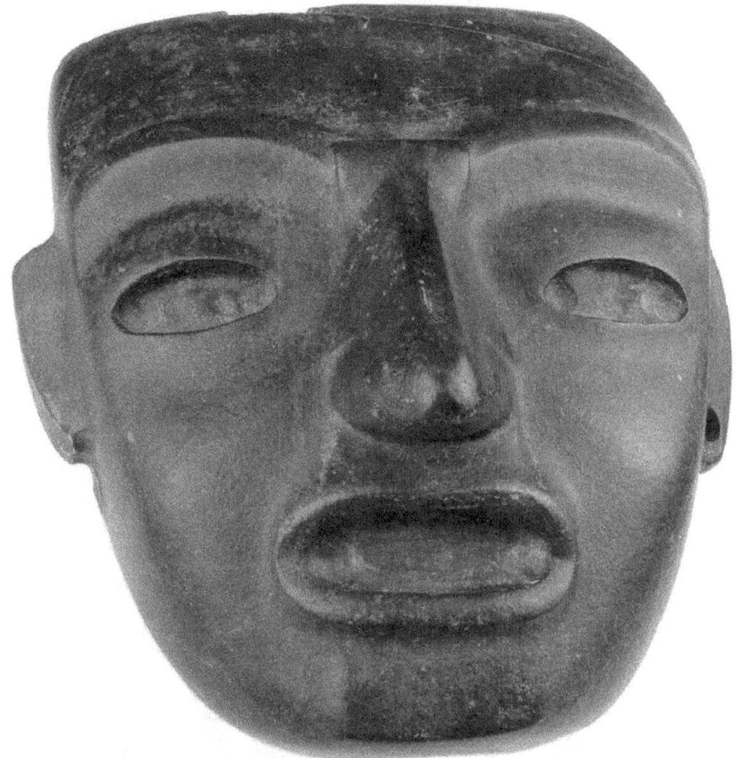

Figure 9.3b   Carved stone face (courtesy of the Musée du quai Branly, Paris, 71.1878.1.171AM).

At least one of the carved stone faces in the Pinart/Boban collection also came from the Museo Nacional. It is in the second row from the top on the far left in this Maximilien Franck drawing. The face is carved from limestone. Boban collected masks from digs in Azcapotzalco in the Valley of Mexico in the 1860s, and there are numerous limestone masks in this collection. However, this particular example is different from those he recovered in Azcapotzalco. The carving of the bridge of the nose, the nose itself, and the gaping mouth make it quite unusual, which may have been what attracted Boban to acquire it.

The Franck drawings allow us to trace other artifacts. A stone figure identified as Ehécatl-Quetzalcoatl, the feathered serpent in his guise as wind god (López Luján and Fauvet-Berthelot 2005: 82), can be seen as depicted by Franck sometime between 1828 and 1830, when it was in the collection of a Mexico City businessman named William Marshall. It is possible that Boban acquired the sculpture from Marshall directly or from his heirs. Here again Boban is

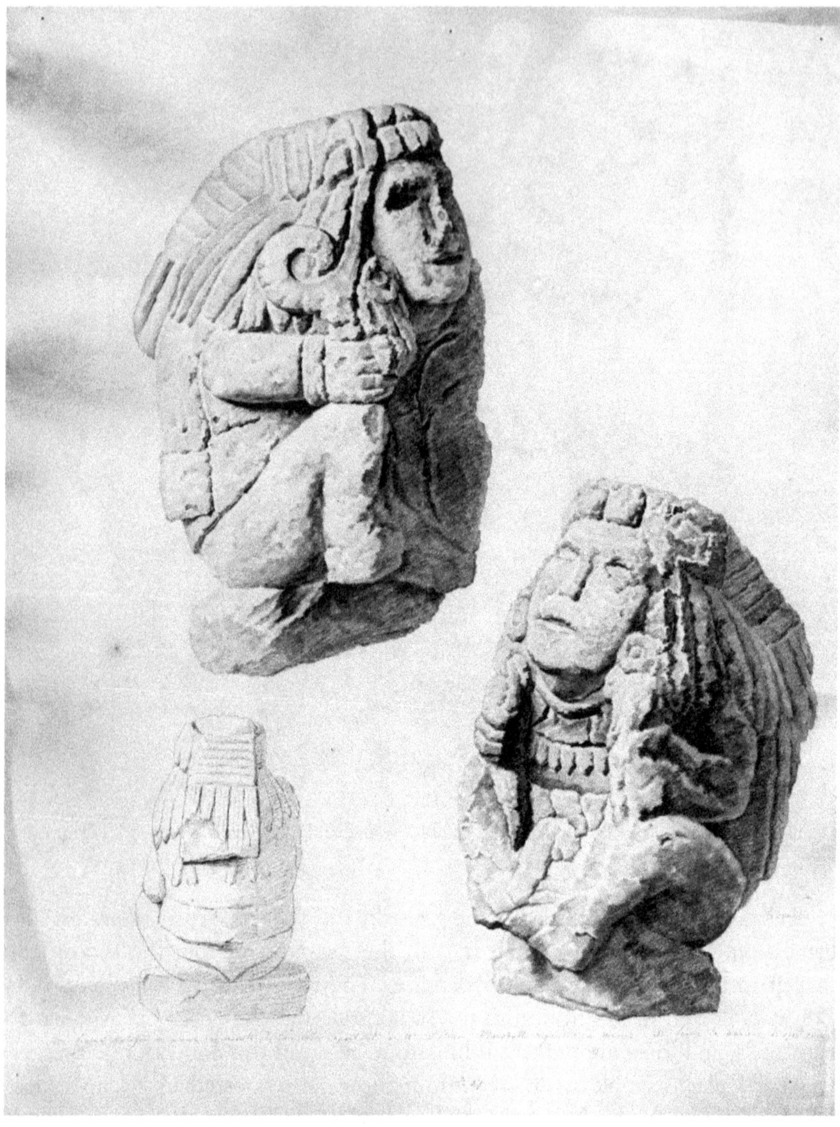

Figure 9.4   Three views of carved stone figure by Maximilien Franck, 1828–30 (courtesy of the British Museum, London, AM2006, Drg.128, pg. 47).

demonstrating his ability to recognize an unusual piece and successfully acquire it for his collection, whether through purchase or trade.

As Boban himself noted, most of the collection that he sold to Pinart was acquired in Mexico, but some pieces were added after his return to Paris. In an October 1874 letter to his "estimado amigo" Boban, José María Melgar y

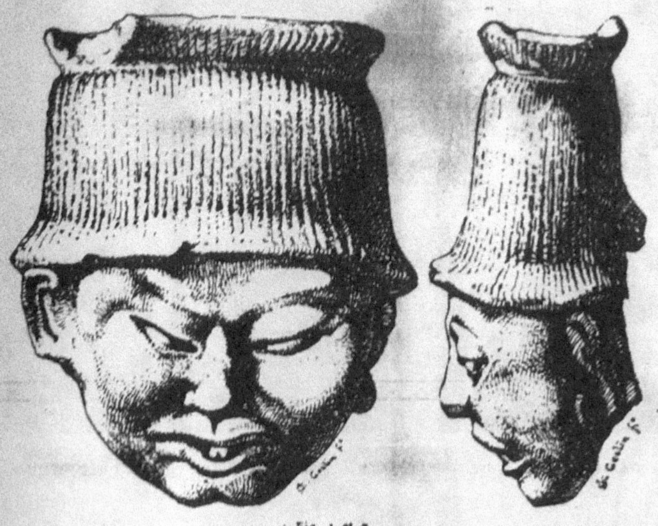

Figure 9.5a "Terra cottas reproducing cranial deformation" from Boban's 1875 article in *Le Musée Archéologique* (Smithsonian Libraries).

Serrano informed him that he was shipping a case of artifacts to Paris, including twelve large ceramic heads for the price of one piastra each. *Piastra* was a term used by the French and other foreigners in Mexico. It was meant to be equal in value to a Mexican peso of the day, which was more or less equivalent to one US dollar. One dollar was equal to five French francs at the time. The items

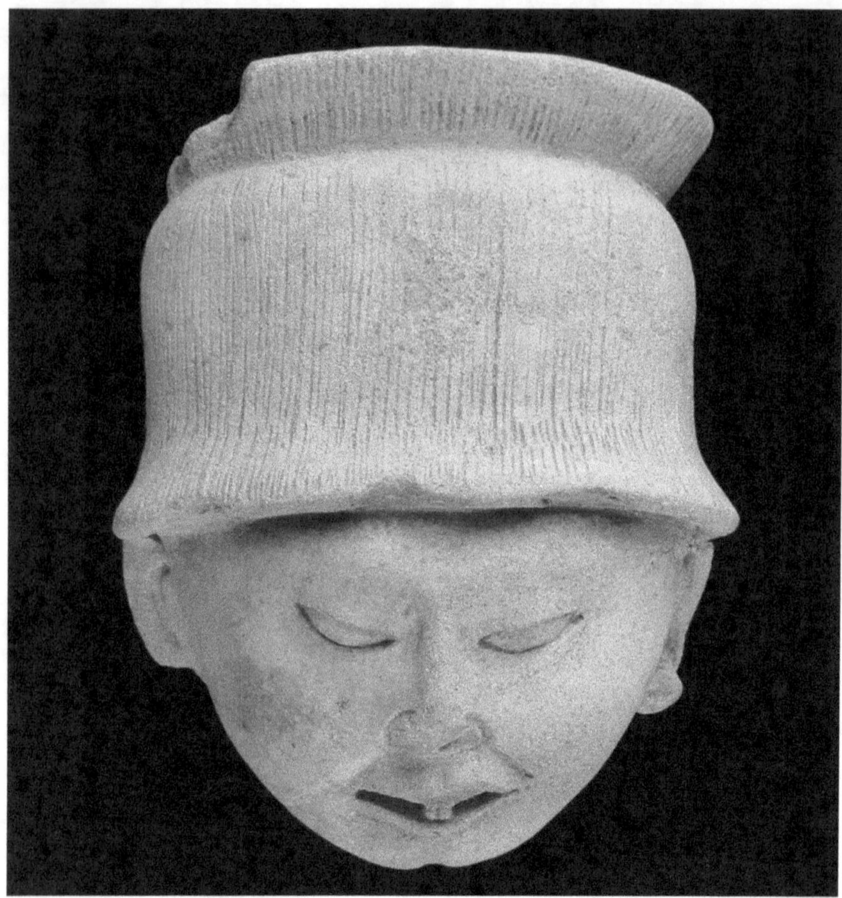

Figure 9.5b   Smiling head in Musée du quai Branly collections (courtesy of Musée du quai Branly, Paris).

Melgar y Serrano was sending had been "taken from a site near Estanzuela, 40 leagues from Veracruz." [3] Boban wrote about some of these large ceramic heads in 1876 in one of the series of articles he wrote for *Le Musée Archéologique*.

A freelance excavator, Melgar y Serrano dug up and shipped off a variety of artifacts from the Veracruz region in Mexico for a number of years. In 1862 he had partially excavated the first known colossal Olmec head near the hacienda of Hueyapan in Veracruz. Because of the head's enormous size and weight, and the difficulties of transporting large objects in the provinces of Mexico at that time, he was forced to leave the head where he had found it (Taladoire and Walsh 2014: 81–85).

In his 1874 letter, Melgar tells Boban that there are several other larger idols he can get for him from the Veracruz region, if he is interested (BNF DMO n.a.f.

21478: item 328). There is evidence in Boban's papers in the Bibliothèque nationale that Melgar continued to send him a variety of other artifacts from Veracruz (BNF DMO n.a.f. 21479 Uhthoff & Co., London, 1877: item 375).

Boban's *Musée Archéologique* article says that the ceramic heads obtained from his friend—beautiful examples of Remojadas ceramic figures—are rare and highly unusual depictions. Some of these *sonrientes*, or smiling faces, are highly individualistic. Although they are now much better known than in Boban's day, they are still prized by collectors.

In addition to well-documented artifacts that came from other collections, some artifact types are simply not found elsewhere. Some of these are considered masterpieces. One such object, exhibited as a sculptural masterpiece in the Louvre Pavillon de Sessions, is the porphyry carving of Quetzalcoatl, the Feathered Serpent.

This sculpture is carved in the round, in itself an unusual practice for pre-Columbian lapidary work. Although it has a monumental quality, surprisingly, it is only 17.3 in. (44 cm) high. The inclusion of hands and feet, in addition to the head of the figure, is unique for depictions of this Mesoamerican deity, as far as can be determined. Occasionally the feathered serpent is sculpted with a man's head inside its open jaws, but this is the only known artifact representing the hands, arms, and legs of the man as well. The Smithsonian Institution maintains three cast copies of this piece, underscoring its importance to the study of pre-Hispanic art.

This sculpture does not appear in the original catalog of Boban's collection. Therefore, he must have acquired it either in Mexico after he prepared the catalog in 1867 and before he departed in 1869, or sometime during the six years after his return to Paris and the sale of his collection in 1875. In a later memoir he describes this extraordinary piece as a Toltec sculpture, but does not say anything else about it.

There was a tendency for collectors of pre-Columbian artifacts in the nineteenth century to describe any particularly handsome or well-executed sculpture as Toltec, in accordance with the Aztec assertion that the Toltecs had been the master stone carvers. Interestingly, Maximilien Franck drew another stone sculpture of a man showing the same odd treatment of the hands and feet when it was in the Museo Nacional in 1829. The seated figure clasping his knees wears an emblem associated with Quetzalcoatl. It is no longer in the Museo Nacional, having somehow become part of the collection of Alice and Nasli Heeramaneck in New York, who donated their collection to the National Museum of New Delhi, in India. The New Delhi sculpture is 8.8 in. (22.5 cm), almost exactly half the height of the Quetzalcoatl, and carved from what is described as "grey stone" in an exhibition catalog (Morley 1968: 32). It may have been the work of the same pre-Columbian carver or perhaps the same workshop. Franck did not draw the Quetzalcoatl figure in Boban's collection, so we can assume that it was not

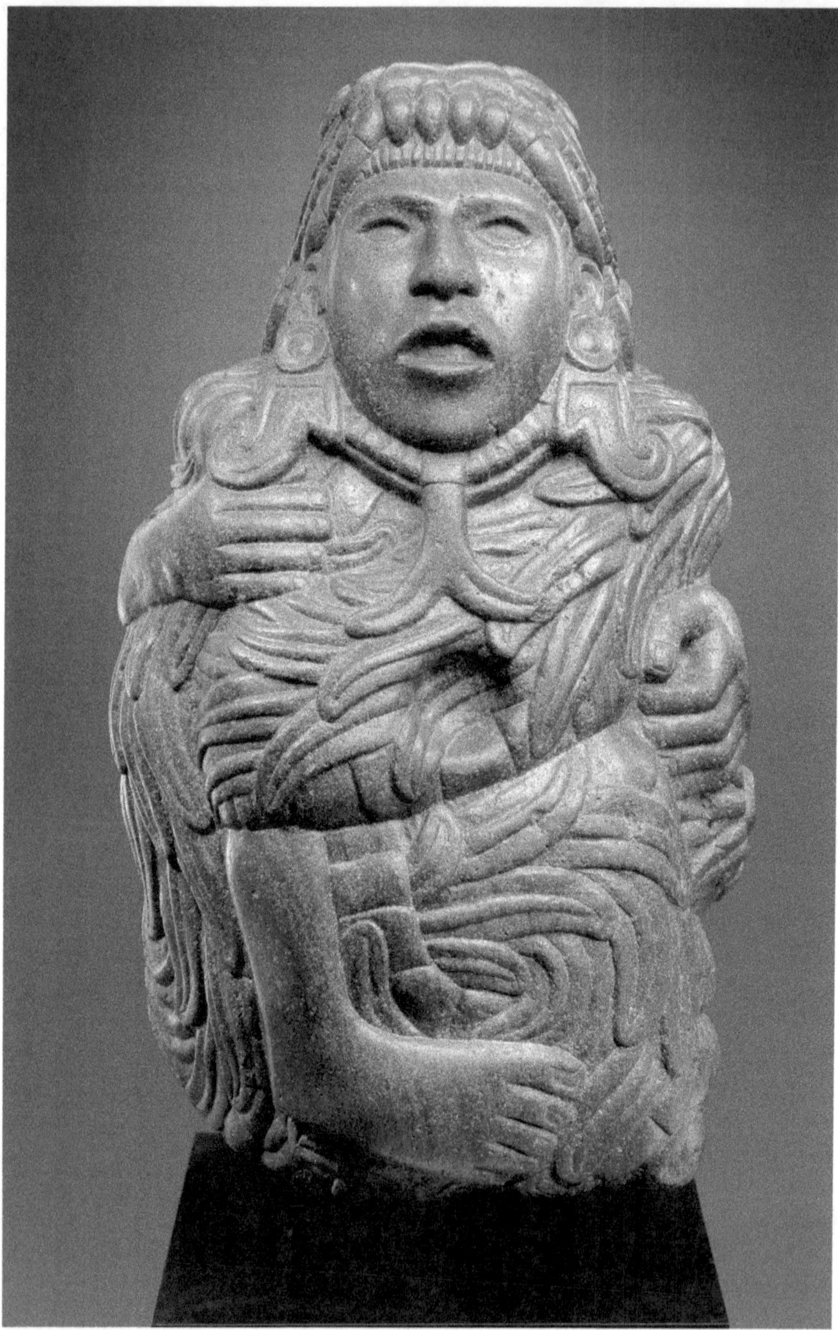

Figure 9.6   Quetzalcoatl carving in Musée du quai Branly collections on exhibit at the Louvre (courtesy of Musée du quai Branly, Paris).

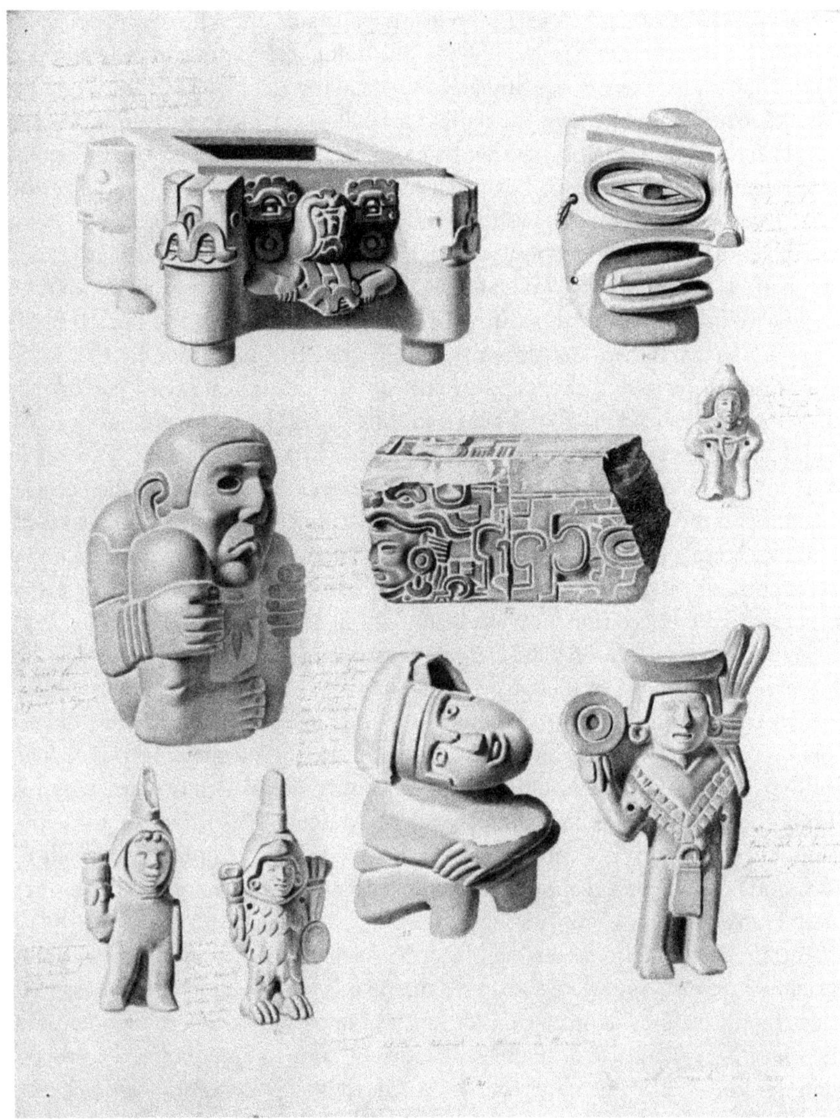

Figure 9.7   Maximilien Franck drawing of seated stone figure (courtesy of the British Museum, London, AM2006, Drg. 128, pg. 41).

in the Museo Nacional in 1829, since he would certainly have depicted it had he seen it.

Another stone sculpture in the Pinart/Boban collection also wears ornaments symbolically associated with Quetzalcoatl. In this case it is a seated monkey. Now in the Musée du quai Branly, its acquisition history is documented in a reminiscence of Boban's found among his papers at the Hispanic Society of America. He wrote that around 1858, while doing excavations in Azcapotzalco near a location where some Indians were making adobes, they uncovered a burial. He noted that he kept the skull in his collection, along with an associated necklace made from shell beads that had a "transversally cut fasciolaria" or tulip-shell pendant (HSA B2246, Box VII). He knew that this was a symbol of the deity Quetzalcoatl in his form as the wind god Ehécatl.

Apparently, he made a point of mentioning the importance and significance of the tulip-shell symbol to those visiting his store. His eagerness to share what he knew with others later paid off. In 1867, with the departure of the French expeditionary forces, Boban was pleasantly surprised by the impression he had made in talking to friends and clients. "M. E. de Jupeause, the paymaster of the French army in Mexico, told me that a Mexican, Mr. X, had found a very heavy stone idol, which [Jupeause] said was of little interest to him. If you want it, I give it to you for your collection, [he said,] and this was even more precious to me because it confirmed the importance of my sharing the significance of the shell necklace. This idol was a large squatting monkey."[4] The Aztec stone carving of the monkey wearing the transversally cut tulip-shell on its own necklace was seen by many who visited the Exposition Universelle in Paris in 1867 (HSA: B2246, Box 7).

While the story is interesting and revolves around an important identification and association made by Boban when finding shell beads and pendants in his excavations, it tells us nothing about where the object was found or any details about its context. Even the person who found it is identified only as Mr. X. The sculpture itself is quite charming. There is even a quick sketch of it in Augustus Wollaston Franks's notebooks in the British Museum (BM). Franks, the chief curator of the Christy collection, must have visited the Exposition Universelle of 1867 and been impressed enough with the sculpture to want to record its features (BM: Franks notebook, 1867, SS20).

Another extremely interesting object in Boban's 1867 catalog demonstrates his familiarity and knowledge about Maximilian's adventure in Mexico, as well as his highly attuned appreciation for rare and important artifacts. He identifies the piece as a "Panache de Plumes de Couleur" (Panache of colored feathers) from the Valley of Mexico. Below that he adds the following etymology: *panache: cuauchictli—plume: yhuitl—plumage: quequetzalli*. Rémi Siméon, who published a Nahuatl-Spanish dictionary in 1885 in Paris, defines *cuauchictli*, the Nahuatl word that Boban provides for panache, as a feather adornment worn by warriors (Siméon 1977: 396).[5] Boban also says that the object belonged to the last Aztec Emperor of Mexico, Cuauhtemoctzin, and that the Emperor of Austria gave the plumed ornament to Maximilian to present to the Museo Nacional (Reichlen 1962: 50).[6]

A later handwritten description by Boban accords with Siméon's viewpoint that the object had a military significance. "About the feathers [*plumes*] I exported

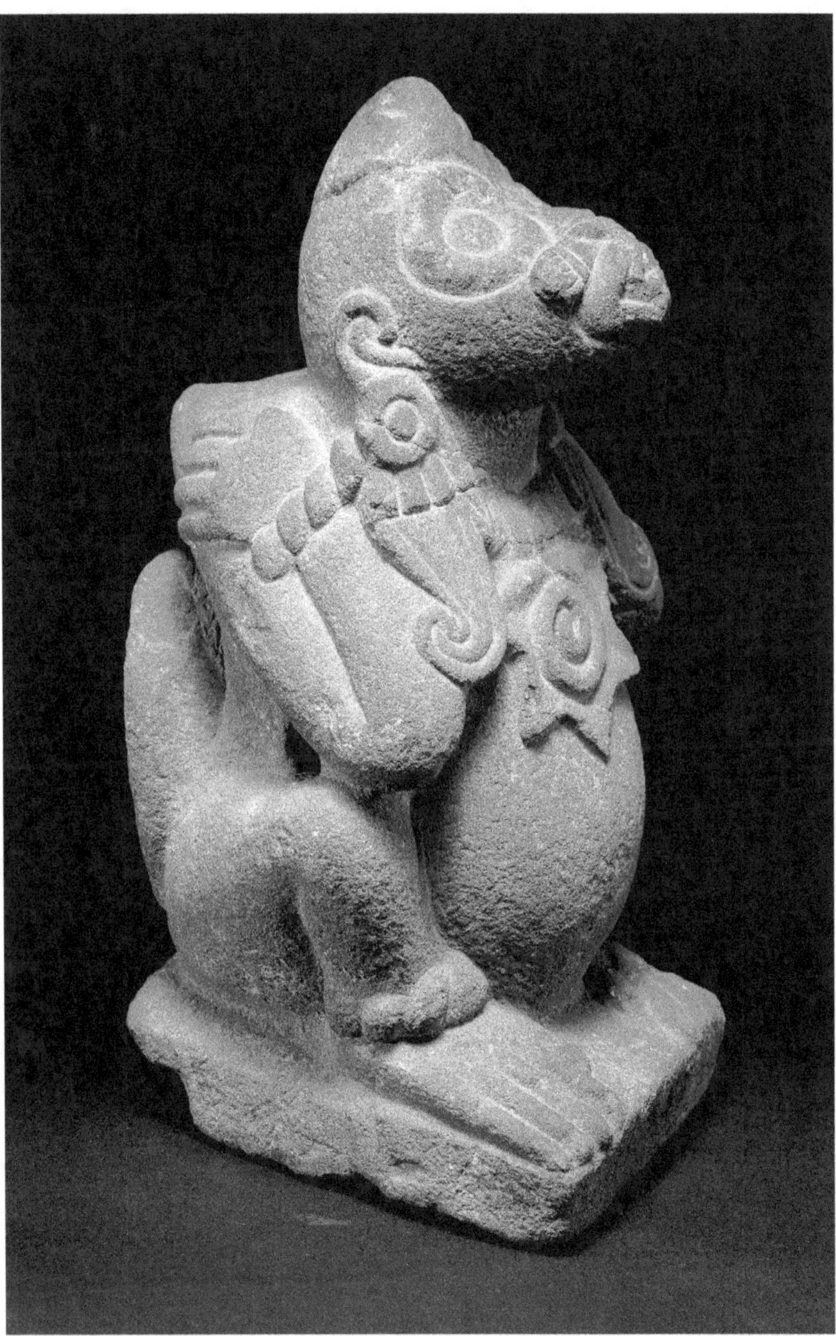

Figure 9.8   Monkey with tulip-shell pendant (courtesy of Musée du quai Branly, Paris, 71.1878.1.81AM).

from Mexico in 1869, now at the Trocadéro—this ornament went with a shield known as the 'Shield of Moctezuma II,' which is at the Museo Nacional in Mexico City, Room 2—item # 1." He then gives the backstory of how the shield ended up at the Museo Nacional and the feathers became part of his collection.

> According to many historians, the shield and the panache, among several other objects, were sent to the emperor Charles V by the Spanish conqueror Cortés. The shield and the panache were brought from the Museum's storerooms in Vienna, Austria, [a gift] from the emperor Franz Joseph. He offered them to his brother Maximilian, and they were brought in 1865 by Count Bombelles and given to the Museo Nacional. The panache did not follow the same path as the shield. It never made it into the museum collections or it was removed from the Palacio Nacional. We purchased it after the fall of the empire of Maximilian (HSA: B2246 Box VII).[7]

Boban is claiming that the panache was removed, perhaps stolen, from the Museo Nacional sometime during or shortly after the French Intervention and was later sold in Mexico City. Count Bombelles, to whom he refers, is Karl Albert Bombelles, a friend of Maximilian's who grew up with him in Austria. Bombelles did indeed bring back to Mexico the feathered shield now in the Museo Nacional and some letters that Cortés had written to Charles V in 1519, but there is no mention in the historical record of a feathered ornament.

Some light on the panache's earlier history may be provided from Austria itself. In 1878 Ferdinand von Hochstetter, the director of the newly formed K. K. Naturhistorisches Hofmuseum (Imperial Royal Court Museum of Natural History) in Vienna, began cataloguing objects that had been part of Austria's imperial and public collections for centuries. In the process, he examined the Ambraser Sammlung (Ambras Collection) assembled by Archduke Ferdinand of Tyrol between 1567 and 1595. According to Christian Feest, the former director of the Museum für Völkerkunde (Museum of Ethnology) in Vienna, who also traced Vienna's early collections, one of the most significant items that Hochstetter documented in the Ambras Collection was the famous feather headdress of Moctezuma (Feest 1990: 1). By examining early inventories, he was able to identify pieces that had disappeared. Among the missing items were "four other pre-Hispanic Mexican feather pieces, i.e., a coat or skirt ('rockh,' listed for the last time in 1788 in an already much worn condition), a shield, a feather bunch, and a fan, all of which he considered lost" (Feest 1990: 2). It is likely that the shield is the one Franz Joseph gave his brother Maximilian in 1865, and which is now found in the Museo Nacional. It may be that the "feather bunch" is Boban's panache. The later history of the coat or skirt and the fan remains unknown.

Ernest T. Hamy, anthropologist, ethnologist, and founding director of the Musée d'Ethnographie du Trocadéro, published the panache in 1897 in a catalog entitled *Galerie Américaine du Musée d'Ethnographie du Trocadéro*. He had selected it as one of the outstanding objects in the Trocadéro's American collection. He describes it as "a curious ornament, feather headdress of ancient construction, and a vague tradition is that it belonged to the unfortunate victim of Cortés, Guatimozin, last emperor of Mexico" (Hamy 1897b: 49–52).[8]

The piece is now in the Musée du quai Branly with the catalog number 1878.1.2963, described as an "insigne." Whatever its provenance, it is the only one of its kind. The feathers are attached to a coiled basketry disk made of sticks and thread, which is covered by a finely woven cotton cloth and topped by green parrot feathers. Suspended from the disk, which is 3.5 in. (9 cm) in diameter, are three layers of feather ornaments—flowerlike tufts of feathers attached to sticks about 3.9 to 4 in. (10 cm) in length, which are wound with thread. The construction of each of these feather flowers, and indeed of the entire ornament, is extraordinarily complex.

There are very few examples of pre-Columbian Aztec feather work, and most of the known specimens are in European collections. If the panache is indeed pre-Columbian, it survives today in part thanks to Boban's knowledge of Mexican antiquities and his understanding of the rarity of Aztec featherwork, perhaps combined with his desire to rescue a unique object that had once belonged to the Emperor Maximilian.

Another extraordinary artifact in Boban's collection is listed in his catalog as number 1969 and described as "Mantle made with feathers—Mexico—this mantle is called Tilmatli by the Aztecs" (Reichlen 1962: 86).[9] Actually this mantle is not a *tilma*, nor is it Aztec. It is an extremely rare example of a California Indian feather blanket (McLendon 2001; Hudson and Bates 2015). According to ethnologists Travis Hudson and Craig Bates, who have published extensively on early California Indians, these warm, luxurious blankets were made by nearly all the Indian groups living in the central valley of California, "where immense flocks of birds provided the feathers for the manufacture of such marks of affluence" (2015: 104). The same authors claim that there are only fourteen such blankets in museum collections in the United States and Europe. Their figure does not take into account the feather blanket collected by Boban.

The blanket is erroneously described in the Musée du quai Branly catalog as having come from Baja California and being made from pelican feathers, due to an inaccurate identification made by the anthropologist Robert Heizer, who did extensive fieldwork in California (Sally McLendon, pers. comm.). The softly-toned white blanket with brown bands at each end is not constructed from pelican feathers, but rather from some other waterfowl, probably ducks and geese.

The catalog number (71.1881.80.110) indicates that Alphonse Pinart donated it to the museum in 1881, some six years after he traded Boban's pre-Columbian Mexican objects to the French government in exchange for financial support for his mission to California. Pinart did not collect the blanket in California in

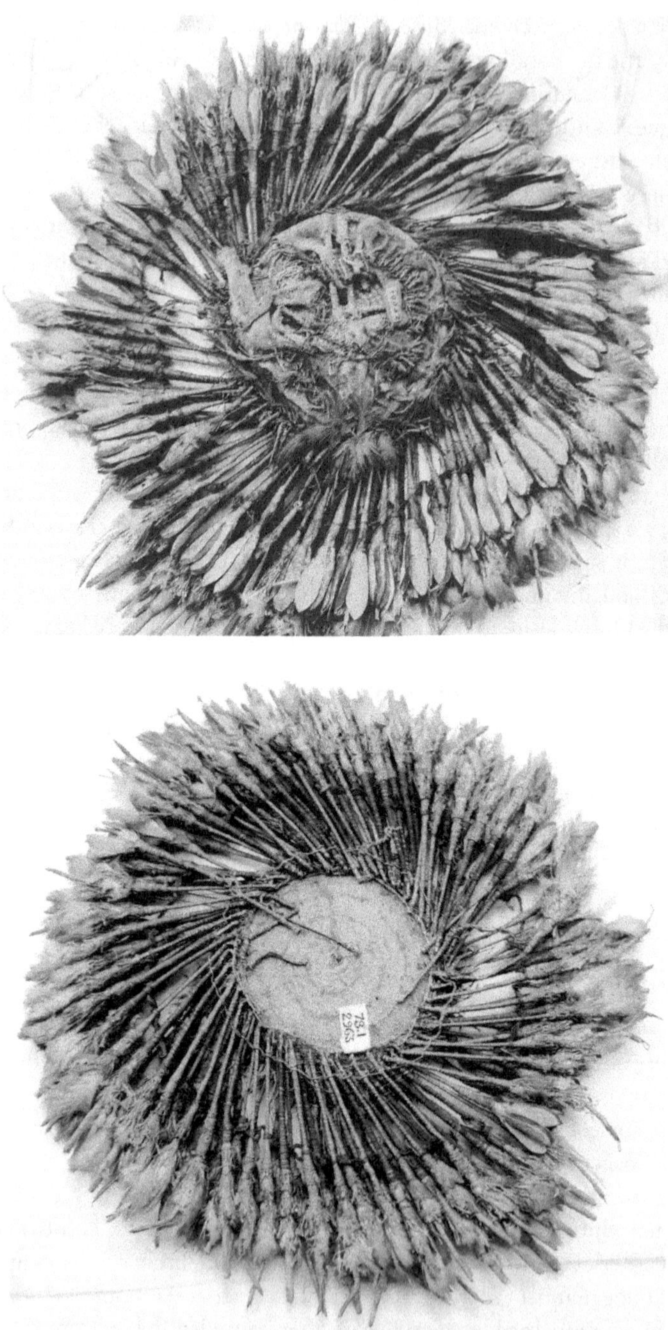

Figures 9.9a–b Front and back of Aztec feather insigne (courtesy of Musée du quai Branly, Paris, 71.1878.1.2963).

Figure 9.10a   Feather blanket from Musée du quai Branly collections (courtesy of Musée du quai Branly, Paris, 71.1881.80.110).

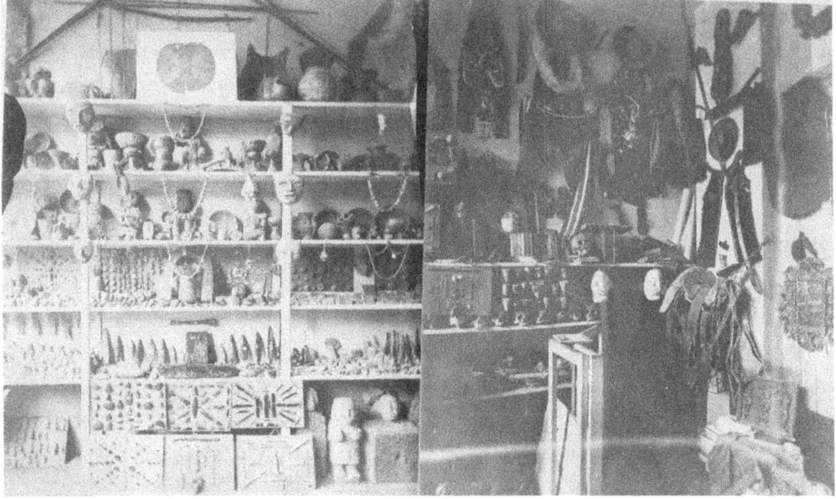

Figure 9.10b   Photograph that Boban sent to Gabriel de Mortillet showing feather blanket in his collection (courtesy of Musée d'Archéologie nationale, Saint-Germain-en-Laye, M5001_1100490_ Album Noir 37, folio 191).

the late 1870s, however, since it is in Boban's 1867 catalog and is clearly visible at the top center of a photograph Boban took of part of his collection between 1869 and 1870. The image is one of a group of photos, all of which are still in the archives of the Musée d'Archéologie national in Saint-Germain-en-Laye, that Boban sent to Gabriel de Mortillet when he offered to sell his entire Mexican collection to the prehistorian in 1873 (f° 191: M5001_1100490_Album Noir 37 folio191_Mexique_Coll Boban).

To make identification easier, a recent photograph of the California Indian feather blanket in the Musée du quai Branly's collection has been provided. Although hard to discern, the same blanket can be seen hanging above the shelves containing Boban's pre-Columbian artifacts.

It is possible that Boban acquired the mantle from a collector in Mexico City, assuming it to be a feather *tilma* worn by Aztecs. It might also have come from the Museo Nacional, since Fanny Calderón de la Barca mentions museum exhibits in the 1840s of "various dresses, arms, and utensils from both the Californias" (1970: 340). Another possibility is that Boban collected it himself in California, when he traveled along the Sacramento River in the early 1850s, where the fourteen other examples of this type of blanket originated, most of which were collected during that same time period. Did he describe the blanket as an ancient Aztec *tilmatl* because he thought it would be considered more valuable, or did he simply not know that it had come from California? Today, because of their rarity, both the Aztec feather panache and the California Indian feather blanket are priceless.

Although Boban provides more documentation about his collection than most collectors of the period, there is a wide spectrum of provenances supplied for the artifacts. Some pieces were excavated with care, along with their associated objects, and their significance and provenance were dutifully recorded. Much less information is supplied for other pieces that he likely acquired through purchase or trade.

The portrait of Boban that emerges from the provenance and collection history of the artifacts he assembled is one of a lively and energetic man. The locations in which he dug for artifacts span the entire Valley of Mexico and much farther afield. He journeyed as far away as Chiapas and the Yucatan, some 650 miles to the south of Mexico City, and to Durango, about 550 miles in the opposite direction. The story about the seated monkey sculpture displaying Quetzalcoatl ornaments suggests that he was passionate about explaining to others what he had learned, and that he did so in such a way that they appreciated and remembered what he had shared with them. He was a man who made friends easily and kept them for life. Such was the case with José María Melgar y Serrano, Col. Louis Toussaint Simon Doutrelaine, Augustin Alexis Damour, and many others. Other personal characteristics that emerge are loyalty, independent thinking, and generosity. But his most important talent was his educated ability to recognize the quality and rarity of archeological and ethnographic artifacts, as demonstrated by his acquisition of the calendar wheel, the porphyry sculpture of Quetzalcoatl, the Xipe mask, the panache, and the feather blanket. It is hard to imagine who else would have appreciated the importance of collecting one of the few remaining pieces of pre-Columbian featherwork or a nearly perfect example of the feather blankets made by the rapidly disappearing Indians from the central valley of California.

Notes

1. Il est étonnant de voir comment les anciens Mexicains travaillaient bien les pierres dures.

2. On remarquera l'expression de calme et de mort de ce masque; il fait, par là, contraste frappant avec la plupart des masques mexicains qui, généralement, sont empreints d'une vie énergique, mais grimaçante. Il représente la face d'une vierge Colhua, sacrifiée et déifiée sous le nom de Teteoinan. L'intention du sculpteur, qui a voulu rappeler la face humaine revêtue de la peau de la victime.

3. Fueron sacados de la Estanzuela, 40 leguas de Veracruz.

4. M. E. de Jupeause le payeur en chef de l'armée française au Mexique me dit [q'un] Mexicain, M. X, vient de trouver une idole en pierre très lourde. Il [Jupeause] me l'a offert . . . [en disant] cela m'intéresse peu; si vous le voulez, je vous le donne pour votre collection. Cette présent était plus précieux pour moi car il venait confirmer ma manière de voir [et partager] un sujet . . . [l'importance du] mon collier de coquilles. Cette idole était un grand singe accroupi.

5. Adorno de plumas que llevaban los guerreros.

6. Panache en Plumes de Couleur (panache : cuachictli – plume : yhuitl – plumage : quequetzalli. Plumes. Vallée de Mexico. Objet ayant appartenu au dernier Empereur du Mexique, Cuauhtemoctzin. Offert à Maximilien par l'Empereur d'Autriche pour le Musée National de Mexico.

7. Au sujet du panache de plumes que j'ai exporté du Mexique en 1869 qui se trouve au Trocadéro – cet ornement accompagnait le bouclier connu sous le nom de Bouclier de Motecuhzoma II qui se trouve au Musée national de Mexico. Salle 2 – portant le #1. Suivant plusieurs historiens ce bouclier et le panache était accompagné de plusieurs autres objets précieux expédié a l'empereur Charles V par le conquérant espagnol Cortés. Le bouclier et le panache ses trouvés au Musée de l'arsenal de Vienna en Autriche. L'empereur François Joseph l'offert a son frère Maximilien. [Ils été] apporté [a Mexico] en 1865 par le Comte de Bombelles et deposé au Musée national.

8. Un curieux ornement de tête en plumes, de fabrication ancienne, et qu'une vague tradition assurait avoir appartenu à l'infortunée victime de Cortez, Guatimozin, dernier empereur du Mexique.

9. Manteau fait avec des plumes—Mexico—Ce manteau est nommé Tilmatli par les Aztèques.

I O

THE RUE DU SOMMERARD DECADE

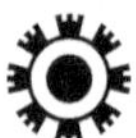

Collectors are a different breed. The need to acquire objects is in their blood. It is as though they have an incurable virus. In the case of Eugène Boban, the illness was exacerbated by the fact that antiquities were not just his passion; they were also his livelihood. Thus, he was constantly searching for new objects, expanding his range, buying and selling a large variety of items of every description.

Having finally sold his impressive collection of pre-Columbian artifacts to Alphonse Pinart in 1875, Boban almost immediately began to form a second Mexican collection. Recalling this period of his life in later writings, he acts as though he had little choice in the matter. "I found myself at the center of meetings about American antiquities and considered to be the expert, while many people still living in Mexico continually contacted me in Paris with offers to sell me artifact collections, that I purchased" (HSA: B2244, Box V).[1] In addition to the Mexican objects that he says his colleagues were more or less forcing on him at this juncture, he had expanded his activities to collect and sell European prehistoric implements and ethnographic material from Asia, North America, Polynesia, and Africa. He also acquired another crystal skull—an object that would complicate his life for many years.

With the addition of objects from new subject areas, Boban explored new ways of presenting them. In 1877 he met Henry Augustus Ward of New York, a man with a passion for natural history who had taught at the University of Rochester. He had launched Ward's Natural Science Establishment in Rochester, which supplied an enormous variety of natural history specimens to colleges, museums, and private collectors (BNF DMO n.a.f. 21479: item 479). According to historian Sally Gregory Kohlstedt, Professor of the History of Science and Technology at the University of Minnesota, Ward had quite an impact on the study and knowledge of natural history in the United States: he "was prominent among a group of naturalists and entrepreneurs who, in the last half of the nineteenth century, shaped the development of museums across the country" (Kohlstedt 1980: 647). He had pioneered the approach of presenting a pseudo museum exhibition in his sales rooms in Ward's Natural Science Establishment. A kindred spirit, Boban may have decided to emulate Ward's sales approach, since at this point he started to exhibit artifacts in his Paris shop with long explanatory labels detailing their history and provenance. Ward gave Boban permission to sell copies of two photographs of the famous mammoth skeleton he had reassembled, with him posing alongside it for scale. He wrote to Boban saying not to sell them for less than thirty francs each (BNF DMO 21479: items 479–80).

Later in 1877 Boban purchased a large collection from the budding archeologist and prehistorian Jacques de Morgan. It comprised some 1,733 objects, including flint tools, spear points, arrow points, and pottery from North America. The price was five hundred francs (BNF DMO n.a.f. 21478: item 352). De Morgan's mentor was Boban's colleague Gabriel de Mortillet, who was then curator at the Musée des Antiquités nationales at Saint-Germain-en-Laye.

In addition to obtaining material from Mexican colleagues, Boban added a number of important pieces to his new collection after the close of the 1878 Exposition Universelle. Among these acquisitions was the Labadie Collection of Mexican pre-Columbian artifacts. Jules Labadie was the owner of a pharmacy called Droguería de la Profesa, located near the church Nuestra Señora de La Profesa, a few blocks from Boban's Callejón del Espíritu Santo shop. The two men had been well acquainted in Mexico City.

Boban augmented his pre-Columbian materials with the artifacts he continued to receive from José Maria Melgar y Serrano. He managed to acquire the pre-Columbian collection that had belonged to Dr. Jean Baptiste Fuzier, an army surgeon assigned to Veracruz during the French Intervention, and another from Colonel Blanco of the Mexican army. He received additional objects through a Mr. Puységur of Mexico, who previously had sent him the items that had belonged to an Italian citizen to whom Boban refers as Mr. X, a subtlety he uses at various times to disguise someone's identity. As we shall see later, this mysterious figure is most likely Luigi Constantini, whom Boban described as the director of the military school in Chapultepec, who had lived in Mexico for more than thirty years (HSA: B2244, Box V; H HSA: B2240, Box 1, Folder III).

Boban published a sales catalog for his collections in 1878, listing himself as *antiquaire* or antiquarian. He calls his shop, still located at 35, rue du Sommerard, across from the Musée du Cluny, a *Comptoir d'archéologie prehistorique*. This means a sales counter, or branch, dedicated to prehistoric archeology. By calling it a branch, he may be alluding to his other shop in Mexico City.

Boban's 1878 shop catalog lists prehistoric artifacts from France, Denmark, Switzerland, and North America. There is a small selection of ethnographic objects from Oceania, perhaps obtained from Alphonse Pinart, who had traveled and collected there after his time in California. Other archeological objects are from Peru, Cypress, and Egypt. Despite the fact that Boban had sold the majority of his Mexican pre-Columbian collection to Pinart three years earlier, he once again lists Mexican archeological artifacts in his sales catalog. Some of these items include obsidian points, cores, scrapers, and blades from the Valley of Mexico, priced between five and ten francs. There are flint points, stone beads, and a large series of stone and terra-cotta idols, along with a number of figurines and ceramic vessels described either as "modern Mexico manufactures" or as fakes (*contrefaçons*) (Boban 1878: 12).

Throughout his career Eugène Boban worked assiduously to broaden his audience and increase his clientele. His activities in Paris in the mid to late 1870s reveal some of his networking strategies. He sent all four of his articles published in the *Musée Archéologique* to colleagues and collectors in Mexico City, and to the Sociedad de Geografía y Estadística. In 1876 he received a letter from the society's director, Ygnacio Altamirano, thanking him for his generosity and informing him that he had been elected an honorary member (BNF DMO n.a.f. 21476: item 30–31). Boban was always proud to mention his membership in an array of scientific societies and made a point of attending their meetings and exhibiting at their conferences.

In the late 1870s and early 1880s Boban increased his sales to museums throughout Europe. In fact, judging from the list of his sales and contacts, it seems as though his shop was an emporium, carrying almost any type of object or specimen a museum or collector might desire.

In 1878 he sold a series of eighty-six casts of prehistoric objects to a M. Stefanesco, director of the museum of Bucharest in Romania, for the sum of 427.50 francs (HSA: B2243, Box IV). Francisco Antonio Pereira da Costa, the director of the Museu da História Natural in Lisbon, Portugal, purchased a collection of human skulls from Mexico in 1879, along with numerous Mexican figurine heads, casts, and complete figures (BNF DMO n.a.f. 21478: item 487).

In October 1878 Ferdinand von Hochstetter, director of the ethnographic department of the K. K. Naturhistorisches Hofmuseum (Imperial Royal Court Museum of Natural History) in Vienna, who was in the midst of cataloguing the museum's far-flung collections, purchased ethnographic pieces from Tahiti, New Zealand, the Admiralty Islands, and the Marquesas, along with prehistoric objects from France and casts of artifacts from Europe and America (Gerard van Bussel, pers. comm.). Boban never traveled to the Pacific, but Alphonse Pinart made large collections from numerous South Sea islands. It is possible that Pinart used ethnographic material from these exotic lands to settle part of his debt for his purchase of Boban's Mexican collection in 1875. It is also possible that Boban acquired these objects from other travelers.

In 1881 Luigi Pigorini, who had founded the Museo Nazionale Preistorico Etnografico Luigi Pigorini in Rome five years earlier, purchased several lots of ethnographic material from Boban's shop for 915 francs. One group included axes and weapons from New Guinea, clubs from the Marquesas, and miscellaneous weapons from Tonga and New Caledonia. The following year Pigorini spent six hundred francs on a number of stone and bronze axes from European archeological sites, some of which were hafted (the blade was still attached to the wooden handle secured by animal hide or vegetable fiber). It would have been unusual to find hafted axes in archeological contexts unless they were found in caves; perhaps Boban was hafting them himself in an effort to create a better, more salable artifact. Pigorini later bought a third group of objects. A beaded-buckskin Indian costume from Canada headed the list of purchases, followed by additional objects from the South Seas (BNF DMO n.a.f. 21478: items 542–44).

In 1880 archeologist and ethnologist Augustus Henry Lane-Fox Pitt Rivers stopped by Boban's shop, where he purchased a varied assortment of ethnographic and archeological pieces. Like many collectors of his era, Pitt Rivers bought in quantity, although rather eclectically. He kept careful records of his purchases—a Japanese helmet, a war club from Samoa, a Mexican pre-Columbian ceramic tripod vessel, rosewood castanets, and other items that caught his eye (Margot McGreevy, pers. comm.). His meticulous note-keeping allowed his assistant, a Mr. Riordan, to write Boban on Pitt Rivers's behalf in May 1881. "Would you kindly inform me," inquired Riordan, "whether General Lane-Fox Pitt Rivers, when visiting your shop in September last, bought a pair of long Mexican Stirrups (Etriers). . . . The Stirrups were hanging in the right-hand window of your shop, just a little to the right . . . looking from the Street. The General thinks he bought them but they cannot be found" (BNF DMO n.a.f. 21478: item 575).

The objects purchased from Boban's shop, along with many thousands more, became part of the Pitt Rivers Museum, founded at Oxford University in 1884, when the ethnologist donated his vast collection of more than twenty thousand artifacts to the University. Pitt Rivers had distinct ideas about cultural evolution and, from the beginning, the objects in his museum were arranged in displays to show the cultural developmental sequences he envisioned (Hicks 2013: 1–15). The exhibits show the enormous variety of objects used by different cultures to solve everyday problems like hunting, making fire, making music, and other day-to-day activities. His accurate visual memory, which he used in arranging and comprehending his collection, is evident in his recollection of the stirrups he had purchased and their exact position in Boban's shop window. Boban sent the stirrups to Oxford after receiving Riordan's missive, and they are in the museum's collection to this day (Margot McGreevy, pers. comm.).

Boban continued to fill out his own collections with purchases and trades, even as he was selling to museums and dealers in the early 1880s. For instance, in 1881 he bought a number of Mexican antiquities and a few drawings for three hundred francs from the widow of Jean Frédéric Waldeck, the renowned painter and explorer of Mexican archeological sites, who had died in 1875, purportedly at the age of 109 (BNF DMO n.a.f. 21479: item 475).

Having survived the early catastrophes of the first two years of the 1870s at rue du Sommerard, Eugène Boban continued in his rented rooms and shop through the rest of the decade, both within walking distance of his parents' home at 22, rue Grands Augustins. It would appear from later correspondence that he was in close contact with his father, mother, and two aunts from Angers. His older sister, Rose Louise, who had married in 1853, the year Boban set sail for California, became a widow in 1878. She and her husband had lost a daughter, Jeanne Laurence, in 1864, a month short of her second birthday (D1M9 735). Papers relating to her husband's will indicate that Rose Louise's profession was making beaded jewelry, an activity in which she apparently did quite well (Christiane Demeulenaere-Douyère, pers. comm.).

A year after her first husband died, Rose Louise married the architect Jean Paul Mabille in 1879. According to an 1895 directory of architects, Mabille was born in Chelles, France, in 1821 and graduated from the École des Beaux-Arts in 1842. In marrying an architect and well-educated man, it is clear that Rose's status had risen from the petite bourgeoisie to the solidly bourgeois class. Both her mother and father were listed as witnesses to the marriage, and the parents were described as *sans profession* or unemployed. It is unclear what their source of income was, although it is likely that some of their children were supporting them.

Two of Boban's younger sisters had not fared so well. They were apparently struggling financially, living in unfashionable arrondissements, and two of them had not married. Marie Françoise, two years younger than Eugène, had had three illegitimate children between 1860 and 1868, before Boban returned from Mexico. Only the first of these daughters, Leonine Laurence Marie, survived into adulthood. Infant mortality was especially high during the mid-nineteenth century for a variety of reasons. One contributing factor was bottle feeding, which had become more common than breastfeeding, and meant that babies had diminished immune systems. Poor hygiene habits and the lack of sanitation also contributed to an unhealthy atmosphere for infants and toddlers (Price 2004: 413).

Although it is uncertain who the father of any of Marie's daughters was, it is likely, due to the similarity of their names, that Philippe-Alphonse de Metz was the father of her second daughter, Philippine Alphonsine Marie, who was born in August 1867 and did not survive to adulthood. An older married man, de Metz was a German-born architect who died in 1879 at the age of seventy-three. The fact that Marie herself was named a beneficiary of de Metz's will further corroborates Philippine's parentage. He left Marie an annual allowance of 2,300 francs, with the stipulation that upon Marie's death her other daughter, Leonine Laurence Marie, would receive a reduced annual allowance of three hundred francs. This portion of the will and testament was read by the notary Émile Jozon in the presence of de Metz's son, his two daughters, and Marie Boban. There is no record of any objection on the part of de Metz's family, so Marie must have been on good terms with them (Jozon 1879; Archives nationales, Paris).[2] The daughter bearing his name is not mentioned in de Metz's testament, nor in subsequent documents. Marie's last daughter was stillborn on 22 September 1868. Evidence for Philippine's death has not been uncovered in the Paris records.

Boban's next younger sister, Julie Félicité, struggled even more than Marie and in far harsher circumstances. She had two illegitimate children, in 1863 and 1865, both of whom died as infants. In their birth certificates Julie's profession is listed as *glaceuse*, a paper or cloth glazer—quite a menial and low-paid job. Unhappily, she died on 14 July 1870, a year after Boban's return, at the age of thirty-one, while giving birth to her third child in a charity hospital only a few blocks from where her parents still lived. There must have been a serious rift in the family, since Julie's death certificate lists her as Julie Félicité Duvergé, with no mention of Boban. Also, despite the fact that her parents, sisters, and brother were close by, no one came forward to take care of her orphaned daughter, who died in a foundling hospital a few days after her mother. According to Claire Goldberg Moses, the French Civil Code did not permit paternity suits, and men were not held legally responsible for supporting illegitimate offspring. In fact, most of these children were either abandoned "or became the charge of women who were hardly able to support themselves alone" (Moses 1984: 28).

The youngest sister, Charlotte Héloise Boban Duvergé, who was seven years younger than Eugène, married Martial Chavanon in 1859 at the age of eighteen. Chavanon died during the Paris Commune revolt, but Charlotte continued to live in Paris, although she apparently never remarried.

Boban's father, René Victor Boban, died at his home on rue Grands Augustins on 28 February 1880 at the age of seventy-one. Although Laurence Michel Simon Boban, who had been married to René Victor for fifty years, was still alive, it was her son who made the declarations recorded in the official death notice. He is listed as "Eugène André Boban, merchant antiquarian, age forty-five, at rue du Sommerard 35, son of the deceased." It appears that it was customary for the man of the family to give the information recorded on death certificates. Whether customary or not, this is the case for all the death notices recorded for the Boban family.

Another government document from these years indicates that Boban obtained an official permit or decree from the office of the Ministre de l'Intérieur in September of 1880 giving him the legal right to exercise the profession of bookseller at his rue du Sommerard location (BNF DMO n.a.f. 21476: item 174). The shop appears to have been expanding, and its proprietor was continuing to broaden the range of his merchandise.

Once Boban assumed the role of bookseller in his shop, he seems to have become more conscious than ever of being an educator as well as a dealer. His *Catalogue d'Ouvrages Scientifique* of 1881 opens with the statement:

We have the honor of announcing to professors, and Directors of Museums and colleges, that as a result of research, purchases, and exchanges made over several years with museums and amateurs, we have succeeded in assembling a considerable quantity of prehistoric, ethnographic, and anthropological objects. In order to facilitate demonstration in courses and meetings, we thought that it would be useful to create a series of casts of representative pieces, which permit us to deliver facsimiles of them at moderate prices. The objects carry labels employing the classification system developed by professor Gabriel de Mortillet (Boban 1881: 3).[3]

After having served as curator at the Musée des Antiquités nationales at Saint-Germain-en-Laye for eight years, Mortillet became a professor of anthropology in Paris in 1876. He is best known for his classification system for prehistoric cultural development during the Paleolithic or Stone Age. The system was the first attempt to chronologically organize the archeological finds from numerous European sites.

Boban was an avid follower of Mortillet's classification system, which used terms related to the location in which specific types of objects had been found by men like the archeologist Edouard Lartet, the banker Henry Christy, and the engineer Peccadeau de l'Isle. The names for different eras he assigned were Solutrean, Mousterian, Magdalenian, Chellean, and so forth. Boban corresponded with Mortillet, attended his lectures, and took courses from him. In the 1878 sales catalog, he included a chart that Mortillet had constructed showing chronological divisions in the Stone, Bronze, and Iron ages (1878: 2).

Numbering fifty-five pages, the 1881 sales catalog for Boban's shop is considerably larger than the 1878 edition. It contains a variety of distinct artifact classes, in addition to scientific books. There are casts and archeological objects from the Dordogne, Charente, the Menton grottoes, Grand Pressigny, Denmark, and Switzerland. There are sections detailing ethnographic artifacts from the South Pacific, Africa, and North America. A few things come from Mexico, Peru, and Canada, and a number are advertised as Mexican fakes, with lengthy commentary.

Then, in a section entitled "OBJETS DIVERS," he lists a rock crystal skull (Représentation en cristal de roche d'un crâne humain), priced at the considerable sum of 3,500 francs. More finely carved and larger than the skull he sold to Pinart, it is the most expensive piece in the catalog. He describes it as life-size and "a masterpiece of the lapidary arts" (Boban 1881: 49).[4]

The price of this object is nearly double that of an ivory figure of Christ offered for two thousand francs. Comparing it to many other items in the catalog—a Mexican saddle for 150 francs and stone axes from Denmark for ten to one hundred francs—it becomes clear how valuable Boban believed this skull to be. Although the price makes it stand out immediately, the description provided, "Representation in rock crystal of a human skull of natural size, masterpiece of the lapidary arts," hardly foreshadows the convoluted schemes and claims that would be required for its eventual sale.

In 1880 and 1881 Boban sold a series of collections to the Musée des Antiquités nationales en Saint-Germain-en-Laye, perhaps after having been introduced to the museum's new director by Mortillet. These included fossils, bronze fibulas (ancient fasteners that resemble safety pins) from Spain, and a steatite or soapstone club (Louvre archives, série G6).

As he expanded his knowledge of the field, Boban decided to take advantage of his bookseller's permit. "Recently we added a special department to our *Comptoir* for a book-selling business where we receive on commission, on deposit any publications, books, brochures, maps, plans, drawings, etc. relating to prehistoric, archeological sciences" (Boban 1881: 3).[5] He added that he intended to publish a bulletin listing the books for sale, to which he would add new books every three months.

Gustave Dumoutier, an archeologist who would later travel to Tonkin, northern Vietnam, for the French government, wrote a study of French prehistoric sites along the plateau of Grand-Morin describing and enumerating their workshops, camps, houses, monuments, and burials, under the title "Les Stations de L'homme Préhistorique." Eugène Boban's establishment in Paris is listed as the publisher of this ninety-eight-page monograph (Dumoutier 1882). There may be other books that he had privately printed and sold in his comptoir, but this is the only one found to date.

In addition to his success with museums, his sales to scientists in France and across Europe soared during the first half of the 1880s. One of these was Eugène Deslongchamps, a professor of zoology at the faculty of sciences at the Université de Caen Normandie, who purchased a tattooed Maori head and New Caledonian axes (BNF DMO n.a.f. 21477: items 59–69).

Correspondence in the Smithsonian Institution's archives documents some of the more elaborate trade arrangements that nineteenth-century collectors engaged in. In 1882 Boban obtained a number of North American antiquities from the Smithsonian Institution through the intervention of Edwin Atlee Barber, curator of ceramics at the Pennsylvania Museum and School of Industrial Arts in Philadelphia (today the school is known as University of the Arts and the museum is the Philadelphia Museum of Art). In 1881 Barber wrote to his friend and colleague Spencer Fullerton Baird, the second secretary of the Smithsonian, requesting North American material for exchange. At the time, the institution had an office of distribution that traded pieces from the national collections widely, in an effort to obtain artifacts and specimens of natural history that were rare in America but relatively common in other parts of the world (Walsh 2002).

Barber, who had exchanged specimens with Baird a number of times, was writing to ask a favor. "Will you kindly inform me whether I can arrange exchanges through the Smithsonian Institution with M. E. Boban of Paris. He wishes to send me a case of ancient pottery, pipes, etc., in exchange for which I am to send him a box of American antiquities" (SIA: Baird corres #16229).

In January 1882 Edwin Atlee Barber wrote Boban apologizing for the delay in sending the material he had obtained from the Smithsonian. "The pottery I send is rare and good and brings good prices in this country." The list of objects he was forwarding described contemporary Southwestern pottery from Laguna and Jemez pueblos. Older, archeologically recovered objects included a seventeenth-century British clay pipe, "found in an Indian grave," stone hammers, axes, and wedges from Ohio, and an "earthen vessel from an ancient mound in Missouri," among a variety of fragments (BNF DMO n.a.f. 21476: item 88–89). It is not known precisely what the Smithsonian received in return for this favor to Barber, other than the secretary's ability to maintain the goodwill of an active trading partner in Philadelphia.

Later in 1882 Boban attended the congress of Americanists in Copenhagen, winning a silver medal for an exhibition of prehistoric artifacts, as well as a sincere letter of thanks from the organizing committee's president (BNF DMO 21479: item 505). He was gaining more and more recognition in the academic and scientific communities, and his clientele had increased considerably—so much so that in March 1882, he sent out a printed announcement saying that his Comptoir d'archéologie was moving to a larger shop, at 85, Boulevard Saint-Michel, opposite the École nationale des mines de Paris.

This new shop featured a library of prehistoric sciences, ethnography, and anthropology, along with maps and photographs of foreign lands. Only about three blocks from the old shop on rue du Sommerard, the new location was still relatively near to his mother's home on rue Grands Augustins, not too far from his own apartment on rue Saint-Jacques, and just up the street from the Sorbonne.

He set up his new shop to resemble a museum, as he had done previously. The objects for sale had labels listing their cultures and provenance, the materials used for their manufacture, customs related to them, and other pertinent details. He did this to educate students and collectors, and his establishment was frequently described as a favored meeting place for pre-historians and Americanists. One of these was Jean-Louis Capitan, who haunted Boban's shop from the time he was fifteen, according to his obituary (Maurer and Vaufrey 1929: 403). The heady intellectual atmosphere Boban provided in his museum-like business setting clearly influenced his visitors. Capitan became a well-known and respected anthropologist and archeologist, who excavated and restored parts of a first-century AD Roman arena in Paris. He taught at the École d'anthropologie, and several times requested Boban's opinion about artifacts, saying that his input was indispensable (BNF DMO n.a.f. 21476: item 456). Capitan even appears to have followed in Boban's footsteps as a collector. The Smithsonian's National Museum of the American Indian houses a pre-Columbian collection that was purchased from an auction of Capitan's possessions after his death in 1930. It comprises a number of Aztec artifacts, including a large coiled feathered serpent carved in stone. Some of these pieces may have come from Boban's shop, further evidence of the ripple effect of the antiquarian's curiosity about and enthusiasm for the cultures of ancient Mexico.

Notes

1. Et malgré moi se me trouvai être l'expert [en] les centres de réunion des antiquités américaines, pluseurs personnes habitants le Mexique durant mon absente de Mexico, m'adressant à Paris pluseurs séries acheter pour moi.

2. Christiane Demeulenaere-Douyère of the Archives Nationales of Paris brought to our attention the information about the relationship between de Metz and Marie Boban.

3. Nous avons l'honneur d'annoncer à messieurs les Professeurs, Directeurs de musées et de collèges que, par suite de recherches, achats et échanges faits depuis plusieurs années avec des musées ou des amateurs, nous sommes arrivés à réunir une quantité considérable d'objets préhistoriques, ethnographiques et anthropologiques. Pour faciliter la démonstration dans les cours et les conférences, nous avons pensé qu'il serait utile de faire exécuter une série de moulages sur les pièces typiques, ce qui nous permet d'en livrer des fac-similés à des prix modérés. Les objets portent des étiquettes rappelant la classification donnée par M. le professeur Gabriel de Mortillet.

4. Représentation en cristal de roche d'un crâne humain grandeur naturelle, chef-d'oeuvre de l'art du Lapidaire. 3,500 fr.

5. Récemment, nous venons d'adjoindre à notre Comptoir un bureau spécial de *librairie*, où nous recevons en commission, en dépôt, toutes les publications, livres, brochures, cartes, plans, dessins, etc., ayant rapport aux sciences prèhistoriques, archéologiques, ethnographiques et anthropologiques.

OF FAKES AND FAKERS

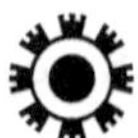

Eugène Boban's passion for educating others about the significance of the broad range of objects he amassed and sold was especially evident with pre-Columbian artifacts, his particular area of expertise. As the years passed, this passion to educate became increasingly entangled with a desire to analyze and unmask fake artifacts. However, the more he writes about fakes, the harder it becomes to distinguish between revelations made as a public service from other, more self-serving interests, such as spiting colleagues, covering his own sale of fakes, or bragging about how cleverly he has fooled the "experts."

Boban began to write about fakes in the mid-1870s, drawing upon the authority conferred by his standing as a long-term collector and dealer. In 1876 Caix de Saint-Aymour, publisher of the journal *Le Musée Archéologique*, wrote to Boban to say that he was copyediting an article of Boban's on *contrefaçons* (fakes), which would be included in the next issue. Unfortunately, the journal folded after the first year, and that particular article evidently did not appear (BNF DMO n.a.f. 21476: item 438). There are numerous drafts and versions of the article in Boban's papers, however, along with other material documenting his evolving ideas about Mexico's long-standing industry of manufacturing fake pre-Columbian artifacts. One of several drafts of an article entitled "Fake Mexican pre-Columbian Antiquities made in Tlatelolco, a Mexico City suburb" is in the collection of the Hispanic Society of America (HSA: B2242, Box III).[1] It may be that a portion of it dates to the 1876 version penned for *Le Musée Archéologique*, although this iteration contains much later information as well.

Boban included some of this material in his 1878 sales catalog to inform his clients about fakes, even giving pointers on how to recognize them and, by implication, guaranteeing the authenticity of the artifacts in his own collection that he wanted to sell. As noted earlier, he also sold examples of modern fake antiquities in his shop at modest prices.

In these instances, Boban wrote with broad-based knowledge and considerable detail about the differences between actual pre-Columbian artifacts and what he considered to be obviously contemporary Mexican pottery. "The black color with brown or red varnish found on these imitations, with snakes or lizards on the handles, are assuredly modern. Ancient Mexican pottery is well fired, burnished with much patience, and above all very thin. If it has ornaments at all, they are painted with great finesse, such as those shown in # 156, 818, 1030 etc. in our catalog." Further underlining the different characteristics of the old and new ceramics, Boban explained that, "The ancient Mexican pottery offers great resistance [it is very durable] in contrast to the imitation pottery, which is very thick, friable, and can easily be broken with handling" (HSA: B2240, Box I).[2]

Continuing this discussion, he shares his own personal knowledge of how and where these newer objects were produced:

> I saw these imitations being made in Santiago [Tlatelolco] and Los Angeles, that is to say in the suburbs of Mexico [City]. The kiln of these potters is composed of a simple low wall, one meter 50 cm high by 1 meter in diameter; it is nothing more than an open-air furnace built to contain the flame and is constructed of unfired bricks (adobe). The combustible [material] is composed of dry herbs, hay or old *petates* [straw mats], and also garbage coming from the city, never wood. The tools of these potters are most rudimentary and primitive, one or two bits of bone for chisels, [and] little reed tubes of differing diameters, which are used to imprint circles and semicircles which cover the bodies of snakes, lizards and ornaments. (HSA: B2240, Box I)[3]

He adds that he is surprised at the lack of ingenuity of the antiquities fakers. Guided by his own experience, he feels that finding actual ancient objects is relatively easy. "Santiago Tlatelolco" Boban notes, where the last remnants of the Tenochtitlan marketplace lay, was in fact "littered with arrow points, idols, fragments, etc. Santiago [Tlatelolco] is an excellent mine for the antiquities hunters, which is still far from being exhausted. It is clear to me that a well-directed dig would produce quite a lot, but these people are so poor that as soon as they find some object, even of the slightest value, they run to sell it in the city *instead of making a mold of it and making copies* [emphasis added]. But No"(HSA: B2240, Box I).[4]

Boban's aside about how foolish the Indians are who find authentic pieces and then sell them immediately without first making a mold so that they can sell copies reflects his own business practices. Whenever he acquired a particularly important piece, he would have molds made. As early as 1875 he was exhibiting casts of his collection in Nancy. In his 1878 and 1881 sales catalogs, he lists numerous casts of the Lartet and Christy material, along with copies of a variety of prehistoric European artifacts. He also includes casts of several important sculptures from Mexico that are no longer in his own collection, having gone to the Trocadéro as part of the Pinart Collection. Thus, with more money to invest, he turns some of his artifacts into gifts that keep on giving. His remark about the Indians of Tlatelolco, of course, is that it would be better for them to sell casts of actual pre-Columbian artifacts than to fabricate the dreadful black-ware fakes that they tried to palm off, sometimes successfully, as authentic ancient pieces.

He next takes issue with what he considers the preposterous sales techniques used by those who manufacture and sell fake pre-Columbian artifacts.

> Some people creating this type of pottery are in the habit of explaining that these vessels [are obviously authentic] because they are far beyond their own capabilities to make. [But in fact] they do make this grotesque type of vessel, which they are certain to sell to novice archeologists, to whom they swear to their great god that they themselves unearthed these atrocious caricatures. They will immediately offer to bring the person to the place where they found the pottery, where they tell them they will discover vases, treasures, and the golden chariot of Moctezuma. This chariot is, in reality, very problematic, since horses did not appear in Mexico until after the conquest; and as to the pottery pieces, one is sure to find them in the hole where they had been placed the night before, still smelling of burnt hay. (HSA: B2240, Box I)[5]

The "novice archeologist" Boban writes about may have been himself early in his career, since there is clearly a piece of the infamous Tlatelolco blackware sitting at his feet in the photograph of his collection taken prior to the 1867 exhibition, although it might have been one of his first examples of a classic Mexican fake.

In his descriptions of the fakery industry Boban writes as an insider who is almost acting as an informant for his readers. He begins by sharing his knowledge about who is actually manufacturing the fake pre-Columbian artifacts. "In the Santiago [Tlatelolco] prison more than one prisoner has taken up the fabrication of idols in stone, in marble, and above all in alabaster. I saw several attempts at faking in obsidian, but these had neither the polish nor finesse of ancient examples." Then he starts to name names. "I also saw several collections in which were found objects in copper and in bronze; these last objects are the work of a foreign jeweler named Pe." This was most likely Philippe Praget, a personal acquaintance of Boban's who was attached to the French legation (HSA: B2240, Box I).[6]

He also shares some insights about the market forces affecting the production of fake stone sculptures. "There are additionally several sculptors and stone cutters who, during work stoppages live by this sort of industry [creating 'ancient' artifacts], which has been going on for a long time. Perhaps the most prosperous [of these work stoppages] occurred during the American invasion in 1847 under the orders of General Scott. When the Americans traveled the route back to their country, hoping to enrich the museums of the United States, they paid very well for found [archeological] objects. The digs did not produce enough, so the counterfeiters joined the party." As Boban points out, foreign interventions had long-term repercussions on the collection and understanding of pre-Columbian art. Continuing with this thought, he adds, "It was the same during the French expedition [intervention]—of such unhappy memory for both countries. Many tourists and personnel attached to the French, Belgian, and Austrian corps brought back to Europe many of these horrors, which are probably in magnificent vitrines and must have given the European savants a sad idea of the art of the ancient Mexicans" (HSA: B2240, Box I).[7]

In his 1881 sales catalog, entitled *Catalogue d'ouvrages scientifiques* (Catalog of scientific works), Boban actually presents fakes for sale, along with an adamant condemnation of their conception and artistry. "These objects are not casts, nor copies of the ancient monuments of the country, they are pure fantasy; it is a type of bizarre caricature, whose inspiration escapes us, but the principal reason for which is to fool the public." He continues a review of his long-term interest in fakes, saying, "It is with the intention of unmasking them, to point them out to amateurs and above all to museum directors, that we exhibited a series at the 1878 Exposition Universelle in the Anthropology section" (Boban 1881: 47–8).[8]

Much of what Boban wrote was later quoted and attributed to him by Paul Eudel, a distinguished Parisian chronicler of the Hotel Drouot auction house, in a chapter on Mexican pre-Columbian fake pottery in his book *Le Truquage* (Fakery). Calling Boban "an honest merchant," Eudel noted that, "having long pointed out these fake antiques, seeing that despite his advice they continued to please, he then proceeded to list them [in his sales catalogs] at their current price: Counterfeit Mexican idols, 5 to 25 francs. It's all spelled out!" Paul Eudel also takes note of the merchant's efforts to inform an even wider audience. "In 1878, at the Exposition Universelle, in the Anthropology section, one could contemplate and study a variety of these [fake] pieces intended to put admirers and museum directors en garde" (Eudel 1887: 54).[9]

Aside from the objects that Boban identified as fakes in his own displays, two pieces (from his previous collection) that he had sold to Alphonse Pinart were fake, but not exhibited as such at the 1878 Exposition Universelle. Pinart, temporarily back from his travels, was on hand to serve as a commissioner for the exposition. He exhibited the artifacts he had purchased from Boban as his own, along with other pieces he had himself collected, in the "Missions Scientifiques" section in the Palace of Industry. The 1878 *Notice sur le Muséum ethnographique des missions scientifiques* takes particular note of two pieces in the Pinart Collection. "An engraved and polished obsidian plaque, discovered at the site of the great temple of Mexico, recording its dedication, [and] a human skull in rock crystal" (Missions Scientifiques 1878: 34).[10]

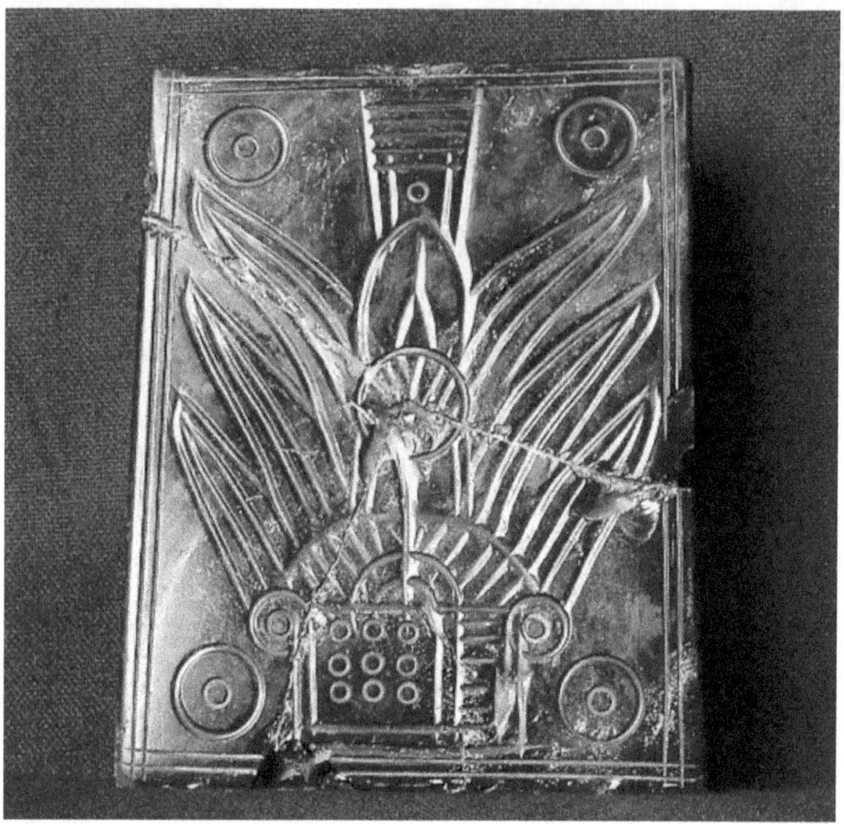

Figure 11.1 Obsidian artifact in Musée du quai Branly collections (courtesy of Musée du quai Branly, Paris, 71.1878.1.498).

There is no doubt that Pinart purchased the obsidian plaque from Eugène Boban. It is the third item in the original catalog and is quite prominent in photographs of the antiquarian's collection. By contrast, the skull does not appear on the list, making it likely that it was added to the collection after Boban returned to Paris in 1869.

The authenticity of both the obsidian plaque and the Aztec crystal skull has been widely challenged. They are now considered to be nineteenth-century fakes, despite the fact that each was the subject of an article published by Ernest Théodore Hamy, then a recognized authority on pre-Columbian artifacts (1883; 1897). Neither Pinart nor Hamy was aware that these objects were not pre-Columbian, but Boban, the expert on fakes who had collected and sold them, clearly was.

When Pinart exhibited it in 1878, the obsidian plaque was said to have been the foundation stone of the Templo Mayor in Mexico City. However, more

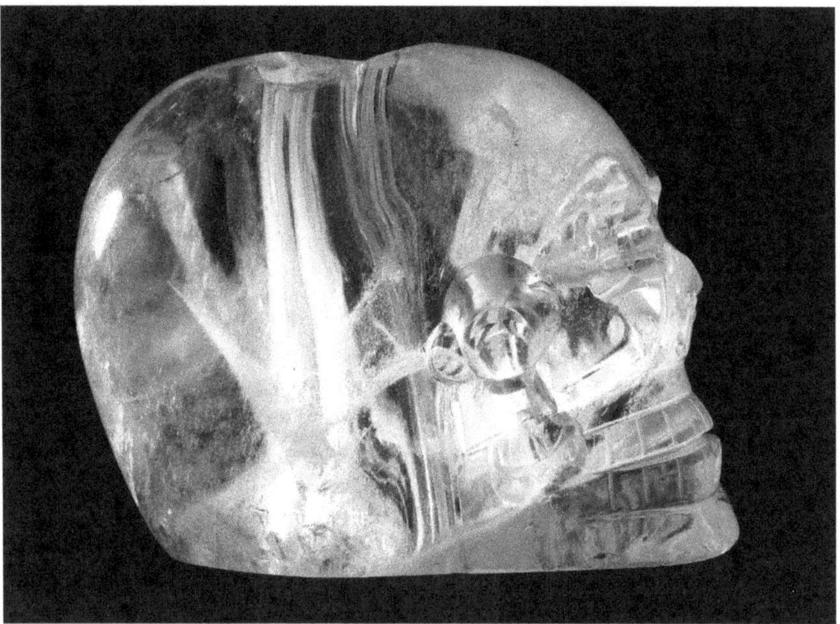

Figure 11.2 Rock crystal skull in the Musée du quai Branly collections (courtesy of Musée du quai Branly, Paris, 71.1878.1.57).

than a decade earlier Boban had written in his catalog that it was "certainly a commemorative stone of the date of a great historic event, which took place in the year 4 Acatl . . . corresponding to the year 1327" (MQB #71.1878.1.495; Reichlen 1962: 5).[11] This description makes no claim that the plaque was related to the construction of the Templo Mayor, although it coyly suggests it, since the year Boban sites is widely accepted as the one in which the first phase of the temple was dedicated. The Musée du quai Branly's online catalog for this piece notes that the "inscription signifies the date 4 acatl which corresponds with the years 1431, 1483 or 1535 of our era" (MQB cat. 71.1878.1.498) and that 1483 is the date of the construction of the fifth stage of the pyramid. These are fifty-two-year cycles, so Boban's 1327 date can also be read from the 4 Acatl glyph.

One fact discrediting this piece is that in his catalog, Boban writes that he acquired the obsidian bas-relief from somewhere in the vicinity of San Juan Teotihuacan, not in Mexico City, where the Templo Mayor was located. Presumably Boban told Pinart that there was a direct link between the plaque and the temple when he sold him the collection many years later.

Hamy's article on the piece, published in 1883, indicates that it was dug up some time around 1865 in the environs of Mexico City and *purchased* by a French collector, Eugène Boban (Hamy 1883: 194).[12] Of the two provenances offered— Hamy's, that it came from near Mexico City, or Boban's that it came from the vicinity of Teotihuacan—Boban's is likelier to be accurate, with the proviso that it was purchased, not excavated. In pre-Columbian times Teotihuacan controlled the production and exchange of obsidian, which accounted for much of the city's wealth and power; however, some of the best obsidian carvers of the nineteenth century, who were responsible for some of the most elaborate fakes in the medium, lived and worked around San Juan Teotihuacan, as they do to this day.

In 2009 the object was examined. It measures 8.3 in. (21.2 cm) in height by 6.4 in. (16.4 cm) in width and is about 2 in. (5 cm) thick. The study revealed the presence of wooden fragments on two of the sides, and the right-hand edge of the obsidian plaque had been cut using a tool different from that used on the other three sides. Both findings suggest that it may have started life as one of the rectangular obsidian mirrors that Wilson Wilberforce Blake described in his 1884 catalog of the Museo Nacional collection. The term *obsidian mirror* describes a rectangular, square, or round piece of obsidian between an inch or two thick, which has a high polish on one side. In the catalog, Blake notes, "the Spanish priests used [these framed obsidian mirrors] immediately after the conquest at the altars of the churches" (Blake 1884: 105). Although many nineteenth- and twentieth-century scholars and collectors believed these objects were pre-Columbian, it is likelier that many are colonial pieces.

A study of two small paintings by Bartolomé Estéban Murillo, the Spanish Baroque painter who lived between 1617 and 1682, recently conducted in the Louvre revealed that the works were painted on obsidian from Mexico, not black marble, as was previously believed. The paintings are almost identical in size and shape to several "pre-Columbian mirrors," whose measurements range from 9.5 to 13.8 in. (24 to 35 cm) in height and 8.7 to 11.8 in. (22 to 30 cm) in width (Calligaro et al. 2005: 576). Boban's obsidian plaque is just about half the size of a standard rectangular obsidian mirror as well as the two painted by Murillo. If the plaque had been carved on the polished side of half of one of these obsidian mirrors, that would account for its fourth, anomalous edge.

Unfortunately, when Boban's obsidian plaque was reexamined in 2013, the wooden remnants were no longer in evidence, having been removed by conservators who may have thought they were part of a previous exhibition mount. It seems quite plausible, however, that the wood pieces were the last vestiges of what had been a colonial frame. A square obsidian mirror in a gilded wood frame exhibited in Dumbarton Oaks has a wooden backing that is carved with Franciscan symbols and is clearly a colonial artifact. Susan Toby Evans, the editor of the most recent catalog of the Dumbarton Oaks pre-Columbian collection, describes this specimen as being in all probability a portable table altar. One reason she gives for that conclusion is that the sixteenth-century priest Juan de Torquemada commented that the "shiny black stone (obsidian) made excellent *aras* and mirrors" (Evans 2010: 284n53). *Aras* were portable polished stones that were placed on altars. "Very soon in Mexico as in Europe, altars were made of stone, with a top slab called the *mensa* (table). On or in the *mensa* was set a small, hard, rectangular stone slab, about 12 by 14 inches: an *ara* which symbolically represented Christ and was the holiest part of the altar. The chalice and some other equipment would be set on it during the Mass" (McAndrew 1965: 353). Evans goes on to say that out of twenty-one "obsidian mirrors" in museum collections that she surveyed, similar to the one at Dumbarton Oaks, "only one appears to be possibly Pre-Columbian, with a dated inscription engraved on its surface" (Evans 2010: 77). She is referring here to the Boban obsidian plaque, which, as has been noted, is certainly not pre-Columbian.

Although Boban described this object as one of his premier pieces, it is undoubtedly the work of a nineteenth-century obsidian carver, who incised a rather uncharacteristic version of the calendrical date of four (or is it six, or nine?) reed or acatl on the polished face of what had formerly been part of an obsidian *ara*. He must have known that it was a fake, since his story and description of the artifact changed over time. Initially, in his 1867 catalog he stated that he had acquired it in San Juan Teotihuacan, an archeological site that had been abandoned six hundred years before the purported date on the plaque. Later he must have told both Alphonse Pinart, who exhibited it as Aztec relating to the foundation of the Templo Mayor, and Ernest Hamy, who published the same information, that he had acquired it in or near Mexico City.

The second Pinart object highlighted in the 1878 *Notice sur le Muséum ethnographique des missions scientifiques* is a rock crystal skull. It is one of at least four, and perhaps more, that Eugène Boban would eventually sell, and it was another highly collectable piece that the antiquarian presented as pre-Columbian, when he knew full well that it was not.

This so-called Aztec crystal skull does not appear in the original 1867 Boban catalog and was presumably added after Boban's return to Paris in 1869. This accords with what Boban wrote about the history of the collection, then in the Trocadéro. "In 1875 this collection [was] much enlarged by objects we had received from our shop in Mexico" (HSA: B2244, Box V).

This Aztec crystal skull is yet another modern artifact, which has been carved and polished employing nineteenth-century lapidary equipment. A study in 2008 at the Centre de recherché et de restauration des musées de France used Elastic Recoil Detection Analysis to measure the water vapor diffused through the quartz. The results made it possible for Thomas Calligaro, the same scientist who had studied the Murillo obsidian paintings, and Yvan Coquinot to estimate that the skull had been created sometime between the late 1840s and the late 1860s (2009: 871–8). Those dates encompass the entire span of Boban's initial stay in Mexico.

A small crystal skull, measuring 1.2 in. (3 cm) high, is listed in the 1867 catalog as an Aztec artifact, and it appears in a drawing done by Col. Doutrelaine's draftsman, Jean Amatus Klein, along with several earspools and polished stone ornaments. Unfortunately, this small skull was damaged before its tool marks and other features could be thoroughly studied, but the illustration indicates that it was very similar to other small skulls that have been studied and found to be nineteenth-century creations. Another of Klein's drawings depicts various other quartz crystal objects, including a crescent moon with a human face. This artifact cannot possibly be pre-Columbian since the man-in-the-moon image is a European concept. Aztecs imagined and depicted rabbits on the moon. Aside from this crystal moon figure, which is still in the Musée du quai Branly collection, four crystal hands appear in the drawing. These are actually typical examples of the *mano fica*—a fist with the thumb placed under the index and middle finger. This amulet, which had its origins in medieval Italy, was used to ward off the evil eye, especially from children. These are not pre-Columbian artifacts either, although presented as such above the caption "Antiquités aztéques." Thus, all of the objects depicted on the page, with the exception of the three small lip plugs drawn toward the bottom, are European in concept, and probably in manufacture.

It seems clear that while Boban acquired artifacts from his numerous archeological digs, he also purchased objects from a variety of artisans, as well as other sources. The smaller Aztec crystal skulls, and perhaps even the larger one in the Pinart Collection, may have come from the sales held by the Mexican government following the destruction of churches and monasteries in Mexico City. If that were the case, Boban would have known that these crystal pieces were colonial, if not even more modern. Regardless of how he acquired them, these objects were always attractive to collectors, particularly those who thought, or had been told, that they were ancient. Apparently, though, not everyone thought they were Aztec or Toltec.

A contemporary account of the 1878 Exposition Universelle, printed in the *Revue scientifique*, describes the remarkable collections of M. Pinart, in which the Mexican objects abounded. It continues, "One can also see a representation of a human skull in rock crystal attributed to Mexican [pre-Columbian] artistry. This piece comes from the Boban collection acquired by M. Pinart. However, its authenticity seems questionable" (Revue Scientifique 1878: 734).[13]

As with so many details surrounding Boban's personal and professional life, this story remains half told, and one is left to wonder just who determined that the skull's authenticity was in doubt. The reviewer may have had some insider information provided by Boban himself. Despite the skepticism of this original review, the piece eventually became an accepted, highly prized pre-Columbian artifact. It took more than a century to confirm that this early suspicion was justified: the sculpture was a nineteenth-century creation—a fact that Boban alluded to in the *New York Tribune* interview in 1900.

Despite the reservations voiced by some about a few pieces that had passed through his hands, friends and colleagues frequently consulted Boban through the

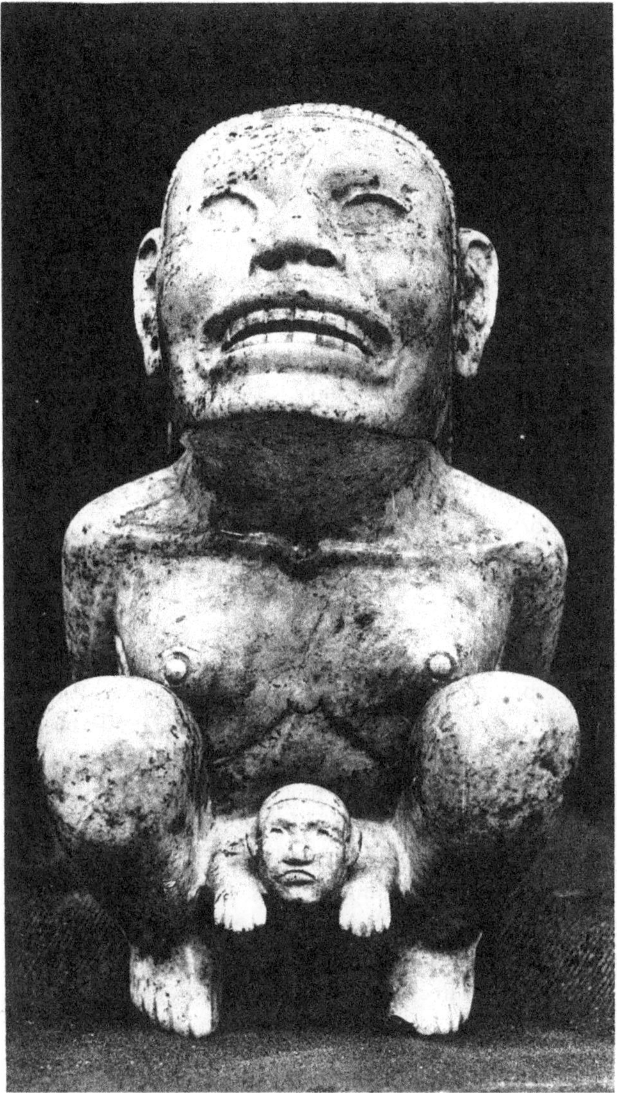

Figure 11.3 Carved stone figure about which Augustin Damour consulted Boban in 1883. Ernest T. Hamy published the piece in the *Journal de la société des américanistes* in 1907, identifying it as Ixcuina (Smithsonian Libraries).

years as an expert on pre-Columbian artifacts and as one of the world's leading authorities on fakes. One of them was the mineralogist Augustin Damour, who visited Boban's shop in an excited state one day in the early 1880s, clutching a carved figure of a squatting woman in the act of giving birth. He was thinking of buying the piece and wanted the antiquarian's opinion of the sculpture.

On a single page written front and back and dated Monday, 28 May 1883, now in the collections of the Hispanic Society of America, Boban recorded his reactions to the object, which he thought was "most likely a Mexican deity." He comments on the fact that it was a rare example of a pre-Columbian carving in the round and that he thinks the piece was earlier than Aztec, but not Maya, at least at first glance. Having only about ten minutes to give his reactions to the work—Damour had to return to a M. Ivan's place of business to complete the purchase—Boban offers his opinion that it might be Toltec. He guesses that it came from the Mexican Gulf Coast, and thinks it was much more valuable than the price asked (HSA: B2245, Box XIII).[14] In fact, he believes it is one of the most original sculptures he has ever seen. "After the Quetzalcoatl carving in red porphyry, which we sold to M. Pinart," he writes, "this is evidently the most curious and most interesting piece of lapidary art" (HSA: B2243, Box XIII).[15] Tellingly, Boban had thought that the Quetzalcoatl carving also was Toltec. After Boban gave his opinion, later recorded in his notes, Damour rushed back and purchased the statue.

Many others besides Damour and Boban have been quite taken with this piece, which is now in the collections of Dumbarton Oaks in Washington, DC. Unfortunately, despite the enthusiasm that it has generated through the years by its unusual three-dimensional carving, exotic material, and realistic theme, recent studies have shown that it, too, is of modern origin (Walsh 2008a: 7–43).

There is really no reason to expect that Boban would have determined that this carving of a female figure giving birth was not authentic after his cursory examination of it, even though he clearly knew a great deal about pre-Columbian artifacts, and pre-Columbian fakes. There is every reason to wonder, however, where he drew the line between the objects he exhibited as fakes and the artifacts he sold as legitimate that he knew full well were fakes, as shown by his records, writings, and direct statements.

Notes

1. Contrefaçons d'antiquités mexicaines fabriquées à Tlatelolco, faubourg de la ville de Mexico.

2. De couleur noire et varnies en brun ou en rouge, ces imitations ont pour ornements ou pour anses des serpents ou des lézards et elles sont assurément modernes. . . . La poterie ancienne est bien cuite, brunie avec beaucoup de patience et surtout très mince; lorsqu'elle porte des ornements, ceux-ci sont peints avec une grande finesse, ainsi que montrent les nos. 456, 818, 1030, etc. de notre catalogue. La poterie ancienne offre une grande résistance; au contraire la poterie imitée est très

épaisse, friable; on peut facilement la briser avec les doigts; la pâte est noire intérieurement, la cuisson n'a été que superficielle.

3. J'ai vu fabriquer ces imitations de poteries anciennes à Santiago et à Los Angeles, c'est-à-dire dans les faubourgs de Mexico. Le four de ces potiers est formé par un simple petit mur de 1 m.50 de haut sur 1 m. de diamètre; ce n'est qu'un fourreau à ciel ouvert destiné à encaisser la flamme et construit en briques crues (Adobes). Le combustible est composé d'herbes sèches, de paille, de vieux paillassons ou d'ordures provenant de la ville, jamais de bois. Les outils de ces potiers sont aussi des plus rudimentaires ou primitifs; un ou deux bouts d'os pour èbauchoirs, [et] des petits tubes de roseau de diamètres différents pour imprimer les cercles et les demi-cercles qui décorent le corps des serpents, des lézards ou autres ornements.

4. Santiago Tlatelolco . . . est jonché d'armes, d'idoles brísées, etc.; Santiago a été pour les chercheurs d'antiquités une mine excellente qui est encore loin d'être épuisée; il est certain pour moi que des fouilles bien dirigées produiraient beaucoup; mais ces pauvres gens sont si malheureux que des qu'ils ont trouvé quelque objet, même de la plus mince valeur, ils courent le vendre à la ville au lieu de le mouler et de le copier. Mais non!

5. Quelques-uns ont crée ce genre de poterie; ils en ont pris l'habitude; ils en donnent pour raison que les vases trouvés sont toujours fort simples et que pour conséquent ceux qu'ils pourraient faire . . . ils se sont donc bornés à ce genre de vases grotesques qu'ils sont certains de vendre à des archéologues novices auxquels ils jurent leur grand dieu d'avoir deterré ces affreuses caricatures et offrent immédiatement de les conduire en un lieu ou se trouvent des vases, des trésors et le char en or de Mocthecuzuma; ce char est, en réalité, fort problématique, car les chevaux n'ont paru au Mexique que depuis la conquête; quant aux poteries, on est sûr de les trouver dans les trous où elles ont été enfouies la veille, sentant encore la paille brûlée.

6. A la prison (carcel) de Santiago, plus d'un prisonnier se livre à la fabrication d'Idoles en marbre, en pierre et surtout en albâtre. J'ai vu plusieurs essais d'imitation en obsidienne, mais ces essais n'avaient ni le poli, ni le fini des modèles anciens. J'ai vu aussi plusieurs collections où se trouvaient quelques objets en cuivre et en bronze; ces derniers objets étaient l'oeuvre d'un bijoutier d'origine étrangère, nommé Pe . . .

7. Il y a, en outre, quelques sculpteurs et tailleurs de pierre qui, pendant ce chômage se livrent à ce genre d'industrie, lequel date d'assez loin. Mais son époque la plus prospère a été celle de l'invasion américaine en 1847 sous les ordres du Gen. Scott. Quand les Américains reprirent la route de leur pays, ils voulurent enrichir les musées des Etats-Unis et payerent fort bien les objets trouvés; les fouilles ne produisant point assez, les contrefacteurs se mirent de la partie. Il en fut de même lors de l'expédition française de si funeste mémoire pour les deux pays; beaucoup de touristes et de personnes attachées aux corps français, belge ou autrichien rapportirent alors en Europe pas mal de ces horreurs qui s'etaient probablement dans de magnfiques vitrines et doivent donner aux Savants Européens une triste idée de l'art chez les anciens mexicains.

8. Ces objets ne sont ni moulés, ni copiés sur des monuments anciens du pays (c'est de pure fantaisie), c'est un genre de caricatures bizarres dont l'inspiration nous échappe, mais dont le but principal est de tromper le public. . . . C'est dans l'intention de les démasquer, de les signaler aux amateurs et surtout aux directeurs des Musées, que nous en avons exposé une série à l'Exposition universelle de 1878, section d'anthropologie.

9. En 1878, à l'Exposition universelle, dans la section d'anthropologie, on pouvait contempler et étudier toute une série de ces pièces destinée à mettre en garde les amateurs et les directeurs de musées.

10. Une plaque d'obsidienne polie et gravée, découverte sur l'emplacement du grand temple de Mexico, et en rappelant la dédicace, [et] un crâne humain en cristal de roche, ...

11. C'est certainement une pierre commémorative de la date d'un grand évènement historique qui dut avoir lieu l'an 4 d'Acatl. Comme époque cette pierre correspond à la date 1327 de notre ère.

12. Exhumée aux abords de Mexico vers 1865 et achetée par un collectionneur français, M. Eugène Boban.

13. On voit aussi une représentation de crâne humain en cristal de roche attribué à l'art mexicain; cette pièce provient de la collection Boban acquise par M. Pinart. Mais l'authenticité en paraît douteuse.

14. Une divinité Mexicain bien probablement m'a été présenter par M. Damour . . . elle ma semble etre Tolteque et doit provenir des bords du golfe Mexicain entre Tampico et Vera Cruz.

15. Après la pièce le Quetzalcohuatl, en porphyre rouge que nous avons cédé à M. Pinart, c'est évident la pièce la plus curieux [et] la plus intéressant comme travail de part lapidaire.

12

From Student to Teacher, Dealer to Curator

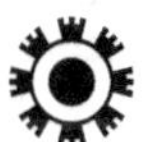

In a surprising turn of events, in early 1885 Eugène Boban sent out a printed announcement to his clientele. It was dated 15 February and headed with the address of his shop at 85, boulevard St. Michel where he had been for three years. The flyer stated, "I have the honor to announce that due to a voyage to America (my address in Mexico: Eugène Boban, antiquaire, Mexico), I am transferring my prehistoric archeological comptoir to 7, rue Daguerre, in Montrouge (near the Lion de Belfort). The persons who will take my place during my absence are my relatives, the Mesdames Duvergé." The notice concludes with the statement, referring to his aunts, "I hope you will maintain the same confidence in them that you have always shown to me" (HSA: B2240, Box 1, folder II).[1]

The Mesdames Duvergé were, of course, his father's two half-sisters—Fanny and Henriette—the former owners of the corset and shirt business in Angers. For a number of years, they had assisted Boban from time to time, and would run their nephew's antique business for him while he was away. Henriette lived at the shop's new location on rue Daguerre, probably sharing the premises with Fanny, her older, widowed sister. The new comptoir was about a mile and a half from Boban's shop on the boulevard St. Michel.

An advertisement heralding his return to Mexico had previously appeared in Hamy's *Revue d'ethnographie* in late 1884. The ad announced the sale of curiosities relating to the prehistoric, ethnographic and anthropological sciences, and antiquities, and it would take place at the Paris auction house Hotel Drouot on Wednesday, 24 December (Hamy 1884b: 557). According to the notice, the reason for the sale was the antiquarian's imminent departure.

In a variety of unpublished manuscripts and notes in the Hispanic Society, Boban composed what he may have intended as an autobiography, or at least a kind of history of his professional career. After sixteen years in Paris buying, trading, and selling his artifacts, he wrote of his desire to return to Mexico, where the "climate is the best in the world."[2] This nostalgic voyage may have been motivated partially by the fact that he was then fifty and had at some point married his second wife, who had been ill, apparently for several years. A list of consultations by Dr. Camille Raspail with Madame Boban includes seven visits in 1879, thirteen in 1880, five in 1881 and three in 1882 (BNF DMO n.a.f. 21479: item 16). As in the case of his first wife from Mexico, this woman is known only indirectly—through friends' greetings to "Madame Boban," a passenger list entry, and this medical bill.

Raspail, a respected physician, had been commander-in-chief of the southern forts of Paris in 1870 and 1871, during the Siege and the Commune. In 1885 he became a member of parliament, representing the far-left. The fact that he was the family physician may give us another clue to Boban's political leanings. His association with Raspail, his friendship with François Fénélon, who wrote about the "tyrants" ruling France, and his own service to the Republic in the fire brigade prior to the end of the Paris Commune all suggests that the antiquarian was something of a radical.

Boban later recorded his own reasons for returning to Mexico after so many years. "The long cold winters in France made us nostalgic for Mexico, and we entertained the idea of returning to the land of the hummingbirds," he recalled (HSA: B2244, Box V—Preface).[3] Curiously, he writes this as though he and his current wife had both lived in Mexico and that they were pining to return, when, in fact, his first wife had died there. This woman, his second wife, as far as can be determined, had not yet visited the country.

Boban had high aspirations for this second chance at a life in the Mexican capital. His ambition was to establish an intellectual center in Mexico City—an institution that would house a museum, a library, a conference room and, eventually, a school of archeology. It would also function as a shop, where he would continue to buy, trade, and sell art and artifacts. "We prepared ourselves over a long period. For this purpose, we made our choice from the collection of all the genres that we possessed in Paris" (HSA: B2244, Box V—Preface).[4]

He packed heavy on his return trip to Mexico, taking with him his extensive anthropological and archeological collection, including numerous first editions from Brasseur de Bourbourg's collection, along with colonial manuscripts he had purchased during the 1850s and 1860s, when he was first in the country. He crated up a selection of antiquities and ethnographic items from around the world—from Europe to Egypt and the South Seas. He took most, though not all, of his Mexican pre-Columbian collection. As he later wrote in autobiographical notes and in his letters to Parisian colleagues, he felt he was bringing back to Mexico not only his expertise as a seasoned archeologist, but also the knowledge that he had acquired in study and conversation with some of Europe's best-known scientists, anthropologists, and historians (HSA: B2244, Box V).

Recalling the momentous move some years later, he wrote, "Once our crates arrived, we rented a large locale for the time being; then after further reflection, we came to appreciate it. It was situated at the 10th street of la Violeta in the Guerrero neighborhood, a new section of the city, which was far removed from the center, it must be said" (HSA B2244, Box V- Preface).[5] Displaying his usual frugality, he found an area of Mexico City that was still affordable. The new section of town was north and west of the Alameda Park, and some distance from Boban's old shop and neighborhood.

All in all, it appears that he was pleased to be back at first and was welcomed with open arms. "We decided to return to Mexico around the first days of the year 1885, where we were very well received when we arrived. After a sixteen-year absence, naturally many of my friends could not be found. The young ones were men and the old ones were dead. Notwithstanding this, we found once again many of our friends and acquaintances" (HSA: B2244, Box V—Preface).[6]

Boban's old friend Juan Francisco Fénélon was still a practicing surgeon residing at Tacuba No. 7, a few blocks from his former residence on Independencia, according to *The Merchants' and Tourists' Guide to Mexico*. Jules Labadie, the pharmacist and collector of pre-Columbian artifacts, still had his establishment around the corner from Boban's old shop (Zaremba 1888: 34). Another pharmacist doing business then was Francisco Kaska, an Austrian who had been part of Emperor Maximilian's cabinet and had remained in Mexico. In his spare time, he worked as an advisor to the Museo Nacional. Boban carried a letter of introduction to him from Teobert Maler, who had first come to Mexico as a soldier and had later been associated with the Commission Scientifique du Mexique. Maler would become a well-known photographer of pre-Columbian sites in Mexico (BNF DMO n.a.f. 21478: item 243). Numerous other French expatriates, either old friends or new acquaintances of Boban's, had thriving businesses in his old neighborhood.

Not only was the weather pleasant, the political climate was good for the French community. Despite Napoleon III's attempt at a second conquest of Mexico, the present government under Porfirio Díaz, one of the generals who had first stopped the invading army at the Battle of Puebla, was decidedly favorable to all things French.

Once the French had been defeated, Díaz campaigned against Benito Juárez in 1870 on a platform of no reelection but lost at the polls. When President Juárez died, in 1872, his vice president, Sebastián Lerdo, took over the presidency. Increasing unrest throughout the country, aided and abetted by Díaz and his military cronies, forced Lerdo into exile in 1876, and Díaz became president a year later. Although one of his first actions was to amend the constitution to prevent presidential reelections, he would go on to rule Mexico for more than three decades, until his government was ousted in the revolution of 1910.

Mexico progressed economically under Díaz, particularly from the standpoint of the upper classes and foreign investors. This was due in part to the input from the president's advisors, known as *los Científicos*. A group of technocrats, they embraced the positivist notion that social and economic progress was most effectively achieved through the collection, study, and practical application of quantifiable data. José Yves Limantour, a French-Mexican, whose father had immigrated in 1836, was a leading thinker in this faction (Kandell 1988: 353–4).

Boban's establishment on 10a Calle de Violeta no. 6 in the Guerrero *colonia* was called the *Museo Científico*, a name clearly intended not only to compliment the ruling elites, but also to differentiate his establishment from those of his competitors. Where Boban had enjoyed more or less a monopoly in the sale of antiquities during his first stay in Mexico, by the mid-1880s numerous shops were selling pre-Columbian artifacts. Some shops offered artifacts along with other merchandise. For instance, a bookstore owned by an American named Hill advertised in Mexico's English-language newspaper, *The Two Republics*, that it offered Mexican curiosities and antiquities (Two Republics, 18 November 1885). However, none of these commercial ventures called themselves a museum.

Violeta Street, a few blocks north of the Alameda Park, was in a relatively new suburb of Mexico City. The area would not have been familiar to Boban, since it had been virtually empty twenty years earlier. However, in his description he wrote that it was well served by a series of new streetcar lines plying the city.

Boban had brought some fifty crates of collections and books for his museum, which he immediately began constructing. Considering that the collection itself was enormous and his exhibits were elaborate, it took many months before the establishment was ready for public viewing. Preparations were further complicated by the fact that the collection was still expanding. Boban continued his practice of acquiring artifacts from the Museo Nacional as he had done in the past, purchasing human mummies from the museum's director, Jesús Sánchez.

Although Boban makes no mention of this in his later recollections of his return to Mexico, his mother died in Paris on 5 May 1885, just a few months after his arrival in the capital. Again, it is striking how little about his personal life and feelings he reveals in his writings. The declaration on her death certificate was made by her son-in-law, the architect Jean Paul Mabille, Rose's second husband. Laurence Michelle's own declaration of succession, a will and testament, named her four surviving children—Rose Louise, Eugène, Marie, and Charlotte—as heirs. Julie, the fourth of her five children, died in 1870.

Laurence Michelle, the family matriarch, who was still residing at the rented flat on Grands Augustins, left only a pittance, which amounted to sixty-six francs to be shared among her four children. This fact is striking, since the economic status of the Boban children contrasts so sharply with that of their mother. At the time of Laurence's death, her oldest daughter, Rose Louise, and her husband owned their own home and had other property. Eugène had shops in Paris and Mexico City. Marie, who never married, was leading a decidedly bourgeois life, having received a pension of 2,400 francs per year in 1879 as a bequest from the respected architect Philippe Alphonse de Metz, who had been her lover. Little is known about the youngest daughter Charlotte, who was widowed in 1870 during the Paris Commune.

Ten months after arriving back in the city, the antiquarian finally began to advertise his museum in the various Mexico City newspapers, including *The Two Republics*. In December 1885 the newspaper took note of Boban's new establishment and listed it under amusements. It informed its readers that the Museo Científico was open from 9 AM to 5 PM and that the admission was one *real*. *The Two Republics* later ran Boban's paid ads about his new shop and museum. Boban had posters printed and distributed to advertise the new venture.

Like some of the more famous entrepreneurs of the nineteenth and twentieth centuries, Boban had concluded that a bit of sensationalism would be the best draw for his museum—come see the collection of historic Mexican mummies! They had been buried in the monastery attached to the Santo Domingo church in Mexico City. The church had been consecrated in 1590, although construction had begun in 1527, just six years after the Spanish conquest. In what some felt was an excess of nationalistic vindictiveness, the mummies had been dug up in 1861 when the major demolition of the convent was ordered by President Juárez. The demolition obliterated the courtyard wall, the gallery of arches, and two chapels. All of this was done to make way for what author and historian Manuel Toussaint described as a "stupid street, . . . one which goes nowhere and comes from nowhere" (Tovar 1992: vol. II, 55).

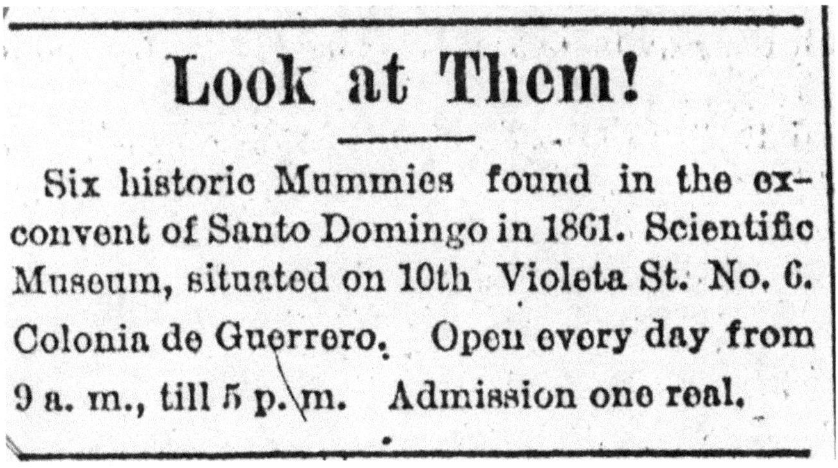

Look at Them!

Six historic Mummies found in the ex-convent of Santo Domingo in 1861. Scientific Museum, situated on 10th Violeta St. No. 6. Colonia de Guerrero. Open every day from 9 a. m., till 5 p. m. Admission one real.

Figure 12.1 The announcement that appeared in *The Two Republics*, 1 January 1886 (courtesy of Hispanic Society of America, New York).

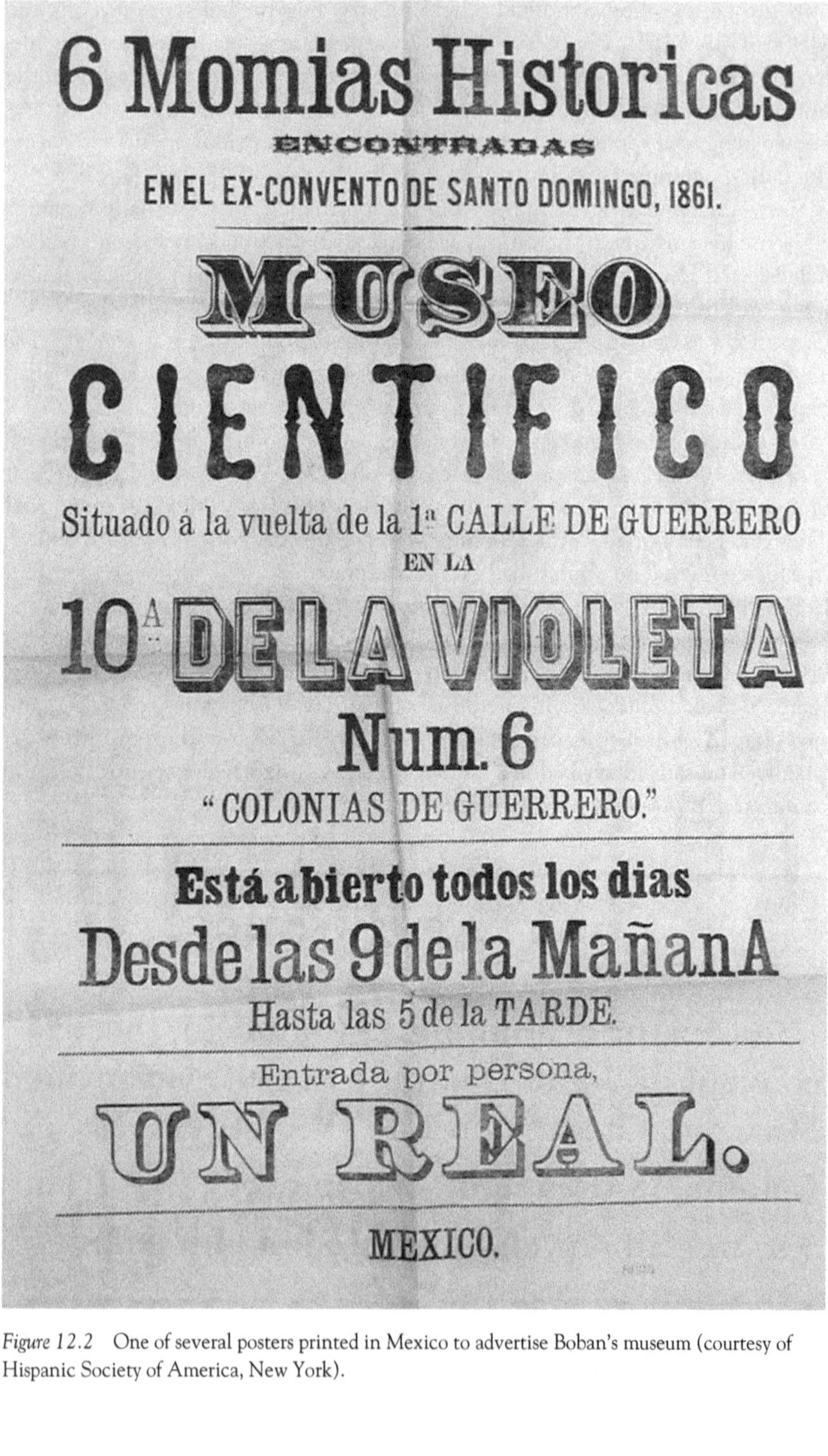

Figure 12.2   One of several posters printed in Mexico to advertise Boban's museum (courtesy of Hispanic Society of America, New York).

Doubtless, the dessicated bodies were those of priests and nuns who had lived and died in the monastery that had been attached to the church. Their corpses had dried naturally in the environment in which they had been interred. According to one historical source, some thirteen bodies had been dug up during the destruction of the buildings. Their names were known from church records at the time of their disinterment. At least some, though not all, of the mummies were sold to a Mexican general, who exhibited them in Europe and America, and despite the historical records he described them in his displays as having been victims of the Mexican Inquisition (Cossío 1994: 115).

While the Office of the Holy Inquisition certainly functioned with grim efficiency in Mexico well into the eighteenth century, these bodies were not the remnants of those who had suffered torture and death at the hands of the Roman Catholic Church. Anyone accused of being a heretic would not have been buried in sacred ground. Since most herectics ultimately were burned at the stake, there would have been nothing to bury anyway. Boban purchased his six mummies from the Museo Nacional in Mexico City, as he states in a later catalog of his collection (Leavitt 1886a: 34), and continued to promote the general's fictional account of their demise during the Mexican Inquisition.

The Museo Científico provided Boban with a venue through which to fulfill his long-held desire to share his knowledge about prehistoric and ancient artifacts—especially pre-Columbian objects—with a large, diverse audience. There he could lecture about Mexican prehistory, using examples from his own collection, and entertain important intellectuals, in addition to political figures and foreign dignitaries. He could also entice prospective collectors and the museum-going public, whom he charged an admission of one peso.

He divided his new establishment into a series of exhibit halls or rooms, featuring related displays in each. As had become his custom for his Parisian stores, Boban published a catalog of the museum's exhibitions, produced by the well-known Mexican printer Antonio Vanegas. He would later become famous for his reproductions of the drawings and lithographs of José Guadalupe Posada, whose acerbic and witty political cartoons employed skeletons engaging in every form of human interaction.

Individual pages of the museum catalog are in the Hispanic Society collection; however, the two complete copies that have come to light are housed in the Bibliothèque nationale, (BNF DMO n.a.f. 21476: item 192) and the library of the Musée de l'Homme now in the Musée du quai Branly (F1220.9 zb). The booklet describes the museum's owner and proprietor as a "member of various scientific societies in Europe and Mexico."[7]

Judging from the catalog, the first room or exhibit hall in the Museo Científico was dedicated to ethnographic exhibits. The book lists displays of weapons, tools, and costumes of tribal people from North and South America, Africa, Oceania, and so forth. The North American artifacts no doubt included some

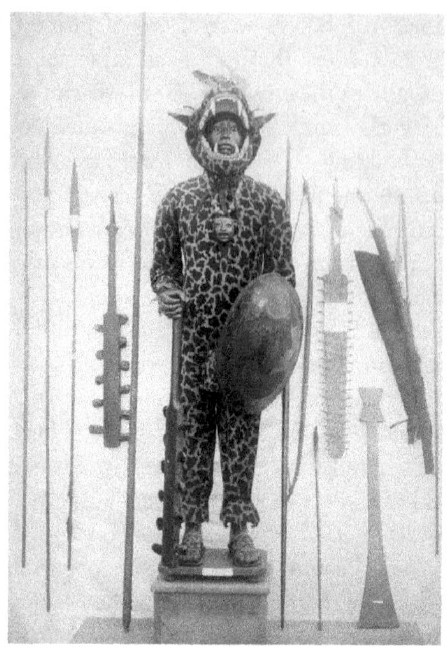

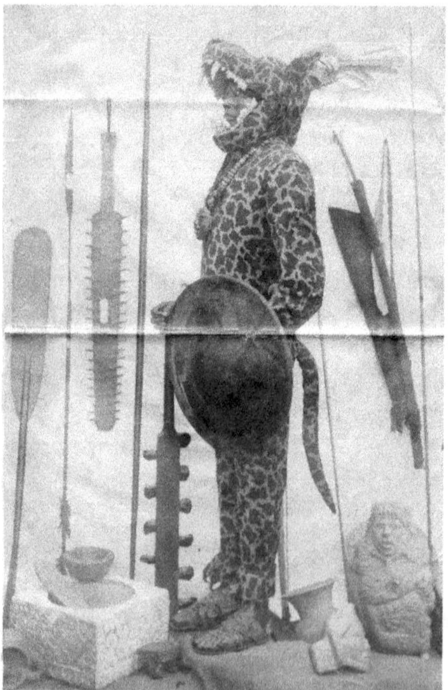

Figures 12.3a–b   Front and side view of Aztec warrior figure exhibited in 1885 in Museo Científico, Mexico City (courtesy of Hispanic Society of America, New York).

of the prehistoric objects Boban had obtained from the Smithsonian Institution through Edwin Barber. However, the main exhibit in this room was a life-size mannequin clothed in faux-jaguar skins, representing an Aztec jaguar warrior with a jaguar head as a helmet. The figure wore a jadeite or greenstone bead necklace, from which hung a miniature face pendant. In the photograph of the figure that Boban had commissioned, it is surrounded by weaponry from a variety of different cultures.

To the left of the photographed figure is an example of one of Boban's reconstructions of the Aztec macuahuitl. To the right is the saw of a sawfish, which Boban believed had functioned as a weapon among precontact cultures and was the inspiration for the war club. It is unclear where the bow and arrows and spears had originated or how they might relate to the pre-Columbian figure. The warrior holds a shield, along with another macuahuitl.

Another photograph of the Aztec jaguar warrior figure includes casts of various artifacts that Boban had sold to Alphonse Pinart in 1875 displayed at the mannequin's feet. The Quetzalcoatl figure on the bottom far right of the photograph is now on exhibit in the Pavillon de sessions at the Louvre. Boban excavated the carved stone box on the left in Chalco in 1857 (López Luján and Fauvet-Berthelot 2005: 121, 174). He may have intended the casts to be reminders of his previous tenure in Mexico, when he advertised himself as archeologist in the Emperor Maximilian's court, and as proof of the significance of his collection, since Pinart had donated the pieces to the Trocadéro. It was also a way of sharing true facsimiles of artifacts of Mexico's ancient heritage that he had removed from the country.

The Aztec jaguar warrior, an impressive centerpiece for any room, appears to have been modeled on images from Bernardino de Sahagún's Florentine Codex. A December 1884 article in *La Nature*, the French journal of popular science, featured the manikin. The author, Gaston Tissandier, who was founder and editor-in-chief of the journal and a colleague of Boban's, found it compelling. He wrote at some length about the figure and of the man who had created it:

> M. Eug. Boban, the antiquarian and voyageur well known to anthropologists and ethnographers, recently invited us to see in his establishment on the Boulevard Saint Michel, the curious reconstruction he made of the costume of a young Aztec warrior, knight of the Tiger order, the army of Montezuma (Moctheuzoma). The figure is a very skillfully executed manikin that we illustrate in the engraving on the opposite page; this truly remarkable object is destined for one of the most important ethnographic collections of Mexico. . . . This extraordinary clothing is assuredly one of the most remarkable examples that one can find among military costumes. The many voyages Boban made to Mexico, and countless documents he collected about antiquities of this very interesting country, [and] the skill that the persevering antiquarian acquired as a result of his studies and research guarantee the accuracy of this reconstruction. (Tissandier 1884: 23)[8]

Tissandier notes that Boban had this figure made specifically for the museum he was planning to create in Mexico. He goes on to say that the face was modeled on an actual inhabitant of the Valley of Mexico, probably one of the life casts Boban had made in the 1860s. He laments the fact that the manikin is not going to be seen at the Trocadéro (Tissandier 1884: 23–24).

The second room of Boban's museum housed a scientific library of books and important early manuscripts on Mexican archeology, along with numerous other published works on world prehistory and prehistoric science. The collection comprised more than a thousand volumes on subjects ranging from geology, mineralogy, paleontology, linguistics, and numismatics to natural history, travel, ethnography, and anthropology. Many of these books are listed in a later catalog as having originated from the private libraries of some of the most famous collectors of early manuscripts, among them Charles Étienne Brasseur de Bourbourg,

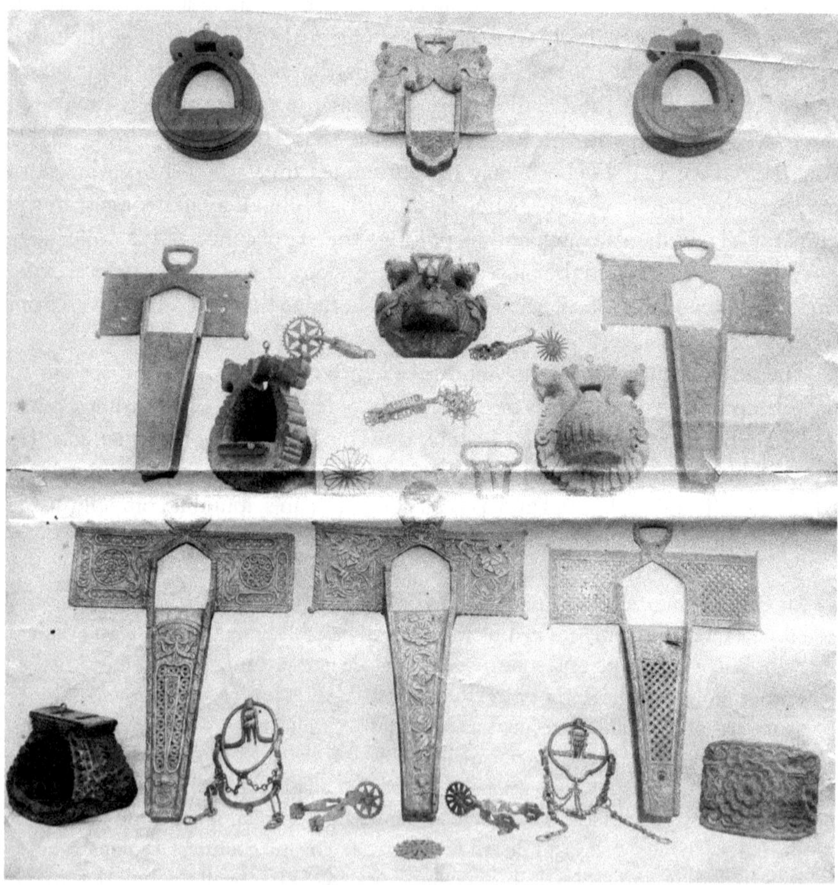

Figure 12.4 Part of Boban's stirrup and spur collection (courtesy of Hispanic Society of America, New York).

abbé Emmanuel Domenech, Joseph Marius Alexis Aubin, and Alphonse Pinart. Filling out the displays in this room were natural history specimens, plaster casts of monuments from the Yucatan, numerous scientific instruments, and an assortment of Greek and Roman coins.

Boban used the third room to present his collection of Mexican antiquities, along with artifacts that he had amassed from North America, Peru, Egypt, Italy, and Greece. Here he displayed stone tools and weapons from European prehistory and paleontological exhibits, including the teeth and bones of fossil animals modeled in plaster. Another part of the room held embossed iron stirrups, bridles, and spurs purportedly dating from the Spanish conquest of Mexico in the sixteenth century.

The fourth room contained the much-ballyhooed historic mummies from the convent of the Santo Domingo church in Mexico City. There was also one mummy of a "young Egyptian prince" dated to 1643 BC, accompanied by all the objects found in his sarcophagus, as well as a collection of human skulls representing the ancient peoples of Mexico and other regions.

One of the highlights of this exhibit was "a life-size rock crystal skull (quartz hyaline) unique in the whole world" (Boban 1885b: 4). This is the same crystal skull that had been advertised in the 1881 sales catalog with a price tag of 3,500 francs.

The elaborate, bizarre, and rather macabre display seen in the photograph of this room shows two of the mummies from the Santo Domingo church in Mexico City, covered for modesty's sake with white cloths, laid out in velvet-lined coffins under a canopy supported by four ornately carved columns, forming a sort of catafalque. There are three human skulls at the foot of the coffins and an arrangement of skulls on a fringed display table just under the window.

A label below these skulls reads *Craneo de Cristal de Roca* (rock crystal skull), which can be seen in the enlargment of the photograph. The human skulls block the view of the rock crystal skull, but its ghostly shine can be made out in the center just behind the other crania. It is interesting that the crystal skull now has migrated from the part of Boban's collection denoted "Objets divers" to the section devoted to pre-Columbian and other ancient Mexican artifacts.

The exhibits in Boban's Museo Científico were flamboyantly eccentric, theatrical, and diverse. To twenty-first-century eyes, they are anything but scientific. However, they have a direct link to the tradition of the cabinets of curiosities displayed by Renaissance princes, wealthy merchants, and European intellectuals from the late fifteenth century onward. The assemblages in the cabinets of curiosities were intended to unite art and science by presenting beautifully crafted pieces and rare natural specimens in a context that "inscribe[d] them within a special setting which would instill in them layers of meaning" (Mauriès 2002: 25). In these wondrous collections could be found nautilus shells made into sumptuous cups, branches of coral carved into representations of the Holy

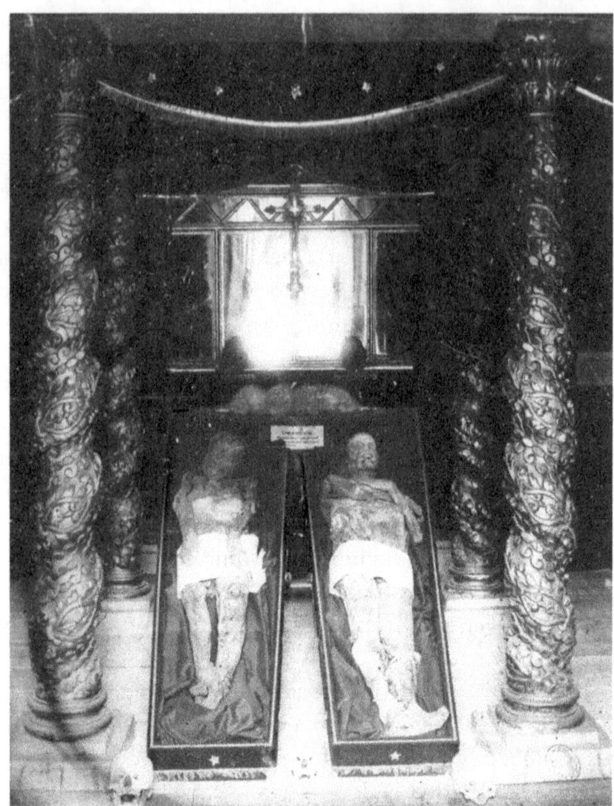

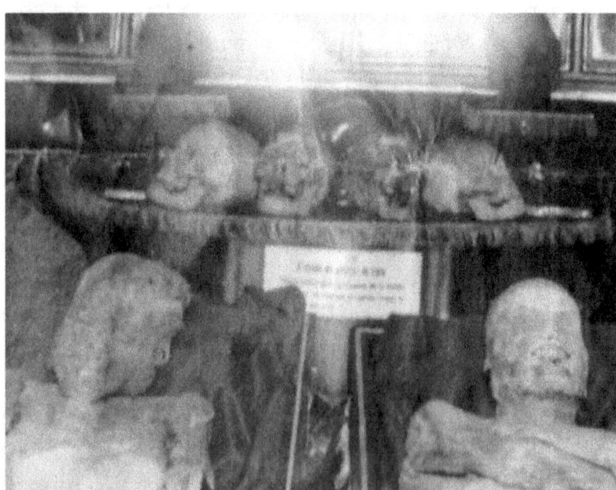

12.5a–b　Two of the mummies from Santo Domingo exhibited in 1885 in the Museo Científico, with detail of the mummies and the table of skulls behind them (courtesy of Bibliothèque nationale, Paris, DMO n.a.f. 21476: item 278).

Family, Greek and Roman vases or ivory tusks ingeniously sculpted into forms within forms, along with exotic tropical birds, a crocodile fetus or extraordinary gems and minerals from faraway places.

Boban's decision to provide as much information as he could about each object he displayed, to include books and artifacts in his museum, and to publish catalogs of his collections on a regular basis all have roots in the earlier cabinets as well. Duke Albrecht V of Bavaria (1528–1579) had a collection that he exhibited in the two top floors of one of his palace buildings. Every piece in the collection, whether laid out on tables or hanging from the ceilings, was labeled. The collection of the craftsman Manfredo Settala of Milan was one of the most impressive of the seventeenth century. The annotated catalog of his massive displays encompassed seven volumes (Mauriès 2002: 38, 54–55).

The tradition of combining the beautiful and the bizarre continued with the formation of public museums in the eighteenth and nineteenth centuries. The well-known 1822 self-portrait by Charles Willson Peale in which he is drawing back the curtain of the Peale Museum, established first in Philadelphia in 1786 and reestablished in Baltimore in 1814, reveals the range of the natural history specimens on display. They include everything from graceful water birds and a wild turkey to mastodon bones that Peale himself had excavated. In addition, the museum presented the portraits of America's founders, most painted by Peale and members of his talented family (Alderson 1992: 78).

The French word *bibelot*, meaning an object of beauty, curiosity and/or rarity removed from its actual context, captures Boban's ideas about artifacts and their uses. Nearly everything exhibited was taken completely out of context and displayed with objects of similar use, shape, or design as he saw fit. This approach undermines some of his stated educational and scientific goals. The arrangement of the mummies from the Mexican Inquisition has nothing to do with the context in which they had actually been buried or accidentally uncovered. Additionally, whatever the historic accuracy of the Aztec jaguar warrior figure, it is diminished by the nineteenth-century Mexican *huaraches* (sandals) on his feet and surrounding displays of weapons and other artifacts that have no relationship to him.

The photographs of the museum's exhibits that were taken and saved by Boban seem rather odd. They cause one to wonder what message he was hoping to impart with these displays, and what audience he was hoping to attract. Perhaps he just wanted to get visitors in the door so that he could offer them a selection of curiosities for sale.

With its emphasis on spectacle, it seems that Boban envisioned his museum venture as a way to return to Mexico and share what he had learned and collected with ordinary Mexicans, particularly Indians, whom he greatly admired. But he also wanted to explore the world's early history through his archeological exhibits. A third vision seems to have been setting up a learning center, complete with an extensive library for scholars and students, along with a conference room in which to host discussions, and offer courses in physical anthropology, ethnology, and archeology. In addition, there was to be the ongoing function of selling artifacts.

All in all, the Museo Científico was a modern and ambitious undertaking, combining as it did the activities of a variety of institutions and businesses, while attempting to attract a broad audience—from the slightly curious to the educated connoisseur. Unfortunately, the times soon proved to be inauspicious for such a venture.

Notes

1. J'ai l'honneur d'annoncer qu'en raison d'un voyage en Amérique (mon adresse au Mexique: Eugène Boban, antiquaire, Mexique), je transfère mon comptoir archéologique préhistorique au 7, rue Daguerre, à Montrouge (près du Lion de Belfort). Les personnes qui prendront ma place pendant mon absence sont mes parents, les Mesdames Duvergé. J'espère que vous conserverez la même confiance en eux que vous m'avez toujours montrée.

2. Où le climat est le plus beau du monde.

3. Les longueur [et] la rigueur des hivers en France, n'était pas faite pour nous guerir de la nostalgie du Mexique, aussi caressions nous l'idée de retourner au pays des oiseaux-mouches.

4. Aussi nous preparions nous de longue main. A cet effet nous avions fait un choix dans les collections de tous genre que nous possedions a Paris.

5. L'arrivage des caisse nous louame provisoirement un grand local. Puis toute reflexion faites nous ré-estimé cet endroit qui etait situé 10a calle de la violeta, dans la colonie de Guerrero, un nouveau quartier. Cetait evidemment assez eloigné du centre il faut en convener.

6. Nous décidions à retourner au Mexique dans le premier jours de l'année 1885, arrivés à Mexico, ou nous fut tres bien accuelles; apres 16 ans d'absence naturellement beaucoup d'amis manquait à l'appel. Les jeunes etaient des homme [et] les vieux etaient morts. Malgré cela nous retrouveront encore beaucoup d'amis et connaissances.

7. Eugenio Boban—miembro de varias sociedades científicas de Europa y de México.

8. M. Eug. Boban, l'antiquaire et le voyageur bien connu des anthropologistes et des ethnographes, nous a récemment invité à aller voir dans son établissement du boulevard Saint-Michel, la curieuse restitution qu'il a faite du costume d'un jeune guerrier aztèque, chevalier de l'ordre du Tigre, de l'armée de Montézuma (Moctheuzoma). Le personnage est figuré en un mannequin très habilement exécuté que nous représentons dans la gravure ci-contre; cet objet vraiment remarquable est destiné à l'une des plus importantes collections ethnographiques de Mexico. . . . Cet habillement extraordinaire est assurément l'une des plus remarquables curiosités que l'on puisse mentionner parmi les costumes militaires. Les nombreux voyages que M. Boban a exécutés au Mexique, les innombrables documents qu'il y a recueillis sur les antiquités de ce pays si intéressant, la compétence que le persévérant antiquaire a acquis à la suite de ses études et de ses recherches, sont autant de garanties de l'exactitude de la restitution.

13

GOOD DEALS AND BAD

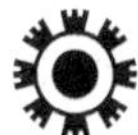

That Boban still had important contacts in Mexico in 1885 is clear from his ability to enter the country after a sixteen-year absence with fifty crates of valuable artifacts for which, according to his own statements, he paid no duty and made no customs declarations. One of those contacts was Leopoldo Batres, a highly placed bureaucrat who was himself extremely well connected. In fact, that same year the president of Mexico, Gen. Porfirio Díaz, had appointed Batres to the post of inspector and conservator of archeological monuments throughout Mexico (Lombardo 1994: 33).

Boban had met Leopoldo Batres in late 1882, when the thirty-year-old Mexican was visiting Paris to conduct informal research on archeological material in the Musée national d'histoire naturelle and the Trocadéro. According to Batres's great-granddaughter, Elvira Pruneda Gallegos, he was the first Mexican to study at the Trocadéro (pers. comm.).

It is clear that Batres was in Paris in 1882, but there is no record of his having any connection to the museum in that year. He might have just stopped by to view the Mexican pre-Columbian collection, as the museum did not offer formal classes in the 1880s. His military records state that he was in Paris from 14 October to 14 December 1882 (Adam Sellen, pers. comm.). In her book about the links between archeology and popular culture in Mexico, *El pasado prehispánico en la cultura nacional*, anthropologist and former director of the Museo Nacional de Antropología Sonia Lombardo de Ruiz describes Batres as a self-promoter. His claim to have been the first Mexican to "study" at the Trocadéro, whether or not he actually did, fits this profile. Certainly, the declaration of having conducted archeological studies in France could have influenced President Díaz's decision to appoint Batres to the post of inspector of monuments.

During his visit in Paris, Batres probably made several contacts among the French intellectual community. According to his great-granddaughter, he studied under Gabriel de Mortillet and presumably met Ernest T. Hamy, then director of the Trocadéro (Pruneda Gallegos, pers. comm.). Both of them were close colleagues of Boban's.

The Boban Collection in the Hispanic Society of America documents the fact that the two men met in Paris. It includes a handwritten transcript of *Vistas fotográficas de las antiguas ruinas de los palacios de Mitla, en el estado de Oaxaca* (Photographic views of ancient ruins of Mitla in the state of Oaxaca) by Emilio Herbinger, published in 1875. On the final page of the manuscript, Boban noted that he had copied the book in December 1882, and that M. Leopoldo Batres had lent it to him (HSA 2246 Box VII). The young Mexican bureaucrat and budding archeologist might have had some influence on Boban's decision to return to his beloved adopted country just two years later. That Batres at first impressed Boban is evident from the fact that the antiquarian nominated him for membership in the Société d'anthropologie de Paris, which Boban stated in his 1886 letter to President Porfirio Díaz (UI CPD leg. 11, caja 28, doc. 13681).

In 1885, within eight to ten months of his return to Mexico City, Boban was touring the country's archeological sites with Batres. Always keen to be in the limelight, the inspector of monuments saw to it that his archeological and museum activities were well chronicled in the Mexican newspapers of the day, in particular *El Monitor Republicano* and the English-language newspaper *The Two Republics* (Lombardo 1994).

The Two Republics first appeared in 1867, after the French army had departed, and continued as a daily publication in the capital for about thirty years. Its editors openly favored the American colonization of Mexico—which gave their views on industrialization, modernization, and capitalism a decidedly US slant. The paper also published articles on Mexican culture and ancient history, particularly stories about excavations and visits by foreigners to archeological sites. Soon after Boban's return to the country, local news reports in the daily newspaper mention that he was visiting several archeological sites across Mexico, and apparently excavating at them, or at least making surface collections.

In November 1885 a story appeared reporting on one of Leopoldo Batres's recent activities. "Mr. Batres, the lately appointed Inspector and conservator of the national archeological monuments, has made a visit to the ruins of Tula, Hidalgo the ancient metropolis of the Toltecas, and after considerable negotiations with the local authorities and private property owners he has succeeded in obtaining permission for the removal of the following thirteen objects which are without doubt relics of the first population of Mexico" (Lombardo 1994: 218; Two Republics, 29 November 1885). After listing the thirteen items, a variety of large stone carvings and architectural elements, the writer continues in a most appreciative manner saying, "This new acquisition for the National

Museum shows the importance of the work to which the President has assigned Mr. Batres, and also the latter's superior qualification" (Two Republics, 29 November 1885). He added, "Mr. Batres was accompanied on this expedition by the Antiquarian Eugenio Boban, proprietor of the museum established in the colonia de guerrero."

The article provided a nice bit of advertisement for Batres's activities, and Boban's own newly opened museum. In addition, Boban's presence seems significant. It may signal that he was acquiring artifacts for his own Museo Científico with the approval of the inspector of monuments. It is not clear what, if anything, Batres was doing from an archeological standpoint at the sites he took Boban to visit. However, as inspector of monuments he acquired thirteen fragments of ruined sculpture, some of which were monumental, from local landowners near Tula, which he arranged to have transported to the Museo Nacional for exhibition (Lombardo 1994: 117–18).

Boban and Batres also traveled to the archeological site of Xochicalco in Morelos, which is about sixty miles (120 kilometers) from Mexico City, although the trip was not heralded in Mexican newspapers. The site is the same one that had so captivated the Commission Scientifique during the French Intervention two decades earlier that they presented a life-size replica of the main pyramid at the Exposition Universelle in 1867. There are five photographs of the principal pyramid at Xochicalco in Boban's papers in the Hispanic Society, and three of them were published in La Nature in October of 1886, in an article "Les ruines

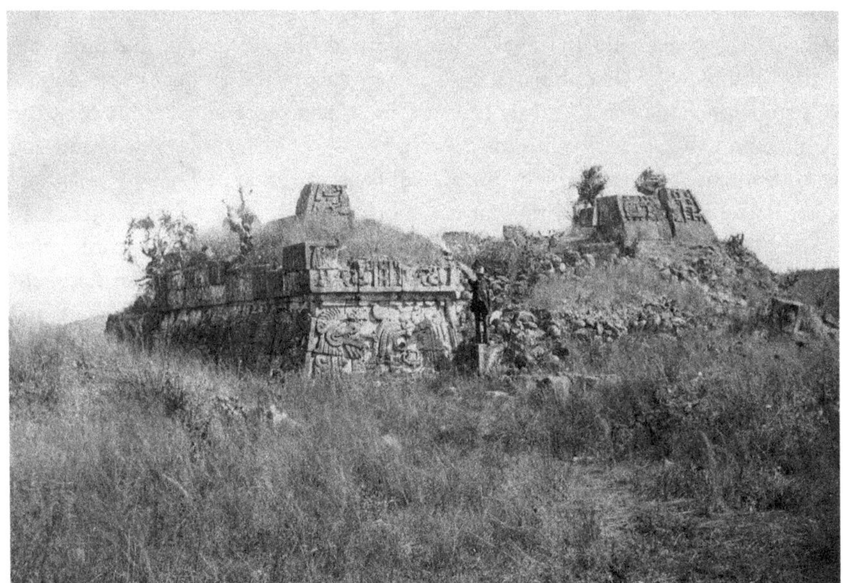

Figure 13.1a   Main temple at Xochicalco, Morelos, Mexico (courtesy of Hispanic Society of America, New York).

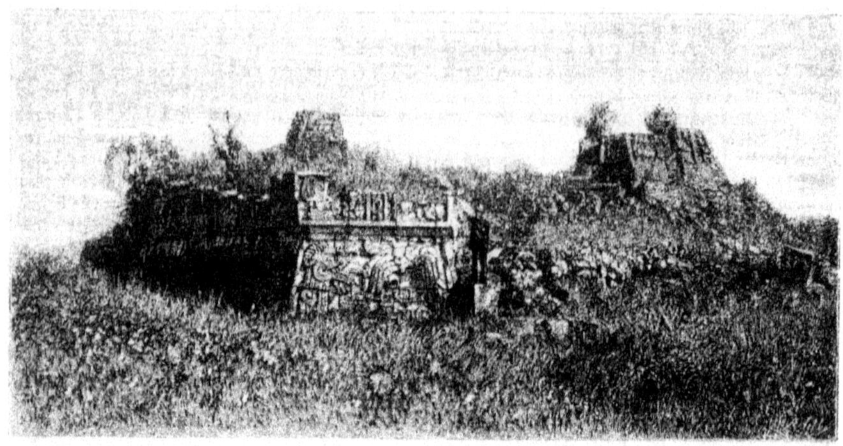

Figure 13.1b   Engraving of same image of temple published in *La Nature* in 1886 (courtesy of Hispanic Society of America, New York).

de Xochicalco au Mexique" purportedly written by Leopoldo Batres. It is likely in view of subsequent events that Boban at least cowrote the article, and presumably arranged for his friend Tissandier, the journal's editor, to publish it.

Some of the publicity Batres received was not as flattering. On several occasions an anonymous reporter for *The Two Republics*, who may have been Wilson Wilberforce Blake, judging from some of his other writing at the time, was rather dismissive in describing Batres's theories about the archeological sites he was studying. This was certainly the case in a short piece entitled "A Mexican Schliemann. What an Enthusiastic Archeologist Proposes to Do. Teotihuacan to be Brought to Light," which appeared in February 1886 in *The Two Republics*. Here Batres is quoted as saying that it was his considered view that Teotihuacan was a Mexican Pompeii. However, he believed that it was not a volcanic eruption that had buried the city, but the Toltecs—the same people who had built it. "I cannot think it occurred as did the burying of Herculaneum, Stabies, and Pompeii, by a rain of ashes from a volcano," Batres asserts in the article. "No, I think the Toltecs did it themselves. It is my impression from what I know of Toltec characteristics that this mysterious people, at incalculable expense, and with the sacrifice of thousands of human lives, buried their own city" (Two Republics, 23 February 1886).

Astonished by the idea—as well he should have been—the interviewing reporter goes on to comment on the absurdity of this notion. In yet another article, the same author, we believe, wrote "Mr. Batres says that in about twenty days the spades will be flying lively, and that within three months' time, he expects to lay bare the great Pyramid of the Moon. He still insists that a great grand city lies under those sandy stretches above which the pyramids lift their grey heads" (Two Republics, 30 March 1886). Ignacio Bernal, later a director of Mexico's Museo Nacional de Antropología, concurred with the reporter's assessment of Batres's capabilities. In his *History of Mexican Archaeology*, Bernal wrote that Batres was a self-taught archeologist who accomplished his explorations "without the benefit of any technical skill and without making a serious study of the subject" (Bernal 1980: 141). Nevertheless, the inspector was certainly correct that there was a ruined city surrounding the pyramids.

At the end of his first year back in Mexico, Boban's connection with Batres was proving to be an asset. Not only did the inspector take Boban on tours of Mexican archeological sites, but from subsequent sales catalogs it appears that he allowed the antiquarian to do at least surface collecting and perhaps even some small excavations at several locations. He may also have sold Boban pre-Columbian artifacts—an activity for which Batres would later become notorious. As 1885 drew to a close the two men teamed up on what they hoped would be a major moneymaking and educational venture—an archeological poster entitled "Cuadro arqueológico y etnográfico de la Republica Mexicana" (Archeological and ethnographical chart of the Mexican Republic). Only a few copies of the poster can now be found in a handful of libraries, including that of the Smithsonian Institution.

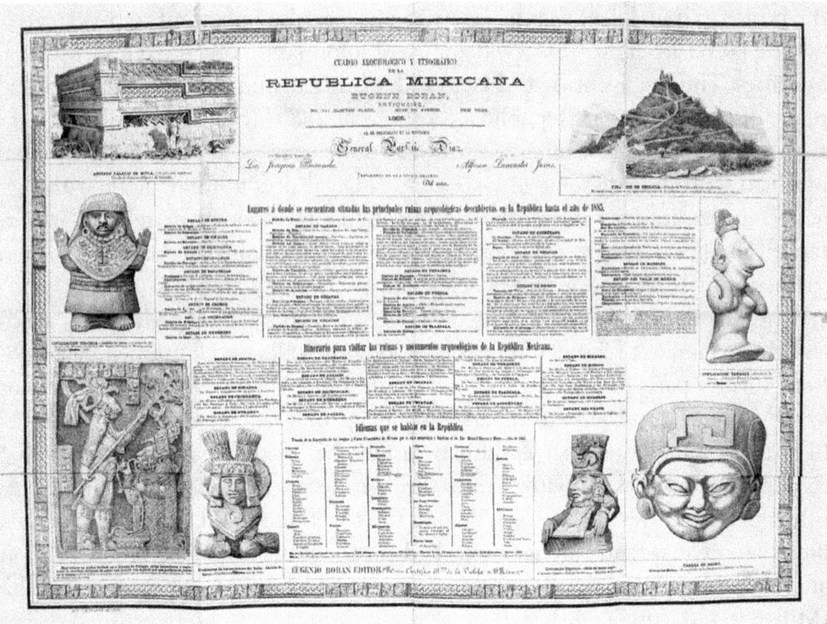

Figure 13.2a "Cuadro Arqueológico y Etnográfico de la Republica Mexicana" (Smithsonian Libraries).

Leopoldo Batres announced the production of the poster in an interview with *The Two Republics* in December 1885. "Mr. Batres, who is an enthusiastic archaeologist, has published a most interesting chart which everyone desirous of studying Old Mexico should secure. It gives sketches of the ancient palace of Mitla, with its quaint and curious Zapoteca architecture; also, the Cholula pyramid, a rival of the celebrated Cheops in Egypt, [and] the extravagant bas-relief in Chiapas in the Lacandones temple, representing the religious sacrifice of piercing the tongue and passing through it a cord covered with thorns, as a self-inflicted penance to the gods" (Two Republics, 29 December 1885).

The poster has dedications to Gen. Porfirio Díaz, Mexico's president; Joaquin Baranda, minister of justice and public education; and Alfonso Lancaster Jones, president of Mexico's congress. Lancaster Jones was a highly respected politician and diplomat, who would become the Mexican ambassador to the United Kingdom. He was the grandson of the renowned English educator Joseph Lancaster. Lancaster's daughter Elizabeth and son-in-law Richard M. Jones had been invited by President Guadalupe Victoria in 1825 to establish schools in Mexico City based on Lancasterian principles. These educational principles, which were popular in the early nineteenth century, were "monitorial," meaning that more capable students taught other students what they had already learned and assisted in monitoring classroom behavior (Bolton 1913: 194). As a political appointment of President Díaz, Batres was being particularly politic in dedicating the poster to him. The other two gentlemen were also important to his career.

The poster itself presents a wide range of information organized under several headings. The first is entitled, "Places where one can find principal archeological ruins, discovered in the Republic as of the year 1885" (Smithsonian Libraries).[1] Beneath this is a list of nineteen Mexican states, arranged geographically from north to south, listing some fifty-six archeological sites in total, along with suggested itineraries for visiting them and commentaries on their relative importance. Finally, there are columns enumerating indigenous languages spoken in Mexico, which are also arranged by state.

The text is framed at the top by images of the Zapotec site of Mitla in Oaxaca and the pyramid at Cholula in Puebla. Along the sides and bottom are figurines from various parts of Mexico and one of the Remojadas-style terra-cotta heads from Veracruz. On the bottom left is an image of a famous limestone bas-relief from a site now known as Yaxchilan in Chiapas of the Maya ruler Lady Xoc running a rope studded with thorns through her tongue. Boban obtained this lithograph from Désiré Charnay, despite the fact that Alfred Percival Maudslay, diplomat, explorer, and archeologist, had cut the lintel from its original location and had it shipped to the British Museum in London three years earlier in 1882 (Miller and Martin 2004: 108).

One of the extended commentaries and descriptions in the first section dealing with the sites in the State of Mexico involves San Juan Teotihuacan. It

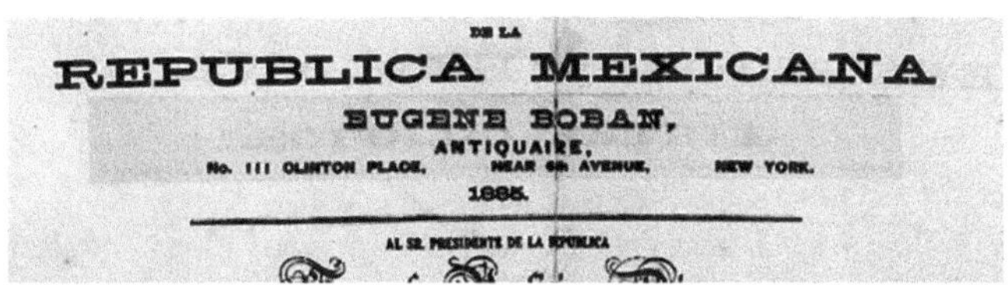

Figure 13.2b   Detail of poster's title and author information (Smithsonian Libraries).

reiterates Batres's strange ideas about the ruined city. "[There are] two pyramids, one called the Sun, which is the larger, and the smaller one is the Moon. In the space between there is a succession of small promontories that are called sepulchers, and by excavations that I have accomplished at some of them I have found their walls and stairways richly decorated, which has allowed me to form the judgment that all those ruined mounds are nothing more than habitations that have been buried, whether by a geological accident, in the opinion of Mr. Boban, or by the hand of man" (Smithsonian Libraries). [2]

All the extant posters have a label pasted just below the title, which bears the name of the author, Eugène Boban, and below that, "Antiquaire" and the address "No. 111 Clinton Place, near 6th Avenue, New York." Since the poster is dated 1885, at which time Boban was living in Mexico City, the label is somewhat confusing. Additionally, at the bottom of the poster, is the legend: "Eugenio Boban; Editor—Museo Científico, 10a calle de la Violeta, México." In Spanish, *editor* can mean either editor or publisher.

If one looks closely at the name of the author under a bright light, it is possible to read another name beneath the label: Leopoldo Batres, whose authorship was mentioned in *The Two Republics* article in addition to what the poster says about the ancient site of Teotihuacan. Perhaps in an effort to provide a more credible explanation, Boban added his own comment to the text about the possibility that a great earthquake had destroyed the ancient urban center.

In this and other ways, both the text and the illustrations make clear that Eugène Boban was much more than just the poster's editor; as we shall see, he was most certainly its publisher. All of the artifacts illustrated are from his own collection, including the smiling head on the bottom right, which he had published in *Le Musée Archéologique* ten years earlier. The depiction of the Mayan bas-relief of Lady Xoc is from a lithograph produced by Boban's friend, colleague, and former Commission Scientifique member Désiré Charnay. However, Charnay's name does not appear on the poster.

The coproduction of this impressive and informative chart represents the high-water mark of the men's personal and professional relationship. By the end of 1885, despite the fact that his collaboration with Batres was affording him access to the Mexican archeological scene, Boban was already regretting his involvement with the inspector's projects. Unfortunately, allying himself with

Batres was turning out to be a miscalculation on many levels. It may even have precipitated his hasty retreat from the capital and the demise of his dream of ending his days in the balmy climate of Mexico City as a respected curator of an archeological museum.

Wilson Wilberforce Blake provides some important clues about the rest of Boban's ill-fated association with Batres in a letter to William Henry Holmes at the Smithsonian Institution. Blake had spent many years in Mexico and knew the cultural scene well. Initially employed by the Mexican Railroad, he went on to become a dealer of books, manuscripts, and antiquities in the capital. He published an English-language guide to the Museo Nacional and occasionally wrote for *The Two Republics*, being listed as one of its editors in later years. The tone of his correspondence with Holmes suggests that Blake may well have been the anonymous reporter whose sarcasm is so apparent in the description of Batres's archeological expeditions.

In early 1886 he had some news to share with Holmes about Batres's plans regarding Teotihuacan: "Sr. Batres, the inspector of museums," Blake wrote, "proposed to employ a regiment of soldiers in exploring the ruins about the pyramids of San Juan Teotihuacan believing that he will unearth a buried Pompeii. His proposition strikes me as absurd" (SIA: USNM Acc#17619).

Blake had an equally unflattering opinion of Eugène Boban, who had apparently contacted Holmes at the Smithsonian offering to sell him objects including a rock crystal skull from his pre-Columbian Mexican collection (Walsh 1997: 127). In a letter dated 29 March 1886, Blake wrote to say, "I was out to the pyramids last week, to see what Batres is doing. He is a fraud—has done nothing but manage to get himself interviewed about twice a week. He is not only a fraud but a swindler." Responding to questions posed by Holmes about crystal skulls, Blake continues, "The only rock crystal skull of any value is the one I got in the Fischer collection." Expounding upon antiquities and dealers, he then offers a description of a recent and apparently well-publicized scandal. "Well, Frenchman named Boban—who has a private museum here—and is a member of various French societies and seems to be very intelligent, although not honest, brought from Germany a glass skull made to imitate rock crystal. Batres persuaded him into a partnership to defraud the National Museum, by selling it as a genuine rock crystal from Orizaba for $3,000. Sanchez was at the point of buying it, but first had Dr. Kaska examine it who at once pronounced it glass and the two busy B's are under a cloud" (SIA: USNM Acc#17619).

As previously noted, Jesús Sánchez was the curator of the Museo Nacional with whom Boban had numerous dealings, including the purchase of six mummies. Dr. Francisco Kaska was a pharmacist who had come to Mexico with Emperor Maximilian, and later coordinated the building of a memorial chapel at the site of the emperor's execution. As a consultant to the museum, Kaska authenticated a variety of objects. He was wrong about the skull, though; it was not glass.

In the same letter Blake offers yet another piece of information. "Boban has closed his museum and will remove to New York, soon. Look out for him. He hopes to sell a great many things to the Smithsonian. He has some valuable antiquities, but his ownership of them gives them a suspicious character" (SIA: USNM acc.17619; Walsh 1997: 127). In evaluating these statements, it should be kept in mind that Blake was himself negotiating with Holmes to sell a small crystal skull to the Smithsonian, along with the rest of a large pre-Columbian collection that he had acquired from Augustin Fischer, Maximilian's confessor and cabinet secretary. Holmes had purchased these pieces from Blake for $1,250.

Blake's March 29 letter dovetails nicely with a series of advertisements for the Museo Científico that had appeared in *The Two Republics*. The first ads ran in January 1886, with the bold headline "Look at them"—referring to the six mummies. These ads gave general information about the museum, intended to attract visitors. The promotions continued to run daily until mid-November 1886. A second paid announcement appeared on the same page on 17 March. It read, "Closed Museum—The Zoological Museum which has had such a successful season in 10a Calle de la Violeta no. 6, has been closed because the proprietor is preparing to leave the city." This is the address of the Museo Científico, the "zoological museum" and the scientific museum were one and the same. This ad also notes that Boban "offers for sale several interesting objects such as antiquities, specimens of natural history, old books, etc. He can be seen from 2 PM to 6 PM at 10a Calle de Violeta no. 6. Eugenio Bobon [*sic*]" (Two Republics, 17 March 1886).

Boban himself tells the end of the tale of his second Mexican adventure in two letters written to his friend and colleague Ernest Hamy. He is writing from 111 Clinton Avenue in New York City—the address on the poster label—to which he moved in June 1886. The draft of the letter, which is much more explicit about his feelings about Batres and more revealing about their relationship, is in the Hispanic Society collection. The letter he actually sent to Hamy, which he substantially edited, is in the archives of the Musée du quai Branly. In that letter Boban never mentions Batres.

Boban was responding to a letter Ernest Hamy had written in February 1886, which begins by thanking him profusely for his efforts in maintaining such good relations with their Mexican colleagues. Hamy goes on to acknowledge receipt of a book by Antonio Peñafiel, who was a member of President Díaz's group of technocrats known as Los Científicos, and to comment on the news of the Leopoldo Batres expedition. He also mentions that he had received a letter from Batres, which was accompanied by a copy of a poster he had authored, for which he was grateful. He confides to Boban, however, that he regretted seeing the lithograph of Lady Xoc without any credit given to Charnay (BNF DOM n.a.f. 21477: item 422).

In the letter he mailed to Hamy, Boban writes "We went to explore San Juan Teotihuacan, where I found a lot of very interesting fragments. Near the pyramids in studying the upheaval of the habitations, it seems impossible that it is man-made; it is likely that this region was the scene of geologic phenomena or seismic disturbances, a terrible earthquake" (MNHN Ms. 2256/153bis).[3] This statement seems designed to put some distance between himself and the "Cuadro Arqueológico," to which Hamy refers. This is virtually the only reference to the unnamed Batres in the letter he posted.

By contrast, in the draft of the letter, which Boban did not send, he writes, "In your last letter you told me that Batres had sent you his poster, [but] it must be said it is my poster; I paid the cost of printing and all the paper. . . . he told me we could not put the name of a foreigner on the finished poster, saying it would hurt sales [referring to the lack of credit to Charnay]" (HSA: B2246, Box VII).[4] Boban continues in this vein, bitterly complaining about Batres, mentioning the fact that the inspector seemed to hate Charnay and conspired to keep him out of Mexico. Additionally, he says that Batres had guaranteed him that the President Díaz would buy one thousand copies at a dollar each, or 5 francs, which would have been a tidy sum.

Indeed, there are a number of letters in the Bibliothèque nationale correspondence from governors of Mexican states thanking Boban for having sent the posters, usually 25, and saying that they would attempt to sell them at the suggested price of one *real*. Other letters, however, indicate that the posters were all eventually returned to Boban, with apologies for not having found purchasers for them. Some protested that the price was too high or that they had not had enough time to find buyers. The dates of these letters correspond with the time when Boban was leaving, or had already left, Mexico, so it seems he was trying to recoup some of his losses in this venture.

However positive his relationship with Batres may have been at first, it appears that Boban mostly felt contempt for him when he wrote Ernest Hamy. In his draft letter he expresses utter incredulity at Batres's ignorance of archeology and anthropology, writing, "This idiotic scoundrel gave a lecture at the Society of Geography, saying that cranial depressions were natural in Mexico, and not artificial as proposed by Broca and Hamy, etc. He is not only stupid and lacking in any real archeological knowledge, I also learned that he is a panderer, swindler, intriguer, and police agent" (HSA: B2246, Box VII).[5] When Boban was on the verge of leaving the country, he adds, he gave Batres "quite a few valuable objects, anthropological instruments, some books, etc." These appear to have been meant as a bribe, since Boban notes darkly, "with his position as inspector he could harm me." According to Boban, Batres quickly sold all the items, and promised not to do anything against him. However, by the time he arrived in Veracruz, Boban learned from the broker shipping his crates of artifacts, books, and luggage that Batres had denounced him "as a smuggler of Mexican antiquities." Furious about the entire episode, Boban seems to believe that he had the last laugh, though, as he recounts in the draft letter to Hamy: "The stupid blowhard imbecile made a mistake of several days and my 50 crates were already on the high seas" (HSA: B2246, Box VII).[6]

Evidently, putting all of his pent-up anger on paper allowed Boban to get it off his chest—either that or someone with a cooler head intervened, perhaps his wife. He also may have decided he needed to be more diplomatic with the director of the Trocadéro. Whatever the case, he included none of the criticism of Batres in the letter he sent to Hamy. Nevertheless, he felt strongly enough about the Batres episode to keep the emotionally charged draft letter in his personal files.

The various versions of his unpublished memoirs paint several different portraits of his difficulties in Mexico. Some add details about his reasons for leaving the country that are not apparent in his angry draft letter to Hamy. The Museo Científico had not fared as well as Boban had hoped. Despite the fact that his time in the country had afforded him the opportunity to meet with other collectors, confer with museum professionals, and profit from his association with Batres, he was never able to attract many Mexican visitors to the museum. The new venture was not profitable and may not even have generated enough revenue to cover expenses.

Boban had spent a little more than a year in Mexico City, and within this short period had experienced considerable disenchantment, which he highlighted in his memoir.

> I was painfully surprised by what I shall call the indifference of the public, despite the fact that I brought many informative documents full of carefully acquired knowledge to that country. I had returned to Mexico full of joy at the thought that I could be useful from the point of view of teaching archeology. With the documents and the experience, I had counted on holding a number of conferences with the artifacts . . . but all was in vain. The times were without doubt not propitious, or the hour had not come. I remember the often-repeated words I heard outside my windows, from those who are called in Mexico, *los Pelados* [a slang term for the poor and homeless]. 'The admission [to the museum] costs one real, better to drink a real's worth of pulque.' (HSA: B2244, Box V—Preface)[7]

The Mexican peso, also called the *real*, was approximately the same value as the US dollar at the time, an amount that the poorer classes would have been unlikely to spend to enter a museum or buy a poster, for that matter. Why the comments of poor people passing by on the street would have wounded Boban in such a way is hard to understand, but his disappointment is palpable.

Perhaps a more important reason for his disenchantment and premature departure from Mexico had to do with the failed collaboration with Batres, and the controversial attempt to sell his crystal skull as an ancient Mexican artifact, as Blake had reported. His willingness to enter into a fraudulent transaction with the Mexican bureaucrat in order to enrich both of them left a bitter taste and would continue to cause problems.

Boban felt compelled to point out in his memoirs that the same indifference to the museum did not "exist at all for me with the foreigners living in Mexico, the French colony, American, English, German, Swiss, Belgian, etc. Groups arrived on the holidays when businesses were closed, to visit our collection, and later would take their place in the lecture hall." (HSA: B2244, Box V—Preface).[8] Presumably these visitors could easily afford the one *real* admission.

In the best of lights, Boban's association with Batres may have resulted from his disappointment with the lack of paying museum visitors. Fearing a total failure and collapse of his business, he may have chosen to turn a blind eye to the ways in which the inspector exploited his position, or perhaps he considered it business as usual. Boban was accustomed to bribing people to achieve his own ends—a fact he mentions several times in his memoirs, and certainly it has been a long-held custom in Mexico. He referred to the bribe, or *mordida*, as the "universal lever" in his story about descending into "the abyss" as a young archeologist, when he paid local people to allow him to enter a large cavern (HSA: B2246, Box VII).

Although his memoirs paint the rosiest picture possible, it is evident that he faced considerable difficulties in extracting himself from this business venture. "Finally, after a fruitless attempt of around eighteen months, I resolved, with the advice of many friends, to close shop and move my establishment to the United States of the North. Upon closing [the museum], with the idea of lightening my baggage, I offered to sell appropriate collections to the director of the Museo Nacional, but the offer fell on deaf ears. They had a unique opportunity that would never present itself again. It would have been easy to enlarge their collection, which is poor in the types of ethnographic objects I possess, and [European] prehistory, which they lack completely. It is the same for Greek, Roman, and Egyptian archeology" (HSA: B2244, Box V).[9]

Exasperated with the museum administrators, Boban is surprised by their lack of insight about the importance of the artifacts he was offering them. In all probability, the crystal skull venture played some role in this refusal. Gumersindo Mendoza, who had long been director, died in February 1886, and Jesús Sánchez succeeded him. Since his attempt to purchase the crystal skull had proved to be an embarrassment to him and the museum, Sanchez's reluctance to buy anything at all from Boban is certainly understandable.

In these memoirs Boban portrays his struggles in Mexico and earnest attempt to enlighten the Mexican public in the best light possible, while being truthful about some of his mistakes. Boban admits in the memoir version of events that he was not as cognizant of the changed legal climate as he might have been. The Mexican government had in fact, become more protective of its patrimony during the years Boban had spent in France, and had begun to prosecute antiquities smugglers. "I was thus threatened with having my Mexican collection seized at the moment of my sailing. I was understandably very upset. I went to see and recount my misgivings to Lic. Don Alfonso Lancaster Jones, who, accompanied by the brave General Sóstenes Rocha, had visited our collection. They had seen the unpacking of our collection and could be witnesses to prove that all our collections that we wished to take with us had been brought by me from Europe" (HSA: B2244, Box V—Preface).[10] As previously mentioned, Lancaster Jones was one of three people to whom Batres and Boban dedicated the "Cuadro Arqueológico." Sóstenes Rocha, a highly decorated liberal general during the War of Reform, had been named director of the Colegio Militar at Chapultepec. Both men held important posts in the Díaz government.

A note to Boban in the Bibliothèque nationale correspondence shows how astute he was in using his contacts. Written on 26 May 1886, on paper mono-grammed ALJ, it reads, "Alfonso Lancaster Jones greets affectionately Mr. and Mrs. Boban and sends them infinite thanks for the precious gift they have given me, and that will be kept as a remembrance of such esteemed friends" (BNF DMO n.a.f. 21478: Item 36).[11] The communication underscores just how win-ning Boban's personality must have been. Many people give presents to well-connected individuals, perhaps intending to influence a particular outcome, but few indeed must receive such heartfelt thanks for their gesture. Throughout the years an array of scholars, museum directors and others went out of their way to express their warm feelings toward Boban and members of his family giving the impression that they were welcoming and interesting people.

Aside from the enhanced and newly enforced antiquities laws, the former museum proprietor seems to have overlooked another small matter, perhaps as the result of his hasty retreat: a bill sent to him by Antonio Vanegas, the printer of the Museo Científico's catalog. Vanegas eventually brought suit against Boban in 1886, although beyond a listing of this court case in the Archivo General de la Nación, there appears to be no documentation of its settlement.

So Boban hastily left Mexico just ahead of the customs inspectors and trail-ing unpaid bills. He had also outfoxed Leopoldo Batres and restrained himself from revealing too much about what had actually gone on to Ernest Hamy, the Trocadéro's director. Nonetheless, this second expedition to Mexico would continue to haunt him.

Notes

1. Lugares á donde se encuentran situadas las principales ruinas arqueológicas descubiertas en la República hasta el año de 1885.

2. Dos pirámides, llamadas la una del Sol que es la grande, y la más pequeña de la Luna. En el espacio que hay entre las dos pirámides hay una sucesión de pequeños promontorios que llaman sepulcros y por las escavaciones que he practicado en algunos de estas he encontrado sus paredes y escaleras ricamente decoradas, lo que me ha permitido formar el juicio de que todos esos montículos en ruinas no son más que habitaciones que han sido enterradas, ya sea por un accidente geológico, en la opinión del Sr. Boban, ó por la mano del hombre.

3. Nous sommes aller explorer San Juan Teotihuacan ou j'ai rapporte pas mal de fragments tres interessants près des pyramides en étudiant le bouleversements des habitations il semble impossible que soit faites de main d'hommes il est fort probable que cette contrée à été le théatre de phénomènes Geologique ou perturbations sismíques, un terrible tremblement de terre.

4. Dans votre dernière vous me disiez que Batres vous avait envoyé son table [mais] c'est le mien qu'il fallait dire, c'est moi qui l'ai disposé payé le dissinateur l'impres[sion] et tout papier. . . . Il m'avait dit qu'il ne fallait pas mettre le nom d'un étranger que cela pourrait nuire à la vente les Dessins terminés.

5. Cette idiote crapule avait fait une lecture à la Société de Géographie en disant que les dépressions crâniennes étaient naturelles au Mexique et pas artificielles comme le prétendent Broca, Hamy, etc. etc. c'était un comble là je le traitait d'imbécile et d'ignorant en lui disant qu'l [n']etait bon qu'à faire des dupes etc. du reste j'ai appris sur son compte de choses infâmes, proxénète escroc intrigant et agent de police; bref au moment de mon départ de Mexico, comme par sa position d'inspecteur il pouvait me nuire je lui donnais pas mal d'objets de valeur: instruments d'anthropologie, livres, etc. qu'il vendit immédiatement.

6. Il me promit ces grands dieux de ne rien faire contre moi en descendant à Vera Cruz j'appris par mon consignataire que j'avais été dénoncé comme contrebandier d'antiquités mexicaines mais le mouchard imbécile il s'était trompé de quelques jours et mes 50 colis étaient en pleine mer sans quoi j'aurais été cloué à Vera Cruz.

7. [J'ai été] surpris peniblement de ce es que j'appelerai l'indiference du public. Et cependant j'apportais dans ce pays, bien des documents, des renseignements, et des connaissances acquises peniblement. Je revenais au Mexique tout joyeaux a la pensé que je pourrais me rendre utile au point de vue de l'enseignements de l'archeologie en general. Avec les documents et l'experiences je comptait faire des conference avec les pieces . . . mais vainement le temps n'etait pas sans doute propice, ou l'heure pas encore sonnée. J'entendais souvent repeter ces mots sous mes fenetres par ce que nous appelons au Mexique Los Pelados, entrada un real, mejor es beber un real de pulque.

8. Cette indiference n'existait point parmi les etrangers etabli a Mexico. La Colonie Francaise, Americaine, Anglaise, Allemande, Suisse, Belge, etc, nous arrivaient enfoule les jours fériés ou le commerce etait fermé, pour visiter nos collection, puis prenaient [leur] place dans la salle de lecture.

9. Enfin après un essais infructueux de 18 mois environs, je resolu sur le conseille de plusieurs amis de fermé et d'aller m'etablir aux Etats Unis du Nord. Apres la fermeture je fis offrir a fin de diminuer mon bagage la vente des series qui pourront convenir a la direction du Musée National de Mexico, on fit la sourde oreille. Ils avaint la cependant un occasion unique qui de longtemp ne se presentera pas. Il leur etait facile d'augmenter la collection si pauvre en classe d'objet d'ethnographie puis le prehistorique qui manque completement, il en est de même pour l'archeologie Grecque et Romaine, [et] Egyptienne.

10. J'etais donc menacé de voir saisir mes colections Mexicaines au moment de l'embarquement, fort inquiet comme ou le comprendra. Je feu voir et compter mes inquietudes au Lic. Don Alfonso Lancaster-Jones, qui en compagnie du brave General Sóstenes Rochas, avaient assisté au deballage de nos collection et pouvrent etre les temoins et prouver que tous les objets que nous desirions emporter nous les avais apportes d'Europe.

11. Alfonso Lancaster Jones saluda afectuosamente al Sr. y la Sra. Boban y les envía un agradecimiento infinito por el precioso regalo que me han dado, y que se guardará como un recuerdo de esos estimados amigos.

14

BACK IN BUSINESS

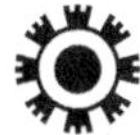

Eugène Boban, his wife, and some fifty crates containing his collection and library sailed from Veracruz to New York City, landing on 7 July 1886. Unlike their arrival in Mexico the year before, this time, the crates were held up for weeks at Tice and Lynch, Custom House Brokers, who excused the long delay with the understatement, "It is quite a job for the examiner." The company finally managed to complete the inspection at the end of August (BNF DMO n.a.f. 21479: item 327).

Following the delivery of his collections, Boban, as was his custom, wasted no time in setting up shop at 111 Clinton Place near 6th Avenue, as indicated on the label of the "Cuadro Arqueológico" poster. Then he began using his contacts and connections to become better known in the city. One of his contacts was George Frederick Kunz, a gemologist who was vice president of Tiffany & Co. at the time. The two men had been buying, selling, and exchanging collections with each other since 1881, when Kunz offered Boban a "small case of relics" for forty francs, while Boban asked if Kunz was interested in a collection of three hundred stone artifacts for $200 cash (BNF DMO n.a.f. 21477: item 512).

Years later George Frederick Kunz would describe Boban as "one of the most amazing men I ever knew." It is clear from these recollections that Boban was adept at using his expertise and showmanship to make an impression. "Eugene Boban," Kunz wrote, "did more than any other one man to show us the wonders of Mexico. I shall never forget my first visit to his home in Tenth Street, where I went to see a wonderful sacred painting depicting in gems the Marriage of Joseph and Mary, in life size, which he had unearthed for me from an ancient Mexican church" (Kunz and Ray 1927: 7). One wonders how Boban managed to "unearth" this life-size work of art, depicted in gemstones, from a church or monastery, and transport it out of the country. This painting was yet another example of the religious artwork Boban had purchased after the demolition of churches during Benito Juárez's presidency.

During this first visit George Frederick Kunz was even more impressed with some truly singular objects. "Boban's room! A tiny cot placed between two mummified women which he had dug out of the walls of that same church, and at the foot of his bed, that he might on retiring and rising, contemplate its never-ending archaeological wonders, the head of a man which, during burial, had been transformed into adipocere, a sort of natural hard soap" (Kunz and Ray 1927: 8).

The gemologist makes no mention of Mrs. Boban, although she arrived with her husband in New York harbor on the steam ship *City of Puebla*. The ship's manifest lists Madame Boban simply as "wife, age 49." His age is given as fifty, although he would have been fifty-two at the time (NY Passenger Lists 1820–1891: 496). Since it seems Boban was congenitally incapable of telling the truth about his own age, perhaps he also subtracted years from his wife's. This passenger list is the last written record of this woman, whose given name is unknown, as is that of his first wife.

Clinton Place, where Boban's shop stood—just a couple of blocks south of his home on 10th Street—no longer appears on any New York City map. It was only a few blocks long and is now known as West Eighth Street and East Eighth Street, located a little north of Washington Square. Now surrounded by New York University, the square is a landmark of Greenwich Village.

Many of the earlier buildings still standing in The Village date to the late eighteenth and early nineteenth century. The tightly packed row houses and narrow streets of this older part of New York are reminiscent of the meandering passageways and alleys of pre-Haussmann Paris and the intimate cluster of Mexico City's colonial center. As an older section of the city near a university, the area must have been comfortably familiar to Mr. and Mrs. Boban. Interestingly, both of Boban's Paris shops were close to the Sorbonne. He preferred to locate his businesses near institutions of higher learning, counting on the fact that professors and students would naturally be more interested than the average person in examining and acquiring his artifacts, manuscripts, and books.

Two early contacts that Boban made in his first months in New York were Augustus and Alice Le Plongeon, who had recently returned from the Yucatan. Since 1873 they had been almost continuously excavating and extensively photographing Maya sites, in particular Chichén Itzá. They held strongly diffusionist ideas and rather unusual notions about Maya connections with Egypt and sunken continents like Atlantis.

As it happened, Augustus had also traveled to California in the early 1850s and established a photographic studio in San Francisco in 1855. He became a prosperous businessman and was elected to the California Academy of Science three years after it was founded (Desmond and Messenger 1988: 3–6). It is possible that he and Boban encountered each other during their California days, although it seems improbable, since the young Frenchman frequently was living among the natives while Le Plongeon was cashing in on the boom created by the Gold Rush.

In November 1886 Boban wrote quite sympathetically about Le Plongeon and his wife to Hamy at the Trocadéro, saying, "He assures me he possesses the key to deciphering the hieroglyphs of the ancient people of the Yucatan" (MNHN Ms.2256: 158). He goes on to comment to Hamy that Le Plongeon reminds him of Livingstone, the apostle of the African continent. His apparent personal admiration for them aside, Boban continues in a rather dismissive vein about the couple's ideas regarding the Troano codex, one of three surviving Maya books. Boban thinks they are following too closely the writings of Charles Étienne Brasseur de Bourbourg, who had offered his own views relating Maya mythology to that of Atlantis and Egypt (1866; 1868). Despite their notions about sunken continents and interest in the eccentric viewpoints of Brasseur and others, Boban asks Hamy later in the same letter whether he thinks Leroux in Paris might be interested in publishing some of the couple's manuscripts.

It may be that Boban was attempting to ingratiate himself with Le Plongeon and his wife by finding a French publisher for them. This might have helped him obtain some of their extensive archive of materials, which he describes to Hamy as containing "documents, drawings, maps, engravings, and photographs of the Yucatan and especially monuments known only to himself" (MNHN Ms.2256: 158).[1] The reference to the monuments relates to the fact that Le Plongeon and his wife had reburied excavated artifacts to keep them out of the hands of the Mexican government, which had seized an important sculpture they had excavated and named "chacmool." This piece, often described as being central to the ritual sacrifice of hearts to the Maya gods, is today one of the most iconic images at Chichén Itzá in the Yucatan. If Boban was trying to befriend Le Plongeon, he was apparently successful, since the two men continued a warm correspondence for more than ten years (BNF DMO n.a.f. 21478: item 167-70).

Another acquaintance Boban made in New York, possibly with the help of friends from Mexico and some French expatriates, was Edouard Frossard. A Parisian by birth, Frossard had arrived in New York as a youth and served bravely in the Civil War. A recognized expert in numismatics, he often helped catalog coin and stamp collections (New York Times, 15 April 1899, 9).

Then in another abrupt change of plans, Boban decided to sell his entire collection in the fall of 1886, at the Broadway auction house George A. Leavitt & Co. This was a hasty decision since he had only just opened his shop. He must have been feeling an increasing urgency to recoup what he could of the massive expenditures associated with his second trip to Mexico and rather quick decampment to New York. Another factor influencing this decision was that he did not speak English and felt less comfortable than he did in Paris and Mexico

City. Once again, the idea of selling his entire collection at one time, rather than in bits and pieces, had a strong appeal.

It was an impressive collection by then. The monthly magazine *Bookmart* announced that Leavitt "Will disperse the extensive 'Collection Boban,' in October. There will be some 5,000 lots in the catalog, which will be divided into two parts. The first consists of some 1,000 objects of the highest antiquarian and archaeological value. Mummies, both Mexican and Egyptian; gods and goddesses; vases, armor, flints, paintings of the time of Montezuma; coins and medals, and in fact every conceivable object of antiquity illustrative of the anthropological, ethnological and archaeological development of the human race will be found in this marvelous collection" (Bookmart 1886: 153).

The *Bookmart* article noted also that the French expatriate and numismatist Edward Frossard would catalog the antiquities, while Charles Sotheran, a bibliographer of note, would catalog the books. "Both will have the personal assistance of the owner, Monsieur Eugène Boban-Duvergé, who is so distinguished as a collector and author in Mexico and Europe. He was the friend and antiquary of the Emperor Maximillian [*sic*] and is a member of a large number of learned societies in America and Europe" (Bookmart 1886: 153). Boban's ability to promote himself is evident in this description, where he is not only a distinguished collector and author, but the emperor's antiquary and intimate as well.

Two catalogs of the collection were published in October 1886, just four months after Boban's arrival in New York. One described about 1,360 artifacts from Mexico alone, with multiple objects under each numbered listing, plus several thousands more from all over the world. The second catalog listed some 2,500 books and manuscripts, many of which had previously belonged to illustrious book collectors. The five-day auction began on 14 December.

"About 25 gentlemen attended" the opening day of the sale, according to a *New York Times* report. The article went on to give the credentials of the potential buyers on hand. "Most of those attending the sale are either dealers or private collectors, but Mr. Holmes, curator of the Pottery Department of the Smithsonian Institution, and Mr. Savage, representing the Metropolitan Museum of Art, were on hand watching for and improving favorable opportunities for enriching the collections of those institutions" (New York Times, 14 December 1886).

Boban wrote the foreword to the first auction catalog himself, although it was signed by Frossard and Sotheran, and presumably translated by Frossard. There are numerous versions of the foreword in the Hispanic Society papers. It describes the "extensive and remarkable Collection" as being mainly pieces "discovered by Monsieur Eugène Boban, or purchased directly from other explorers." It says that the collection "drew largely from the following sources: The Mexican Section of Antiquities, at the Paris Exposition of 1868 [*sic*]." Boban must have been referring to the 1878 exposition.

The other sources for the collection Boban cites are diverse and provide insight into his contacts and business practices. They include: "the Zapotecas series of Funereal Vases, obtained from the heirs of Monsieur Martin, formerly Consul in Mexico; the collection, gathered on the Gulf Coast, of the late Dr. Fuzier, Chief of the Polytechnic School, Paris; the Collection of Señor Don José M. Melgar, Mexican Archaeologist; [and] the remainder of the collection made by Count de Waldeck, the well-known explorer of Yucatan" (Leavitt 1886a: 5).

In its descriptions of the "Mexican archaeology" collection, the catalog includes numbers 1 to 226, comprising some "1,360 different specimens in bronze; obsidian, rock-crystal, jadeite, agate, steatite, jasper, serpentine, lava, marble, basalt, bone, shell, wood, and terra-cotta when no other term is used" (Leavitt 1886a: 8). A great number of the objects listed are small items such as stone and shell beads, spindle whorls, arrow points, obsidian blades and cores, along with a rather large group of ceramic figurines. Quite a few large and important ceramic artifacts are also listed, particularly the collection of Zapotec figures originally owned by Martin. Additionally, the catalog notes, "The materials of this part of the collection were originally classified by M. A. Damour, a distinguished mineralogist, member of the French Institute" (Leavitt 1886a: 7; SIA RU:7084).

Boban always gives credit to this friend for helping him classify the minerals in his collection. Damour was influential, had an international reputation and was a member of the Académie française, the most important scientific and intellectual society in France. Of course, being able to refer to him as a colleague added to Boban's own stature.

A number of the pre-Columbian objects in this catalog were clearly the products of recent excavations or surface collections carried out by Boban while in Mexico the previous year. For instance, number ninety-one is a "Terra cotta idol's head in basso-relievo, representing Quetzalcoatl or the god of air." It is listed as having been found by "Mons. Boban in Tula, in 1885, measuring 19 x 14 cm" (1886a: 15). The newspaper accounts stating that Boban accompanied Batres to Tula at the end of 1885, combined with the catalog description, indicate that he made a small collection while there. In addition to the Tula objects, there are some eighty other specimens, including "ceramic human heads," a large variety of obsidian pieces and assorted pottery artifacts, described as having been "excavated" by Mr. Boban at Teotihuacan.

The New York auction of Boban's artifact collection contained 1,925 numbered lots, with only slightly more than 10 percent coming from ancient Mexico. The pre-Columbian section ends at item 226 and is followed by two objects described as "Tlatelolco fabric," meaning modern fakes. The catalog continues with Mexican colonial objects, including an oil painting of Montezuma II. The "life size portrait" is described as follows: "Crowned and clothed in robes of state;

curious Mexican work, probably made by a Spanish monk, a few years after the Conquest. Excessively rare and valuable from a historical point of view. In good preservation. 165 cm by 125 cm" (Leavitt 1886a: 34). Mr. Savage, who represented the Metropolitan Museum of Art, purchased this item for $50, according to the 14 December 1886 *New York Times* report on the auction. The painting, which sounds much like the famous portrait in the Uffizi Gallery in Florence, has not been located at the Metropolitan Museum. In fact, inquiries have produced no information about the painting or Mr. Savage who purchased it.

Although his dream of displaying the collection in his Museo Científico had vanished, Boban obviously hoped that some other institutions would be able to do so for educational purposes. Following the pre-Columbian artifacts is item number 233, "A series of about 45 moulds in papier-maché taken by Dr. Antonio Pañafiel [sic], from the most interesting hieroglyphical monuments in the National Museum at Mexico. Made to order for Mr. Boban and never used. 25 cent. to 1 meter. Valuable lot for a museum" (Leavitt 1886a: 28). Item 236 is the "Skillfully executed mannequin, life size, representing a Knight of the Order of the Tiger," described as a superb centerpiece for an ethnological collection (Leavitt 1886a: 29).

Item 303 is also familiar. It lists "Mummies, Period of Spanish Inquisition in Mexico. At the time of the demolishing of the Convent of San [sic] Domingo, 1861, these mummies were found in one of the walls." The mummified corpses are listed as "four pieces" (Leavitt 1886a: 34). In today's museum world the description of the remains of four human beings as "pieces" is jarring, as is the notion of shipping them from one country to another for exhibition and sale. It is not known what had happened by this time to two of the "six historic mummies" that Boban had been exhibiting in Mexico City.

Despite the lavish and erudite sales catalog and presale advertisements promoting the auction of his objects and natural history specimens, Boban once again found it difficult to sell his collection, particularly the pre-Columbian artifacts. An item appearing in *The New York Times* on 19 December 1886, five days after the sale began, described the results of the auction. "In the opinion of competent judges of the current value of such luxuries, the collection would have brought between $30,000 and $40,000 in Paris, and the net result of the sale, about $10,500, brings disappointment to the collector" (New York Times, 19 December 1886).

The article goes on to review what sold and why more items did not. "Competition among the small audiences in attendance was tame, and many fine specimens were bought very cheap. In the case of curiosities from the South Sea Islands the reverse was the rule, and in many instances, notably that of a jade axe, which brought $175, high prices were obtained." The report continues with a bit of a shocker in terms of the item referenced and its price. "The highest price paid for a single article was $950, for which a Mr. Ellis obtained a human skull carved by ancient Mexicans from a large block of hyaline rock crystal" (New York Times, 19 December 1886).

Despite the "disappointment of the collector," Boban had realized more than fifty thousand francs for the objects he did sell. In another piece of good news, the crystal skull that he and Batres had tried to sell to the Museo Nacional was now being described by *The New York Times*, the paper of record, as having been sculpted by ancient Mexicans.

The second auction catalog for his library, prepared by Charles Sotheran, described Boban's printed books and manuscript collection. This part of the auction seems to have done quite well. Many of the books were personally inscribed to Boban by the authors, and quite a few had originally come from the libraries of Brasseur de Bourbourg and Alphonse Pinart.

Pinart had nearly become bankrupt in the 1870s and had been forced to sell his library for much-needed cash during an eight-day auction in Paris in 1883. Boban purchased numerous important editions. His name appears repeatedly in an annotated copy of the sales catalog, although he is referred to as "Beaubone." Notable among these was Brasseur's own copy of Fray Francisco Maldonado's Sermons in Cakchiquel Maya, quite a rare text published in 1671, for which Boban had paid 125 francs (Pinart 1883: 94).[2] This book sold at the New York auction for $32, which would have been about 160 francs at the time.

A *New York Tribune* article on 18 December 1886, provides an overview of the book auction, complete with the hammer prices of the pieces sold. "The printed books in the collection of M. Boban were sold yesterday, with the addition of some part of the manuscripts. With the exception of representatives from Yale and from Lehigh University, the bidders were chiefly private collectors. The sale showed a fair valuation of the different bibliographical treasures offered."[3]

The sale of Boban's books and manuscripts may have provided the largest portion of the money realized from his collection. Many of the books he sold were extraordinarily rare, certainly difficult to come by, and today can be found in only a handful in libraries of the United States and Europe. The manuscripts, including records of the Inquisition, presumably purchased from demolished churches, were equally important and rare.

Although Boban was finally able to sell the problematic crystal skull, in December of 1886 he was still forced to deal with the repercussions of his ill-considered association with Leopoldo Batres. Apparently, the inspector of monuments was informed of Boban's upcoming auction, perhaps having obtained a copy of the Leavitt & Co. catalogs from someone in the Mexican Consulate or a business associate.

In an open letter to the editors of the Mexico City newspaper *The Two Republics*, which appeared on the second and third of December of 1886—two weeks prior to the New York auction's opening day—Batres gives his version of the events that transpired in Mexico:

Through a letter just received from New York I am informed that Mr. Boban, a gentleman well known in this city, has stated to a number of scientists in the United States that on account of his thorough knowledge of the archaeology of Mexico, he had been appointed by the President to conduct excavations in the interest of science, and to re-arrange the exhibits in the National Museum which, he said, were in a horrible condition. According to my information he furthermore stated that he had already made important excavations, collecting a great many valuable specimens of ancient civilizations, and that he made the classification of the National Museum, where he was deceived by me and the employees of the institution, and so relentlessly persecuted that he was compelled to take his collection and leave for a foreign country in order to escape our malice. I will not discuss the absurd statement made by Mr. Boban that he was persecuted here, for it is well known that all scientific men have, at all times, been courteously received in this city. But I desire to give the lie to the other statements made by Mr. Boban. He never was appointed by the President to any charge, because we have in Mexico a great many men competent for the mission which he falsely claims to have filled. He never did any classification work in the National Museum. He never was consulted on any doubtful points in the archaeology of the country, and the museum never purchased any of the goods he offered, because the professors considered them unworthy of the establishment. As to his claims that he has made excavations and explorations, he can furnish no evidence, especially as it is well known that he never left this city during his stay in the republic (Two Republics, 3 December 1886, 2).

The published diatribe continued,

About the personal reflections which Mr. Boban has endeavored to cast on me I shall not say a word, as I do not think that the scientific or social world in which I am well known, both in this country and Europe, will credit anything that may emanate from the animosity of that gentleman. Before closing this communication, I desire to warn the scientific men of the United States of the fact that Mr. Boban's collection of Mexican antiquities were all obtained in Paris, and that he can give no authentic information whatever on the archaeology of Mexico. Yours very truly, Leopoldo Batres (Two Republics, 3 December 1886, 2).

It is clear in this letter that Batres is attempting to cover over his own transgressions with a blanket of accusation against Boban, thus stifling any questions about how and where Boban had obtained some of the pieces in his second pre-Columbian Mexican collection. *The Two Republics* ran the letter on consecutive days without comment, despite the fact that Wilson Blake, one of the paper's contributors and later an editor, knew Batres's screed was untruthful in many respects.

The statement that Boban never left Mexico City is patently false, since his tours of both Tula and Teotihuacan in the company of Batres were reported in several city newspapers, including *The Two Republics*. Although it is certainly true that Boban purchased a large part of his second collection in Paris from sources in Mexico, he added considerable material after he returned. At a minimum, the artifacts collected at Tula and Teotihuacan were excavated in 1885, and were removed with Batres's assistance, or at least his acquiescence. Batres's claim that Boban has no evidence to show that he made excavations and explorations can be interpreted to mean, "Whatever he says, he can't prove it." However, Boban did have physical proof of his excavations in the form of the artifacts from Teotihuacan and Tula.

While functioning as inspector of monuments, Leopoldo Batres purportedly extorted money from archeologists and collectors, as asserted in Boban's personal (unsent) observations to Hamy, and apparently sold authentic artifacts and fakes to foreign tourists. He sold artifacts to Mexico's national museum, too. The archives of the Museo Nacional contain numerous receipts from Batres that demonstrate he was selling to the museum what he excavated or collected at the government's expense, as though the collections were his personal property.[4] How he got away with this is another matter.

Boban's relationship with Batres was promising at the beginning. Clearly Boban felt that working with the inspector of monuments would help him in his goal to educate the Mexican public about their pre-Columbian heritage. Visiting sites and digging up artifacts with Batres could only enhance the appeal of the Museo Científico exhibits, since visitors would know that the pieces displayed had recently been excavated. The collaboration on the creation and publication of the archeological chart is another indication that Boban was trying to work with Batres to share knowledge and insight with scholars, students, and the public at large. With Batres assuring him that President Díaz would purchase one thousand posters himself, Boban ordered a first run of two thousand, so he could sell other posters to educators and administrators throughout the country.

Then everything changed. Boban found himself burdened by debt when the museum admission fees and poster sales did not materialize. Financial pressures may have led him to justify his partnership with Batres in the attempted sale of the crystal skull to the Museo Nacional, from which he would have recouped a considerable amount of money. When that scheme was publicly denounced, Batres apparently turned on his collaborator and threated to expose him as an antiquities smuggler. This turn of events led Boban to flee the country, taking the precaution of bribing Batres with a variety of scientific instruments and books to smooth the way. Now Batres had gone too far. He had publicly attacked the very thing Boban lived by, and considered sacrosanct, his honesty and his reputation as an expert on pre-Columbian archeology and cultural history. Boban was furious.

If Boban managed to constrain himself in reporting to his colleague Ernest T. Hamy about what had happened during his eighteen months in Mexico, this was not the case with a letter he sent to Gen. Porfirio Díaz, the president of Mexico. Cooler heads did not prevail in this instance. The letter is similar in its uncensored tone to the draft that was never sent to Hamy and reads as a stream of consciousness rant against Batres. The style is overly familiar, as though writing to an old pal. Devoid of the respect due to the office of the president, it is full of errors in grammar, punctuation, and spelling. The document is now in the archive of the Universidad Iberoamericana in Mexico City.

Dated 20 December 1886, after the auction of his collection had been completed, the letter, written in French, begins by addressing Díaz as "Mr. President and dear F." This is a Masonic salutation—the F stands for frère (brother) followed by three dots in the shape of a pyramid indicating that a fellow Mason is writing. Boban became a Mason during his first sojourn in Mexico, sometime between 1857 and 1869. Freemasonry played a large and important role in Mexican politics, starting with the War of Independence from Spain. Later, during the War of Reform, President Benito Juárez was a Mason, as were nearly all liberals and reformers. At the time it was a way to establish one's credentials as a revolutionary and free thinker who opposed the Catholic Church and its conservative backers. Boban begins his letter to the President with "I write in the name of Freemasonry to beg you to chastise the miserable person who is shockingly in your midst. I refer to Leopoldo Batres, a despicable and wicked man, who armed with some letters he received from you, and who you unfortunately treat as a friend, shows these letters to everyone and uses them to profit from and influence people" (UI CPD leg.11, caja 28, doc 13681, p.1).[5]

Boban goes on to call Batres every name in the book in this four-page, handwritten communication. He describes incidents in which the inspector speaks ill of nearly everyone of any importance, including the president himself. Boban informs President Díaz that Batres knows nothing of archeology, and accuses him of being nearly illiterate, saying he is incapable of writing a letter even in his own language. For a corroborating evaluation, he suggests that the President consult the respected Mexican archeologist Ignacio Altamirano, who also happened to be president of the Sociedad de Geografía y Estadística.

Boban continues his letter by writing that he had met Batres in Paris in 1883 when he had traveled to France. "He begged me to nominate him as a member of our society of Anthropology, saying that he had published many scientific papers in Mexico. . . . Upon my return to Mexico City in March 1885, I was unable to find any [publications] and had him erased from the [society's] list since he is an infamous swindler."[6]

"Recently," Boban fumes, "in revenge" for a disagreement he had with Batres, "when I dealt with him as he deserved—he was too cowardly to demand satisfaction but slandered me from afar."[7] Following this reference to the letter in *The Two Republics,* he says he would not answer this "venomous beast" in the American press.

Up to this point Boban has pulled out all the stops in an attempt to do as much damage as possible to Batres. He then moves on to flattering the president and professing his constant support for the liberal cause since the 1850s. "I myself have great affection for everything that relates to Mexico and particularly for you personally. [It is] the country, where I spent 20 years of my youth, and where I constantly worked for the Liberal Party."[8]

In closing Boban once again appeals to the president as a fellow Mason, "So my dear . . . On behalf of the Grand Orient of France and the American Lodge, I beg you to make an inquiry of this scoundrel Leopoldo Batres. From this inquiry you will learn many sad things, and then you will give the miserable scoundrel what he deserves—a good whip lashing" (UI CPD leg.11, caja 28, doc 13681, p.3).[9]

It is hard to imagine that Boban actually believed that President Díaz would fire his inspector of monuments after reading his letter. It is likelier that in sending this uncensored document he was more interested in relieving himself of a lot of bad feelings. This letter, written by a consummate salesman and self-promoter, who is normally exceedingly polite, diplomatic, and in many ways charming, is utterly uncharacteristic in its rude and vulgar tone. Boban clearly has been wounded and has temporarily lost his self-control. There is no evidence that Porfirio Díaz responded.

All in all, Boban's feud with Batres was relatively short-lived, compared to others the inspector of monuments conducted. Batres's nasty public letter about the Frenchman in *The Two Republics* pales in comparison with the ten-page diatribe attacking American archeologist Zelia Nuttall that he had privately printed in 1910. He was responding to Nuttall's own attack against him, which she presented in a paper given at the Society of Americanists meeting held in New York and published in *American Anthropologist* earlier the same year. Nuttall was extremely blunt in her accusations, which echo Boban's:

> The present 'Inspector and Conservator of Archaeological Monuments' is also Director of the Government Explorations at San Juan Teotihuacan besides being a Contractor and Museum Classifier. Although he draws salaries for all of these monopolies, this government official has for years, as many tourists and scientists are willing to testify, openly dealt in antiquities from different parts of Mexico, as well as from Teotihuacan, and received payment for 'affording facilities' for taking said purchases out of the country, although its laws forbid their exportation. (Nuttall 1910: 282)

Her comments spurred Batres to publish a screed called "La Isla de Sacrificios, la Señora Zelia Nuttall de Pinard [*sic*] y Leopoldo Batres." Employing his usual tactics of personal attack, he insultingly and continually refers to her as "Mrs. Pinard," despite the fact that she had been divorced from Alphonse Pinart for more than two decades and had gone to court to reinstate her maiden name

(Parmenter 1966: 32). In one particularly mean-spirited passage, Batres avers that "Mrs. Pinard" had always treated him with a marked ill will, owing to the fact that she knew that he never took her seriously in any sense. He justifies this low opinion by adding, "I have known her from many years ago when she lived in Paris with her husband 'Mr. Pinard,' and I knew then what to expect of her" (Batres 1910b: 4).[10]

Eugène Boban's 1886 letter to the president of Mexico lambasting Leopoldo Batres's character and thoroughly deprecating his work and intelligence did not have the desired effect. Batres maintained his position as inspector of monuments for another twenty-four years. It is difficult to know whether Zelia Nuttall's spirited public attack made a significant dent in the inspector's reputation. Batres would only keep his job for a few months after Nuttall's article appeared, but his ousting resulted from the Mexican Revolution, which toppled the administration of President Díaz.

Notes

1. M. Le Plongeon possede beaucoup de documents, dessins, plans, estampages, photographies du Yucatan et surtout de monuments connus de lui seul.

2. This information was gleaned from an annotated published catalog belonging to Harvard University library, which has been digitized by Google and is available online.

3. Some of the prices were as follows: for Baradère's 'Antiquities Mexicaines,' $45; for the Bulletin of Mexican Geography and History in ten volumes, $440; for Froehner's "Verrerie Antique" with plates colored by hand, and of which only 150 copies were printed, $31; . . . Among the manuscripts in highest estimation . . . a bundle of Mexican manuscripts dating from the Sixteenth Century, including a portion of the original archives of the Holy Inquisition of Mexico with plans and drawings, for which $80 was given (New York Tribune, 18 December 1886).

4. *f. 78—Recibí de la Tesoreria del Museo Nacional . . . 137 pesos para 21 antiguedades Zapotecas, de distintas localidades, adquiridas por mi en el Estado de Oaxaca, y que he vendido a este establesimiento, Mexico, 14 May 1881 Leopoldo Batres.* I received from the treasury of the National Museum 137 pesos for 21 Zapotec antiquities, from different locations, acquired by me in the State of Oaxaca, and which I have sold to this establishment.

f. 80—Recibí . . . 120 valor de una colección de antiguedades Mexicanas compuesta de un cuadro que contiene dos escudos y un colgante de oro, varios dijes agata y porfido y ademas unas basos de barro decorados que vendi para dicho establecimiento—Mexico 30 de Julio 1881—Leopoldo Batres, I received 120 [pesos]—the value of a collection of Mexican antiquities composed of a box containing two shields and a gold pendant, various household idols in agate and porphyry and also some decorated ceramic vessels which I sold to the said establishment.

f. 144—Recibí . . . 28 pesos, 7 pieças antiguas y son las siguientes, una cabeza de vivora, de porfiro, una ollita de barro . . . una careta de tecali. 8 junio 1882, L. Batres, I received 28 pesos for 7 ancient objects . . . a snake head of porphyry, a small olla of clay . . . and a travertine mask.

5. Je viens aux nom de la maçonnerie vous suplier de faire châtier un miserable qui par surprise est arrive au près de vous. Je veux parler d'un nommé Leopoldo Batres, un ètre abject et mechant, qui armè de quelques lettres qu'il à reçu de vous ou par malheur vous le traitez de cher ami il les faits voir a tout le monde et s'en sert a son profit, et pour influencer plusieur personnes.

6. En 1883 lors d'un voyage qu'il fit a Paris . . . il me suplié de le faire nommè membre de notre societe d'Anthropologie en me disant qu il avait boucoup publie d'ouvrage sur les sciences a Mexico ce notad qu un Mansonge a mon retour a Mexico en Mars 1885 apres information je n'ai pu que constate que des enfamie et nombreuses escroquerie sur son compte, jai d'u le faire rayer de la liste des membre comme infame chevalier d'industries.

7. Dernierement il m'a calomnie dans les journaux de Mexico entre autre Les Deux Republiques du 2 de Dicembre 1886. Simplement pour se venger d'une querelle qui nous avons en ou je le traitait comme il le meritait. Trop làche pour m'en demander raison, il me calomnie de loin, c'est plus facile.

8. Comme j'ai personnellement baucoup d'affections pour tout ce que touché le Mexique et votre personnalite en particulier ce pays ou j'ai passe 20 ans de ma jeunesse ou j'ai constamment travaille pour le Parti Liberal.

9. Je viens donc Mon cher.: Comme Maçon du nom du Grand Orient de France et des loge Americaine vous suplier de faire lever une Enquète sur ce chenapan de Leopoldo Batres. Cette enquète vous apprendrez des chose bien triste et alors vous ferez chassez ce miserable coquin comme il le merite à coups de cravaches.

10. Para juzgar de la conducta seguida por la Sra. Pinard en este escabroso asunto, basta saber que siempre que se ha tratado de mí ha manifestado una marcada mala voluntad, debido tal vez á que ha comprendido que nunca la he tomado en serio en ningún sentido, pues la conozco desde hace muchos años, desde que vivía en París con su esposo Mr. Pinard, y sabía yo desde entonces cuales eran los alcances de la protagonista de este denuncio.

15

FINGERPRINTS ON CRYSTAL SKULLS

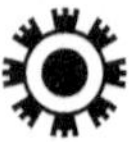

The description of item #1491 of the Leavitt auction catalog, in the "Geology, Mineralogy, Gems" section reads "Human skull, natural size, dolicephalous in shape, deep eye-sockets, nose cavity, upper and lower jaws, cut from a large and solid block of hyaline rock-crystal. Smooth polished surface. A magnificent, perfect and unique specimen. Length 20, height 14 ½, width 13 centimeters. Mexico" (Leavitt 1886a: 84). Following this physical description, the catalog goes on to present a series of essentially truthful statements through which Boban adroitly misleads potential buyers into thinking that this skull and others like it are actually pre-Columbian artifacts. This expanded description reads, "The human skull played an important part in the religious ceremonial of the Ancient Mexicans, and small specimens in terra-cotta, green stone and rock crystal are not infrequently found in museums and private collections, but the Boban specimen is by far the largest and finest one known, and is considered by him one of the most curious and important, as well as one of the most valuable objects in his collection" (Leavitt 1886a: 84). Although the large skull is not listed among the Mexican pre-Columbian artifacts, its provenance is given as Mexico, and its connection to Ancient Mexican cultures and rarity is emphasized.

This is not the only crystal object for sale. There is another rock crystal skull listed in the catalog, although it is much smaller and is placed prominently within the Mexican antiquities section. It is item five: "Human skull, carved in rock-crystal, 3 ½ cent. Valley of Mexico." Accompanying it are a rock crystal lip plug, a rock crystal hand that is 4 cm long, and two fragments of other rock crystal lip plugs, all of which are described as Aztec (Leavitt 1886a: 8, 12). Also included in the auction catalog, although not in the pre-Columbian section, are three rock crystal balls, one rock crystal cup, two polished pieces of rock crystal

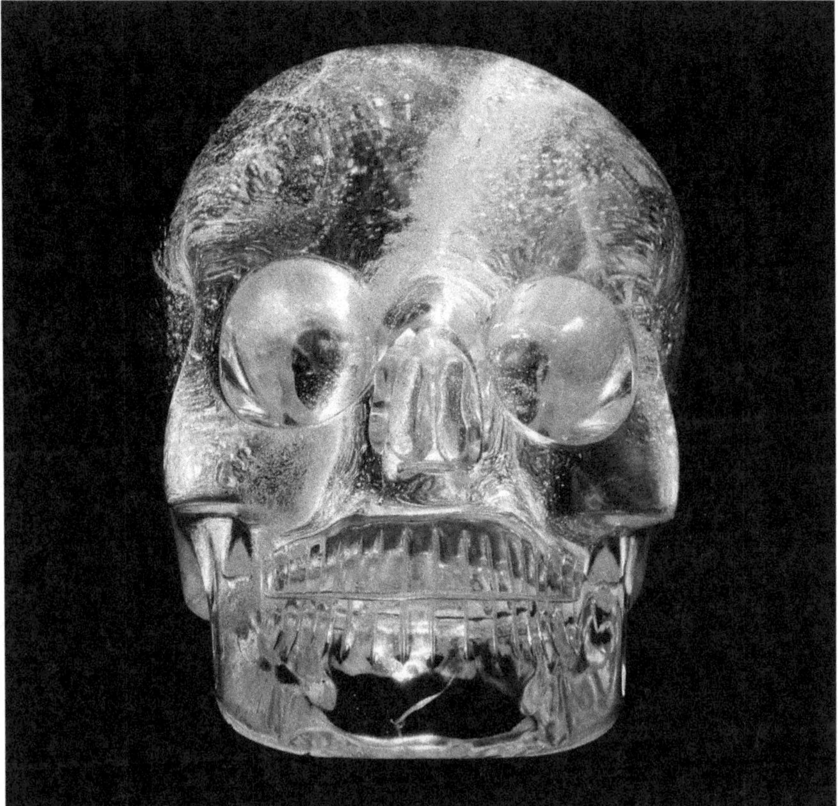

Figure 15.1   Boban skull auctioned to Tiffany & Co. and later sold to the British Museum (courtesy of the British Museum, London, Ethno 1898.1).

and something described as a "rock crystal stand; death's head, etc. engraved, 5 cm" (Leavitt 1886a: 85).

William Henry Holmes, who attended the auction, annotated his copy of the catalog, which is now in the Smithsonian Institution Archives. He listed the buyers of many individual items and the prices paid, along with sketches of particular pieces that interested him. His notes indicate that the large crystal skull was sold to a Mr. Ellis for the grand sum of $950, making it by far the most expensive item sold in the auction. The carrying case for the skull, which was covered with iguana skin and presumably made in Mexico, sold for $50, rounding up the total for the large crystal skull to $1,000.

The life-size crystal skull, purchased by Ellis at the New York sale, ultimately entered the collections of the British Museum. It took a while to get there, however, leaving a public trail. It is the same skull that Boban first offered in his Paris store as an exemplary work of lapidary art sometime between 1878 and

1881. It is the skull that he exhibited in his Museo Científico, carefully placed on a table behind two of the Santo Domingo mummies. It is the same skull that he and Leopoldo Batres attempted to sell to the Museo Nacional as a pre-Columbian artifact from Veracruz—the failed transaction that ended Boban's museum career in Mexico.

When Boban first listed the piece in his Paris sales catalog in 1881, his asking price had been 3,500 francs. In 1886 the exchange value for the French franc remained five to the dollar, meaning that the troublesome skull finally brought five thousand francs to its owner—a rather large sum. The majority of artifacts in the auction did not do as well. A Mr. Douglass purchased the small crystal skull included under item five, according to William Henry Holmes's annotation, for $2.50 (Leavitt 1886a: 7).

Mr. Ellis, who bought the large skull, was associated with Tiffany & Co., and George Frederick Kunz, Tiffany's vice president, sent an assistant to complete the transaction. A postcard signed by George F. Kunz is in the antiquarian's papers in the Bibliothèque nationale in Paris. It is addressed to Mons. E. Boban, 111 Clinton Place, and reads, "Please deliver to bearer wooden case for skull" (BNF DMO n.a.f. 21477: item 524).

Within a few months of its purchase by Tiffany's, the skull was sold to a private collector and Kunz was exhibiting it at a variety of venues, while it was on loan from the new owner. "At a recent meeting of the American Association for the Advancement of Science, held in New York in August, a paper read by Mr. George F. Kunz, with the house of Tiffany & Co., excited a lively interest," reads a *New York Times* report on the gathering. "It described a crystal skull and a jadeite votive axe, both objects being exhibited to the audience, and referred to during the reading of his paper by Mr. Kunz, who, at our particular request, has permitted us to print his remarks as they will appear in the forthcoming reports of the Association" (New York Times, 13 August 1887).

By this point the story of the skull's origins and journey had become more elaborate. No longer had Boban had it in his possession in Paris since 1881 and auctioned it off in 1886. According to Kunz, it came from Mexico, was sold to an Englishman and later to Boban. Next it went to a client of Tiffany's. He is quoted as saying, "The skull, which I herewith exhibit, was originally brought from Mexico by a Spanish officer, before the Maximilian conquest [prior to 1862], and was sold to Mr. Evans, the English collector, at whose death it passed into the hands of Mr. E. Boban. It is now in the possession of Mr. George H. Sisson of this city, who has kindly loaned it to me for exhibition to-day" (Kunz 1887: 40).

The *New York Times* article gives a sense of the drama with which the skull was presented at the meeting. "Mr. Kunz produced a curious cabinet made of the skin of a Mexican lizard, which, when opened, revealed a skull of nearly natural size and almost transparent" (New York Times, 13 August 1887). One can almost hear the gasps of the scientists in the audience.

Kunz, who published a great many articles on his gemological studies, was not above embroidering a story, even a good story, as illustrated by the description of his first visit to Boban at his 10th Street address. The gemologist most likely embellished the crystal skull's history, since nowhere does Boban claim to have acquired it from the late Mr. Evans. Boban did correspond with the English collector John Evans, who purchased Solutrean artifacts, including actual human skulls and bones. Their correspondence occurred in 1884, several years after Boban had acquired this particular crystal skull. Additionally, this Evans did not die until well into the twentieth century.

George Frederick Kunz also altered his story about the jadeite votive adz, now known as the Kunz Axe in the American Museum of Natural History, which he also presented at the meeting of the American Association for the Advancement of Science. In a book published in 1913, he claimed to have come into possession of the axe in 1890. However, the Smithsonian's National Anthropological Archives contains a letter of his dated 4 December 1886, which states, "I have recently come into possession of what I have reason to believe from my knowledge and recollection of foreign cabinets to be the finest [object] of true jadeite ever found on the American continent. It is said to be of Mexican origin" (NAA Powell Corres #335). Kunz adds that he hopes the Smithsonian will publish an article about the remarkable object, and includes a tracing of it, front and back. The enormous Olmec jadeite votive adz is perhaps the most impressive, certainly the largest and most exquisitely carved example of this rare type of object. The letter is dated nine days before Boban's auction. It is likely Kunz purchased the votive adz from Boban despite the fact that he never revealed his source for the artifact. Kunz clearly knew Boban well. They had corresponded since at least 1881, and Kunz himself described his visit to Boban's home in New York shortly after he had arrived from Mexico.

One part of Kunz's embroidered story—the statement that Boban had not acquired the skull in Mexico—is accurate. Recent studies have shown that the rock crystal in this skull and its inclusions are consistent with quartz from Madagascar (Sax et al. 2008). Since France had colonial interests in Madagascar in the 1870s and 1880s, it is probable that the skull was carved in France, and not long before Boban first acquired it.

George Frederick Kunz was not only interested in the crystal skull purchased by Tiffany's, but in crystal skulls in general. In 1890, in his book *Gems and Precious Stones*, he summarized where they could be found. "Small skulls are in the Blake Collection at the United States National Museum [the Smithsonian], the Douglas [*sic*] Collection, New York, The British Museum and the Trocadéro. A large skull, now in the possession of George H. Sisson of New York, is very remarkable" (Kunz 1890: 285). Here he is accounting for five crystal skulls—walnut-sized skulls at the Smithsonian, the British Museum and the Douglass Collection and the grapefruit-size skull at the Trocadéro. He mentions the life-size skull that Tiffany's sold to George Sisson. What is remarkable about this list is that three of the five crystal skulls have a direct link to Eugène Boban, and the other two have a possible link to him.

Kunz's list accounts for half of the ten crystal skulls now known to have appeared in museum or private collections during the nineteenth century. Number one is a small skull 1 7/16 in. high (3.7 cm) identified by Kunz as being part of the Blake Collection in the United States National Museum (Smithsonian Institution; cat. #98949). William Henry Holmes purchased the skull and other objects in 1886 from Wilson W. Blake. The skull itself came from the collection of Father Augustin Fischer, Maximilian's confessor. It is possible that Fischer purchased this crystal skull from Boban while he still had his shop in Mexico City in the 1850s and 1860s. He could also have purchased it during Boban's second visit to Mexico. The two men knew each other, and Boban kept Fischer's business card with an 1885 address, indicating that he visited the Museo Científico. This small skull disappeared from the Smithsonian's collections some time after it was taken off exhibit in the early 1970s.

Number two is the one that Kunz identifies as part of the Douglass Collection (human skull carved in rock-crystal; 3.5 cm high) or 1.5 in. high (Leavitt 1886a: 7). This one came from Boban's 1886 New York auction, as shown by Holmes's annotation listing Douglass as the buyer. In 1901, Andrew Ellicott Douglass donated this skull to the American Museum of Natural History in New York, along with a crystal hand and twenty-three thousand other artifacts from his collection (AMNH Douglass Collection, cat. # DN 28).

Skull number three is a small skull that Kunz says was in the British Museum (cat. # Am, St.420). This skull is 1.2 in. high, 0.9 in. wide and 1.4 in. deep or 3 cm by 2.4 cm by 3.5 cm (Sax and Meeks 2009: 48). According to the museum's records, Henry Christy purchased it before his death in 1865. However, it was not mentioned in a catalog of Christy's entire collection published by the museum in 1868. Since crystal skulls were considered to be so remarkable, one would assume it would have been included had it been part of the collection at that time. If Christy did not acquire the skull himself, one of the collection's curators, Augustus Wollaston Franks or Charles Hercules Reed, might have added it to the collection after Christy's death, using funds that were provided in his will. Both Franks and Reed corresponded with and made purchases from Boban's Paris atelier.

The fourth skull on Kunz's list in the Trocadéro collections is the grapefruit-size crystal skull that Alphonse Pinart bought from Boban in 1875 (cat. # 71.1878.1.57—4.5 in. high or 11.3 cm). This skull was exhibited at the Exposition Universelle of 1878.

The fifth skull Kunz mentions is the "very remarkable" natural-size Sisson skull. It was in Boban's collection from 1881 onward, purchased by Tiffany's in the 1886 auction, and sold to Sisson in 1887. In 1897 Tiffany's sold it to

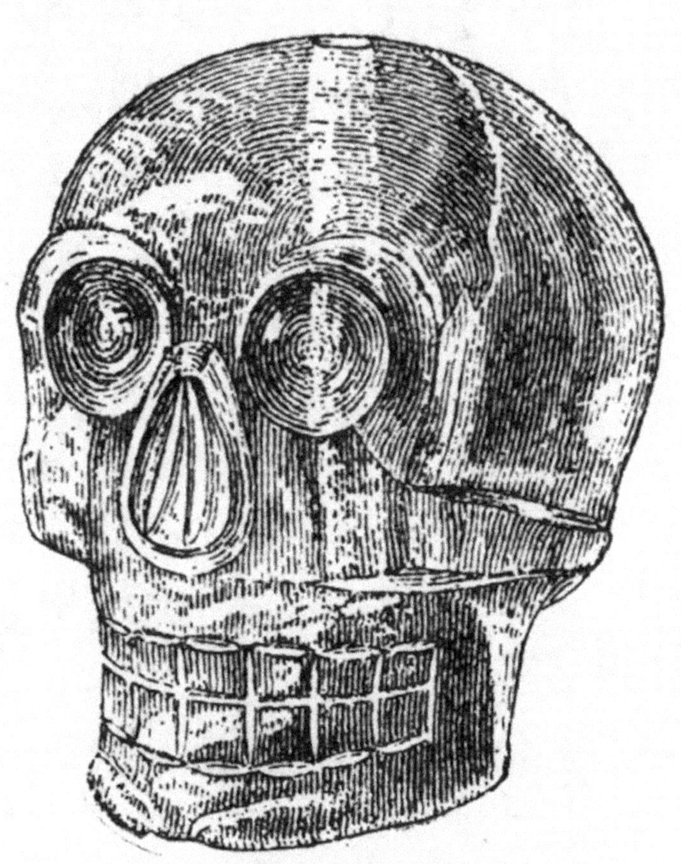

Figure 15.2 Crystal skull in Smithsonian's Blake Collection (Smithsonian Institution, Department of Anthropology, 98949. Annual Report 1896: 463).

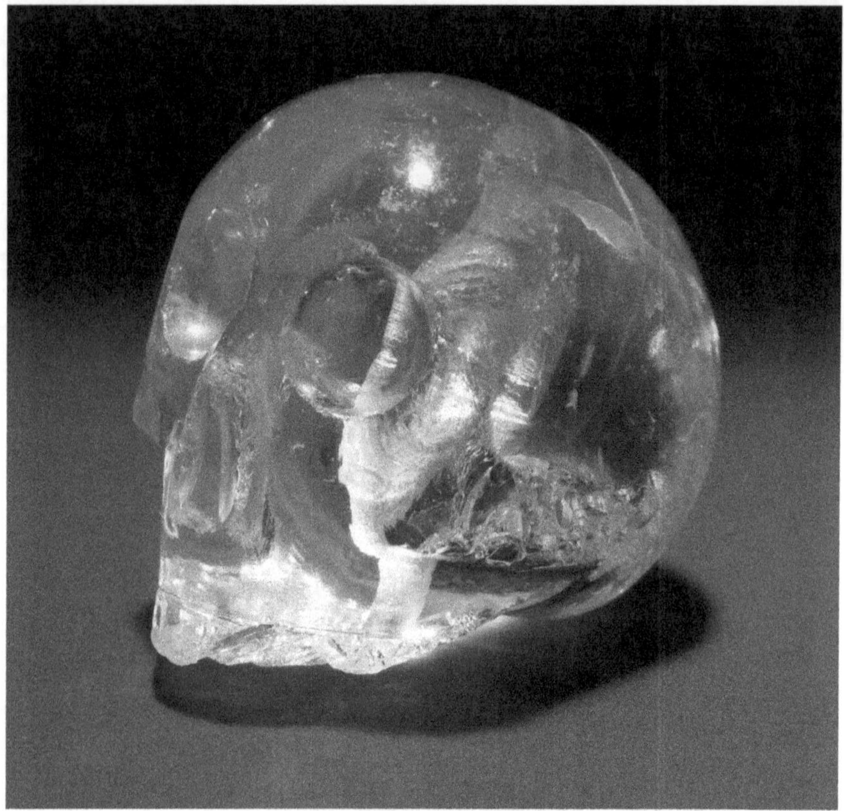

Figure 15.3   Crystal skull in the Christy Collection at the British Museum (courtesy of the British Museum, London, Am, St.420).

the British Museum for $950 or £220, the equivalent of £27,000 today (cat. # Am1898-1; 8.25 in. or 21 cm high).

In addition to the skulls that Kunz enumerated in 1890, five other documented crystal skulls entered European and Mexican museum collections before the publication of *Gems and Precious Stones*. The first of these is the very small skull that was sold by Boban to Pinart in 1875, which had been exhibited at the Exposition Universelle in 1867 and drawn by Jean Amatus Klein in 1866. It is now in the Musée du quai Branly with the catalog number 71.1878.1.216 AM; and is 0.7 in. or 1.8 cm. high. This skull has suffered some damage during its years in the museum's collection.

There are two small skulls in Mexico's Museo Nacional. They were both purchased from local collectors, with the earliest coming from Luis M. Costantino. He sold it to the museum for twenty-eight pesos on 30 July 1874 (#108—f. 109). Coincidentally, Eugène Boban acquired a large collection of Mexican antiquities

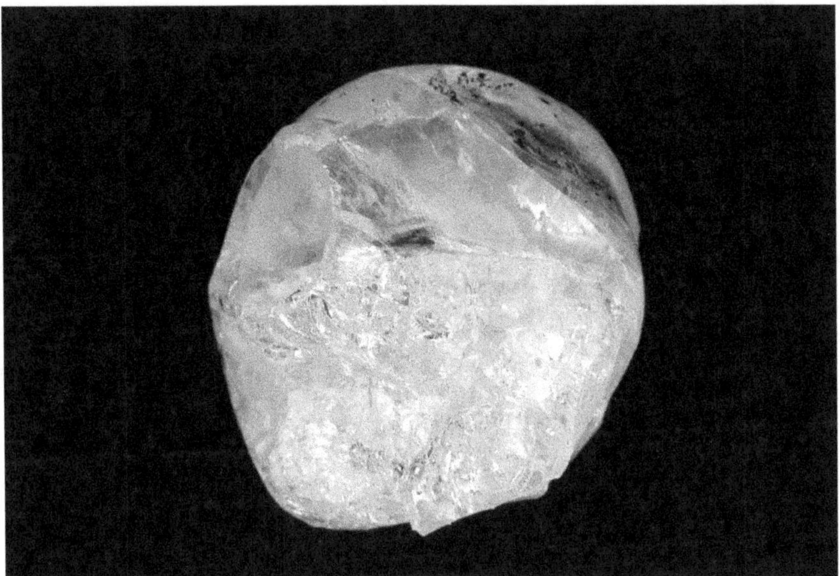

Figure 15.4 Small crystal skull in the Pinart collection of the Musée du quai Branly (courtesy of Musée du quai Branly, Paris, 71.1878.1.216).

from Luigi Constantini in 1878, which he exhibited at the Exposition Universelle the same year. Constantini, an Italian who had lived in Mexico for thirty years, had been, according to Boban, governor of the military school at Chapultepec (HSA: B2244, Box V). Certainly, Luis Costantino and Luigi Constantini could be the same person, and the antiquarian and this crystal skull collector knew each other. The museum's director Gumersindo Mendoza purchased a second small skull on 1 January 1880, from Felix Mala for thirty pesos (#239—f.237). One skull now is exhibited in the Valley of Mexico or Aztec hall, while the other is on display in the Valley of Oaxaca hall as a Mixtec artifact.

There is a small crystal skull attached to a sixteenth-century German reliquary box made of ebony, silvered metal, and rock crystal. It sits at the base of a crystal crucifix. Vincenzo Funghini, the well-known nineteenth-century collector of early ceramics and other antiquities, who was a native son of Arezzo, donated the reliquary to the Museo Nazionale d'Arte Medievale e Moderna in Arezzo, Italy in the 1880s.

There is recent information (Eric Taladoire, pers. comm.) about yet another small crystal skull that entered another Italian collection during the last quarter of the nineteenth century. Zaverio Calpini owned an establishment called Calpini Hermanos that sold toys, luxury items, and eyeglasses and was listed in the Mexican Empire Commercial Directory in 1867. Calpini donated the skull to the museum in Turin, Italy, in 1876. The Calpini Brothers' address was at the

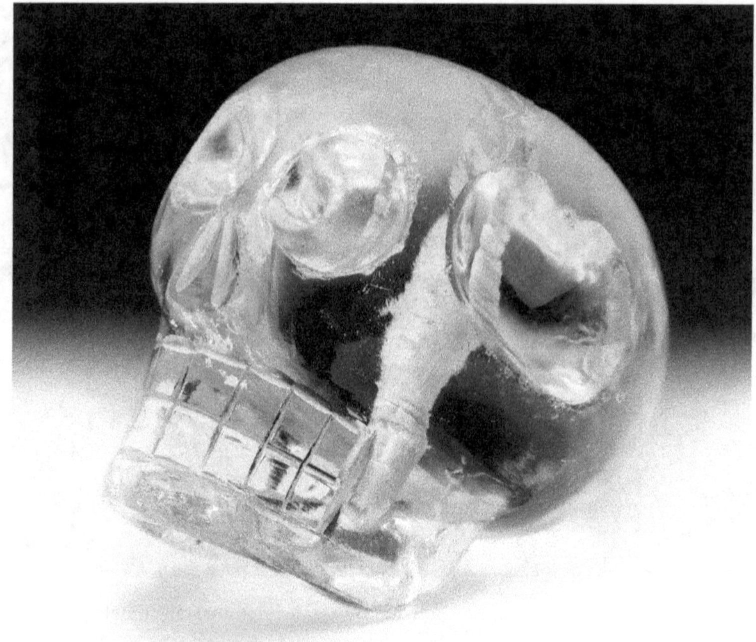

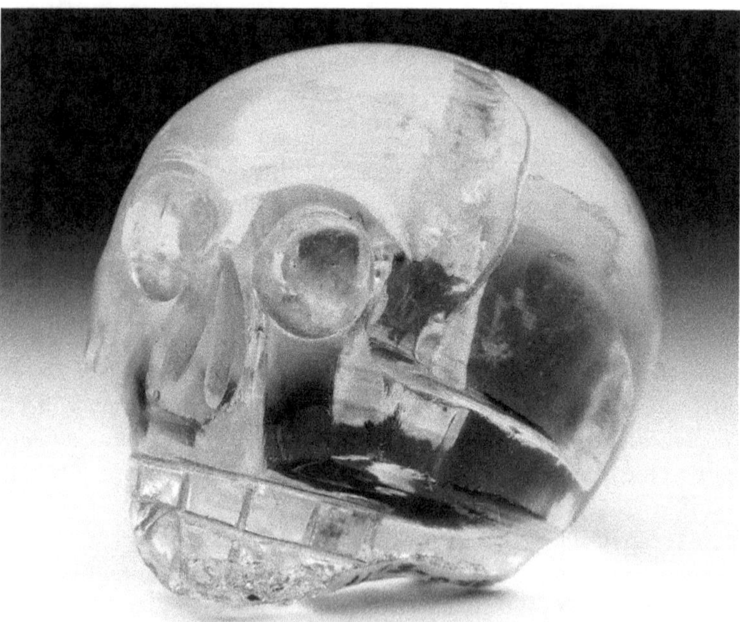

Figures 15.5a–b Costantino and Mala crystal skulls in the collections of the Museo Nacional (courtesy of the Museo Nacional de Antroplogía, Mexico City).

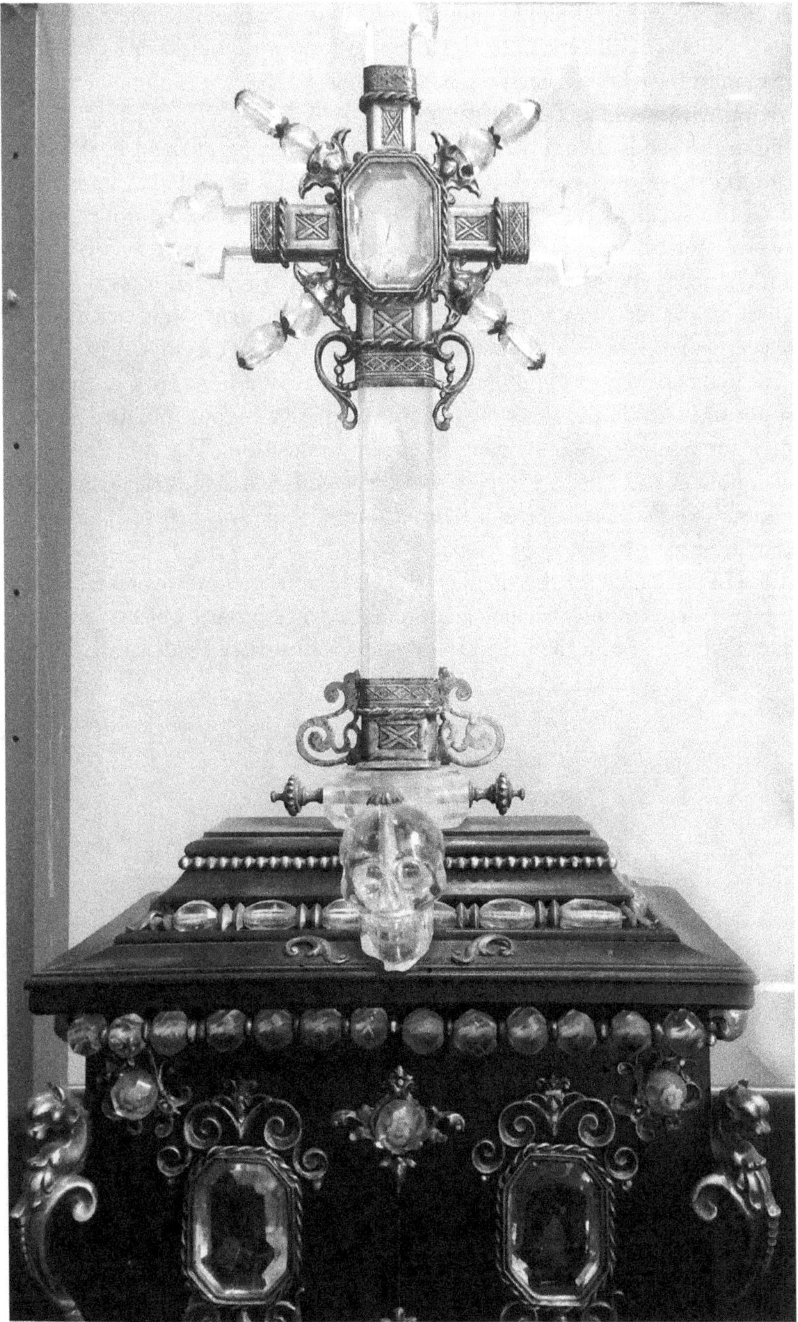

Figure 15.6 Crystal skull on a reliquary in the Vincenzo Funghini Collection (courtesy of Museo Nazionale d'Arte Medievale e Moderna, Arezzo, Italy).

corner of San Francisco and Callejón del Espíritu Santo, just a few doors from Boban's shop (Maillefert 1992: 260). Since they were neighbors, Calpini and Boban must have known each other, and it may be that the skull now in Turin is yet another one sold by Boban (cat. # 731).

From the skulls themselves, or visual documentation of them in the case of those that have disappeared, it is easy to see a strong similarity among them. All of the smaller crystal skulls that are or were in museum collections are approximately the same size—between slightly less than 1 to 1.5 in. or 1.8 to 4 cm high, about the size of a walnut. They all have wavy lines incised in a cross pattern on the top to indicate sutures (a feature the larger skulls lack). They all have vertical drill holes and resemble each other in their carving—with deep eye sockets, concave cheeks and flattened temples. In addition, most of them were first documented during the same twenty-year period—from 1867 to 1887—and except for one, all have a strong Mexican connection. The two large Boban skulls, now in the British Museum and Musée du quai Branly, appeared during the same two decades, although neither one of them was first seen in Mexico, and neither has sutures.

One likely source for the smaller skulls that appeared in Mexico City during those two decades is Catholic devotional and ceremonial objects. They may originally have been attached to the crucifixes on rosary beads carried by nuns

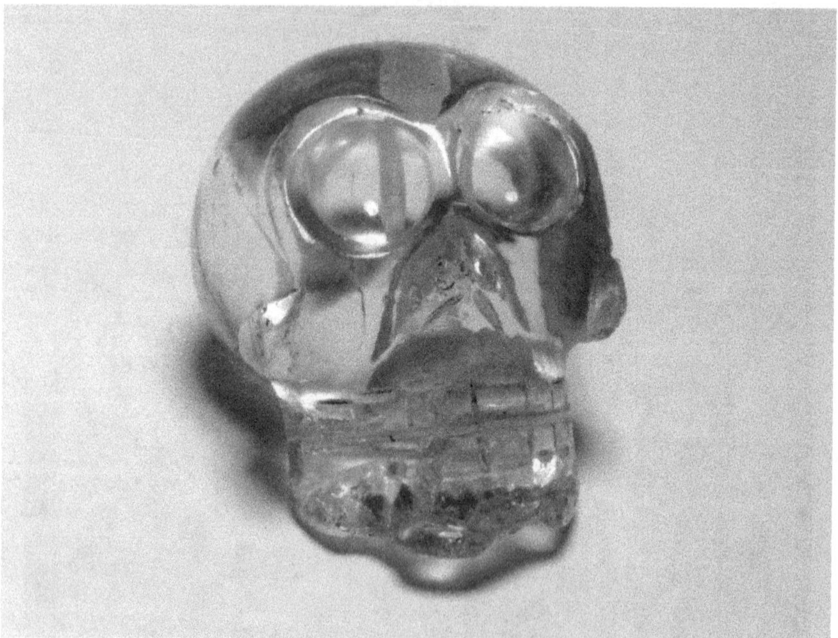

Figure 15.7 Crystal skull in the Zaverio Calpini Collection, Turin, Italy (courtesy of the Fondazione Torino Musei).

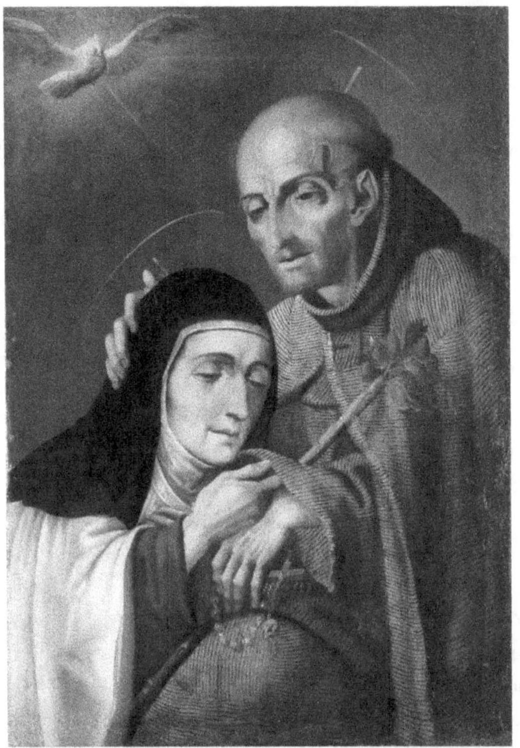

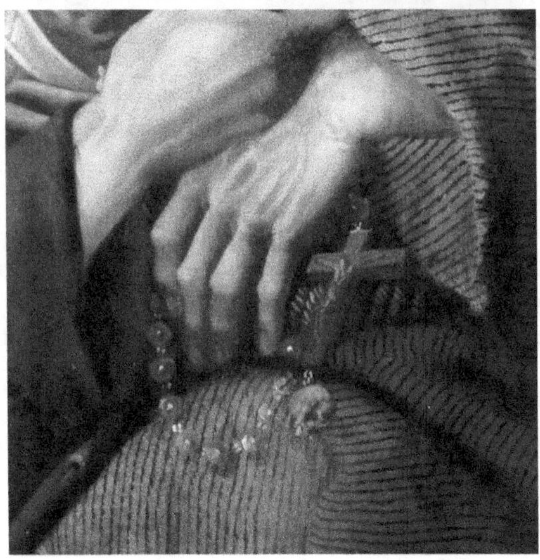

Figures 15.8a–b *Saints Peter of Alcántara and Teresa of Avila* by Melchor Pérez Holguín, with detail of a hand holding a rosary with a skull bead below the crucifix (courtesy of Hispanic Society of America, New York).

residing in the many convents demolished by President Benito Juárez. A painting entitled *Saints Peter of Alcántara and Teresa of Avila* by Melchor Pérez Holguín, a Bolivian artist working in the late seventeenth and early eighteenth century, now hangs just outside the reading room of the Hispanic Society in New York. In the image one of the saints holds a rosary with a small skull, possibly rock crystal, suspended from the bottom of the crucifix. Along with the many other objects he acquired in this manner, it is quite possible that Boban purchased rosary beads like those in the painting following the destruction of the monasteries and convents. Later he repurposed these skulls minus the rosaries as Aztec artifacts.

The grapefruit-size skull in the quai Branly collection that Boban sold to Pinart has a vertical drill hole like those in the small skulls. One of the photographs showing a group of Mexican religious objects in Boban's shop includes a crucifix that has a Christ figure hanging from what appears to be tree limbs. The crucifix has a curved extension on the bottom that resembles the slightly curved hole drilled through the quai Branly's skull. It is likely that this larger crystal skull supported that crucifix, or one like it, at some point in its history. Boban transformed this Catholic object into an Aztec artifact simply by identifying it as such.

The association of the skull of Adam with the crucifixion was first seen in Christian iconography of the West in the ninth century AD and continued as a feature of Catholic art (Hall 1996: 85). The imagery comes from the Byzantine church, which portrayed the skull at the foot of the cross. The skull thus became a multivalent symbol of death, redemption, and resurrection (Jover 2010: 39), and was a particular feature of the art of the Counter-Reformation from 1545 to 1648. The skull is also one of the attributes of St. Francis of Assisi, along with the stigmata, crucifix, and lily (Hall 1996: 131). In 1524, twelve members of the Franciscan order were the first missionaries to arrive in Mexico to convert the country's indigenous population. Many of the objects used for reverence and worship by the Franciscan friars and members of other orders could well have incorporated smaller and larger crystal skulls. It may not have been at all coincidental that Boban listed the rock crystal skull in his 1881 sales catalog just above the "very beautiful ivory Christ on an ebony cross atop a gilded wooden base" more than a meter high (Boban 1881: 49).[1] This figure is the second most expensive item in his shop at two thousand francs. Perhaps the crystal skull would have been set before such a splendid image.

Eugène Boban sold quite a number of rock crystal artifacts, starting with his original 1867 collection, which contained several crystal items in addition to the small skulls. These included labrets and pendants, as seen in the Klein sketches now in the Hispanic Society of America's collection.

Aztec crystal skulls have been celebrated features of important museum collections for 150 years despite the fact that not a single one has ever been found in a controlled excavation nor recorded by any archeologist (Calligaro et al.

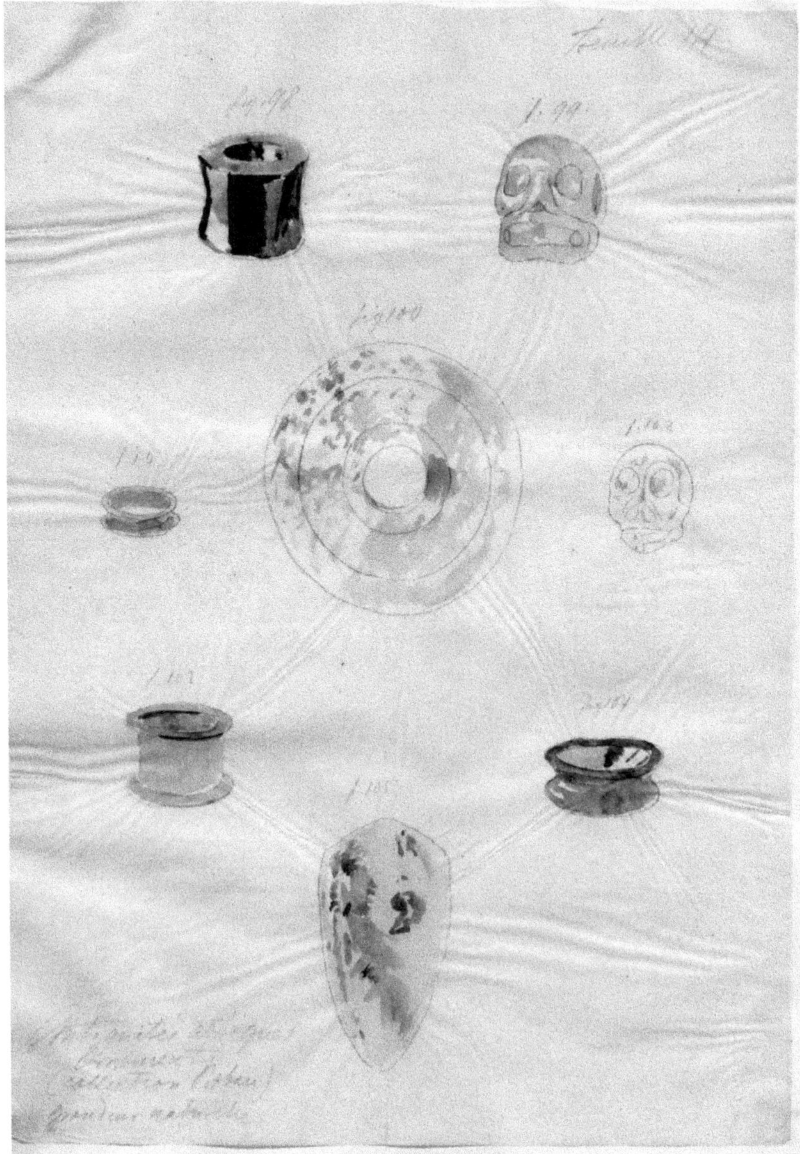

Figure 15.9a   Jean Amatus Klein drawing of a small crystal skull, obsidian earplugs, and another crystal adornment (courtesy of Hispanic Society of America, New York).

2009; Sax et al. 2008; Sax and Meeks 2009; Walsh 1997; 2008b). Nevertheless, numerous examples are still exhibited in museums and private collections and are frequently characterized as proof of the incredible artistry and craftsmanship of pre-Columbian carvers.

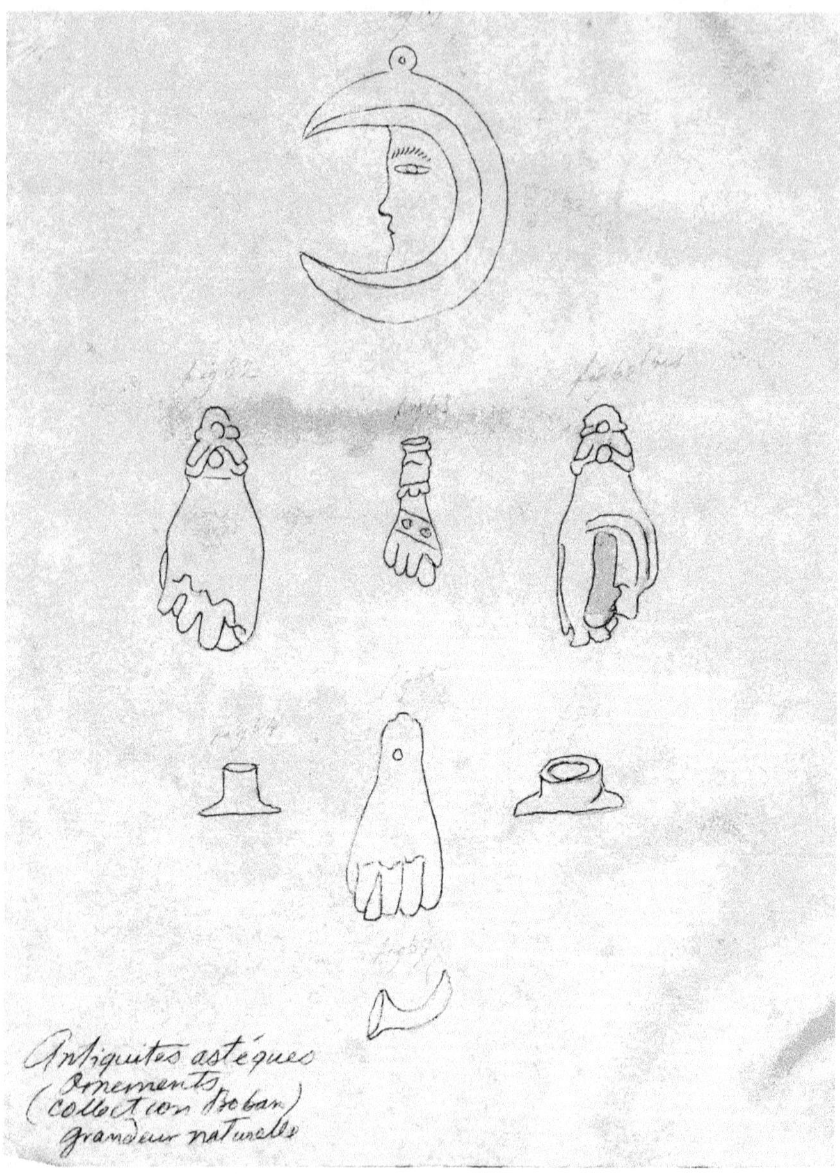

Figure 15.9b Jean Amatus Klein drawing of Aztec antiquities and ornaments (courtesy Hispanic Society of America, New York).

As previously mentioned, Smithsonian geologist William Foshag said in 1952 that the Blake skull was a fake, carved and polished with modern lapidary tools. It is strikingly similar in size, shape, incised cranial sutures, carving, and vertical drilling to the two small skulls exhibited in the Museo Nacional in Mexico City, the two small skulls in Italy, and the small skull in the British Museum. A joint Smithsonian–British Museum study in 1996 determined that both the large skull bought from Tiffany's by the British Museum and the smaller one purchased with Christy funds had also been carved with modern tools (Sax et al. 2008; Sax and Meeks 2009).

The two skulls in the Musée du quai Branly were not part of the joint 1996 study, but each of them is modern, and each was carved with nineteenth-century lapidary equipment. The larger crystal skull was the focus of a 2008 study, which was discussed earlier, using Elastic Recoil Detection Analysis to measure the water vapor diffused through the quartz. The results made it possible for Thomas Calligaro, Yvan Coquinot et al. to estimate that the crystal was carved sometime between the late 1840s and late 1860s (2009: 871–78).

The authenticity of this artifact class is questionable not only because not a single one has been found in an archeological context, but also because every skull that has been scientifically examined has proven to be modern.[2]

Eugène Boban himself ultimately provided his own frank appraisal of the validity of these ancient crystal skulls, which accords with these recent findings. As reported by *New York Tribune* Paris correspondent Charles Inman Barnard on 20 August 1900, "M. Boban, the well-known Paris dealer in Mexican antiquities, says that numbers of so-called rock crystal pre-Columbian skulls have been so adroitly made as almost to defy detection, and have been palmed off as genuine upon the experts of some of the principal museums of Europe."

Notes

1. Un très beau Christ en ivoire, hauteur 0m, 60, sur un piédestal en bois doré. La croix en ébène. Le tout plus d'un mètre de haut. 2,000 f.

2. Margaret Sax and Nigel Meeks of the British Museum determined that the large crystal skull, anonymously donated to the Smithsonian Institution, which first set this investigation in motion and was only anecdotally tied to a nineteenth century collection, had not only been carved by modern tools, but had been polished using a product unavailable until after World War II. In all probability, it was created in Mexico shortly before it was purchased in 1960.

16

COURTING THE SMITHSONIAN

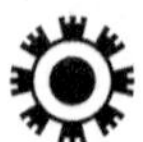

Having failed to sell a large part of his inventory for the prices he had hoped
at the Leavitt & Co. auction in New York, Eugène Boban shifted tactics once
again. Now he attempted to sell what remained of his pre-Columbian collection to the United States National Museum at the Smithsonian Institution. A
master at developing and maintaining business connections, he had already corresponded with a number of curators at the Smithsonian. Thomas Wilson, who
was appointed to oversee the prehistoric archeology collection at the National
Museum early in 1887, had been a friend and colleague for several years, since
Wilson had served as United States vice-consul in Nice, France, in the early
1880s (Schwarz 1996: 9).

Boban wrote to Wilson at the Smithsonian in January 1887 and included a
recent carte de visite photograph of himself taken in a New York studio. By his
own admission, he had been forced to buy back many of the auctioned pieces
that had not achieved a price he felt he could accept. Wilson replied with an
apology for not writing immediately, saying that he was still unpacking from his
return from France. He added that he had seen Boban's aunt Henriette at the
shop at 7, rue Daguerre, and thought she looked very well (BNF DMO n.a.f.
21479: item 443).

In February Wilson wrote again to say that he and William Henry Holmes
had been discussing the possibility that Boban might visit Washington, and that
he looked forward to seeing him again soon. As further enticement, he added
that he would like to show Boban his own personal collection of European
prehistoric artifacts (BNF DMO n.a.f. 21479: item 440).

Wilson, who was fluent in French, acted as translator and middleman between
Boban and the institution. Boban also corresponded with the Smithsonian
ethnologist James Constantine Pilling, who was producing a bibliography of

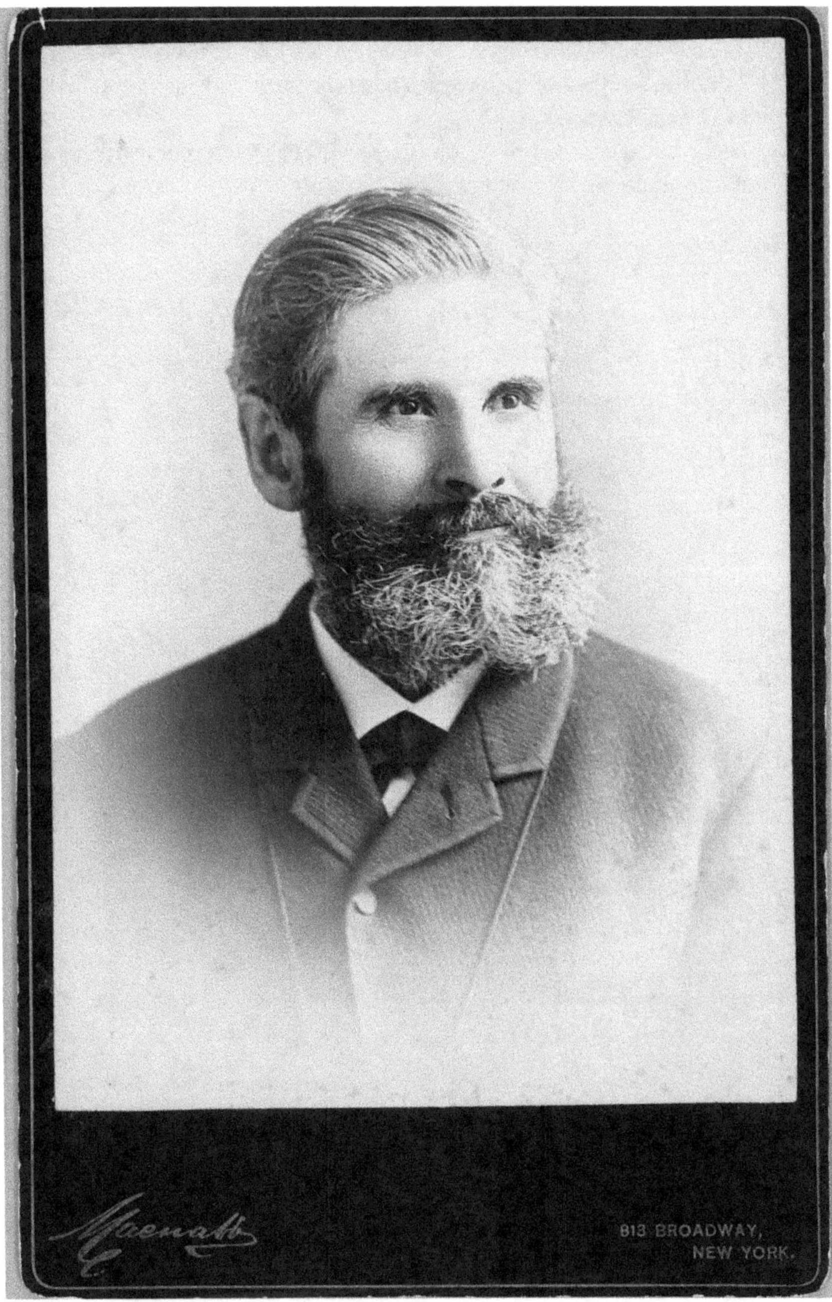

Figure 16.1   A carte de visite photograph from a Manhattan studio that Boban sent to Thomas Wilson at the Smithsonian Institution in 1887 (Smithsonian Institution, National Anthropological Archives, NPC 028770.00).

Uto-Aztecan languages, part of his series of publications on New World languages. Boban's principal contact, however, was Holmes, who was interested enough in Boban's collection to have attended the New York auction (New York Times, 14 December 1886).

Eugène Boban did travel to Washington to speak personally with Holmes. While at the museum he examined the Smithsonian's collections of Native

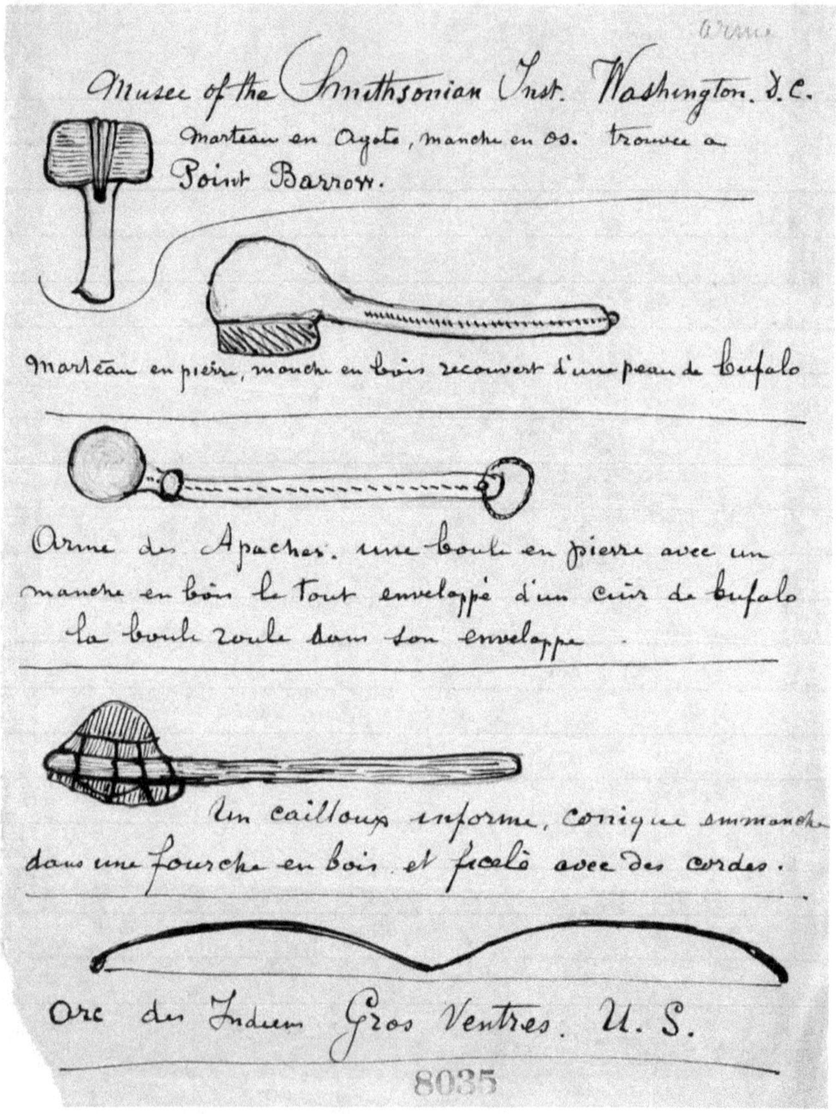

Figure 16.2   Notes Boban took during his visit to the Smithsonian (courtesy of Hispanic Society of America, New York).

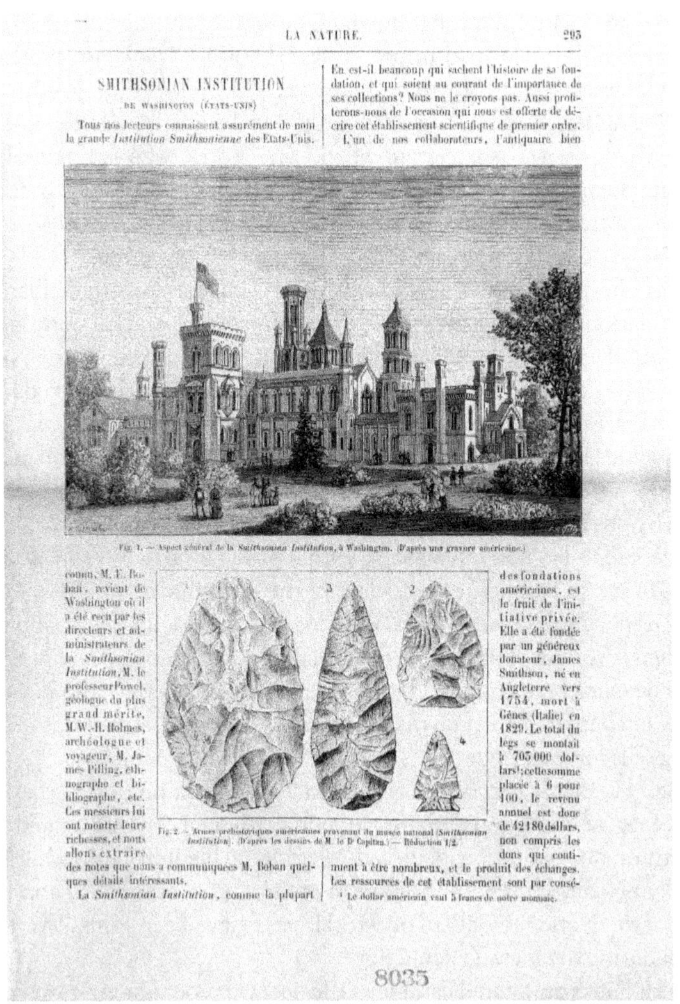

Figure 16.3 Boban's note to the editor of *La Nature* (courtesy of Hispanic Society of America, New York).

American ethnographic and archeological materials. Holmes evidently guided him on a tour of both exhibits and artifacts in storage, during which Boban recorded his impressions of the Smithsonian holdings on numerous pages. One note indicates his interest in a variety of Native American clubs and a bow in the Smithsonian's collection (HSA: B2043, Box IV).

As ever the master self-promoter, he sent a detailed report of his Washington visit to the Paris journal *La Nature*, which published the account from "one of our collaborators, the well-known antiquary, M. E. Boban." In it he described his meetings with important Smithsonian scientists. According to the three-page article, Boban "visited Washington where he was received by directors and officers of the Smithsonian Institution, Professor Powell, Geologist of great merit, Mr. W. H. Holmes, archeologist and voyageur, Mr. James Pilling, ethnographer and bibliographer, etc. These gentlemen showed him the wealth of their collections which we will share from M. Boban's notes, who has provided more interesting details" (HSA: B2243, Box IV).[1] The article goes on to discuss the history of the creation and expansion of the United States National Museum and the enormous collections already amassed by it.

One of the most interesting aspects of the Eugène Boban–William Henry Holmes relationship is that it is transparent, because all of their correspondence is preserved. Holmes kept Boban's letters, along with a copy of the New York auction catalog and the archeological poster that the antiquarian produced with Leopoldo Batres. This material is now in the Smithsonian Institution Archives (SIA: RU 7084). Boban filed Holmes's letters in one of his albums of correspondence now in the Bibliothèque nationale in Paris. This allows us to measure the men's reactions to each other (BNF DMO n.a.f. 21477: items 461–71).

Each wrote in his native language. Despite the fact that Wilson Wilberforce Blake had warned Holmes to steer clear of the Frenchman and his crystal skull, their correspondence reveals a growing respect for each other's abilities and knowledge. It records Boban's gift for geniality in his business dealings, and the methods he employed to entice perspective buyers. The letters also illustrate the problems encountered by underfunded museum curators attempting to acquire new materials for their collections.

In 1887 Holmes was curator of aboriginal American pottery in the Division of Ethnology of the United States National Museum (which would become the Smithsonian Institution National Museum of Natural History). He would eventually be named chief of the Bureau of American Ethnology, and later the director of the National Gallery of Art. He may have been formally introduced to Boban during the New York auction.

From Holmes's annotated catalog of the auction proceedings, it would appear that most of the items listed had been sold for rather meager amounts. This meant that Boban had to take action to save himself from what may have been a financial disaster. As he explained in an early letter to Holmes, "I have the honor of sending you my catalog by mail. The x mark indicates the objects that I purchased back at the sale, which are in my possession and of which I can dispose. See if there are some things that might interest your museum. We will deal with this in the best manner possible. . . . Please present my greetings to Mr. James C. Pilling" (SIA: RU7084).[2] Boban was already acquainted with James Constantine Pilling, since he, Father Augustin Fischer, and Antonio Peñafiel all had contributed to Pilling's *Proof-sheets of a Bibliography of North American Indian Languages*, which ran some 1,200 pages. Only one hundred copies were printed in 1885.

Boban soon moved on to a more direct approach to selling his collection to the Smithsonian—he shipped many of the artifacts to the museum. This would allow the curators to view and handle the materials in their home territory. On 17 March 1887 he wrote Holmes,

> I have just come from sending by train, addressed to Prof. S. F. Baird at the National Museum in Washington, eight packages of antiquities, seven cases, and one package of wooden weapons of the natives of the South Seas. Enclosed is the list of the catalog numbers of the items I sent in those eight packages. If you wish I can send you another catalog with the prices of the objects, [giving] the lowest prices possible in order that you might keep many of the items for your museum. If you see my excellent friend Mr. Thomas Wilson, many compliments, also to Mr. Pilling". (SIA: RU7084)[3]

Holmes had the packages opened and the artifacts set out on tables to be photographed. He himself carefully examined each one, making notes and sketches of individual pieces. Boban had sent more than 160 objects from his collection, about half of which were pre-Columbian artifacts from Mexico. One particular ceramic vessel caught Holmes's eye. His somewhat cryptic notes read, "Most remarkable American vessel is much like metal in looks and feel that its material would not at first be suspected—stone ware—dark throughout" (SIA: RU7084). He was describing a plumbate vessel from around 1100 AD, correctly assessing the piece's metallic effect as coming from a glaze-like slip. Plumbate vessels were quite rare in early nineteenth-century collections, so, once again, Holmes proved he had a very good eye.

Among the items Boban sent were many of his most important artifacts, including the entire Zapotec funerary series. Boban considered these to be among his most prized possessions. As described in the New York auction catalog, "The series from 101 to 116 inclusive, was brought to Europe in 1845, by Monsieur Martin, Consular Agent of France at Oajaca [sic], who made long and very successful explorations in the country of the Zapotecas" (Leavitt 1886a: 20). Holmes had all of the Zapotec pieces photographed, and wrote notes describing elements and features he found interesting.

Boban was not exaggerating the collection's importance. The series represents a group of Zapotec ceramic urns that are typically found in a funerary context with several richly attired seated figures and two unusual depictions of warriors. The figures and urns were purportedly found near the site of Mitla in Oaxaca. Boban had succeeded in acquiring this collection in 1879, after the death of the French Consul M. Martin.

Holmes was keenly interested in the Zapotec figures and kept the collection for several months. Then, at the end of May 1887, Thomas Wilson received a letter from Boban writing from the Clinton Avenue address that contained sad news. "I regret to announce to you the death of my aunt Madame Duvergé in

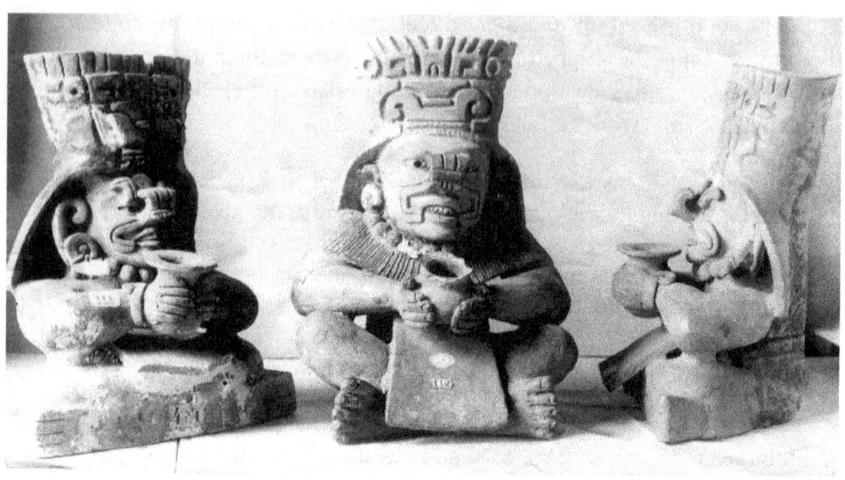

Figure 16.4   Three Zapotec funerary vessels excavated near Mitla (Smithsonian Institution Archives, RU 7084).

Paris, May 12, this year. I find that I am forced to return to Paris, in time to see to family affairs."[4]

Madame Duvergé was Boban's aunt Henriette —the younger of his father's two half-sisters. After Boban and his wife left for Mexico in 1885, she took over the running of the shop, which had been moved from boulevard St Michel to 7, rue Daguerre. She lived at this location as well. Henriette was seventy-three when she died at that address in the 14th arrondissement. Her death certificate took note of the fact that she was *celibataire*, meaning she had never married.

Boban added in his letter to Wilson,

I would be very grateful to you if you would question the gentlemen of the Smithsonian to find out if they intend to acquire all the objects which I sent on 17 March to Washington. It is the reason that I am staying in the United States, although I have recently sent to Paris the remaining ethnographic objects—spears, bows, arrows, axes, clubs, etc. from Africa and Oceania and also [European] prehistoric objects.[5]

Now, in view of the sad event of the death of my relative, I am forced to return to Paris. I've decided to bring about a sale here in New York of everything that I have left . . . I know that you are on good terms with all these gentlemen. Try to have them keep all the objects and buy the whole lot for the museum at Washington. That would simplify things very much for me. Otherwise, I would like them to let me know how many objects they do not want to buy for the museum, so that I can begin the catalog here in New York. I am counting on your experience and kindness to do your best for my interests. My compliments to Madame. Cordially, E. Boban. (SIA: RU7084)[6]

Wilson translated the note and passed it on to Holmes, adding only that he had meant to go in to see him, "but have been much engaged." He did not press Boban's case in writing, although it is certainly possible that he met with Holmes privately to discuss the matter.

Holmes wrote several times to Boban in New York apologizing for keeping the objects so long and saying that he could take no immediate action due to a lack of funds. A letter from Boban on 13 June offered him advice as a museum curator, asking Holmes to consider the importance of the pieces and to leave aside the financial question. "One must not forget that among these antiquities are some that will never pass through your hands again and will never be found at any price again. Concerning the money there is always some. I constantly produce it" (SIA: RU7084).[7] Boban is amazingly glib, not to mention blunt, in this letter, indicating perhaps that he had lost patience and also might have felt somewhat desperate. He was correct, of course. Given the right circumstances and the right people, money can usually be found.

Boban continued in the same vein. "Look out," he wrote in English. "Do not deprive the great Smithsonian museum of procuring these unique pieces, [they are] well-authenticated, and at relatively moderate prices. Above all, the Zapotec terra-cotta series is assuredly of greatest archeological value for the American continent, a value that can only grow with study. You better than anyone can judge this to be true since you have traveled to Mexico" (SIA: RU7084). [8]

Finally, he added, "This Zapotec series is very well known by the learned European world. The director of the ethnographic museum of the Trocadéro at Paris, before my departure in February, 1885, had offered me 25,000 francs or 5,000 dollars for my Mexican Collection, and in this collection what interested him most was the Zapotec series which they lacked in their museum." He then explains why the sale did not go through. "At that time I had the intention of setting up a museum in Mexico, and I did not want to give up these pieces. You may ask Dr. E Hamy, he will give you the details on this affair." The letter concludes with more words of curatorial advice. "In the interests of your Institution keep the most objects possible, which you will later be pleased for having made these acquisitions. I'm depending on you to choose best of what is useful to your museum and to return the rest to me at New York" (SIA: RU7084).[9]

Boban seems passionate here, sincere in his intent to leave these important pieces at the Smithsonian. He is candid in his explanation for why he refused Hamy's offer to buy them for the Trocadéro, and it fits with other things he has written.

One of the most important objects of the Zapotec collection is the figure of a warrior carrying a ceremonial bat-claw cup, wearing a necklace of human maxillae (the upper section of the jaw), and a human trophy head. It clearly was of intense interest to Holmes. His notes surround the photograph of the object taken while it was at the National Museum.

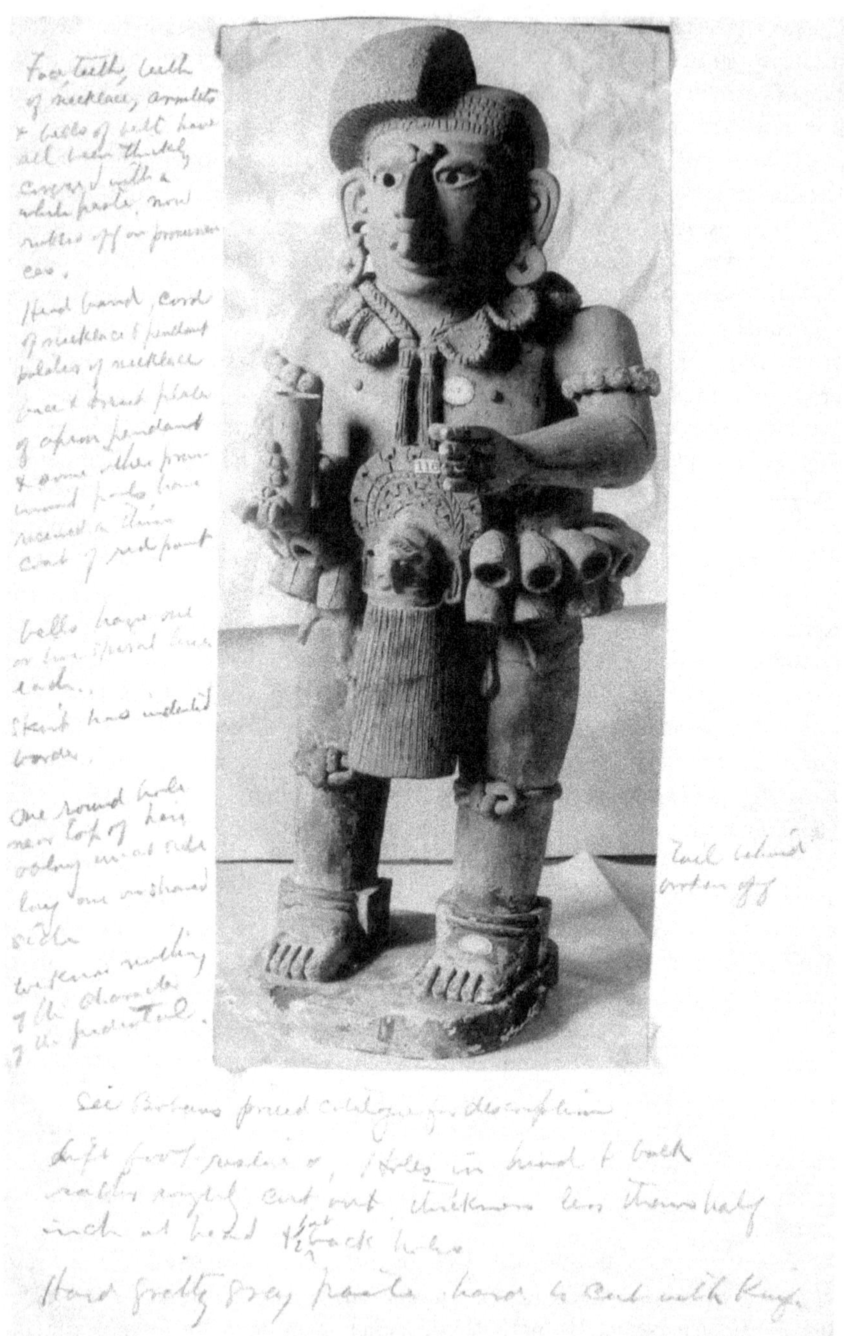

Figure 16.5 Zapotec warrior figure with notes by W. H. Holmes (Smithsonian Institution Archives, RU 7084).

Face, teeth, teeth of necklace, armlets & bells of belt have all been thickly covered with a white paste, now rubbed off on prominences. Headband, cord of necklace & pendant palates of necklace, face and breastplate of apron, pendant & some other prominent parts have received a thin coat of red paint. Bells have one or two spiral lines each. Skirt has indented border. One round hole near top of hair, oblong one at side, long one on shaved side—We know nothing of the character of the pedestal. See Boban's priced catalog for description. Left foot restored. Holes in head and back rather roughly cut out. Thickness less than half inch at head & at back holes. Hard gritty gray paste hard to cut with knife (SIA: RU7084).

Holmes responded to Boban's final sales pitch with reassurance, but he made it clear that he was unable to get the money to purchase what he wanted.

Your letter of June 13th is before me. You impress upon me the importance of Mexican antiquities—especially of the Zapotecan material, to the greatest American Museum, but you already know how fully I agree with you in this matter. *I want everything I can get* [emphasis added], but the indisposition of our authorities, who have what they believe to be more important matters in hand, is in my way. (BNF DMO n.a.f. 21477: item 469)

In making additions to the collection, Holmes relied on the interest and purse strings of the Smithsonian's second Secretary, Spencer Baird, who had supported his interest in collecting Mexican archeological pieces in the past. Unfortunately, Baird was seriously ill in June 1887, and died just two months later.

In a final note, addressed to "My Dear Mr. Boban" and written on 2 July 1887 Holmes lamented the bad timing of their negotiations.

The disability of Prof. Baird renders me almost powerless in the negotiation of archaeological purchases. He is the only one that favored such purchases, who at the same time had command of money. It was in his support that I built my hopes of securing part or all of your Mexican series. The poor professor will probably not come back to us. He cannot recover, and I suppose that the best thing I can do for you—and for myself for that matter—is to send your collection back to you. This I shall do with much regret. I am having boxes made for the purpose.

Then Holmes proposed one last possible method for acquiring some of the pieces. "At one time something was said in regard to exchanges of specimens. Have you a desire to secure a series of our pueblo ware from Arizona and New Mexico? Perhaps something can be done in this way. I am very much obliged to you for your kindness in this matter and I appreciate your patience in considering my poor and insufficient offers for your fine antiquities" (BNF DMO n.a.f. 21477: item 470). There is no evidence that Boban took him up on this exchange offer. At this stage he wanted to lighten his load prior to returning to Paris, not collect more artifacts.

Holmes could only afford to offer the paltry sum of $175 for the Zapotec warrior figure, and Boban, who had originally hoped to get $600 or $700, would not let it go for less than $400. In the end Holmes managed to purchase only nine of the smaller ceramic pieces, which are still in the museum's collections and still bear Boban's catalog numbers and stickers. Holmes reluctantly returned the rest of the collection to 111 Clinton Place in New York.

William Henry Holmes might have regretted somewhat the fact that he had spent quite a bit of money that Spencer Baird had allocated to him for archeological collections just a few months before. Principal among the material he had purchased from Mexico was the Wilson Wilberforce Blake collection (formerly owned by Augustin Fischer), on which he had spent $1,200. The Blake/Fischer collection was much inferior to Boban's and contained a number of fakes.

It is a testament to the quality of Boban's collection and Holmes's highly discerning eye that the few pieces he managed to acquire from Boban are all excellent examples of their type. The small collection consists of eight ceramic vessels from several locations in Mexico, including the Yucatan, Veracruz, and the Valley of Mexico. Two ceramic effigy vessels are of the unusual plumbate ware, the metallic-looking pottery that Holmes had found to be so captivating.

Ironically, the impressive Zapotec warrior figure that so intrigued Holmes, but which he was unable to purchase, would eventually find its way into the Smithsonian collections. George Gustav Heye, the collector of ethnographic and archeological artifacts from the Americas, who founded the Museum of the American Indian in New York, purchased Boban's warrior from the dealer Charles Ratton in Paris in 1937. The figure is now on exhibit in the Smithsonian's National Museum of the American Indian.

Notes

1. L'un de nos collaborateurs, l'antiquaire bien connu, M. E. Boban, revient de Washington où il a été reçu par les directeurs et administrateurs de la Smithsonian Institution, M. le professeur Powel, géologue du plus grand mérité, M. W. H. Holmes, archéologue et voyageur, M. James Pilling, ethnographe et bibliographe, etc. Ces messieurs lui ont montré leurs richesses, et nous allons extraire des notes que nous a communiquées M. Boban quelques détails intéressants.

2. Cher Monsieur, J'ai l'honneur de vous envoyer par la poste mon catalog. La marque X indique les objets qui j'ai racheter à la vente et qui sont en mon pouvoir en ce moment dont je puis disposer. Voyez s'il y a quelque chose qui puisse interesser votre Musée. Nous traiterons cela dans les meilleurs conditions possibles . . . avec prier de presenter mes Salutations a M. James C. Pilling.

3. Je viens de remettre au chemin de Fer à l'adresse du Prof S. F. Baird au National Museum à Washington. 8 colis antiquites, 7 caisses et un paquet d'armes en bois des Sauvages des Mers du Sud. Ci inclue la liste des numeros du catalog qui j'ai expedie aujourd'hui dans ces 8 colis. Si vous le desirez je puis vous adresser un autre catalog avec les prix des objets, les prix aussi bas que possible afin de vous engager a garder beaucoup des ses objets pour votre Musée. Si vous voyez Mon excellent ami Mr. Thomas Wilson bien des Compliments et aussi à M. Pilling.

4. Jai le regret de vous annoncer la mort à Paris de ma Tante Madame Duvergé Decedée le 12 mai courant. Je me trouve donc force de retourner à Paris dans quelque temps pour affairs de Famille.

5. Je vous serais bien obligé de questionner ces Messieurs du Smithsonian Institution, afin de savoir s'ils ont l'intention d'acquerir d'acheter tous les objets que j'ai expedier le 17 mars a Washington. Voici pourquoi pensant rester quelques temps aux Etats Unis. J'avais fait venir de Paris dernierement ce qui me restait d'objets d'Ethnographie, lances, arcs, fleches, haches, casse tetes, etc. de l'Afrique et Oceanie et aussi de objets prehistorique.

6. Aujourd hui en vue du triste evenement de la mort de ma Parente je suis forcé de retourner à Paris. J'ai decider de faire une vente ici à New York de tout ce qui me reste. . . . Je sais que vous êtes en tres bons termes avec tous ces Messieurs tâchez qu ils gardent tous les objets, qu ils m'achetent tout le lot pour le Musée de Washington. Cela simplifierait boucoup les choses pour moi. Dans le Cas contraire qu ils veuillent me signaler les numeros des objets qu ils n'ont pas l'intention d'acheter pour le musée. Afin que je puise faire commencer le catalogue ici à New York. Je compte du reste sur votre experience et amabilite pour faire au mieux de mes interets. Tous mes compliments a Madame Wilson je vous serre cordialement la main.

7. Veuillez prendre en consideration que laissant de coté la partie commercial il ne faut pas oublier que parmi les objets d'antiquites ils s'en trouvent qui ne vous passent par les mains qu'une seule fois et ne se retrouvent jamais a aucuns prix. De l'argent il y en a toujours il s'en produit constamment.

8. Look out, ne privez pas le grand musée du Smithsonian de profiter de la chance qu il a de pouvoir le procurer des pieces uniques bien authentiques surtout et a des prix relativement moderés. Surtout la serie de terre cuite Zapotèque à assurement une grande valeur archéologique pour le continent Americain.

9. Cette serie Zapotèque est tres connue du monde savant Européen. Le Directeur du Musée Ethnographique du Trocadero à Paris lors de mon depart (Fevrier 1885) m'avait offert 25,000 Fs soit 5,000 $ pour ma collection Mexicaine et dans cette collection ce qui l'interesait le plus était la serie Zapotèque qui manque dans les musées. A cette epoque javais l'intention de monter un Musée a Mexico et je n'ai pas voulu me separer de ces pièces, vous pouvez du reste demandez au Docteur E. Hamy il vous donnera des renseignement sur cette affaire. Dans l'interet de votre institution gardez le plus d'objets possible et plutard vous saura gre d'avoir fait ces acquisitions. Je m'en rapporte a vous faites pour le mieux choisirez ce que vous croyez utile à votre musée et retournez moi le reste ici a New York.

17

OF FAKES, FORGERS, AND FRAUDS

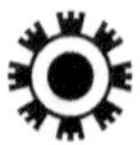

In addition to their mutual appreciation for pre-Columbian cultures, William Henry Holmes and Eugène Boban shared an interest in the thriving nineteenth-century industry producing fake pre-Columbian artifacts.

By all appearances, Boban became ensnared in the business of circulating fakes (principally crystal skulls) early in his career. It is possible that some forged artifacts had initially fooled him, such as the blackware pot shown at his feet in the early photograph. After all, the Museo Nacional exhibited many dubious objects as genuine at the time. However, he eventually went out of his way to expose certain types of fake artifacts to the public.

In the late 1870s he began selling the obviously fake, at least to his educated eye, blackware figurines and pots from the Tlatelolco factories. Describing them in his catalogs as modern or fake, he sold them for nominal prices—to educate buyers and students of pre-Columbian art and culture, he said (Boban 1878: 12).[1] In a later "Catalogue d'ouvrages scientifiques," Boban wrote about these fake antiquities in detail. "Fabricated these days in the suburbs of Mexico [City] by the Indians (from Santiago [Tlatelolco] and Los Angeles). These objects are not casts nor are they copies of the ancient monuments of the country (they are pure fantasy) a type of bizarre caricature, whose inspiration escapes us, but whose principal goal is to fool the public."[2] He goes on to say that it is clear that these objects have no value, but that they have brought disfavor on actual pre-Columbian artifacts since they are so easy to acquire "and so cheap in the country [Mexico] that careless travelers bring back lots of them, and then these monsters strut about in the best showcases of our museums of Europe" (Boban 1881: 47–48).[3]

William Henry Holmes's acquaintance with faked pre-Columbian artifacts began when he first visited Mexico in 1883 and 1884, a year before Boban returned to the country, at the invitation of the Ferrocarril Central Mexicano (Central Mexican Railway). While in Mexico City he lived in a specially equipped railroad car located in the city's main railway station, from which he visited the Museo Nacional and important archeological sites. Wandering about the train yard, he became fascinated by what he discovered. "The old walls and fortifications of the city, dating back perhaps to early Spanish times, lie just outside of the enclosure of the station. . . . The section exposed by the railway cuttings exhibits a curious agglomeration of the deposits of all past human periods" (Holmes 1884: 68–9). As suggested in this quote, Holmes was one of the first archeologists to recognize and write about the importance of stratigraphy, whereby the age of the remnants of past civilizations is determined by the level at which they are found in undisturbed areas.

As Holmes discovered, Mexico City's train yards were littered with potsherds, so much so that he made a surface collection of pottery pieces, some rather large, and perhaps did a bit of freelance digging in the exposed strata as well. The collection of the fragments of ceramic vessels he amassed is impressive for the range of shapes, rims, sizes, and decoration it contains. It still forms part of the Smithsonian's holdings.

Many of the pieces appear to be typical of the elaborately decorated wares produced by pre-Columbian potters of Cholula, from around 1000 AD until the Spanish conquest. This pottery, known to archeologists as Mixteca-Puebla ware, exhibits beautifully painted, exuberant designs using geometric and figurative patterns. According to some chroniclers, and certainly most dealers, this was the preferred tableware of the Aztec emperors. In his train-yard wanderings Holmes also collected many examples of post-Classic Aztec ceramics, such as black-on-orange and red-on-orange wares. All the potsherds Holmes was collecting dated to post-Classic Aztec times, between the twelfth and the sixteenth centuries.

As curator of aboriginal ceramics at the United States National Museum, Holmes knew a great deal about potsherds and their role in reconstructing the activities and achievements of earlier cultures, so he was surprised to find that there were few examples of the beautiful polychrome pottery, like the sherds he was collecting, on exhibit in Mexico's Museo Nacional. Instead he saw many of the large, bulky, black and dark-brown vessels he considered to be recent fakes. "I was much perplexed thereby," he wrote. "It is not surprising that the archaeologists in the United States or in Europe should make mistakes in interpreting this work, as they have taken the word of unscientific collectors who rely upon the statements of native dealers; but it is strange that Mexican scholars should so long have passed the work by without remark" (Holmes 1889: 320). He quotes Professor Gumersindo Mendoza, the director of the Museo Nacional, saying the black- and brownware pottery should "be classed as ordinary domestic Aztec ware, thus implying that it probably constituted a normal feature of Mexican art originating in the distant past, and extending down to the present." Holmes dismissed this notion, "This was a rather easy way of dealing with the matter, but it was not all that science demanded, and I undertook to examine into the subject more closely" (Holmes 1889: 320–21). Mendoza's explanation was that Mexican Indians were making the same pottery today as the Aztecs had five hundred years before, and that the everyday domestic wares were unchanged through the centuries. Holmes knew that this was simply not true, since he had collected Aztec pottery all around his train car.

He completed two articles on the subject of contemporary, faked Aztec pottery. The first, titled "The Trade in Spurious Mexican Antiquities," was published in the journal *Science* in 1886. The second, a much longer version titled "On some spurious Mexican antiquities and their relation to ancient art," appeared in the Annual Report of the Smithsonian Institution's United States National Museum in 1889.

Although Eugène Boban was living in Paris when Holmes visited Mexico City in 1883 and 1884, he later learned about and was interested in his American colleague's activities and opinions. In the Hispanic Society's collection of Boban's papers, there is a copy of a Mexico City newspaper article dated May 1886, a month before Boban left Mexico for the second and last time, covering the sale of fraudulent Mexican and Peruvian pre-Columbian artifacts in New York City. The author quotes Mr. William Henry Holmes extensively. In fact, the newspaper piece is essentially an excerpted translation of Holmes's article "The Trade in Spurious Mexican Antiquities," published a month or so previously in *Science* (HSA: B2242, Box III).

Holmes and Boban began corresponding about Boban's proposed sale of artifacts to the Smithsonian early in 1887. With the subject of fakes still fresh in his mind, Holmes asked Boban what he could tell him about the Mexican industry of forging artifacts. As we know, Boban was well versed in the subject, having recorded his ideas on fakes as early as the mid-1870s.

In his correspondence, Boban is eager to discuss the topic with Holmes, who not only shared his interests, but also might become a client and ally. Boban presents himself as being vigilant about fakes. He intimates that he is capable of passing on information about the authenticity of specific Mexican pre-Columbian objects and eager to critique collections in other parts of the world for their inclusion of fakes. His claim to having such a keen ability to discern fakes adds luster to the quality of his own collection, of course.

To entice Holmes even further, Boban details in one letter a number of people he personally knows to be engaged in the manufacture of faked pre-Columbian artifacts. He begins by listing, "A Mexican lapidary named Juan Bobadilla," and goes on to provide his address, "Plazuela de Santo Tomas no. 17." This gentleman, he notes, "has fabricated and still fabricates numerous statues or idols in hard stone, obsidian, jadeite, etc."[4] Plazuela de Santo Tomas is a small square in what was once the separate town of Azcapotzalco, where Boban did some of his earliest collecting.

Continuing with his list, Boban writes, "Another Mexican lapidary, Mr. Amador, resident of Mexico [City] and a former employee of the *diputación* [Mexican government administrative office], I know for certain has fabricated several counterfeit pieces of antiquities in hard stone" (SIA: RU7084).[5] One wonders how he knows this for certain. When he refers to hard stone, Boban means jadeite and quartz. Both of these are difficult to carve because of their hardness and tough crystalline structure, requiring sophisticated know-how, the right tools, and some talent. Mr. Amador must have been a skilled artisan.

Next Boban writes that there were numerous other forgers, but that he does not really know their names. Then remembering yet one more faker in particular, he names Philippe Praget, then deceased, who was of "French origin, and had been a jeweler and a miner. He had the specialty of counterfeiting bronze objects, which *had* [fooled] many amateurs—one could see a sample of his work among the objects carried from Mexico by Mr. Benito Nichols y Orrin."[6] Nichols and his colleagues the Orrin brothers were the owners of the Aztec Fair, then exhibiting in Boston and New York. In 1887 the fair was held in Washington, DC.

Boban concludes this letter by saying that there were "four pieces, one copper fish, 8 to10 inches long with the tail ending in an ax, another rather strange piece much like an American hand ax with a point, and a human figure that looks like it has wings, and two thick axes. These four pieces were fabricated in Mexico and sold to the Italian collector Mr. Tangassi, who is now dead."[7] The Frenchman named Praget apparently manufactured all these metal artifacts (SIA: RU 7084).

Tangassi owned a marble emporium in Mexico City (Maillefert 1992: 301). He may or may not have known that numerous pre-Columbian fakers were using broken pieces of marble that the Tangassi firm had discarded to create "ancient" objects, according to Boban. Many of these pseudo pre-Columbian marble creations are now in museum collections around the world—the British Museum, the University of Pennsylvania Museum, and the Smithsonian Institution, to name but a few (personal research). Most, if not all, could not even be described as good fakes.

With regard to types of stone used to manufacture fakes, what seems odd to Boban, as he is describing his own research to Holmes, is that the fakers seemed not to have noticed the fact that "the ancient Mexicans never made statues or idols out of obsidian, nor did they make ground axes out of this stone." He says he believes that the small and larger masks of obsidian are actually ancient, however. He thinks that obsidian lip plugs, earplugs, and small obsidian disks that were once embedded in the eyes of masks and idols are all authentic. He also vouches for the "small animal heads that served as pendants in *cozcapetlatl*, or necklaces, *itztli tezcatl* round mirrors, and the *coxcatl* or beads of necklaces, [as well as] large blades in the form of scrapers that served as arms for a *macuahuitl* or Mexican mace" (SIA: RU7084).[8] Boban always enjoyed displaying his knowledge and facility with Nahuatl.

Boban is still insisting on his idea that obsidian scrapers were the cutting implements used on the Aztec war club, or *macuahuitl*, despite the fact that few scholars agreed with him. Then, getting to the crux of Holmes's questions about the validity of different types of stone artifacts, he writes categorically, "All obsidian statues representing small idols with arms and legs should be considered false" (SIA: RU 7084).[9] The subject of fakes and who was making them all, appear in the same letter, which has no date, but was apparently sent along as an addendum to one of the communications he had with Holmes.

Interestingly, another topic of their correspondence—the human remains that Boban was also trying to sell to the institution—had a connection to their mutual interest in fakes. He had initially offered the Smithsonian a collection of two dozen human skulls and other skeletal material, presumably the remains he had exhibited in the Museo Científico. Holmes responded to Boban's inquiry about this by writing, "Mr. Wilson showed me your letter to him in regard to crania etc. I advise you to send all the articles mentioned, excepting the mummies. Our Medical Museum people are making a collection of crania and may buy from you" (15 March 1887—BNF DMO n.a.f. 21477: item 461).

A short note from Holmes addressed "Dear Doctor" informed the director of the Army Medical Museum (AMM), which was just off the Mall behind the Smithsonian Castle, that Boban's collection of skulls and casts could be viewed in the National Museum, just east of The Castle. Ultimately, the Army Medical Museum purchased the collection for $99. It consisted of twenty-seven human skulls and two plaster casts of skulls. Most of the skulls were Mexican, although two were cataloged as "Gallo Roman" and another described as an Egyptian skull. Three skulls, which had been presented to Boban by Dr. Raspail of Paris, the physician who had treated Madame Boban in the late 1870s, were from the Cimetière des Innocents, or children's graveyard (AMM 2587-2615—NAA). The removal of skeletal remains from Paris cemeteries was a common occurrence. Burials were maintained only for a period of ten to fifty years. If no money was forthcoming for ongoing care of the grave after a specified time, the skeleton would be removed and placed in one of the many ossuaries in and around Paris, or otherwise disposed of.

One of the Mexican skulls in Boban's collection, number 1389, was described as "Skull of Antonio Rojas, ferocious chief of Guerillas killed by a soldier of Capt. Berthelin's Co., French Army time of Maximilian" (Leavitt 1886a: 80).[10] As it happened, Holmes had recently attended the Aztec Fair in Washington, produced by Benito Nichols and the Orrin brothers, who were circus owners from Mexico. These were the same people who had exhibited the fake pre-Columbian artifacts, such as the bronze fishes that Boban claimed had been made by Philippe

Praget. By the time it arrived in the nation's capital, the fair had already had successful runs in Boston and New York City.

Like many fairs and expositions of the day, this one had live performers, who demonstrated to the visitors the ways and customs of Mexico. It also exhibited a variety of antiquities, which, judging from the photographs, were comprised largely of nineteenth-century fakes. There were historical sections, one of which contained two mummies, which may be the two missing mummies of the six Boban originally exhibited in Mexico.

Another section of the fair was entitled "Relics of Highway Robbers in Mexico," where the organizers exhibited the "Skull of the blood-thirsty Rojos, [*sic*] shot by the Mexican troops in 1864 at Guadalajara" (Orrin, Nichols, and Orrin 1886: 17). The similarity of Boban's "Skull of Antonio Rojas, the ferocious chief of Guerrillas" and the Aztec Fair's "skull of the blood-thirsty Rojos" was a bit too intriguing for Holmes to overlook. In another letter to Boban, he mentioned the problem of the multiheaded bandit.

Boban's response in a letter dated 3 April 1887 provides a series of interesting facts about the collection of human skulls he was offering to sell to the Army Medical Museum. "On the subject of the provenance of the skulls—numbers 1372—1374—1368—1383—1375—1377—1370—1385—these eight skulls come from the *Chenapan* [rascal, scalawag] Leopoldo Batres."[11] Evidently, the antiquarian cannot pass up the opportunity to denigrate the intelligence and character of the inspector of monuments, particularly to a prominent archeologist and museum curator. Boban continues his explanation to Holmes, saying,

> If you wish to take off or carefully unglue the tags which carry the numbers in my catalog, you will find underneath other tags, his numbers written in his hand on a little band of white paper with deceitful provenances such as Zapotec, Tehuantepec, etc. . . . He had assured me of the provenance of these skulls and said that he wished to form an anthropological collection of ancient Mexican races for the museum of Mexico and produce a publication on this subject (of which he is perfectly incapable). A little time before my departure from Mexico a certain person named Swans came to my shop—he was interested a bit in natural history. . . . On seeing the skulls in question, he said, I recognize these skulls, we dug them up a little while ago in the small Indian village near the Villa de Guadalupe. [Boban's client Swans is describing Tepeyac, a town just north of Mexico City, where the Virgin of Guadalupe was said to have appeared to the Indian Juan Diego in the sixteenth century.] He told me, this worthless Batres is a liar, to say that they are from Oaxaca or Tehuantepec. I give you my word of honor, Swans said to me, these skulls truly come from the environs of Mexico City. It is in view of this rectification, due to chance, that I now classify [these skulls] in my catalog as Valley of Mexico. (SIA: RU7084)[12]

Boban continues to lay waste to Leopoldo Batres. "I have learned that he had sold others to travelers with these completely made-up provenances. Moreover, with a bit of attention one would remark that these skulls have certainly the same racial characteristics, and above all the same patina, the same color, produced by the same milieu" (SIA: RU 7084).[13] Although he admits to being initially fooled, he presents himself as a keen observer and is correct in his assessment of these human remains; they are too similar in features and color to have come from different ancient burial sites.

Responding to Holmes's question about the Rojas skull, Boban writes:

> Number 1389 was given to me by a friend, Col. Tamisey, of the 60th Regiment, whom I knew during the French occupation of Mexico. Since my [recent] departure from Mexico, Mr. B. Nichols [of the Aztec Fair] wanted to buy this skull from me, but found it too expensive, so he asked me to sell him another. I was surprised to find the skull I had given him in Mexico [exhibited] in New York with the title 'head of Rojas' etc. on the display and in his catalog. I do not doubt that my friend Mr. Nichols will happily rectify this little error, because now he would have us believe that Rojas, this terrible brigand, had two heads, but the original is assuredly our number 1389. (SIA: RU 7084 4/3/1887)[14]

Boban's collection of twenty-seven skulls and casts that he sold to the Army Medical Museum was transferred to the Smithsonian's Department of Anthropology in 1904 as part of a larger transfer of "normal" human skeletal material. At that time, the AMM was divesting itself of these normal specimens to make room for the burgeoning collections of pathological and trauma-based specimens they were acquiring from the Army Medical Corps. Boban's was the first collection cataloged in the division of physical anthropology.

At some point since the skull entered the Department of Anthropology's collection, a physical anthropologist examined it and annotated the catalog card with the information that the skull was that of a female, approximately thirty to forty years of age. This assessment (taken with the Holmes–Boban correspondence and the Aztec Fair catalog description) raised some questions about Eugène Boban's honesty as a dealer of human remains from Mexico. Since the "ancient Aztec" crystal skulls he sold to museums turned out to be nineteenth-century creations, it began to seem possible that this was not the real Rojas.

The bandit or guerilla fighter Antonio Rojas was, by all accounts, a blood-thirsty, illiterate warlord who routinely shot prisoners—as many as several hundred at a time—and torched entire towns on a whim. He rode with a secretary, Don Pedro Leos, who read him documents, legal and otherwise (Paz 1895: 37). Leos was at least as cruel and vengeful as Rojas. According to a contemporary journalist, Ireneo Paz, General Rojas signed papers with an insigne that, appropriately enough, took the form of a skull. It appears that he meant to strike terror in the heart of any recipient of a letter bearing his rubric (Paz 1895: 38).

Rojas and his band of cutthroats, known as the Galeanos, terrorized Mexicans throughout the state of Jalisco in the late 1850s and early 1860s, during the

War of Reform. After the French invasion of 1862, President Juárez called upon all Mexicans to resist the invaders when he was forced to flee the capital. In the words of the journalist Ireneo Paz, "Of all the chiefs [or warlords], whom we invited to join our grand combined forces, none answered the call (unfortunately) except general Antonio Rojas, . . . well-known by the inhabitants of Jalisco, where there was not a town that had not experienced the horrors of his presence" (Paz 1997: 59).[15]

Ireneo Paz, who fought alongside Rojas, was horrified at nearly every turn. One incident the journalist chronicled occurred when Rojas and his men were headquartered in the town of Zapotlán. A stagecoach arrived from Guadalajara, the capital of the state of Jalisco, when the general was suffering from a recent painful wound and in a terrible humor. Because of his annoyance at the racket caused by the coach, Rojas ordered it burned, along with the passengers, the coachman, and everything it contained. "Those of us present had to proceed with caution, trying to cajole this furious crazy man, to dissuade him from committing such a barbarity" recounts Paz (1997: 75).[16]

First, they managed to save the mail by convincing Rojas of the strategic advantages they would obtain from reading it. Then they were able to suspend the execution of the passengers, saying they would be able to give the soldiers news about enemy emplacements. Finally, they "managed to remove the death penalty from the horses, saying they could serve in the cavalry. . . . We had to resign ourselves to watching the stagecoach in flames in the middle of the plaza. The unlucky coachman was shot" (1997: 75–76).[17]

Rojas was extremely effective against the French forces, and thus became a target for a captain who was a kindred spirit. "Berthelin, . . . [was] if possible, worse than Rojas. The Frenchman was a bloodthirsty racist, a tiger in victory. . . . He killed perhaps five hundred Mexicans in Colima and Jalisco" (Vanderwood 1992: 6).

The end of the bandit-turned-patriot was as violent and blood-soaked as his life had been. On 28 January 1865 Captain Berthelin, with fifty dragoons under the command of Captain Miranda, surprised him at Potrerillos. Rojas had five hundred cavalry and three hundred infantry (Galvan Rivera 1987: 146). Diego Barrientos, a member of Rojas's own forces, betrayed the general by informing the French Captain Berthelin where Rojas would be camped and helping set up the ambush. Barrientos had joined the Galeanos to avenge his sister, who had been raped by Rojas. His older brother had attempted to defend their sister, only to have Leos, Rojas's secretary, gouge out his eyes (Paz 1895: 125). Diego Barrientos finally avenged his siblings by shooting Rojas in the back while the general and his men were trying to hold off the French attack. When the dust and smoke cleared, there were fifty or sixty dead, with Rojas and Barrientos among them. By the time he died Rojas had become a legendary figure. He then became a war trophy and, finally, a museum specimen.

An additional piece of documentation was found on the Internet. During searches for references and archival information about the bandit, a photograph of Antonio Rojas appeared for sale. The photograph was one of ninety-four carte de visite images—postcard-size albumen portraits reproduced on thin paper mounted on heavier stock—kept in a leather-bound album. The photographs in the album were being sold individually and included images from the French Intervention—portraits of Benito Juárez and many members of his cabinet, Maximilian and his court, French generals and their Mexican allies, as well as Mexican generals and individuals involved in the resistance. The photograph of Rojas was one of the few still available.

The image documented Rojas's features, making it possible to compare them to the skull in question. In forensic anthropology, an individual's identification is made from the remains—the skull and skeleton. The photographic image could be superimposed on the skull to see whether the features match, particularly in the upper half of the head.

David Hunt, a forensic anthropologist colleague at the Smithsonian, used a Siemans Somotom CT scanner to make a three-dimensional surface rendering

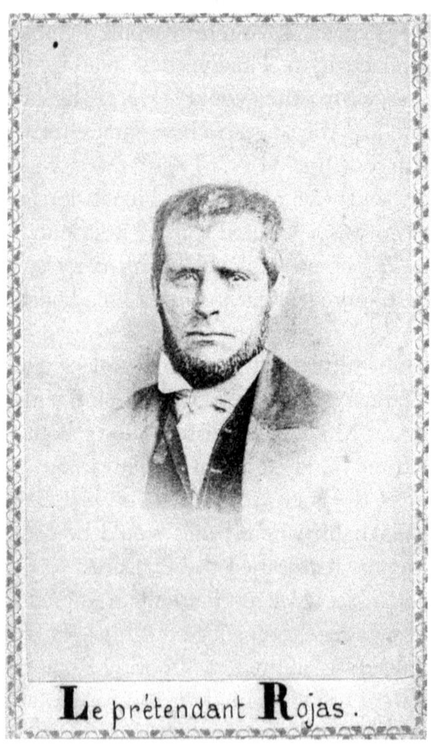

Figure 17.1 Photograph of Antonio Rojas (Smithsonian Institution, National Museum of Natural History).

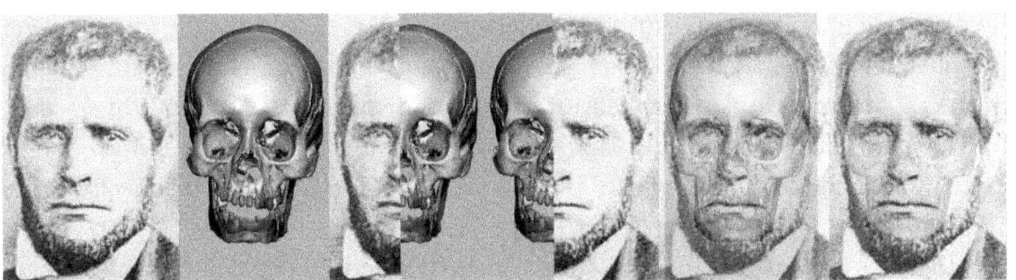

Figure 17.2 Superimposition of face on Rojas skull (courtesy of Joe Mullins, Forensic Imaging Center, National Center for Missing and Exploited Children, Washington, DC).

of the Rojas skull. This image was then taken to the Forensic Imaging Section at the National Center for Missing and Exploited Children, where forensic artist Joe Mullins, with whom Dr. Hunt has worked for many years, superimposed the three-dimensional cranial image over the photograph of Rojas. To more accurately assess the match to the photograph, Mullins used Free-Form layering software to virtually reconstruct the face. He placed the eyes back into their orbits, estimated the nasal shape from the shape of the bony nasal aperture, located eyebrows along orbital ridges, and built up the mouth edges and forehead (Walsh and Hunt 2013).

The results: the human cranium that Eugène Boban sold to the Army Medical Museum in 1887 is, in fact, the head of Antonio Rojas, as far as can be determined presently. The skull is authentic, and Boban told the truth about this specimen.

Holmes and Boban were not the only people studying and writing about faked pre-Columbian artifacts. The subject of fakes also fascinated Paul Eudel, the chronicler of the Hôtel Drouot, a Paris auction house. In several editions of his famous volume *Le Truquage* (Fakery; 1887), he expressed admiration for Eugène Boban's work, describing him as an honest merchant who warned his clients by sharing his superior knowledge of authentic and inauthentic artifacts.

Many years later, in 1910, Boban's work on fakes was referenced once again by none other than Leopoldo Batres in his book *Antigüedades Mejicanas Falsificadas: Falsificación y Falsificadores* (Faked Mexican Antiquities: Faking and Fakers). The book is an exercise in irony, since nearly every page is filled with passages taken directly, only sometimes with quotation marks, from a 1907 reissued edition of Paul Eudel's book. Adding another layer of ironic appropriation, much of the rest of the book is reproduced verbatim from Boban's writings, although his name is never mentioned.

Eugène Boban and William Henry Holmes were the two men who knew most about faked pre-Columbian artifacts in the late nineteenth century. Boban's public pronouncements on the subject appear in his sales catalogs beginning in 1878, the year he began exhibiting blackware fakes to educate his clientele. From there he went on to write letters to others notifying them that they had fakes in their collections. In a draft letter to Léon de Rosny, he protests the publication of an issue of *L'Amérique Préhistorique* that he insists illustrates fake artifacts. He mentions a publication in the Smithsonian Contributions series, "The Archaeological Collection of the United States National Museum," dated 1876, which includes among its illustrations those of obvious blackware fakes (HSA: B2244, Box V; Rau 1876:82-87).

Holmes's interest in the subject was sparked when he noticed that his surface collections of Aztec pottery made in early 1884 differed so greatly from what he saw exhibited in the Museo Nacional. It also stemmed from his education as an artist, which included studying many examples of ancient ceramics in the Smithsonian and other museum collections. This caused him to appreciate the work of Mexicans who had lived centuries before. "In pre-Columbian times the native potter of that country had reached a high degree of skill in the handling of clay" (Holmes 1886: 170). It caused him to judge the blackware objects—so lacking in artistry and sophistication and so prevalent in artifact shops in Mexico City and Teotihuacan at the time—to be obvious frauds. "The whole genius of aboriginal methods of procedure goes to discredit them" (1886: 172).

Boban and Holmes shared an eye for beauty, an understanding of quality artisanry, and a passion for authenticity and meaning. They also shared a high level of mutual respect.

Notes

1. Modern ou contrefaçons.

2. Fabriquées de nos jours dans les faubourgs de Mexico par les Indiens (à Santiago et à Los Angeles). Ces objets ne sont ni moulés, ni copiés sur des monuments anciens du pays (c'est de pure fantaisie), c'est un genre de caricatures bizarres dont l'inspiration nous échappe, mais dont le but principal es de tromper le publique.

3. Comme ils sont très faciles à acquérir et très bon marché dans le pays, des voyageurs peu soucieux et ont apporté beaucoup et, alors, ces monstres se pavanent dans les belles vitrines de nos Musées d'Europe.

4. Un lapidaire Mexicain nommé Juan Bobadilla. Plazuela de Santo Thomas No. 17 (Mexico) a fabrique et fabrique encore plusieur statuette ou idoles en roches dures, obsidienns, jadeite, etc.

5. Un autre lapidaire Mexicain aussi El Sr. Amador demeurant à Mexico, ex employé à la Diputacion on m'a assure qu'il a fabriquer plusieur contrefaçons d'antiquités en roches dures.

6. Un autre contrefacteur nommé Ph. Praget (mort aujourd'hui) Français d'origine, Bijoutier et Minero, il avait la specialité de contrefaire les objets en bronze, qui avaient beaucoup d'amateur à Mexico.

7. 4 pièces un poisson en cuivre de 8 a 10 pouces de long. don la queue se terminait en hache, une autre piece assez etrange de forme rappelant le coup de poing Americain avec une pointe, et une figure humaine qui semblait avoir des ailles plus 2 haches très epaisse ce 4 pieces avaient été fabriqués à Mexico et vendu à un collectionneur Italien, M. Tangassi, qui est mort aussi.

8. Chose singuliére les imitateurs n'ont pas remarquer que les anciens Mexicains n'ont jamais fait de statuette d'idoles en obsidienne pas plus que des haches polis avec cette roche . . . de petites

tetes d'animaux qui servaien de pendentifs dans les Cozcapetlatl ou collier puis des itztli tezcatl miroirs rond, carrés, etc, des Coxcatl ou grains de colliers de longue lames en forme de grattoirs qui servaient à armés le Macuahuitl ou Massues des Mexicains.

9. Toutes les statuettes en obsidienne representant des petites idoles avec le corps les bras et les jambes peuvent être considérées comme fausses.

10. Mexique—Rojas—Chef de Guerillas—tué par un soldat cie. Du capitain Berthelin du 81e.

11. En réponse a votre lettre du 2 courant au sujet de la provenance des crânes les nos. 1372—1374—1368—1383—1375—1377—1370—1385 ces 8 crânes provident de ce chenapan Leopoldo Batres.

12. Si vous enlevez ou decollez avec soins les étiquettes qui portent les numéros de mon Catalogue. Vous retrouverez en dessous d'autres étiquettes les ecrites de sa main sur une petite bande de papier blanc avec des provenances mensongères telles que Zapoteco—tehuantepecano, etc. Il m'avait assure la provenance de ces crânes et disait qu'il voulait former une collection anthropologique de races anciennes du Mexique pour le Musée de Mexico, et faire une publication sur ce sujet (ci dont il est parfaitement incapable) peu de temps avant mon depart de Mexico, est venu chez moi un nommé Swans qui s'occupé un peu d'histoire naturelle . . . en voyant les crânes en question il me dit mais ces crânes je les reconnais nous avons ete dernièrement les deterrer dans les petits villages Indiens pres la Villa de Guadalupe. Avec ce vaut-rien de Batres me dit il c'est un menteur de dire qui ils viennent de Oaxaca ou Tehuantepec. Je vous donne ma parole d'honneur me dit Swans que ces crânes viennent bien des environs de Mexico. C'est en vue de cette rectification due au hasard, qui j'ai alors classes dans mon catalogue Vallée de Mexico.

13. Jai appris qu'il en avait vendu d'autre à des voyageurs avec des provenances de pures fantaisies. Du reste avec un peu d'attention on remarquera que ces crânes ont bien les mêmes caracteres de race, et surtout la même patine la même couleur produit par le même milieu.

14. Le no. 1389 m'a été donné par un ami Le Colonel Tamisey du 60 de Ligne que j'avais connue l'ors de l'occupation Français au Mexique. Lors de mon depart de Mexico Mr. B. Nichols desirait m'acheter ce crâne mais il le trouvait trop cher. Il me pria de lui en donner un autre, et ce même crâne ancien que je lui avait donné à Mexico. J'ai été surpris de la revoir a New York a son Mexican Exhibition et sur son catalogue avec le titre tete de Rojas etc. Je ne doute pas que mon ami M. Nichols rectifie cette petite erreure avec plaisir, car alors il ferait supposer que Rojas ce terrible brigand avait 2 tetes. Mais l'originale est bien notre numero 1389.

15. De todos los jefes a quienes invitamos para nuestra grandiosa combinación no concurrió a la cita (por desgracia) más que el general Antonio Rojas. Los lectores saben ya quién era Antonio Rojas y más saben los habitantes de Jalisco, en cuyo estado no hubo tal vez un pueblo que no tuviera que resentir los horrores de su presencia.

16. Los que estábamos allí presente tuvimos que proceder con la cautela de quien engaña a un loco furioso para poderlo disuadir de que se cometiera tal barbaridad.

17. En seguida logramos que levantara la pena de muerto para los caballos, diciéndole que podrían servir para la descubierta de un cuerpo de caballeria. . . .Tuvimos que resignarnos a ver arder la diligencia en medio de la plaza. El infeliz cochero fue fusilado.

18

"El Tocayo's" Triumph

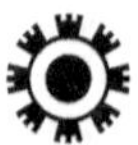

Eugène Boban and his wife returned to Paris in early 1888 without much fanfare. He may have been seeking some solitude after the experiences of the past three years. His hopes had been so high in February 1885, when he left for Mexico City to establish his Museo Científico. He had envisioned his museum as a center for the study of archeology and history, through which he could reconnect with his adopted homeland. But circumstances had conspired to prevent him from making a success of his dream venture.

Perhaps the expenses of setting up and maintaining the Museo Científico played a role in its eventual failure. Boban had borne the cost of shipping thousands of artifacts and books from Paris to Veracruz, and then by rail on to Mexico City. Renting his museum and shop, not to mention a home for himself and his wife, would have added further costs. The elaborate catafalque for the mummies, along with other exhibit settings, constituted yet another cash outlay.

The capital city was prosperous and on the verge of modernity. The Díaz regime had created order and economic growth in the country, certainly for the rich. As Jonathan Kandell, an American journalist who spent many years in Mexico City, commented, "For a wealthy urban elite, this was a self-assured, gilded era—the Mexican equivalent of the Belle Époque in Paris" (1988: 354). Despite this affluence, the economy may have played a part in torpedoing his plans as well. The wealthy elites certainly had disposable income, but the common people, who might have earned between one and three *reals* per day, could hardly have afforded the one *real* entry fee to Boban's museum (Challú 2015: 20). The rather small middle class was unable for the most part to purchase luxury items, making it difficult for the general public to afford the admission at all. A usual Sunday outing for working and middle classes was a picnic in Chapultepec Park, as is still the case to this day.

Leaving for New York following the disastrous business partnership with Batres seems to have been an astute move that paid off financially in the end. Despite his complaints of not achieving the desired prices for a large number of his Mexican collection, Boban actually made a considerable amount of money selling numerous South Pacific artifacts and the crystal skull, as well as a large part of his library. According to some sources the auction brought more than $10,000 or 50,000 francs (New York Times, 19 December 1886).

Just short of three years after the start of his second trip to Mexico, he returned home to Paris with what was left of his collection and his dream. A memorandum dated 18 October 1887 from the Compagnie Générale Transatlantique (French Line Steamers) introduces Boban and his wife to the commissaire of the steamship they were about to take on their return home. "Permit me to recommend to your good care Mr. and Mrs. Boban Duvergé, passengers on Champagne" (BNF DMO n.a.f. 21479: item 12).[1]

The first indication that Boban was once again in the French capital is a letter dated 11 February 1888 from the wealthy industrialist E. Eugène Goupil, who was born in Mexico City in 1831. He was the son of a Mexican mother, whom he usually described as a descendant of Aztecs, and a French father who owned a clothing and jewelry shop. The Goupil family returned to France in 1851 (Cohen 1998: 21).

Following his father in the jewelry business Goupil opened a factory north of Paris in Chaumontel that produced "metallic beads in all colors." He had business dealings in both France and Mexico. By 1888 the two men seem to be old friends, judging by their correspondence. E. Eugène Goupil's first letter is addressed to "Cher Tocayo." This is a Mexican Spanish word, originating from Nahuatl that is used to describe someone who has the same first name—one's "namesake."

Obviously glad to hear his friend was back home, Goupil writes, "It was just last Monday that I found out you had been living in the capital for a month."[2] Mentioning that he had been at the Drouot auction house and had seen Mexican archeological objects going for ridiculously low prices, Goupil says he had discovered that his own brother, Louis Goupil, knew Boban's whereabouts. He then asks Boban to meet with him between 1:30 and 2:30 on 16 February at his home at 40, boulevard Magenta (BNF DMO n.a.f. 21480; item 14).

Goupil sent the letter to 122, avenue d'Orléans, Paris—Montrouge, Seine, which was not only Boban's new business address, but also his home, which he shared with his wife. According to French cadastral records, the avenue d'Orléans address was that of a tall building over a basement, with a ground floor and two upper stories. The property was considerably larger than his previous domiciles, and included a tannery, stables, and house with an office, kitchen, dining room, living room, and bedroom. Presumably it is where Boban warehoused his remaining objects and the collection from the shop on rue Daguerre (AD Paris, D.1P4/827: 122 route d'Orleans).

It seems that Goupil had had more on his mind than simply reconnecting with an old friend when he sent his first letter in early February. A bit more than a week later, he wrote to his "Cher Tocayo" again on 20 February saying, "According to what was verbally agreed upon yesterday, you will kindly give me your entire Mexican collection, and modern things, except the stirrups and absolutely [not] the three mummified human bodies." He concludes that his friend should not add any other objects to the collection, in return for "the sum of eight thousand francs (8,000)" (BNF DMO n.a.f. 21480; item 16).[3] This letter marks the beginning of an extremely close financial and creative venture between the antiquarian and the industrialist—the *tocayos* Eugène.

Boban's fortunes had changed just that fast. A month or so after his return to Paris, he had successfully sold to E. Eugène Goupil virtually all of his remaining Mexican collection. From later photographs of the objects included, it still comprised a considerable amount of material, even aside from the "three mummies" (there were actually four) that, from the tone of his letter, made Goupil shudder.

As with other Mexican objects in his collection, Boban returned to Paris with the four unfortunate cadavers following the New York auction. He had apparently been able to buy these back, along with numerous artifacts whose hammer prices he considered too low. An item in the *New York Tribune*, on 14 December 1886 "Sale of the Boban Collection" noted that, "The four mummy figures from the Convent of San Domingo brought $22 each" (New York Tribune, 14 December 1886). This was clearly too paltry a sum for such exotic items that could thrill the public in the right setting.

The eight-thousand-franc sale price that Boban received from Goupil is less than a third of the twenty-five thousand francs Ernest Hamy had offered for the collection in 1884 (SIA: RU7084). However, the $10,500 he purportedly realized from the sale of his artifacts and library in New York should be added to this figure, representing an additional 52,500 francs, a fairly grand sum, which does not even take into account any other sales he made along the way. Among these are the jadeite votive axe and the gem painting to George Kunz, the human crania to the Army Medical Museum, the ceramic pieces to the Smithsonian Institution, and the sale of a number of other objects now in the collections of museums such as Yale University, the University of Pennsylvania, and a variety of other institutions.

After reiterating their verbal agreement, Goupil's letter of 20 February continues by saying that he will go to Boban's house on the twenty-third of the month to identify with him the items that are most fragile and most significant, and together they will oversee the packing. The next day he will bring a vehicle to transport the remaining material, which he has already decided to place on the first four shelves of the large vitrine in his living room. The other artifacts will go in his Norman armoire. Goupil closes this letter by saying that he sends his greetings to his *tocayo*'s "amiable entourage" (BNF DMO n.a.f. 21480; item

68). In another letter written in the same month, Goupil sends his "civilités a Madame Boban et a Madame votre parente," in other words he sends his regards to Mrs. Boban and to his older aunt, Madame Duvergé (BNF DMO n.a.f. 21480: item 66).

Boban and his wife were then living with Fanny Duvergé, the elder of his father's two half-sisters from Angers, who had presumably helped her younger sister take care of his Paris antiquities shop while he was in Mexico. Since Fanny was a widow, it may be that she had been living with Henriette, who died in May 1887 at the address on rue Daguerre, not too far from avenue d'Orléans where her nephew had moved.

At last Boban had succeeded in selling his second major assemblage of Mexican pre-Columbian artifacts. In his memoirs he referred to it as "the collection of the dead or deceased," since he had purchased some of the pieces from the estates of M. Martin, Dr. Fuzier, Count de Waldeck, and other such early collectors (HSA: B2244, Box V). Selling the collection in its entirety maintained the integrity and educational value of its important series and groupings, such as Martin's Zapotec warrior from Mitla and the accompanying terra cotta figures. Although Boban had not received top dollar for these artifacts, he had been paid a reasonable amount for the great effort and attention spent putting together the collection. And perhaps most important, he had sold it to someone who truly appreciated the objects themselves and respected the erudition of the man who had assembled them.

Goupil quickly developed into an extremely enthusiastic collector himself, making plans to exhibit his newly acquired Mexican objects at the 1889 Exposition Universelle. Boban had exhibited at the previous two expositions. This turn of events recalls the sale of his original Mexican collection to Alphonse Pinart, who then exhibited Boban's artifacts as his own in the 1878 Exposition Universelle.

In March Goupil writes to Boban to inform him of the death of Mr. Labadie, the owner of a pharmacy located a block or so from Boban's first shop in Mexico City. Boban had known the pharmacist when he was first in Mexico and had reconnected with him during his second stay. Goupil, who was still in touch with the French community in the Mexican capital, especially the Labadies, who were cousins (John Charlot, pers. comm. and JohnCharlot.org) writes a few weeks later giving minute details of Labadie's last hours (BNF D.O.M n.a.f. 21480: item 22).

His friendship with Goupil ripens very quickly. Boban soon reconnects with numerous other European friends and clients as well. As the months go by, Goupil becomes a regular correspondent, sending letters every few days to set up meetings and discuss plans for a catalog of his new collection. In March 1888 Boban received a letter from Philipp J. Becker of Darmstadt, Germany, a fellow collector of pre-Columbian Mexican artifacts. "My dear friend Boban," he writes, "your letter gave me great pleasure, hearing that your trip to Mexico and the United States was crowned with such complete success." Jokingly, Becker adds that Boban will probably be retiring soon, living the life of a good bourgeois, and "taking a demitasse every afternoon in one of the cafes on the Boulevard Saint Michel" (BNF DMO n.a.f. 21476: item 115).[4] The merchant from Darmstadt had lived in Puebla and had resided in Mexico for some twenty years (Van Meer 2006). While there he made an important collection comprising pre-Columbian artifacts and two Mixtec painted manuscripts that now bear his name, Codex Becker I and II (Museum für Völkerkunde, Vienna cat. 6036). The two collectors would have known each other since their time in Mexico overlapped; Becker arrived in 1850 and Boban in 1857.

Despite the fact that Boban soon was nearly consumed by his work with Goupil on the exhibition and the catalog of his collection, he still found time to keep up with his correspondence and share some of the highly specialized knowledge he had acquired as a result of his unusual travel experiences. Julien de Saint Venant, a colleague whose card said he was Adjunct Inspector of Forests in Bourges, writes to Boban on 7 April 1888.[5] His letter says in part,

> When I saw you in the month of February last, you told me that you witnessed, at least once, the manner in which the wild Indians of California, I think, made their small flint arrowheads. I will cite you in a paper I am doing for a Society, and would ask, if it is not too indiscrete of me, if you have any details about the way the tools were made, and if they were metal or stone, from pressure or fracture, and with or without the aid of a mallet. . . . If you know the province and the name of the Indian tribe and so on. . . . Recognizing that you are one of the few people lucky enough to have witnessed the entire process. (BNF DMO n.a.f. 21479: item 399)[6]

That same month, Goupil invites Boban to accompany him to the Trocadéro to compare his collection with Mexican artifacts on exhibit, most of which are from Boban's original collection sold to Alphonse Pinart. Another letter from Goupil asks for Boban's advice on a Gallo-Roman collection that he is interested in purchasing. By this stage Boban seems to have taken on the role of private curator for Goupil, helping him plan how to display his artifacts and advising him on other collections to buy.

Their master plan was to mount a grand exhibition of the collection, along with large-format photographs of groupings of objects, at the 1889 Exposition Universelle opening in May. The photographs were to be compiled into a limited-edition publication as well. Goupil soon informs Boban that he has hired a photographer, Mr. R. Guillen, to produce a variety of plates of different artifacts in the collection for publication and exhibition.

Boban had met his match in Goupil—someone who took the collecting and exhibiting of pre-Columbian artifacts as seriously as he did. Goupil was involved in every aspect of the photography and exhibition of the collection. This is evident in his letter of 3 June 1888, in which he writes that he thinks it is a good idea to have the photographer's name and address printed on each image, but in small type. He discusses how to handle the title that is to be printed at the top of each photograph. Goupil proposes that the main heading be: "Antiquités Mexicaines Collection de E. Eug. Goupil." Below that he suggests a subtitle in a smaller typeface reading, "Anciennes Collections E. Boban." He says they should make one hundred imprints of each of the twenty groupings Guillen is photographing, some two thousand photographic reproductions all told. Then Goupil goes on to give three pages of suggestions and edits for the captions for each of the photographs (BNF DMO n.a.f. 21480: item 37).

In a letter written later in June, Goupil comments that the "printed articles" are very good, referring to the long captions for each of the photographs. He also has some corrections to make on the printed and matted photographs. For instance, he thinks the photographer's name is too large and the subtitle "Anciennes Collections E. Boban" too small (BNF DMO n.a.f. 21480: item 37).

Throughout 1888 the two men planned the exhibition, micromanaged the photography of the collection, and crafted the detailed captions for the mounted photographs. In August, the fifty-seven-year-old Goupil complained about feeling debilitated by his diabetes after being laid up for several weeks. Toward the end of November 1888 Goupil signaled the state of his physical and emotional health when he wrote to "Mon cher Monsieur Bauban," forgetting his usual "tocayo" greeting, not to mention how to spell his friend's surname. Goupil's letter says he picked up several packages of Boban's publications from 1876 in the *Musée Archéologique* and delivered them to several people, who were all quite pleased. The communication underscores how much Goupil appreciated Boban's work and the efforts to which he would go to assure that others shared his enthusiasm (BNF DMO n.a.f. 21480: item 48).

In the midst of the feverish preparations for the 1889 Exposition Universelle— photographing the objects, deciding which artifacts to display, preparing captions and labels, editing all the text repeatedly—came a communication that would transform Boban's career and legacy. He received a long letter from the Mexican physician, archeologist, and historian Antonio Peñafiel, written in March 1888. Peñafiel, a member of Díaz's Científicos, was in charge of organizing the Mexican government's exhibit at the Exposition.

Writing in response to a letter from Boban written on 24 February, Peñafiel addresses him as "Very esteemed friend." He says he is working on a variety of projects, several of which will be displayed at the upcoming Exposition. In this endeavor he asks for help from his friend: "Can you give me some idea of how much it would cost, monthly, for five people [to stay in Paris], my wife, a servant, my son Julio, and perhaps another of the children and myself; you understand that it would be for housing and board, not a hotel." Peñafiel ends the letter by saying he will wait for Boban's answer before making preparations for his trip

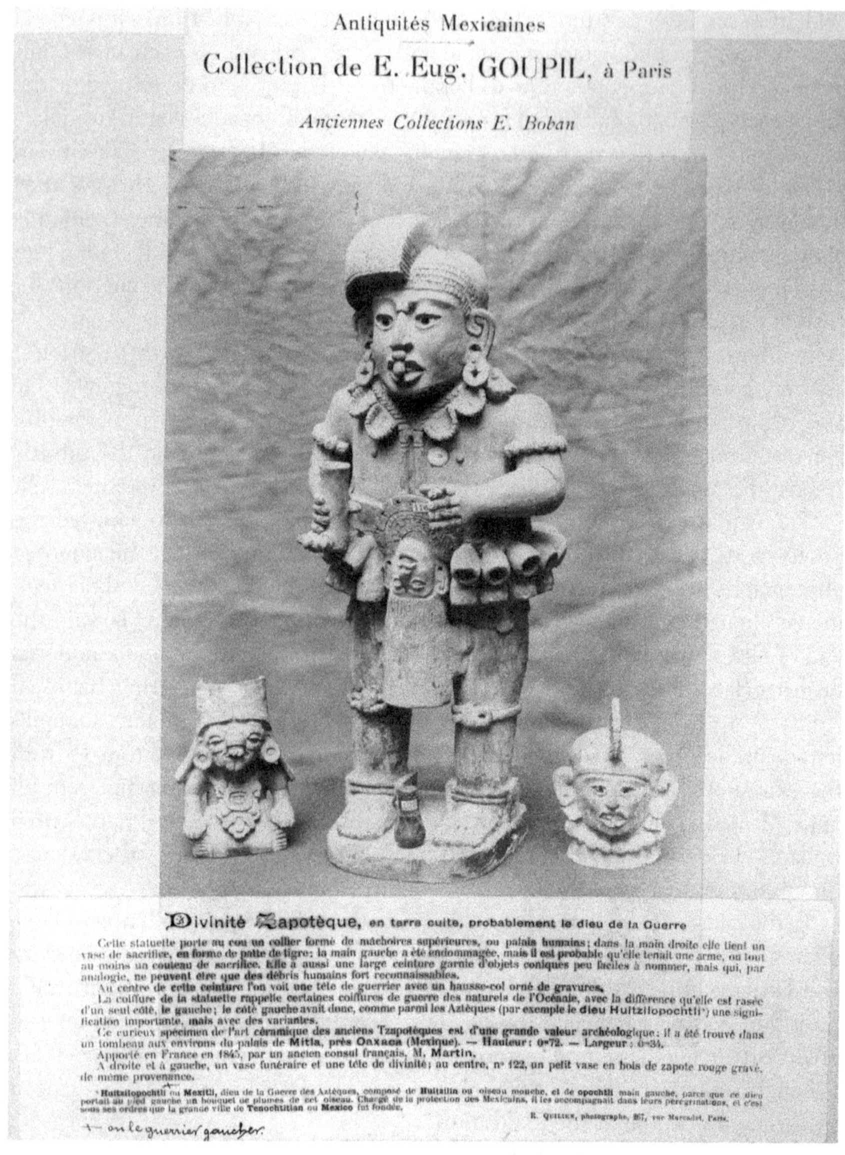

Antiquités Mexicaines

Collection de E. Eug. GOUPIL, à Paris

Anciennes Collections E. Boban

Divinité Zapotèque, en terre cuite, probablement le dieu de la Guerre

Cette statuette porte au cou un collier formé de mâchoires supérieures, ou palais humains; dans la main droite elle tient un vase de sacrifice, en forme de patte de tigre; la main gauche a été endommagée, mais il est probable qu'elle tenait une arme, ou tout au moins un couteau de sacrifice. Elle a aussi une large ceinture garnie d'objets coniques peu faciles à nommer, mais qui, par analogie, ne peuvent être que des débris humains fort reconnaissables.

Au centre de cette ceinture l'on voit une tête de guerrier avec un hausse-col orné de gravures.

La coiffure de la statuette rappelle certaines coiffures de guerre des naturels de l'Océanie, avec la différence qu'elle est rasée d'un seul côté, le gauche; le côté gauche avait donc, comme parmi les Aztèques (par exemple le dieu Huitzilopochtli*) une signification importante, mais avec des variantes.

Ce curieux spécimen de l'art céramique des anciens Tzapotèques est d'une grande valeur archéologique; il a été trouvé dans un tombeau aux environs du palais de Mitla, près Oaxaca (Mexique). — Hauteur: 0ᵐ72. — Largeur: 0ᵐ34.

Apporté en France en 1845, par un ancien consul français, M. Martin.

À droite et à gauche, un vase funéraire et une tête de divinité; au centre, nᵒ 122, un petit vase en bois de zapote rouge gravé, de même provenance.

*Huitzilopochtli ou Mexitli, dieu de la Guerre des Aztèques, composé de Huitzilin ou oiseau mouche, et de opochtli main gauche, parce que ce dieu portait au pied gauche un bouquet de plumes de cet oiseau. Chargé de la protection des Mexicains, il les accompagnait dans leurs pérégrinations, et c'est sous ses ordres que la grande ville de Tenochtitlan ou Mexico fut fondée.

R. QUILLIER, photographe, 267, rue Marcadet, Paris.

— ou le guerrier gaucher.

Figure 18.1 Exhibition photograph of objects in the Eugène Goupil Collection (courtesy of Hispanic Society of America, New York).

to Europe, and closes by saying, "Tell your wife that if she knows how to speak Spanish she can talk with mine, who doesn't speak a word of French!" (BNF DMO n.a.f. 21478: item 488–89).[7] Peñafiel wrote another letter in January 1889, with more news about his plans. He arrived in Paris just before the opening of the Exposition in late March.

Boban must have been on top of the world in 1889 exhibiting his collection of Mexican antiquities. The French had hosted four of the largest and most impressive international exhibitions of agriculture, industry, and arts presented in Europe up to that time, and Boban had exhibited Mexican antiquities in three of them. The 1889 show, commemorating the centennial of the French Revolution, had as its centerpiece the newly constructed Eiffel Tower. It was the largest exposition yet and, for him, certainly the most important.

Boban had spent more than a decade assembling the pre-Columbian artifacts on display. Representing countless sites and sources, it was the largest single collection of Mexican antiquities ever seen in Europe. He and Goupil filled the enormous display cabinet with all manner of artifacts, large and small, stone and ceramic. Commanding the center was the standing Zapotec warrior, excavated in the 1840s and acquired by Boban after the death of the original collector. This is the same figure that William Henry Holmes had so wanted to acquire for the Smithsonian Institution. Judging from the height of the figure, which is described in the notes as being approximately 28.4 in. (72 cm), the mahogany cabinet overflowing with riches was about 12 ft. tall (3.5 m).

The French journal *La Nature* offered a glowing review of the Mexican exhibits at the Exposition. "The Mexican government has stopped at no sacrifice to display the treasures of its history at the Universal Exhibition of 1889, and has built, at its own expense, a special pavilion for Mexican antiquities. . . . They have sent rare plants, geological and mineralogical specimens, marbles, and gemstones. All organized under the direction of Dr. Antonio Peñafiel, a most distinguished archeologist." The article continues with a description of Goupil and Boban's exhibition, which was displayed in another location nearby. "Among the most remarkable collections to be included in the special Mexican antiquities section, we will mention that of Goupil of Paris, born in Mexico; this collection contains objects of great value and beauty" (Tissandier 1889: 119).[8] Boban's name appears only in the caption of a photograph of the Zapotec warrior, which indicates that it is from the Goupil collection, originally from E. Boban. Thus, despite years of work assembling, cataloging, maintaining and promoting the collection, he has once again been relegated to the role of an offstage player, at least in this article.

However, less than a month before the Exposition's opening, Boban had facilitated a sale that would guarantee that his name and reputation as a pre-Columbian scholar would live on. Boban's friend Antonio Peñafiel, the "most distinguished archeologist" mentioned in the *La Nature* article, had asked him to arrange a meeting while he was in Paris with the aging and reclusive Joseph Marius Alexis Aubin to see his famous collection. It was the largest and most important assemblage of pre-Columbian and postcontact painted Mexican manuscripts in the world. Boban, who had known Aubin for years, was delighted to arrange for Peñafiel to meet with him.

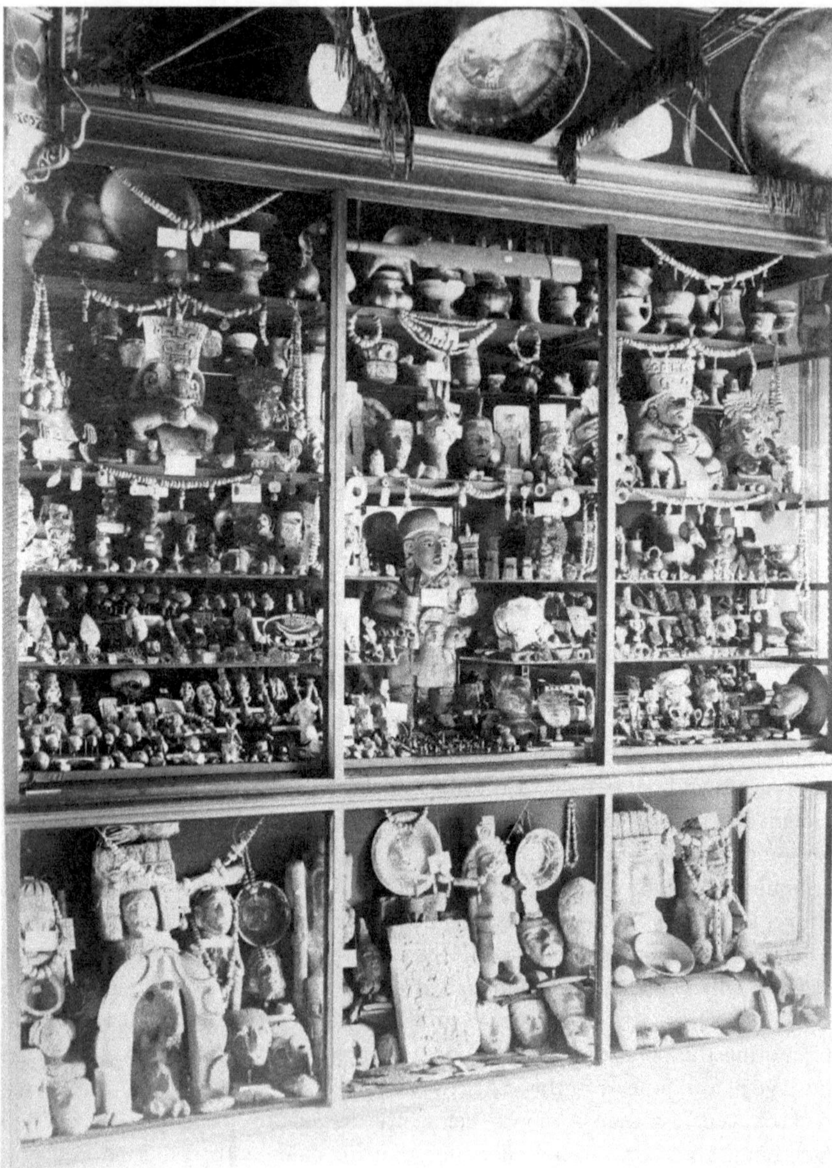

Figure 18.2 Eugène Goupil's exhibition cabinet at the 1889 Exposition Universelle in Paris (courtesy of Hispanic Society of America, New York).

The Aubin Collection of early Mexican manuscripts had been a principal focus of scholarly curiosity and interest of nearly every Americanist in France from at least the mid-nineteenth century. It may even be said that it was the raison d'être for the formation of several of the scientific societies intent on studying Mexican antiquities, including the Société Americaine de France. Aubin had spent the 1830s in Mexico looking for the remnants of the magnificent collection amassed by Lorenzo Boturini Benaducci, and had managed to acquire quite an amazing hoard of painted codices.

The Italian nobleman Lorenzo Boturini Benaducci amassed a collection of pre-Columbian and postcontact painted manuscripts in the early eighteenth century, searching for examples between 1735 and 1743. He then ran afoul of the Spanish authorities in Mexico. He was arrested, imprisoned, and finally deported from the country. In the process of investigating his activities while in Mexico, the vice-regal government seized his manuscript collection, and later dispersed it to scholars and collectors.

When Joseph Marius Alexis Aubin left Mexico in 1840, he hid his manuscripts in his luggage, fearing that the Mexican customs agents would seize them. He separated and mixed up the pages of the codices, "erasing the numbers and labels from public or private libraries, so that the confused jumble looked like a pile of worthless papers and would pass unnoticed by customs. Mr. Aubin was indeed successful. He left Mexico carrying his entire collection, but in such a disarray that he himself never had the courage to catalog it" (Boban 1891: 14).[9] Boban's description leaves little doubt that Aubin removed many of the manuscripts from museums, libraries, and archives, possibly even from the Museo Nacional. He does not say whether Aubin acquired them through purchase, trade, or theft, although his erasure of numbers and labels would indicate that his methods would not withstand official scrutiny.

Boban's published account of the history of the Aubin Collection describes the momentous encounter between Peñafiel and Aubin. "Previously, I had the opportunity on a number of occasions to show M. Aubin the important work being done by Doctor Peñafiel. He became interested and told me I could show his documents to him, [and so] I introduced the two scholars to each other, and we took time to examine the collection" (Boban 1891: 11).[10] He added that he had wanted to share this singular opportunity of examining Aubin's precious manuscripts "with some of the scholars that it might interest, [so] I wrote to M. de Quatrefages, the learned Professor of the Museum of Paris, and asked him to join us on the day of our visit to Mr. Aubin" (BNF DMO n.a.f. 21479:item 1)."[11]

Jean Luis Armand de Quatrefages de Bréau was an important figure on several fronts—he held the chair of anthropology and ethnography at France's Musée national d'histoire naturelle, and he was a member of the l'Académie des science and commander of the Lègion d'honneur. He and Boban had known each other for nearly two decades. In fact, a letter to Boban in the early 1870s from the Mexican archeologist José Melgar y Serrano closes with, "Give my best to Quatrefages" (BNF DMO n.a.f. 21478: item 328). He naturally invited his friend, patron, and *tocayo*, Eugène Goupil, to see Aubin's collection as well.

Boban's published description of this encounter continues:

The visit took place on 28 March 1889. Quatrefages, Peñafiel, his two sons, Goupil, and I were all present. M. Aubin received us well and showed us his principal documents. To our astonishment, after we left Aubin's house, Peñafiel made every effort to convince me and Goupil that these manuscripts, with their paintings and hieroglyphics, had no real rarity or value, and even tried to convince us that the Museo Nacional was littered with similar documents. I knew where I stood on this subject because I had just spent nearly two years in Mexico City. I had seen and reviewed all the collections of the Museo Nacional, and I had firsthand knowledge that manuscripts were almost completely absent there. (Boban 1891: 11)[12]

As it turned out, part of Antonio Peñafiel's mission in asking Boban to introduce him to Aubin was to find a way to restore his country's priceless heritage of codices and manuscripts by purchasing the material from the aging and impoverished collector. After Armand de Quatrefages, Eugène Goupil, and Boban had departed, Peñafiel returned to Aubin's apartment and offered to purchase the old man's entire collection with an annuity set up by the Mexican government. Aubin agreed, and Peñafiel assured him that the deal would be completed within a few days, once he had informed his government.

Unfortunately for Peñafiel and the Museo Nacional de México, his plan came to the attention of Eugène Boban. "While his goal was excellent and he had a good strategy," Boban later wrote, "he was working for his country, no one could fault him, but he did not succeed" (1891: 12).[13] According to Boban's version of the events, Peñafiel had told Aubin to keep silent about the deal, especially with regard to Boban. But the aging and fearful Aubin could not hold his tongue about the possible sale. He told Boban that he was in dire straits and had decided to sell his collection for cash. Boban asked him to give him two days and to make no decision before he could see him again. Aubin agreed and Boban went straight to E. Eugène Goupil.

In his own words, Boban informed his friend, "I am going to surprise you, I told him. The Aubin collection is for sale, and in a few days it may be on its way to Mexico. It is Doctor Peñafiel, who offers to buy the collection, and the sale will be concluded within forty-eight hours unless you buy these precious documents to keep them in France" (Boban 1891: 12).[14] Then, despite their long and deep connections with Mexico and feelings of friendship toward the Mexican archeologist, Goupil and Boban triumphantly snatched the collection from under Peñafiel's nose, blocking the return of the precious manuscripts to their country of origin.

It was Goupil and Boban's express intention that the collection should remain in France, where they believed it would be best kept and preserved. It would also be made widely accessible to scholars, for whom it had become a kind of Rosetta Stone of pre-Columbian Mexican culture.

Following this extraordinary purchase, Goupil and Boban were able to exhibit at the 1889 Exposition Universelle not only the collection of pre-Columbian artifacts, but also specially mounted, large-format photographs of Aubin's painted manuscripts. The exhibition took place in another structure, beyond the special Mexican pavilion organized by Peñafiel.

Linguist and ethnographer Leon de Rosny, who had founded the Société d'Ethnographie in 1859 and had been interested in publishing items from the Aubin Collection for many decades, described their displays in the *Journal officiel de la République française*, which publishes information about France's national government.

> The small exhibition is composed of two parts, each absolutely distinct from the other. One is comprised of statuettes, utensils, tools, objects ... and other sorts of industrial productions of the ancient country of Montezuma. The other is composed of photographic facsimiles of the largest and most beautiful collection of Mexican figurative manuscripts that has ever been gathered together to date. The first of these collections comes from M. Eugène Boban; the second from M. Aubin; both are today in the possession of M. Eugène Goupil." (Rosny 1889: 5938–40)[15]

Having completed the purchase of the Aubin Collection for twenty thousand francs on 11 April 1889, Goupil made plans for the publication of an elaborate *catalogue raisonné* of the newly acquired codices. For this important undertaking Boban would reassemble, catalog, describe and annotate Aubin's collection for the benefit of scholars of pre-Columbian history worldwide.

Demonstrating his enthusiastic support of this project, Goupil wrote to Boban a month later saying he wanted to meet to discuss a plan that the two of them could agree upon. He said he wanted to talk about "pezetas," so that he could arrange for Boban to have "zero material worries to distract you from your passion—your grand passion and goal" (BNF DMO n.a.f 21480: items 35–36).[16] The letter is Goupil's offer to employ Boban as the sole researcher and curator of the manuscript collection, as well as the author of the planned *catalogue raisonné*. He wanted Boban to dedicate all his time to the project and was more than willing to compensate him for his efforts.

Their grand passion was, of course, Mexican archeology and history, and the goal was the publication of a two-volume, six-hundred-page tour de force, *Documents pour servir à l'histoire du Mexique*, accompanied by an atlas of eighty photographic reproductions of the manuscripts. Published in 1891, it has since become a primary reference resource on the subject of Mexican pre-Columbian codices and manuscripts.

The eminent American archeologist and ethnologist Daniel Garrison Brinton wrote in *Science* in 1893 that "M. Boban's task was to make an analytical catalog of the 372 pieces of which the collection consists. He has completed that task in a manner in the highest degree creditable to his own scholarship and to the discriminating liberality of M. Goupil" (1893: 127). More recently John B. Glass, the Library of Congress's specialist in pre-Columbian manuscripts, writing for the *Handbook of Middle American Indians*, described the volumes as a "work of major importance" (1975b: 565). This is high praise indeed from two renowned specialists in the field for the achievements of a completely self-taught scholar.

Boban's description of Peñafiel's attempt to purchase the collection for Mexico, which he published in the forward of the two-volume work, seems in many ways an unkind and undeserved reproach to a friend. Here, at the pinnacle of his career, he is not particularly generous. Instead he represents himself as being smarter, craftier, and better connected, and boasts about his success at the expense of his Mexican friend and colleague.

Peñafiel wrote to Goupil a few years later, in February 1894, after receiving a copy of *Histoire de la nation mexicaine* (1893), a textual and pictorial history of the Aztecs published by Boban and Goupil. After thanking Goupil for the gift, he shared his grievances. "I regret that I have been treated so badly by the editor of the Aubin manuscripts. I never thought to buy the manuscripts for principles of chivalry, but rather on the part of my government, when they were in Aubin's possession, which I was duty-bound to do, knowing that all those documents were taken from the archives and libraries of Mexico" (HSA: B2245, Box VI).[17]

Despite the fact that Boban placed his most important letters from illustrious people, including those of Antonio Peñafiel, in the five albums that he donated to the Bibliothèque nationale in Paris, he kept his copy of this letter separate. It is in Boban's private papers in the Hispanic Society collection. The German book dealer Karl W. Hiersemann purchased these papers after Boban's death in 1908, presumably from his widow, and sold them to Archer Huntington in 1910. At the top of this document Boban carefully noted, "Copy of a letter addressed to Mr. E. Goupil from Dr. Antonio Peñafiel about the gift of the volume 'History of the Mexican Nation after the Departure from Aztlan'" (HSA: B2245, Box VI).[18] Boban may have at some later date regretted his decision to publicly belittle Peñafiel's attempt to recover the collection for Mexico.

Boban and the French intellectual community considered Eugène Goupil's purchase of the Aubin Collection an act of extreme generosity and patriotism, particularly since Goupil's metallic bead factory had burned down several days before he agreed to spend 20,000 francs for the manuscripts. In his own description of events, Goupil wrote that he had acquired the collection to honor the memory of his mother, who was Mexican and a "descendant of the Aztecs," as he liked to describe her. The reason that he insisted that the collection stay in France was to "aid Mexicanists in their work." Because of that, he had "decided that my collection would remain in Paris, which is the center of the learned world" (Boban 1891: viii).

Goupil's thinking on the subject concurs with a certain nineteenth-century French intellectual mindset about how best to research other cultures. As Paul N. Edison pointed out in his PhD dissertation *Latinizing America: the French*

Scientific Study of Mexico 1830–1930, most French scholars of the nineteenth century agreed that "The study of Mexico was best done in France" (1999: 111).

The Goupil–Boban partnership yielded the sale of Boban's second great Mexican archeological collection and the acquisition of the most important collection of Mexican codices ever assembled. They were the crowning achievements of a life dedicated to acquiring, selling, and trading antiquities. In many ways, however, the amazing accomplishment of acquiring the Aubin Collection, particularly his retelling of the manner in which he saved the collection for France, seems to have been a way of severing the ties he still had to Mexico, his adopted homeland.

Notes

1. Permettez moi de recommender à vos bons soins Monsieur et madame Boban Duvergé, passagers sur "La Champagne."

2. Ce n'est que lundi dernier qu'il m'a été appris que vous habitiez la capitale depuis de une mois.

3. Suivant ce qui a été convenu verbalement hier—vous avez l'obligeance de me céder toute votre collection Mexicaine, tant en choses anciennes qu'en choses modernes, n'en exceptant absolument ques les étriers et les 3 corps humains momifiés.

4. Mon cher ami Boban, Vos lignes du 9 courant, m'ons fait grand plaisir, puis qu'elles m'apprennents que votre voyage au Mexique et aux Etats Unis a été couronie d'un plein succes, attenda que vous voila retiré des affaires, ou à peu près, menant la vie d'un bon bourgeois, ce qui vous permet de prendre chaque apres-midi la demi-tasse dans un des cafés du boulevard Saint Michel.

5. Inspecteur Adjoint des Foréts.

6. Quand j'ai été vous voir au mois de fevrier dernier, vous m'avez raconté avoir été témoin, au moins une fois, de la manière dont les sauvages Indiens, de la Californie, je crois, fabriquaient leurs petites pointes de flèche en silex. Je vais peut être citer ce fait dans un petit travail que je redige pour une Société; mais je serais desireux, si ce n'est pas indiscret, d'avoir de vous quelques details relativement à la manière dont les outils étaient faits; si les instruments employés étaient en métal ou en pierre, leur nature; si c'est par choc ou par pression de poinçon d'éclateur avec ou sans l'aide d'une maillet. Enfin tous les détails que vous croirez pouvoir me dire sur cette intéressantes questions, sur le lieu, le province, le nom de la tribu indienne etc. reconnaissant, car peu de personnes ont été assez heureuses comme vous, pour assister deprès à un pareil spectacle et surprendre les procedes.

7. Muy estimado amigo: le ruego mucho que me haga un pequeño presupuesto de lo que podremos hacer de gasto mensualmente cinco personas, mi esposa, una criada, Julio mi hijo y tal vez otro de los chicos y mi persona; se entiende por casa y asistencia, que no sea en un hotel. . . . Digale U. a su Señora que si ya sabe hablar castellano platicará con la mia, que no habla una jota de frances.

8. Parmi les collections les plus remarquables qui figureront dans le pavillon spécial aux antiquités mexicaines, nous citerons celle de M. E. Eug. Goupil, de Paris, né à Mexico; cette collection renferme des objets de grande valeur et de toute beauté.

9. Quand il quitta le Mexique, en 1840, craignant avec raison que la douane de Vera-Cruz n'examinat ses bagages et ne fit main basse sur ses collections de documents historiques, il s'ingénia à les diviser, à les mélanger, à en effacer les numéros et les cachets de bibliothèques publiques ou particulières afin que ce mélange confus eût l'air d'un amoncellement de papiers sans valeur et passât inaperçu à la douane. M. Aubin réussit fort bien. Il quitta le territoire mexicain en important sa

collection entière, mais dans un désordre tel, que lui-même n'eut jamais le courage de procéder à son classement.

10. Précédemment, j'avais eu l'occasion d'entretenir à diverses reprises M. Aubin des importants travaux de M. le docteur Peñafiel. Il s'y intéressa et parla de lui montrer ses documents. Je présentai les deux savants l'un à l'autre, on prit date pour examiner la collection et voulant faire profiter de cette bonne fortune l'un des érudits que cela pouvait intéresser, j'écrivis à M. de Quatrefages, le savant professeur au Muséum de Paris, pour le prier de se joindre à nous le jour de notre visite à M. Aubin.

11. A letter from Quatrefages dated 16 March 1889 saying the invitation to Mr. Aubin was an unexpected event, which he would happily join.

12. Cette visite eut lieu le 28 mars 1889. Étaient présents: M. de Quatrefages, le docteur Peñafiel et ses deux fils, M. E. Eugène Goupil et moi. M. Aubin nous reçut fort bien et nous montra ses principaux documents. A notre grand étonnement, M. Peñafiel, après notre sortie de chez M. Aubin, fit tous ses efforts pour me convaincre ainsi que M. Goupil que ses manuscrits, ces peintures hieroglyphiques de toute rareté n'avaient qu'une valeur relative; il essaya même de nous faire croire que le Musée de Mexico était encombré de documents semblables. Je savais à quoi m'en tenir à ce sujet, car je venais de passer près de deux ans à Mexico, j'avais vu et revu toutes les collections du Musée National et je m'étais assuré *de visu* que les manuscrits y faisaient presque complètement défaut.

13. Certes, son but était excellent et son stratagème de bonne guerre; il travaillait pour sa patrie, nul ne saurait l'en blâmer, mais il ne réussit point.

14. Je vais bien vous étonner, lui dis-je, la collection Aubin est à vendre, et dans quelques jours, peut-être, elle reprendra la route de Mexico. C'est le docteur Peñafiel qui propose de l'acheter et l'affaire sera conclue dans quarante-huit heures, à moins que vous ne vous rendiez acquéreur de ces documents précieux pour les conserver à la France.

15. Cette petite Exposition se compose de deux parties absolument distinctes. L'une comprend des statuettes, des utensils, des outils, des objets de toilette et diverses autres sortes de productions industrielles de la vielle patrie de Montézuma; l'autre des fac-similés photographiques de la plus grande et de la plus belle collection de manuscrits figuratifs mexicains qu'on ait jamais pu réunir jusqu'à ce jour. La première de ces séries providient de M. Eugène Boban; la seconde, de M. Aubin: toutes deux sont aujourd'hui dans la possession de M. Eugène Goupil.

16. A notre prochaine entrevue n'oubliez pas que je vous parle d'un plan pour nos rapports (de vous à moi) de "pezetas" nous arrangerions pour que nulle préoccupation materielle ne vous distraite de votre passion, de votre grandissime passion et préoccupation.

17. Siento que tan mal me haya tratado, el editor de los manuscritos de Aubin, pues nunca pensé en comprarlos por un principio de caballerosidad, ni tampoco di parta á mi Gobierno de que existian en poder de Mr. Aubin como podria haberlo hecho, supuesto que todos esos documentos han sido substraidos de los Archivos y Bibliotecas de Mexico.

18. Copie d'une lettre adressée par L. Dr. Antonio Peñafiel a to à Mr. E. Goupil relatif à l'envoi d'un volume Histoire de la nation Mexicaine depuis le depart d'Aztlan, ou Codex de 1576.

19

Later Life

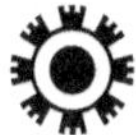

After the publication of *Documents pour servir à l'histoire du Mexique* in 1891, Eugène Boban and Eugène Goupil moved on to produce *Table analytique*, a sixty-one-page analytical table of contents of the two-volume *catalogue raisonné*. Boban continued to write about pre-Columbian manuscripts and objects from Goupil's archeological collections. He maintained his role as curator for Goupil, advising him on purchases of pre-Columbian artifacts from a variety of collectors and dealers. He produced a privately printed catalog with photographs of the collection he had sold to Goupil. The only known complete copy of this catalog is in the Musée du quai Branly, although large-format photographs from the catalog are in numerous other institutions, including the Getty Research Institute, Yale University, and the Hispanic Society of America.

To get *Documents pour servir* into the hands of those who would appreciate it most, Boban and Goupil sent complimentary copies of the two volumes to important scholars and directors of museums and cultural institutions throughout Europe, Latin America, and the United States. In France they went to the Trocadéro and the main library of Angers, the birthplace of Boban's father, aunts, and grandparents, as well as a variety of other important institutions of learning throughout Europe. A letter from James Pilling, the bibliographer of the Smithsonian's Bureau of American Ethnology, thanked Boban profusely for sending the volumes to the Smithsonian. "What a work it is to be sure! And how much labor you must needs have put upon it! Even Icazbalceta must look to his laurels now, while Viñaza and Peñafiel and the rest of us must take back seats as bibliographers. Well, I congratulate you with all my heart" (BNF DMO n.a.f. 21478: item 525). This is the highest praise: Joaquín García Icazbalceta was Mexico's preeminent historian at the time; Cipriano Muñoz, second Count of la Viñaza, was a Spanish linguist and philologist of great renown; and Peñafiel is the same Antonio Peñafiel, the widely published archeologist and historian who organized the Mexican Pavilion at the 1889 Exposition Universelle. In comparing Boban to the greatest intellects in the field, James Pilling expresses himself with the warmth and enthusiasm that Boban seems to have elicited from colleagues worldwide.

Aside from distributing their publications and receiving accolades for it, some administrative matters remained to be taken care of. Goupil's original agreement with Aubin for the purchase of his collection said that any books and manuscripts that had been removed from his library for research, publication, or other purposes were to be included in the sale. Thus, one of Boban's principal tasks during this period, while researching the extant codices and books, was to attempt to locate the collection's missing pieces. Joseph Marius Alexis Aubin could not be of help in this effort, since he had died on 7 July 1891, eleven days short of his ninetieth birthday.

Aubin, who was quite paranoid in his last years, was convinced that some of his manuscripts had been pilfered. For instance, he believed that the artist and collector Jean Frédéric Waldeck had taken one manuscript and replaced the original with a copy he himself had painted. After meeting with Waldeck's widow, Goupil recounted Aubin's speculation in a letter to Boban. In the same letter he recalled that Boban had once told him that Waldeck was a first-class faker of artifacts (BNF DMO n.a.f 21479: item 64). This is an interesting accusation by Boban, who would certainly know.

During the early 1890s Goupil and Boban's correspondence dealt mostly with printing costs, corrections, and changes to their various publications. The letters, in which they share a number of private jokes, provide ample evidence of Goupil's openness, sense of humor, and playful personality. For instance, there are numerous references to meetings with someone they called "Chupamirto," which means hummingbird in Spanish. This was Goupil's nickname for Mlle. Sidonie Verhagen, a "protégée" of Aubin's.

In the late spring of 1892, Boban was diagnosed with diabetes, and Eugène Goupil, who also suffered from the disease, wrote a long letter to his *tocayo* telling him exactly what he should avoid. "Remember," he counsels, "for your diabetes: No flour, no nuts, . . . no liquor nor fruit wines nor beer, nor milk, . . . especially no pastries and none or very little bread. . . . Charcuterie is recommended, even for the fat, then cheese and butter . . ." (BNF DMO n.a.f. 21480: item 294). The rest of the letter is about personal hygiene and exercise, which he humorously labels bedroom gymnastics.

Despite their health issues, the two men worked assiduously to share their collections of artifacts and manuscripts as widely as possible. Their efforts were well received. In March 1893 Daniel G. Brinton, professor of linguistics and archeology at the University of Pennsylvania, and founder of the anthropology museum there, wrote an article for the journal *Science* about the "Boturini-Aubin-Goupil

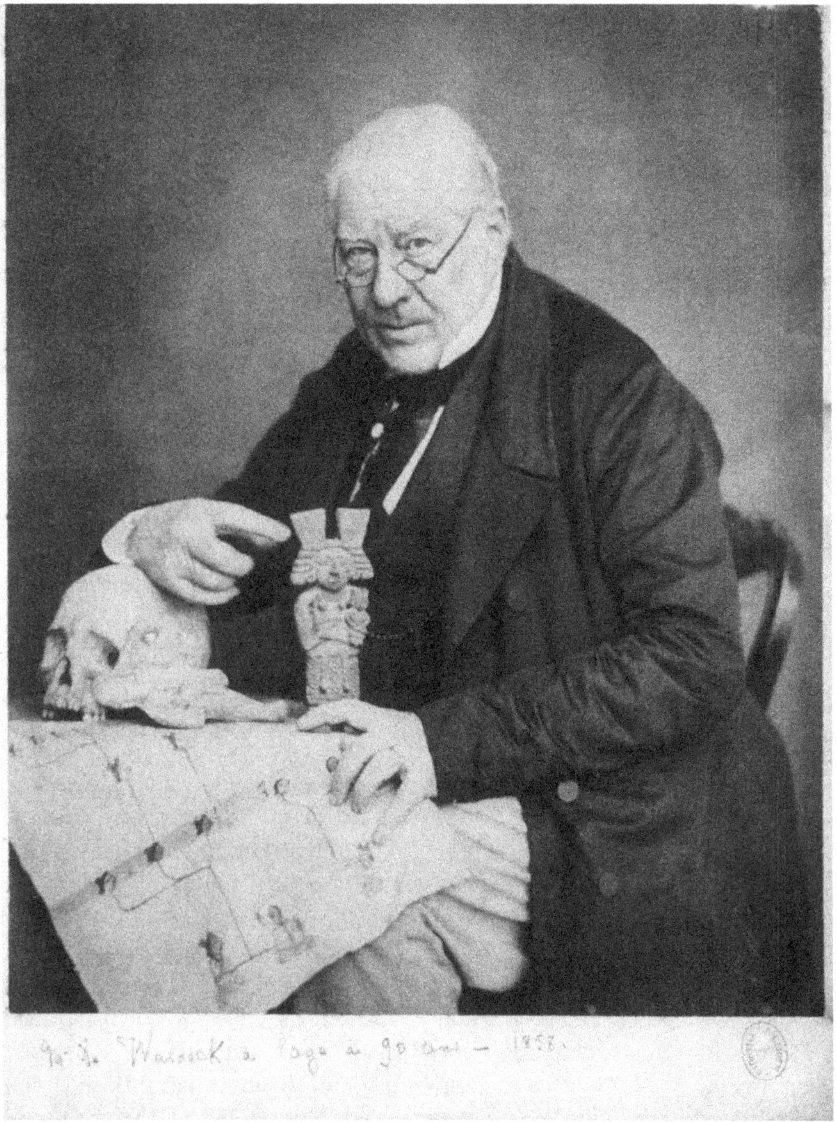

Figure 19.1   Photo of Jean Frédéric Waldeck at ninety displaying a questionable codex, a cast of a jade Olmec statue, and an Aztec ceramic figurine while leaning on a human skull (courtesy of Bibliothèque nationale, Paris, DMO n.a.f. 21479: item 471).

Collection of Mexicana." In it he praised the work of the "distinguished antiquary, well known in the cities of Mexico, New York, and Paris . . . To his kindness I owe the privilege, enjoyed by few, of a leisurely inspection of this wholly unrivalled collection" (Brinton 1893: 127).

Brinton, considered one of the early pillars of American anthropology, played a key role in the anthropological exhibits at the 1893 World's Columbian Exposition in Chicago. He became an important contact for Boban and his *tocayo*, and at Brinton's urging Goupil sent a case of materials for display at the exposition. In a letter to Brinton dated 28 April 1893, he lists what he sent: "2 Boban volumes on the x-Aubin collection, now my property; 80 photo types of the x-Aubin collection; 17 photographs of the same Aubin collection, and 17 photographs of the x-Boban collection of antiquities; 1 photograph of my vitrine of antiquities, 1 portrait of Eug. Boban" (BNF DMO n.a.f 21480: item359). These large-format photographs were all exhibited at the exposition commemorating the 400th anniversary of the discovery of America.

They also had some success in tracking down missing manuscripts. In October 1893 a letter from Goupil to Boban discusses the "reintegration of the original 1697 *Relación de Chimalpahin* (1258–1612) which had disappeared from the Aubin Collection." Apparently, the manuscript had been sent to Rémi Siméon, the author of a Nahuatl dictionary who had known Aubin in Mexico. Siméon published a translation of the work in 1889 entitled *Anales de Domingo Francisco de San Antón Muñón Chimalpahin Quauhtlehuanitzin, Sixième et Septième Relations (1258–1612)*. The publisher was Maisonneuve and LeClerc of Paris. Siméon had died in 1890, and his family took steps to return the manuscript to the new owner of the Aubin Collection (BNF DMO n.a.f. 21480: item 417). Goupil and Boban recovered another of Aubin's Mexican manuscripts from the same publisher. Maisonneuve had purchased this manuscript from Mlle. Sidonie Verhagen (Chupamirto) for twenty francs, although Goupil paid 350 francs to rescue it. In 1893 Goupil and Boban published *Histoire de la nation Mexicaine depuis le départ d'Aztlan, ou Codex de 1576*. This manuscript, also known as the Codex Aubin, contained the original Nahuatl with French translation alongside the illustrations.

In May 1894 Goupil travelled to Frankfurt, Germany, where he owned another factory—Goupil Metallperlin-Fabrik—that also produced metallic beads or pearls. While there he visited Philipp J. Becker, the collector who had owned a department store in Puebla, Mexico, and had been an acquaintance of Boban's. Goupil wrote about Becker's interesting pre-Columbian artifacts. Boban, who knew his collection quite well, kept a series of photographs of Becker's pieces taken at various times. Goupil wrote to Boban saying that one of Becker's daughters had made a colored copy of one of the Mexican manuscripts in her father's collections (BNF DMO n.a.f. 21480: item 482). The two Becker codices are important Mixtec histories, which are now in the Museum für Völkerkunde in Vienna, Austria.

There are just a few letters from Goupil to Boban written in September and October 1894 in the correspondence at the Bibliothèque nationale, quite a change from his usual three to four postcards and letters a week. Then on 17

December 1894, Goupil wrote again to his *tocayo*, introducing the letter with the comment, "You must have thought I died because of my long silence." He explains that he had been extraordinarily busy installing some new machinery in his factory, and that he had obtained more Mexican objects from Mrs. Lohse of Frankfort, which had been brought back by her late husband (BNF DMO n.a.f. 21480: item 492). The following month, on 26 January 1895, Goupil invites Boban to come over to talk and have dinner with him. He tells him to warn Mrs. Boban that they might be eating late (BNF DMO n.a.f. 21480: item 494).

On 22 March 1895, Eugène Boban's remaining aunt, Fanny Duvergé, died. Almost eighty, she had lived her last years with her nephew and his wife. Louis Goupil, Eugène Goupil's younger brother, who had once owned a department store in Mexico City, wrote him a kind note in Spanish. "My dear friend, I am very sorry not to have attended the funeral of your venerable aunt, and I beg you to receive my condolences, which I send you with all my heart (BNF DMO n.a.f. 21477: item 349).[1] From the tone of his letter, he was a close friend. It was he, after all, who first told his brother Eugène that Boban had returned to Paris from New York.

On 25 July 1895, Goupil began a long letter addressed "Dear Tocayo" telling Boban about correspondence from a representative of Phillip Becker, who had recently died. Goupil says that Becker's family was hoping to sell his pre-Columbian collection in its entirety, but had no idea of its worth, and they were wondering whether Goupil could give some sort of appraisal of it as a friend.

Goupil goes on to write that, of course, he immediately thought of Boban, the most knowledgeable person in the world on the subject. Then in this July 1895 letter he asks Boban for some specifics concerning the appraisal that he can pass along to Becker's family. Goupil closes by expressing his regret that he himself cannot afford to buy the collection because of poor sales during the past few years.

Boban and he may have discussed the matter of Becker's estate in person since it does not appear that Goupil sent the letter in July. On the second page of the same letter he writes "My dear Mons Boban—as you can see despite my long silence I am not dead, but yes—I am at the moment '*acabado moralement*' [*acabado* is a Spanish word meaning finished or exhausted with the French word *moralement*, it seems to say he is mentally exhausted]. A [more] favorable reaction will probably be produced in the right direction with time. . . . When you go to my office, if you do not find me there, ask M. Borame to deliver to you an envelope with your name on it, which is on my desk—this envelope contains a newspaper clipping that you will kindly send me at Vichy. . . . My regards to Madame Boban, and good wishes to you in friendship" (BNF DMO n.a.f. 21480: item 496). Vichy was the famous spa that Goupil often visited when his health was poor.

This must be the last letter Boban received from his *tocayo*, since it is the last one in the album, and is followed by samples of the ironic cartoons and drawings

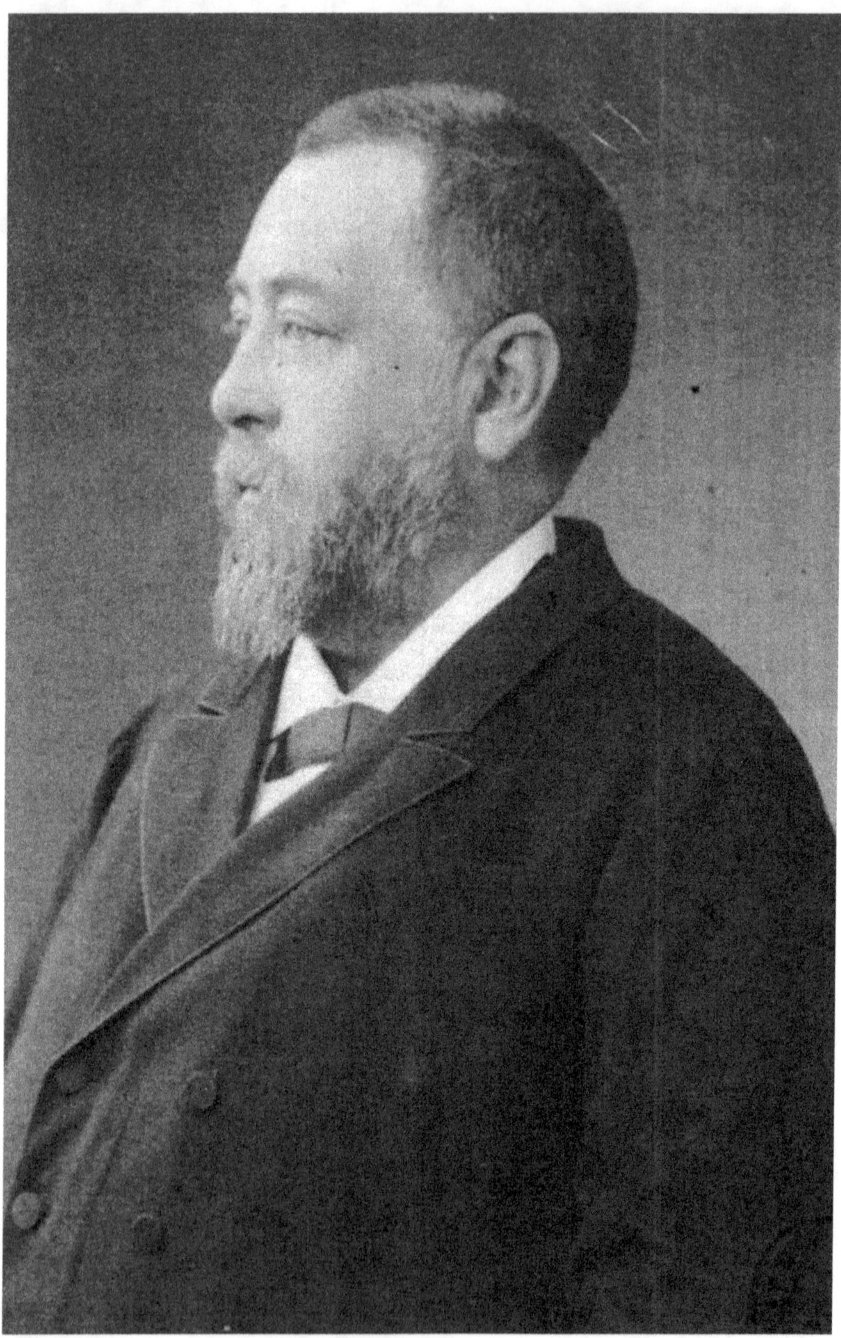

Figure 19.2 Charles Espiridion Eugène Goupil (courtesy Bibliothèque nationale, Paris, DMO n.a.f. 21480: item 7).

with which Goupil embellished the envelopes he used in his correspondence with his curator. Charles Espiridion Eugène Goupil died on 24 October 1895, at his home in Chaumontel. The unusual name Espiridion is after Spyridion, a fourth century Bishop of Tremithus, who was born in Cyprus. Goupil's Mexican mother was following a custom of her country by honoring the saint on whose feast day her child was born. Goupil's birthday, 14 December, is Saint Espiridion's day. Goupil was sixty-four at his death. He was buried a few days later in Père Lachaise cemetery.

A little over a week after Goupil's funeral Boban reconnected with colleagues and friends when he attended a *"Diner préhistorique"* (a prehistoric dinner). The dinner was organized by the École d'Anthropologie and Professor Gabriel de Mortillet. The invitation showed two bearded ancients hunting mastodons. This so-called lacustrian repast, inspired by early Swiss lake dwellers, was held on 4 November, featuring a menu that included Magdalenian fish, a cake from the first glacial period, and Solutrean wine (BNF DMO n.a.f. 21478: item 389). A bit later, Boban received a note from the Duc du Loubat, the American philanthropist and founder of the Loubat prize for anthropological publications, asking if he could visit the Goupil Collection, which Boban arranged (BNF DMO n.a.f. 21478: item 181).

On 5 December 1895, a month after the dinner with prehistorians and archeologists, Eugène Boban married Marie Héloise Langlois. This marriage is certainly a surprising turn of events, considering that it seemed he was already married to the woman constantly referred to as Madame Boban, the woman who traveled with him to Mexico City and New York, and to whom Goupil sent greetings in nearly every letter he wrote to his friend and curator. His very last letter closes with "my regards to Madame Boban and to you as well in friendship" (BNF DMO n.a.f. 21480: item 496).

The marriage certificate does not allow for the possibility that Boban had finally *officially* married the woman with whom he had been living for so many years. French marriage documents provide considerable information about both bride and groom, and this one is no exception. Boban is listed first, followed by details such as his birth in Paris on 11 March 1834, although his actual birth certificate says it was on 10 March. His parents are named, and it is recorded that they are deceased. His bride, Marie Héloise Langlois, is listed as a *rentière* (retired with an independent income) whose parents are also both deceased. While no previous marriage is recorded for Boban, this is the bride's third marriage, according to the document. She had been married for the first time to Eléonor Henri Cauvin in the late 1840s and was widowed when he died at the age of sixty in April of 1876. Two years later she married Eugène Appollodore Nigon, a widower and resident of the 2nd arrondissement, on 16 March 1878. They lived together as husband and wife but were divorced on 24 February 1890. Divorce was legalized after the French revolution in 1792 but abolished in 1816. In 1884 it was once again legalized. However, the principal reasons for granting a divorce were the wife's infidelity or inability to produce offspring. Madame Langlois had two sons from her first marriage, who were witnesses to this third marriage, as was Émile Deshayes, a conservator at the Musée Guimet in Paris, and a friend of the groom. Boban was sixty-one at the time, and his new wife was six years older, at sixty-seven.

Marie Héloise Langlois cannot be the same woman he had been living with since at least 1879, when she was visited at their home by Dr. Camille Raspail (BNF DMO n.a.f. 21479: item 16). She is not the same wife who went to Mexico with him in 1885 and sailed with him to New York at the age of forty-nine in 1886. That woman would have been almost ten years younger than Madame Langlois. It is not known what happened to that wife, and it may be impossible to discover her fate since her name is unrecorded. Likewise, there is no record of the name of the other woman Boban married (or did not marry) in Mexico in the 1860s. It is probable that he did not legally marry either woman. The second "Madame Boban" just disappears between Goupil's last letter, dated July 1895, and Boban's marriage to Marie Héloise Langlois in December of that same year, four and a half months later. Did she die? Did she decide he was never going to marry her and moved on? Did he abandon her in favor of a wealthy older woman? This is yet another mystery enveloping his personal life.

The following year Boban and his new wife moved to a rather grand, newly constructed apartment at 18, rue Thibaud. They would live there for the rest of their married life, although as with his two previous relationships, she, too, would largely disappear from the record of his activities. She is occasionally mentioned in letters, and usually, as before, in their closing lines with "my regards to Madame Boban."

After Goupil's death, Boban maintained a close relationship with his widow, Augustine Elie, and Goupil's younger brother, Louis, fulfilling his continuing obligations as curator of the artifacts and manuscripts. Boban expressed his gratitude to Madame Goupil in a sales catalog of her husband's library published in 1898, recalling her "extreme generosity" as well as his admiration for the entire Goupil family for respecting the wishes of his late benefactor. It seems apparent from reading the catalog, which Boban wrote, that many of the books in Goupil's library had been purchased from Eugène Boban's own library. The descriptions of the volumes are identical to those in the New York auction catalog, so Boban kept those rare books that didn't bring the desired price, as he had done for the important artifacts that he eventually sold to Goupil. Additionally, in a discussion of the history of the two collections written by Albert Reville, a professor of religion in the Collège de France, it was Eugène Goupil's desire to bequeath his "magnificent collection of painted Mexican manuscripts to the Bibliothèque nationale," which was accomplished three years after his death, the same year the library catalog was published (Boban 1898: IX; Reville 1898: XVIII).

Despite having focused largely on the Goupil materials for nearly a decade, Boban still actively maintained his connections with other colleagues in the field. On 10 September 1896 he received a letter written on stationary with a London address from Augustus Le Plongeon, the archeologist and explorer of the Maya in Yucatan, thanking him for his letter and news, and informing him that he will visit him soon in Paris. He adds that he will present his French manuscript on Queen Moo, the Maya ruler he imagined was the consort of Chac Mool and inspiration for the Egyptian myth of Isis and Osiris. The book, which the Le Plongeons had been working on for many years, had recently been published in English in New York and London. He confides to his friend that he wants to get it published in French and German, and hopes to win the Loubat prize (BNF DMO n.a.f. 21478: item 165). This award, endowed by the American Joseph Florimond, Duc de Loubat, was presented by Columbia University every five years for the best published work in English about the history, arts, and cultures of North America. Boban's *Documents pour servir* was exactly the kind of publication that the Loubat prize was intended to honor, but it was published in French only. However, his work was to receive other tributes.

In July of 1897 Eugène Boban received a letter from the Société Américaine de France informing him that he had been named "membre Titulaire perpetual," joining a group whose number was limited to fifteen. He would take the place left vacant by the death of Eugène Goupil. The writer said they hoped he would consider this election as "a testimony of the esteem of our association for your work and the service you have rendered to Americanism" (BNF DMO n.a.f. 21478: item 565). That same year he corresponded with Heber Bishop, a wealthy businessman and philanthropist who had a large and impressive collection of jade objects. He privately published *Investigations and Studies in Jade*, in two enormous volumes, with contributions from such notables as Augustin A. Damour, Thomas Wilson, Zelia Nuttall, and George Frederick Kunz. In his letter to Boban he asks about a jade figurine from Guerrero (BNF DMO n.a.f. 21476: item 82) and writes that Thomas Wilson had recommended that he consult Boban, who sent him a manuscript on jade and other stones from Mesoamerica that he had written. Bishop sent his thanks and eventually returned it.[2] In 1898 Boban received the news that James Pilling had died after a long illness. His close friend and mentor, Gabriel de Mortillet passed away the same year. Boban, who had provided the professor with many examples of prehistoric artifacts for his classes, attended his funeral at Montparnasse in September. The following year, 1899, his friend and founding editor of the journal *La Nature*, Gaston Tissandier, who had escaped the siege of Paris by balloon in 1870, died at the age of fifty-five. Tissandier had been responsible for publishing a number of notes from Boban, including the one reporting on his visit to the Smithsonian Institution.

In 1899 Georges Raynaud, who had translated the Maya holy book *Popol Vuh* into French and published widely on pre-Columbian religion, recognized

Boban's important contribution to the study of Mesoamerican civilizations by naming him a member of the organizing committee for the Congrès des sciences ethnographiques to be held in 1900 in Paris (BNF DMO n.a.f. 21479: item 48). Boban also had continued throughout these years to attend the annual and semi-annual meetings of the numerous intellectual societies to which he belonged.

In 1900 Boban attended the Americanist Conference on Ethnographic Sciences in Paris, which was held to coincide with the fifth Exposition Universelle. Just before the opening of the conference he was interviewed by the *New York Tribune* reporter Charles Inman Barnard, about fake pre-Columbian manuscripts associated with the Duc de Loubat, as well as other fraudulent arti-facts. At this point in his life Boban had achieved quite an amazing array of accomplishments: he was extremely well-known, a perpetual member of the Society of Americanists, an officer of the Academy of Science, and was appar-ently happily married. Yet, in his sixty-sixth year he throws caution to the winds and announces to the world, or at least the New York audience, that he has pulled the wool over the eyes of some of the world's best-known experts in archeology and ethnology. It is unclear what his motivations were in making this revelation. As the *New York Tribune*'s Paris correspondent Barnard reported, "M. Boban, the well-known dealer in Mexican antiquities, says that numbers of so-called rock crystal pre-Columbian skulls have been so adroitly made as almost to defy detection, and have been palmed off as genuine upon the experts of some of the principal museums of Europe" (20 August 1900). He may have been set-tling old scores, wanting to set the record straight, or trumpeting the breadth of his knowledge. As in so many other instances, the rationale behind this action remains a mystery. We will never know why he chose this time and place to essentially confess to fraud.

As the years passed, attending funerals seems to have become a regular event in Boban's life, starting just before the turn of the century onward, as so many of his longtime friends and clients died. There are numerous funeral announcements in his albums of correspondence. Augustin Alexis Damour, one of his oldest friends, died at the venerable age of ninety-six in 1902, and Boban attended his funeral. Thomas Wilson of the Smithsonian died the same year in Washington. The abbé Emmanuel Domenech, who had known Boban in Mexico when he served as chaplain for Maximilian, passed away in 1903. He had once addressed Boban in an 1893 letter, "Ah, my old Mexican and dear friend."

Eugène André Boban Duvergé died at his home in Paris, on 2 May 1908, at the age of seventy-four. He outlived all four of his sisters: Julie Félicité, who died in 1870 at the age of thirty-two; Marie Françoise, who was sixty-three when she died in 1899; Rose Louise, the eldest, was seventy-one when she died in 1902; and Charlotte, the youngest, who passed away at sixty-six in 1907, about seven months before her brother. His death occurred in the same year as that of Ernest T. Hamy, the director of the Trocadéro; John Evans, the British geologist and archeologist, who had traded artifacts with Boban; Albert Gaudry, the geologist and paleontologist whose lectures Boban had attended at the Musée d'histoire naturelle; and Augustus Le Plongeon, the Maya archeologist he had met in New York.

At least three obituaries announced Boban's passing, and all of them were written by old friends. René Verneau, a paleoanthropologist at the Musée d'histoire naturelle in Paris wrote the obituary that appeared in *L'Anthropologie*. Adrien de Mortillet, Gabriel de Mortillet's son, wrote another, that was published in the *Revue Mensuelle Illustrée d'Archéologie et d'Anthropolgie Préhistoriques*. A third remembrance appeared in the *Revue de l'École d'Anthropologie*, signed C, which might be Emile Cartailhac or Louis Capitan. Both men were longtime friends of Boban's.

Mortillet, who certainly knew him well, would have visited Boban's shop with his father when he was a young man in his teens and early twenties, and apparently had vivid memories to share. He was a lecturer at the École d'anthropologie in Paris from 1889 until his death in 1931, and his large assemblage of amulets is now exhibited at the Pitt Rivers Museum in Oxford. He begins his assessment of Boban's career by reclaiming for Boban his role in forming the Trocadéro's first collection of pre-Columbian artifacts while he was living in Mexico. Since Alphonse Pinart had traded his collection to the museum in 1878, its connection to the original collector had been obscured after three decades.

Then from firsthand experience Mortillet expands upon the unique role his friend played in the field of archeology.

> On his return to France, Boban installed his collections in a shop on the rue du Sommerard, and transformed it into a veritable museum, which was visited profitably by all prehistorians. Then to the American objects he possessed, he began to add a very complete prehistoric European collection as well. Through the catalogs, exhibits, and notes he published in French, Spanish, and English, he made a powerful contribution to the diffusion of useful knowledge about European and American prehistory. (Mortillet 1908: 188)[3]

Mortillet takes time to highlight the crowning achievement of Boban's career. "And it is to him also that we are indebted for the great work, begun in 1891 under the title: *Documents pour servir à l'histoire du Mexique* containing a description of the Eugène Goupil Collection, which was arranged and cataloged by Boban."

His final words are a tribute to Boban's preeminence as a teacher and scholar, and his hope that others would continue to benefit from his work.

> In daily contact with innumerable documents that passed through his hands, Boban acquired a very real knowledge. He was one of the men in France with the surest grasp of American archeological material. His uncontestable competence

about this subject enabled him to give serious and far more informative lessons than [even] those taught by Dr. Capitan, which may indeed be used to teach even more by mining the papers left by the departed. (Mortillet 1908: 188)[4]

René Verneau succeeded Hamy as director of the Musée d'Ethnographie du Trocadéro. In 1888 and 1889, he published three different articles in the journal *La Nature* that all focused on Boban's ideas and artifacts. He considers Boban's most important contribution to be his role in convincing Goupil to purchase the Aubin Collection, and later persuading Goupil's widow to donate the collection to the Bibliothèque nationale. "Thanks to this donation, our great institution is richer today in Mexican manuscripts than all other libraries worldwide."[5] He noted also that Boban published two handsome volumes, which elucidated and cataloged these precious manuscripts (Verneau 1908: 369).

Verneau goes on to describe some of the imaginative techniques Boban used to share his knowledge and engage students and amateurs in the study of prehistory. "For a long time in Paris he had a trade in antiquities and used his relationships with archeologists to obtain a quantity of stone implements. He had the idea to guide the novice to choose from an array of typical tools and to place them [in their appropriate locations] on classification charts."[6] The charts were based on Mortillet's system (1908: 369).

The desire to use his shop to instruct collectors and students in the finer points of European prehistory is certainly unusual in the antiquities trade, but the acquisition and diffusion of knowledge seems to have been a primary motivation of Boban's throughout his career. Verneau acknowledges this trait in the conclusion of his obituary, "Eugène Boban has rendered real service to prehistory, and especially to the Americanists" (1908: 370).[7]

Notes

1. Muy estimado amigo, siento mucho no poder estar al entierro de su venerada tía y le ruego reciba el pésame que le mando de todo Corazón. L. Goupil. 15 Marzo 1895.

2. The unpublished manuscript is in the Hispanic Society of America archives (Box XIV).

3. A son retour en France, Boban avait installé ses récoltes dans un magasin de la rue Du Sommerard, transformé en un veritable musée, qui visitèrent avec profit tous les préhistoriens. Puis aux objets américains qu'il possédait, vinrent s'ajouter des séries préhistorique européennes très complètes. Par les catalogues, les tableaux et les notes qu'il a publiés, tant en langue française qu'en langues espagnole et anglaise, il a puissamment contribué à répandre d'utiles connaissances sur la préhistoire de l'Europe et de l'Amérique."

4. Au contact journalier des innombrables documents qui lui passèrent dans les mains, Boban avait acquis un très reél savoir. Il était un des hommes ayant, en France, les connaissances les plus sûres en matière d'archéologie américaine. Son incontestable compétence l'aurait mis à même de faire sur ce sujet des leçons bien autrement sérieuses et instructives que celles que professe le Dr. Capitan, qui pourra du reste, en glanant dans les papiers laissés par le regretté défunt, trouver de quoi relever un peu son enseignement.

5. Grâce à ce don, notre grand établissement est plus riche à l'heure actuelle en manuscrits mexicains que toutes les bibliothèques réunies du monde entier.

6. Pendant long temps il avait fait à Paris le commerce d'antiquités et il avait mis à profit ses relations avec les archéologues pour se procurer une quantité d'instruments en pierre. Il eut l'idée, pour guider les debutants de choisir dans ce lot des instruments typiques et de les disposer en tableaux qui furent répandus à profusion.

7. Eugène Boban a donc rendu de réels services aux préhistoriens, et surtout aux Américanistes, et il n'était que juste de consacrer quelques lignes à sa mémoire.

20

Afterlife

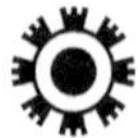

Eugène André Boban Duvergé spent more than fifty of his seventy-four years of life in the amassing and selling of antiquities and collectables. His incessant pursuit of new objects for his collections is not unusual among avid collectors and dealers; however, his ardent desire to share information about his artifacts is unusual. He undeniably added to the knowledge base of pre-Columbian studies in the nineteenth century—through his two wide-ranging collections of artifacts with their extensive descriptive inventories, his numerous published articles, and his scholarly and erudite two-volume *catalogue raisonné* of the Aubin manuscripts.

Eugène Boban pioneered the profession of dealer/expert in the fields of pre-Columbian archeology, pre- and postcontact manuscripts from Mexico, and European prehistory out of his own interest, knowledge, and passion. He acquired his expertise through fieldwork and intensive research into sources published in a language not his own, and with only minimal formal education. Most collectors at the time were highly educated people with the money and leisure time to amass objects that interested them. At first, lacking the funds with which to purchase objects, Boban traveled through Mexico and uncovered in his own digs most of the material that constituted his original collection. In some instances, he purchased, traded, and appropriated objects as well. He made every effort to educate people and express his love for archeology, using his collections to instruct his clients, visitors, and friends. He even exhibited certain classes of fake pottery as a warning to his customers and museum colleagues.

Boban was very much a man of his time. The nineteenth century was a period of easier and more affordable travel, which expanded people's contacts with and interest in the cultures of the world, both ancient and contemporary. Travelers began collecting fine art from earlier centuries and ethnographic and archeologi-cal material from cultures worldwide. The growing demand for art and artifacts created a specialized profession of experts in a range of fields and increased the number of dealers as well. Eugène Boban and other experts often generated interest in previously unexplored areas of collecting and were called upon to identify and authenticate objects for collectors and museum curators.

The increase in demand for ancient, exotic objects created a strain on the supply side, ever a spur for creative invention and elaboration. Paul Eudel, the chronicler of the Hotel Drouot auction house in Paris and an authority on fakes, pointed out that as the number of experts in all fields multiplied around the mid-nineteenth century, so did the number of counterfeiters or fakers. Not every supplier was prepared to go out into the field and dig up artifacts as Boban had; many found it easier and more lucrative to employ others to fashion their own artifacts. The relationship between the rise of the experts and the rise of the fakers was a mystery to many, including Eudel, although it follows the laws of supply and demand. As Paul Eudel comments, "it could not be said that 'This had spawned that,' or that one had at least slowed the other, as simple logic would demand" (1907: 20). In other words, it is not at all clear why, as the numbers of experts increased so also did the number of fakes. Were the experts working to stop the counterfeiters, working in league with them, or were they themselves fooled by the fakers? Whatever the case, the increase in expertise did not diminish the increase in fakes entering public and private collections.

Eugene Boban's own history indicates that he might have been fooled by fakes in some instances when he wasn't sophisticated enough to recognize them as inauthentic, although this assertion does not hold for the crystal skulls. It is abundantly clear that he knew they were not pre-Columbian, even by his own admission. He invented a new type of object, the likes of which has never been seen in an archeological dig and sold them to major museums. Many people have insisted that an important dealer or recognized expert would never jeopardize his reputation by selling objects of dubious authenticity, yet Eugene Boban's own statements prove the contrary. As a recognized expert in pre-Columbian archeology, his word was never doubted, despite the fact that his other role as dealer, might have, or perhaps should have caused some concern.

The nineteenth century was an extraordinarily innovative and creative time, when a wealthy elite and an array of public and private museums were forming collections of fine art, ethnology, and archeology. Boban was not alone in using his expertise to authenticate objects that were not what they were purported to be in the interest of making money. A parallel example at a higher and more remunerative level can be seen in the fine arts expert Bernard Berenson's secret activities with the dealer Joseph Duveen, which netted nearly $2.5 million during just fourteen years of their quarter-century relationship (Simpson 1986: 222). Both Duveen and Berenson profited enormously from the sale of inaccurately attributed (through carelessness or intent) paintings and sculptures, some of which have only recently been recognized for what they are or are not (Simpson 1986: 184, 211–12).

Boban and Berenson shared a passion and erudition in specific areas of art and antiquities. Boban developed a depth and breadth of knowledge about pre-Columbian Mexico unmatched in Europe or the United States at the time. His collection contained objects never seen before on either side of the Atlantic, and hundreds of clients relied upon his insights for their purchases. Bernard Berenson, an expert in Italian Renaissance painting and sculpture, sought to create a scientific method for determining the period, the region, and the painter of each of the art works he helped his wealthy clientele to purchase. While his clients paid him a commission on paintings he advised them to buy, most did not know that Joseph Duveen, a dealer in, among other things, Italian Renaissance painting and sculpture, was supplying the art and paying Berenson a fee as well.

As his correspondence with William Henry Holmes of the Smithsonian Institution indicates, Boban knew fakers of pre-Columbian objects by name and even address. Joseph Duveen and Bernard Berenson had a stable of artisans, restorers, and painters who altered works of art and produced fakes for them (Simpson 1986: 155). There are other famous examples of fine art dealers who were regularly supplied by fakers. The nineteenth century Viennese art dealer Frédéric Spitzer, a contemporary of Boban's who had also arisen from poverty, moved his gallery to France in 1852. He owned a "grand house in the most fashionable quarter of Paris [which] became known as 'Le Musée Spitzer'" (Tait 1992: 117). Shortly after he opened this establishment he commissioned the art restorer and goldsmith Reinhold Vasters of Aachen, Germany, to create hundreds of fake enameled and bejeweled Renaissance pendants and scent bottles, elaborate gold cups, and other decorative objects. In 1918 the London dealer Lazare Lowenstein purchased an archive of Vasters designs, which he donated to the Victoria and Albert Museum in 1919. The 1,079 illustrations that Reinhold Vasters had drawn "disappeared from view and remained effectively buried until the mid-1970s," when Charles Truman rediscovered them and recognized their significance (Tait 1992: 117). It soon became evident that the Victoria and Albert's own collection included many fakes that Vasters had crafted. The Metropolitan Museum of Art in New York, among others, uncovered a similar problem in their collections.

Like fine art forgeries, archeological fakes have an equally colorful history, and have been a problem from time immemorial throughout Europe. At the height of the Renaissance, Cardinal Raffaele Riario proudly displayed his collection of Roman artifacts, many gathered from recent excavations. Michelangelo Buonarroti, then twenty-six years old, was invited to see the collection as part of an interview for a commission. Among the ancient objects he recognized a sleeping Cupid that he himself had made and had sold to a Milanese dealer named Baldassari. Michelangelo admitted the fraud when he discovered that the Cardinal had paid two hundred ducats for the figure, considerably more than the thirty ducats Baldassari paid him. Consequently, Michelangelo's reputation was firmly established when the story spread that his fake Roman antiquity was of such high quality that it had fooled a recognized authority and connoisseur (Sabatini 1900: 228).

Centuries later an archeological faking industry arose practically on the heels of the first excavations and discoveries of prehistoric sites in France and Switzerland in the 1860s. The sheer numbers of fakes produced during the mid-nineteenth century confounded collectors and curators alike. In 1870, Eduard Lartet, the French geologist and pioneer Paleolithic archeologist, sent a collection of stone tools, that he himself had excavated, to Spencer Baird, the second Secretary of the Smithsonian Institution. Lartet wrote Baird,

> You tell me, sir, that your museum is destitute of specimens from the lacustrine habitations of Switzerland, Denmark and the repositories of France which have become celebrated from the discoveries made therein. As many objects from these different localities have long been articles of commerce, I suppose it will be easy for your correspondents to procure them for you, only they should take care not to be imposed on by the counterfeiting, which has been exercised on a grand scale, whether in France or elsewhere; to furnish you an example, I have placed in the box an authentic hatchet taken by myself from St. Acheul, and another, reputed false, proceeding from the celebrated repository of Moulin Quignon near Abbeville. (SIA USNM accession #1959 1870; translation of Lartet's letter for Baird)

The intellectual, academic, and collecting communities of Paris, New York, and Mexico City accepted the combination of expert and dealer as legitimate in Eugène Boban, Frédéric Spitzer, and Bernard Berenson's time. The possibility of a conflict of interest does not appear to have arisen, at least in the minds of most of their clientele. No one seems to have wondered whether their opinions, particularly if they involved art or artifacts they were selling themselves, could or should be trusted. In most cases, no other reliable authorities were sufficiently versed in their particular field to call their pronouncements into question, and the dealer/experts knew that.

Boban's sale of the few documented fakes may have been motivated more by the need to make a living than anything else. The migration of the large crystal skull, the most expensive item in his catalog, from an extraordinary example of lapidary art presented in the "objet divers" section in 1881, to an ancient Aztec artifact from Veracruz just five years later in Mexico City would indicate that he was adept at inventing new and more exotic provenances for inventory that failed to sell. Given his personality, it seems likely that his sale of the crystal skulls and the few other obvious fakes might also have been motivated, in some circumstances, by his sense of mischievous fun. He certainly enjoyed creating drama and suspense while in the "abyss" or accompanying the amateur diggers

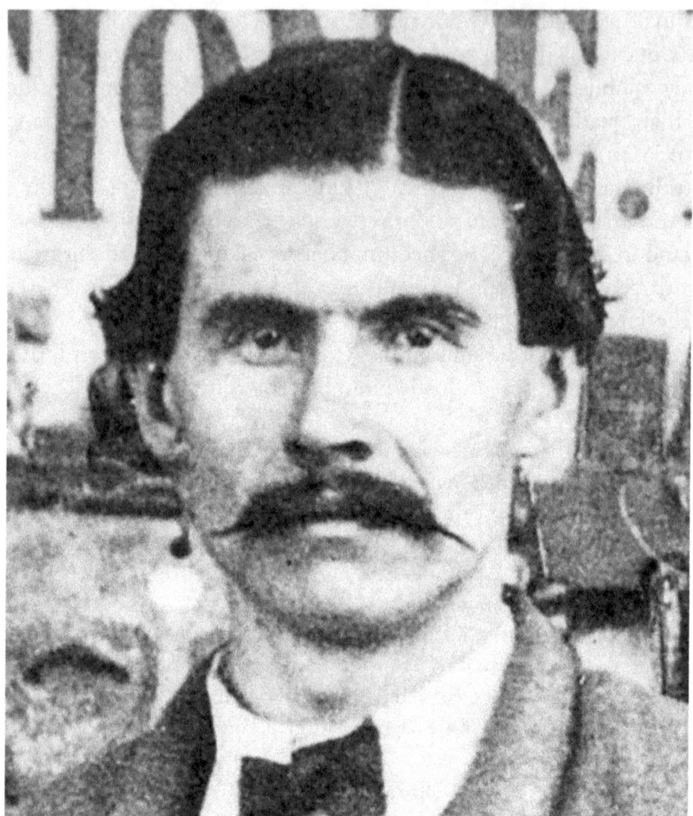

Figure 20.1   Detail of 1860s photograph of Eugène Boban (courtesy of Museo Nacional de Historia, Chapultepec Castle, Mexico City).

looking for Montezuma's chariot. It seems he was always willing to have a quiet laugh at the gullibility of his friends, clients, and colleagues. Surrounded as he was by highly educated and well-to-do members of the establishment, he found it hard to resist opportunities to gently tweak their noses while pulling the wool over their eyes. In his remarks to the *New York Tribune* reporter, Boban is trying to set the record straight—to show that he had not been fooled by these outrageous objects, while other experts had been.

The few photographs we have of Boban graphically capture his life's trajectory. The earliest image shows enormous bravado. He seems to be challenging the viewer; looking straight ahead with arms akimbo—confident, serious, ready to take on the world. One can almost see him descending the precipitous path to the "abyss" in search of artifacts and adventure while villagers anxiously called after him. He looks fearless. After all, he had survived the revolution of 1848 as a youngster in Paris, the chaos of the California gold fields at nineteen and the

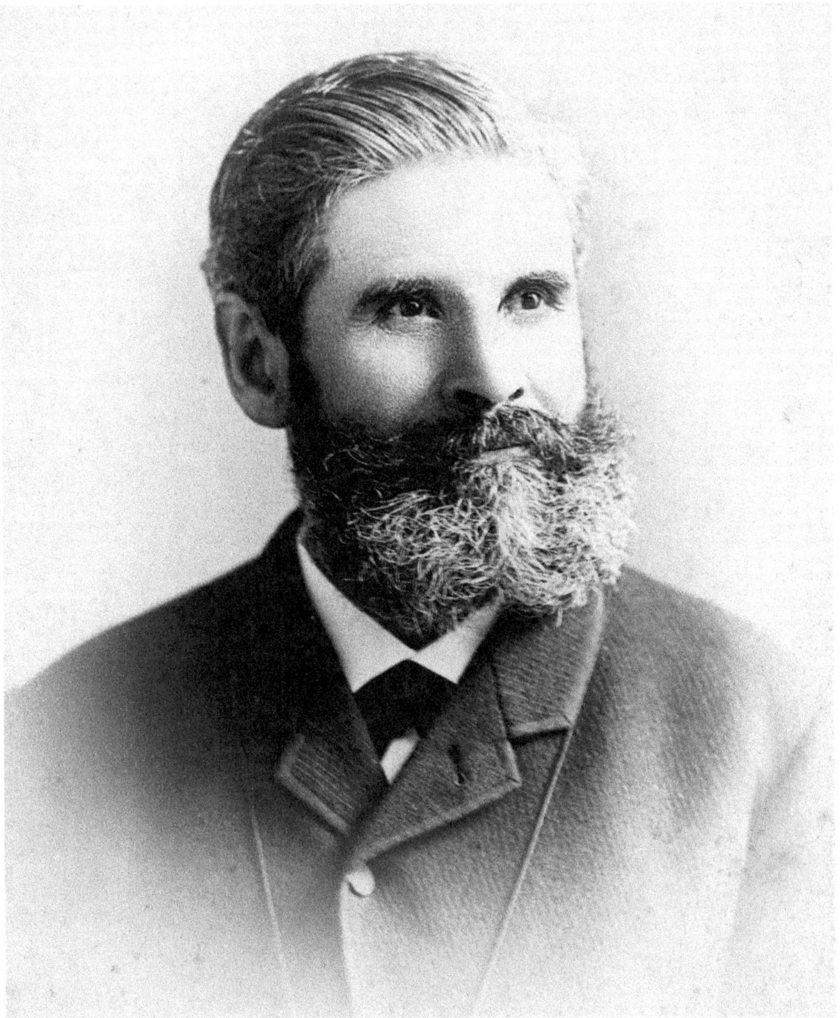

Figure 20.2 Carte de visite photograph of Eugène Boban in 1886, age fifty-two (Smithsonian Institution, National Anthropological Archives).

war of Reform in Mexico during his twenties. He would manage to stay alive through the Prussian siege of Paris in 1870 and the subsequent massacres of the Commune suppression the following year.

He commissioned this later photograph during his two-year stay in New York, one that he sent as a greeting to Thomas Wilson at the Smithsonian. Now fifty-two, he remains handsome, and looks both intelligent and prosperous.

The portrait of Boban taken in his late fifties, which served as a frontis-piece for the first volume of *Documents pour servir à l'histoire du Mexique*, depicts

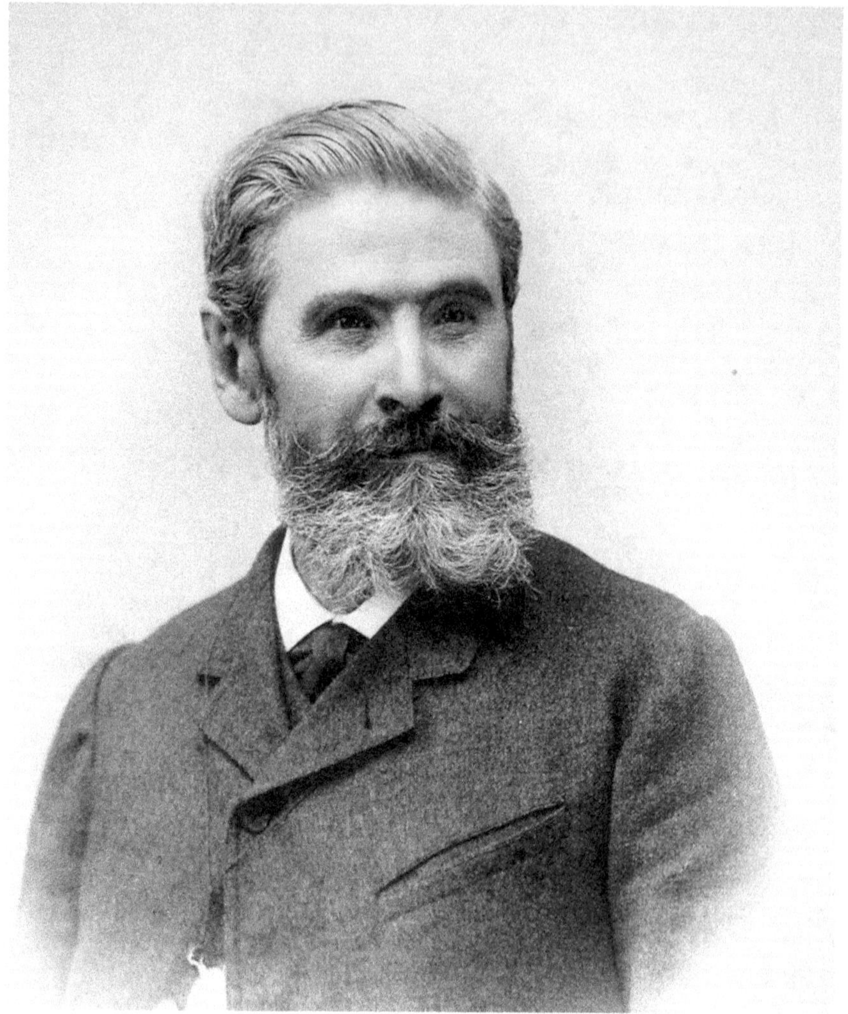

Figure 20.3 Frontispiece photograph of Eugène Boban in 1891, age fifty-seven, *Documents pour servir à l'histoire du Mexique* (Smithsonian Libraries).

the antiquarian and pre-Columbian expert who had finally arrived, taken his place in society as a fully realized authority and gentleman. This image exhibits a profound assurance, unusual good humor, and sweetness of expression for nineteenth-century portraits. He was then at the pinnacle of his career. In 1897, Ernest T. Hamy published sixty photographs of what he considered to be the most important artifacts from North America, Mexico, and Central and South America in the Trocadéro's collection. These same images had been exhibited at the World's Columbian Exposition in Chicago in 1893. More than half of the twenty-one plates depicting the celebrated pre-Columbian objects from Mexico were from Boban's first collection. One of these "master pieces" was the infamous crystal skull, which he denounced three years later.

In his last years his powers gave out, and by the end of his life, he was almost deaf and nearly blind. Following his interment at Montparnasse in 1908 his gravesite was lost after some years, when it was no longer maintained by family or friends and his skeleton was removed to a common ossuary. His reputation largely disappeared as well.

Ironically, Boban's story resurfaced as a result of research into the artifact that he had invented: the Aztec crystal skull.

EPILOGUE

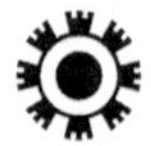

The story of crystal skulls entering respected pre-Columbian collections continued well into the twentieth century. In the 1920s George Gustav Heye, who founded the Museum of the American Indian, purchased a small skull, approximately 1.5 in. (3.8 cm) in Paris. The skull was part of a collection of pre-Columbian objects sold to him by Leo Stein, brother of Gertrude. The catalog card for number 163418.000 describes it only as a "small human skull of crystal" and does not give its dimensions, although it does say it is from Mexico. Heye's wife, Thea, presented the Stein Collection as a gift to the Museum of the American Indian in 1928, but the skull disappeared when the collections were moved to Washington to become part of the Smithsonian Institution. This was the same fate that befell the Smithsonian's own small skull, which William Foshag determined was a fake in the 1950s. The smaller skulls, once probably pendant from rosary beads, are apparently irresistible—and certainly easily pocketed.

The Museum Volkenkunde in Leiden, the Netherlands, still has a small crystal skull, 0.9 by 1.2 in. (2.5 by 3 cm) about the size of the two previously mentioned (Martin Berger, pers. comm. 2016). Leiden received this crystal skull in the early 1950s as a transfer from the Rijksmuseum van Oudheden (National Museum of Antiquities), also in Leiden, which had acquired it in the 1930s.[1]

There is a small crystal skull in the pre-Columbian collection at Dumbarton Oaks in Washington, DC. At 2.7 in. (6.8 cm.) it is slightly bigger than the two just enumerated. Its catalog listing describes it as hollow with a hole in the top: "presumably it was a pendant" (Lothrop, Foshag, and Mahler 1957: cat. # 62, p. 244).

In terms of rock crystal skulls entering private collections in the twentieth century, there is the famous Mitchell-Hedges skull, which has been in private hands since at least 1933. In February of that year, the art gallery owner and dealer Sydney Burney of London offered to sell "a life-size crystal skull with separate jaw, from Mexico"[2] to the American Museum of Natural History in New York. The museum's curators apparently decided not to acquire it, perhaps because it was too expensive. Burney lent the skull to the British Museum in 1936 for research and to compare it with their crystal skull—the one they had acquired from Eugène Boban via Tiffany's in 1898. The journal *Man* published notes on the study of the two skulls, remarking upon their amazing similarity in size and carving (Morant 1936: 105–9).

When Burney placed the skull in a Sotheby's auction in October of 1943, he described it in terms similar to those Boban had used for the British Museum skull in his 1881 catalog, saying in effect that it was a beautiful example of the lapidary arts. Burney's description read, "A superb life-size crystal Carving of a Human Skull, the lower jaw separate, the details are correctly rendered and the carver has given the orbits, zygomatic arches and mastoid processes the similitude of their natural forms."[3] The buyer, who paid £400 for it, was Frederick Mitchell-Hedges, a collector, deep-sea fisherman and adventure writer who dabbled in archeology.

Mitchell-Hedges soon began spinning yarns about his latest purchase. In a letter he wrote to his brother a month later, the skull had already acquired an extraordinary history. "It is fashioned from a single block of transparent rock crystal, exactly life size; scientists put the date at pre-1800 BC and they estimate it took five generations passing from Father to son, to complete."[4]

Six years later, when interviewed by a local Bournemouth newspaper in May 1949, Mitchell-Hedges claimed to have *found* the skull when he "led a British expedition to uncover traces of the lost Maya civilization in Central America in the 1930s." Adding to the lurid details of the legend he was contriving, he said, "It had been taken by the High Priest into the depths of the Temple where he concentrated on it and willed Death (Bournemouth Echo, 31 May 1949)." This yarn may have been inspired by a popular adventure story, "The Crystal Skull," published by Jack McLaren in 1936 and later compiled in *Four Thrilling Adventure Novels* in 1938. The story featured an ethnologist who funds his research by stealing a crystal skull with mystical powers. At one point in the story, he regrets that he cannot tell where he got it, but vows to bequeath it to the British Museum.

When Mitchell-Hedges died in 1959, his adopted daughter, Anna Mitchell-Hedges, inherited the skull. In the early 1960s she went into full promotion mode to enhance its visibility and value. One of her associates in this cause was an art restorer and dealer named Frank Dorland, who helped her develop an extensive publicity campaign. A document produced by Dorland now in the archives of the National Museum of the American Indian claims that rather than her father, it was Anna, at the age of 21, who had found the skull in the ruins of a Mayan complex in 1928, and that the skull has special powers, including warding off evil eyes and defeating all witchcraft with benevolence and angelic forces.[5]

The new story had Anna finding the skull under a stone altar in Lubaantun, a Maya archeological site in what was then British Honduras, now Belize. On different occasions she said she had found it in 1924, 1926, 1927, and 1928, but eventually settled on having found it on her seventeenth birthday, which would have been 1 January 1924. This was actually the only year that Frederick Mitchell-Hedges was at Lubaantun, but his companions on the trip were Lady Mable Richmond Brown and a pet monkey named Michael, not his adopted daughter (Gann 1997: 128). There is no evidence that Anna ever visited the site until shortly before her death, when she went there with a film crew.

In 1972–73 the Museum of the American Indian in New York, under the directorship of Frederick J. Dockstader, exhibited the Mitchell-Hedges crystal skull as a Maya artifact. This, inevitably, endowed it with a legitimacy that it had not enjoyed previously. During preparations for the exhibition, the renowned British archeologist J. Eric S. Thompson, who had himself worked at Lubaantun, tried to warn Dockstader that the skull had not been found at the archeological site, but rather had been purchased from a dealer. This caused the museum director to write anxiously to Anna Mitchell-Hedges requesting clarification. She claimed that her father's purchase of the skull resulted from the fact that Burney had lent him money, and the skull had been the guarantee.[6] Against all advice to the contrary, Dockstader went ahead with plans to exhibit it. Since its first exhibition, the Mitchell-Hedges skull has been extremely well publicized, including in the book *Holy Ice: Bridge to the Subconscious* by the skull's original promoter, Frank Dorland, which appeared in 1992.

Eugène Boban employed subtlety and finesse in his selling of crystal skulls, quietly placing them among legitimate pre-Columbian artifacts to convince purchasers of their authenticity. Mitchell-Hedges used bombast, exaggeration, and tall tales to enhance the credibility of his crystal skull. His daughter certainly followed his example, which others have continued and expanded upon.

When Anna Mitchell-Hedges died at the age of one hundred in 2007, the skull passed into the hands of her widower, Bill Homan. He brought it to the Smithsonian for study the same year and returned with it the following year to appear in a film that the Smithsonian Channel was making about crystal skulls.

The study of the Mitchell-Hedges skull was conducted in the Smithsonian's National Museum of Natural History, with colleagues Tim Rose and Scott Whittaker from the Departments of Mineral Sciences and Scanning Electron Microscopy taking part. The Smithsonian's examination determined that the skull, long claimed to be Maya in origin and nearly four thousand years old, was carved with even more modern tools than those that had been used to fashion the Boban skull now in the British Museum. The rock crystal from which it is carved is extraordinarily free from flaws and inclusions and is polished to an almost mirror-like brilliance. The researchers concluded that the skull was a nearly exact copy of the Boban skull, probably made sometime around the date it first appeared, in 1933 (Walsh 2008b, 2010a). The Mitchell-Hedges skull has the added flourish of a separate mandible, which has drill holes in the underside that align neatly with the pegs in the box made to carry it. Anna Mitchell-Hedges told the well-known British archeologist Norman Hammond, who also excavated at Lubaantun, that the holes were there when she found it (Norman Hammond, pers. comm.). In a 1978 interview, while Dr. Hammond was excavating at other Maya sites, he offered his opinion of the skull saying, "there is not one scrap of evidence to prove that it is even of Pre-Columbian American origin. It could as easily be a memento mori fashioned for some Renaissance ecclesiastic" (Hammond 1978: 4–6). This is exactly the conclusion we have come to regarding the possible origins of all of the crystal skulls we have examined.

There is now in the twenty first century a booming industry in the sale of carved "crystal" skulls. This growth in sales was spurred by the expanding interest in the perceived beneficial effects of crystals in general since the early 1980s and the legacy of the New Age cults that developed in the 1960s and 1970s. On any given day one can find a huge variety of carved skulls for sale online. A recent search yielded skulls ranging in price from $75 for a Tiger Iron Eye skull 2 in. high sold by Etsy to $14,990 for a thirty-two-pound Titan Agate Amethyst Geode skull that is 9 in. high, available from the Chinese carving operation Skullis.com. Although the term "crystal skull" suggests that the skull is carved from clear, colorless quartz, those for sale may be carved from other types of quartz, such as amethyst, citrine, rose quartz, or smoky quartz. One can also purchase "crystal" skulls carved from materials that have little or nothing to do with quartz, such as lapis lazuli, obsidian, dolomite, and even amber (fossilized pine resin). Many of them are natural looking and quite beautiful, seeming to project an aura of mystery. Others are streamlined and rather Deco. Still others call to mind aliens from outer space or Darth Vader of *Star Wars*.

Those who like to do their skull shopping in person can visit the famous stone-carving town of Idar-Oberstein in the Rhineland-Palatine region of southwestern Germany. Here artisans have been carving agate, jasper, and quartz for more than five hundred years and will gladly fulfill a commission to expertly carve a skull from citrine, ruby, or some other beautiful material for $10,000 or more. In Mexico, there is a large workshop selling carved stone objects within view of the Pyramid of the Moon at the archeological site of Teotihuacan north of Mexico City where carvers also manufacture a variety of crystal skulls in quantity for tourists.

As the legends surrounding the Mitchell-Hedges skull invented by father and daughter demonstrate, people seem to like a good story. Some of the skulls are now said to be "ancient" Aztec, Mixtec, Maya, or Tibetan. Other claims are that they were made by higher beings from outer space and bestowed on mankind to aid in the maintenance of our most sacred and ancient traditions, or that they originated with the people of Atlantis. They can become activated through interaction with other powerful skulls, through meditation, and by becoming part of crystal grid networks and matrixes. Skulls carved from different materials have different beneficial properties. Some substances increase clairvoyance, promote beauty, attract wealth, heal stress, or spark passion. The attributes of clear quartz are that it promotes thought and intention. It increases energy and, acting like a radio receiver, enhances intuition. To help a friend or loved one with these or any other issues, you can purchase a skull fashioned from the appropriate material and present it to him or her, or you can meditate on that person's behalf using your own or someone else's skull.

One of the most bizarre legends about the skulls is that they have the capacity to unlock the knowledge of the universe. According to this, there are thirteen large skulls, or possibly four sets of thirteen adding up to fifty-two. The number thirteen is composed of "twelve representing the planets" and the thirteenth is the holder of all knowledge.[7] This skull is usually thought to be the Mitchell-Hedges skull because it has a separate mandible and can therefore speak. When the time is right, uniting the twelve clear crystal skulls in a circle, with a thirteenth skull in the middle, will allow each skull to act as a separate volume of an encyclopedia of all human knowledge. This legend is sometimes attributed to Cherokee or Navaho wisdom traditions, and alternatively to Aztec or Maya beliefs.

These stories are not at all affected by scientific research. Although the internet site CrystalSkulls.com happily posts research findings showing that the crystal skulls in the collections of the British Museum, Musée du quai Branly, and the Smithsonian Institution are modern, it still classifies as "ancient" (i.e., carved more than 1,500 years ago) Sha-na-ra, a crudely carved milky quartz skull found in Mexico in 1995 using "Psychic Archeology"; the Mitchell-Hedges skull; and Max, a well-traveled skull that is purported to have curative powers. Max was given to its present owner by a Tibetan "red hat" lama called Norbu Chen.

In 2011 the producers of a National Geographic Channel documentary visited the stone carving enterprise Skullis in Beijing to conduct their own research on crystal skulls. They wanted to see whether Chinese carvers could recreate the famous Mitchell-Hedges skull to its exact dimensions. Their reasons for this were twofold. First, they wanted to know whether the artisans could create an exact replica, given that one legend now associated with the Mitchell-Hedges skull is that carving it from a single block of crystal is impossible, and yet there it is. Second, they needed a stand-in for the actual skull because Bill Homan refused to lend it for any further study, following the Smithsonian's filmed conclusions about its age and origins. The Chinese carvers managed to accomplish the impossible in relatively little time. It took eight days to carve the replica and three days to polish it.

Skull aficionados got a big boost from Steven Spielberg's fourth Indiana Jones movie, the blockbuster *Indiana Jones and the Kingdom of the Crystal Skull*, whose plot combines several of the standard skull themes. Soviet agents are on the trail of the ancient skull of Akator from Peru, believing that it belongs to an alien life form and will give them the edge in psychic warfare. Indiana Jones and his newfound son, Mutt, beat them to the mountain temple to which they have tracked Akator. They find the temple inhabited by thirteen crystalline skeletons, a familiar number. One of the skeletons is lacking its head!

In the course of the film's climactic ending the missing head appears. It definitely resembles a space being and is much larger than life-size—at least twice the size of the Smithsonian's skull, which weighs thirty-one pounds. Yet Indiana Jones and company toss it around as though it is light as a feather, not sixty or seventy pounds of quartz crystal. Once the skull is reunited with its skeleton, the thirteen beings become a single entity, creating a vortex of overwhelming knowledge. Ultimately, the entire temple collapses into the vortex, uncovering in the process a flying saucer that lifts off and quickly vanishes. At various points in the movie Indiana Jones refers reverently to Mitchell-Hedges, his predecessor in archeological adventuring.

One of the latest entries on the skull scene is Canadian actor Dan Ackroyd's Crystal Head Vodka. This sip of deliciousness is made from quadruple-distilled alcohol mixed with the purest of Newfoundland waters. It is then triple-filtered through carbon and triple-filtered through Herkimer diamonds to achieve its "supernatural purity." Finally, it is hand-poured into an accurate, life-size glass rendering of a human skull. Cheers!

When Eugène Boban made the decision to sell his rock crystal skulls as authentic Aztec artifacts, he could not possibly have imagined the enormous industry in carved skulls—Aztec, Mayan, Tibetan or what have you—that would develop a little over a century later. In the twenty-first century it is possible to buy a crystal skull to deal with any life circumstance or relational problem that might arise for you or any member of your family. The vast industry marketing crystal skulls relies on people's desire to believe that these iconic objects are somehow more than they appear to be. Regardless of their extreme commercialization, however, the crystal skulls retain their beauty, mystery, fascination, and power—at least the power to generate legends and attract avid devotees.

Notes

1. Leiden # RV-3117-1, a bequest in 1931 to National Museum of Antiquities, who transferred it to Leiden in the early 1950s.

2. Burney letter (AMNH 2/17/1933).

3. Sotheby's catalog, 1943.

4. Mitchell-Hedges Official Website, accessed November 2008, since taken down from the internet.

5. National Museum of American Indian—OC 276, folder # 11.

6. National Museum of the American Indian—OC 276, folder # 11.

7. It is currently agreed that there are eight planets in our solar system, and nine if Pluto is reinstated. The identities of the additional three have yet to be revealed.

References

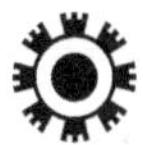

Unpublished Sources

American Museum of Natural History Burney letter 17 February 1933
Archives nationales, Paris
    Ministres central – Emile Jozon, Notaire (XCVI/1033)
Archivo General de la Nación
    Movimiento Marítima
    Segundo Imperio
Bibliothèque central du Musée national d'histoire naturelle
    Boban letters to Hamy MS 2255/245; 2256/153bis & 2256/158-159
Bibliothèque nationale de France
    Albums of Boban letters DMO n.a.f. 21476—21480
British Museum, Anthropology Library and Research Centre
    Maximilien Franck drawings
    John Oliver, 1868 letter to parents
    Augustus Wollaston Franks notebooks
    Hercules Reed notebooks
Hispanic Society of America
    Eugène Boban papers
Library of Congress—Manuscript Division
    Riggs Family papers, 1763–1945 (box 125)
Musée du quai Branly
    Reichlen, Henry. 1962. *Archéologie Mexicaine, Collection E. Boban Duvergé Catalog*. Typed
        manuscript in archives of Musée du quai Branly, Paris.
    Alphonse Pinart papers
Musées d'Angers
    Boban collection of artifacts and notes
Museo Nacional de Antropología archives
    Batres receipts
Museo Nacional de Historia, Chapultepec Castle, Mexico City
    Photograph of Eugène Boban
National Anthropological Archives (NAA)
    John Wesley Powell correspondence (3335)
    Army Medical Museum Records (2587-2615)
National Museum of the American Indian
    Anna Mitchell-Hedges letters (OC 276)

New York Passenger Lists, 1820–1891
  Page 496, City of Puebla
Smithsonian Institution Archives
   United States National Museum (USNM), Accession #17619 W. W. Blake
   The Edward Nelson and Edward Goldman collection, RU 7364
   The William Henry Holmes collection, RU 7084
Universidad Iberoamericana, Mexico City
   Colección Porfirio Díaz (CPD leg. 11, caja 28, doc. 13681)

Published Sources

Acevedo, Ester. 1995. *Testimonios Artísticos de un Episodio Fugaz (1864–1867)*. Mexico City: Museo Nacional de Arte, Instituto Nacional de Bellas Artes.

Alderson, William T. 1992. *Mermaids, Mummies and Mastodons: The Emergence of the American Museum*. Washington, DC: American Association of Museums.

Anderson, Arthur J. O. and Charles Dibble. 1954. *Florentine Codex—General History of the Things of New Spain—Fray Bernardino de Sahagún. Book 8—Kings and Lords*. Santa Fe: School of American Research.

Archives de la Commission Scientifique du Mexique, vol. 1. 1865. Paris: Imprimerie Imperiale.

Archives de la Commission Scientifique du Mexique, vol. 2. 1867a. Paris: Imprimerie Imperiale.

Archives de la Commission Scientifique du Mexique, vol. 3. 1867b. Paris: Imprimerie Imperiale.

Arróniz, Marcos. 1991. *Manual del viajero en México, 1858*, facsimile ed. Mexico City: Librería de Rosa y Bouret; Paris: Instituto Mora.

Baker, Alan R. H. 2001. "Military Service and Migration in Nineteenth-Century France: Some Evidence from Loir-et-Cher." *Transactions of the Institute of British Geographers* 23(2): 193–206.

Bancroft, Hubert Howe. 1889. *History of the North Mexican States and Texas*, vol. 2, 1801–1889. San Francisco: The History Company.

Barnard, Charles Inman. 1900. "Pre-Columbian America The International Congress of Americanists at the World's Fair." *New York Tribune*, 20 August, 9.

Barradère, abbé H. 1834. *Antiquités mexicaines—Relation des trois expéditions du capitaine Dupaix*. Paris: Bureau des antiquités mexicaines, impr. de J. Didot.

Barrister, A. [Alexander Clark Forbes]. 1851. *A Trip to Mexico, Or, Recollections of a Ten-months' Ramble, in 1849–50*. Cornhill, London: Smith, Elder, and Co.

Batres, Leopoldo. 1886a. "Les Ruines de Xochicalco au Mexique." *La Nature* 698(October).

______. 1886b. Letter to *The Two Republics*, 2 December, 3 December.

______. 1910a. *Antigüedades Mejicanas Falsificadas; Falsificación y Falsificadores*. Mexico, DF: F. S. Soria.

______. 1910b. *La Isla de Sacrificios: La Señora Zelia Nuttall de Pinard y Leopoldo Batres*. Mexico City: Tipografía económica.

Baudez, Claude François. 1993. *Jean-Frédéric Waldeck, peintre: le premier explorateur des ruines mayas*. Paris: Editions Hazan.

Behrman, Samuel Nathaniel. 1972. *Duveen*. Boston and Toronto: Little, Brown and Company.

Bellamy, Alex J. 2003. *The Formation of Croatian National Identity*. Manchester: Manchester University Press.

Bernal, Ignacio. 1980. *A History of Mexican Archaeology*. New York: Thames and Hudson.

Bezucha, Robert. 1988. "The French Revolution of 1848 and the Social History of Work." In *Global Crises and Social Movements*, ed. E. Burke, 469–484. Boulder: Westview Press.

Blake, Wilson Wilberforce. 1884. *Catalog of the Collections, Historical & Archaeological of the National Museum of Mexico*. Burlington, Ohio: Hawkeye Job Prints.

———. 1891. *The Toltec Teocallis and Aztec Antiquities: The Antiquities of Mexico as Illustrated by the Archaeological Collections in its National Museum*. New York: C. G. Crawford's Print.

Blumberg, Arnold. 1971. *The Diplomacy of the Mexican Empire, 1683–1867*. Philadelphia: American Philosophical Society.

Boban, Eugène André. 1867. *Inventaire des pièces de la Collection Boban*. Handwritten catalog of 2741 objects now in Musée du quai Branly (D. T. 78.1).

———. 1876a. "Antiquités Mexicaines: Terres Cuites Reproduisant des Déformations Crâniennes." *Le Musée Archéologique*: 45–51.

———. 1876b. "Antiquités Mexicaines: Grelots d'Or Trouvés dans un Tombeau Zapoteco." *Le Musée Archéologique*: 142–47.

———. 1876c. "Antiquités Mexicaines: Le Macuahuitl ou Massue des Anciens Mexicains." *Le Musée Archéologique*: 147–52.

———. 1876d. "Antiquités Mexicaines: Emmanchement de Haches Mexicaines." *Le Musée Archéologique*: 153–4.

———. 1877. "Anciens Etriers Mexicaines." *Le Musée Archéologique*. A. Caix de Saint-Aymour, vol. 2. Paris: Morel et cie.

———. 1878. *Comptoir d'Archéologie Préhistorique: Catalogue des Collections*. Paris: Tremblay.

———. 1881. *Catalogue d'Ouvrages Scientifiques: Bibliographie Paléoethnologique*, 1er partie Science Préhistorique, Archéologique, Ethnologique et Anthropologique, Voyages, etc.; 2ème partie, objets d'antiquité et des collections—Chez Eugène Boban, antiquaire, Comptoir d'archéologie préhistorique. Paris: Tremblay.

———. 1884. *Catalogue d'Ouvrages Scientifiques*. Paris: Tremblay.

———. 1885a. "Le Vase en Obsidienne de Tezcoco au Musée National de Mexico." *Revue d'Ethnographie*: 70–71.

———. 1885b. *Museo Científico*. Mexico: Vanegas.

———. 1891. *Documents pour servir a l'histoire du Mexique—Catalogue Raisonné de la Collection de M.E.–Eugène Goupil*. Paris: Ernest Leroux.

———. 1893. *Histoire de la nation mexicaine depuis le départ d'Aztlan jusqu'à l'arrivée des conquérants espagnols* (et au dela 1607). Manuscrit figuratif accompagné de texte en langue nahuatl ou mexicaine suivi d'une traduction en français par feu J. M. A. Aubin. Reproduction du codex de 1576 appartenant à la collection de M. E. Eugène Goupil, ancienne collection Aubin. Paris: E. Leroux.

———. 1899. *Catalogue de la Bibliothéque de Feu M. E. Eugène Goupil*. Avant-Propos, by E. Boban—V to X ; Notes Explicatives [re] Lord Kingsborough sur les Antiquités du Mexique by Eugène Boban p. 69–114. Paris: Guillemin.

Bolton, Herbert E. 1913. *Guide to Materials for the History of the United States in the Principal Archives of Mexico*. Washington, DC: Carnegie Institution.

Bookmart. 1886. *A Monthly Magazine of Literary and Library Intelligence*. vol. 4. Pittsburgh: Bookmart Publishing Co.

Bournemouth Echo. 31 May 1949. 'The Skull with an Evil Eye'. Bournemouth.

Bragge, William. 1880. *Bibliotheca Nicotiana*. Birmingham: Hudson and Son.

Brands, H. W. 2002. *The Age of Gold*. New York: Doubleday.

Brasseur de Bourbourg, l'abbé. 1866. *Monuments anciens du Mexique*. Paris: Arthus Bertrand.

———. 1868. *Quatre lettres sur le Mexique*. Paris: Maisonneuve.

Bresler, Fenton. 1999. *Napoleon III: A Life*. New York: Carroll & Graff.

Brinton, Daniel G. 1891. "The International Congress of Americanists." *American Anthropologist* 4(1): 33–38.

———. 1893. "The Boturini-Aubin-Goupil Collection of Mexicana." *Science* 21(527): 127–28.

Bullock, William F. L. S. 1824. *Six Months Residence and Travels in Mexico*. London: John Murray.

Bullock, W. F. 1866. *Across Mexico in 1864–1865*. London: Macmillan and Co.

Burke, Edmund. 1988. *Global Crises and Social Movements*. Boulder: Westview Press.

C. 1908. "Eug. Boban." *Revue de l'École d'Anthropologie*: 184.

Calderón de la Barca, Frances. 1970. *Life in Mexico: The Letters of Fanny Calderón de la Barca*. Edited and annotated by Howard T. Fisher and Marion Hall Fisher. New York: Anchor Books.

Calligaro, Thomas, J. Dran, S. Dubernet, G. Poupeau, F. Gendron, E. Gonthier, O. Meslay, and D. Tenorio. 2005. "PIXE reveals that two [of] Murillo's masterpieces were painted on Mexican obsidian slabs." *Nuclear Instruments and Methods in Physics Research Section B: Beam Interactions with Materials and Atoms* 240(1–2): 576–82.

Calligaro, Thomas, Y. Coquinot, I. Reiche, J. Castaing, J. Salomon, G. Ferrand, and Y. Le Fur. 2009. "Dating study of two rock crystal carvings by surface microtopography and by ion beam analysis of hydrogen." *Applied Physics A* 94(4): 871–78.

Cañizares-Esguerra, Jorge. 2001. *How to Write the History of the New World*. Stanford: Stanford University Press.

Capaldi, Nicholas. 1967. *The Enlightenment: The Proper Study of Mankind*. New York: Putnam & Sons.

Castillo, Edward D. 1978. "The Impact of Euro-American Exploration and Settlement." In *The Handbook of North American Indians, California*, vol. 8, ed. Robert F. Heizer, 90–127. Washington, DC: Smithsonian Institution.

Challú, Amilcar. 2015. *Mexico's Real Wages in the Age of the Great Divergence, 1730–1930*. Bowling Green: Bowling Green State University, History Faculty Publications.

Chalmers, Claudine. 1998. "The French in Early California." *Ancestry Magazine* 16(2): 15–21.

Charlton, Cynthia L. Otis. 1993. "Obsidian as Jewelry Lapidary Production in Aztec Otumba, Mexico." *Ancient Mesoamerica* 4: 231–43.

Charnay, Désiré. 1885. *The Ancient Cities of the New World*. New York: Harper Bros.

Christiansen, Rupert. 1996. *Paris Babylon: The Story of the Paris Commune*. New York: Penguin Books.

Ciudad de Mexico. 1976. *La Ciudad de México en 1855–1858*. Mexico City: Talleres Gráficos.

Cohen, Monique. 1998. "Goupil, un collectionneur et un mécène." *Journal de la Société des Américanistes* 84(2): 21–33.

Cohen, Rachel. 2013. *Bernard Berenson: A Life in the Picture Trade*. New Haven: Yale University Press.

Comptoir d'Archéologie Préhistorique. 1908. *Catalogue general: Ages de la Pierre, du Bronze, du Fer; catalogue special des objets provenant de la collection de Boban*. Paris: Schleicher Frères.

Congrès International des Américanistes. 1875. *Compte-Rendu de la Premiére Session*, vol. 1. Nancy and Paris: Maisonneuve et Cie.

Conklin, Alice L. 2013. *In the Museum of Man: Race, Anthropology, and Empire in France, 1850–1950*. Ithaca and London: Cornell University Press.

Cossío, José L. 1994. *Guía Retrospectiva de la Ciudad de México*. Mexico: Inversora Bursatil.

Crimp, Douglas. 1993. *On the Museum's Ruins*. Cambridge: MIT Press.

Cumberland, George. 1827. *An essay on the utility of collecting the best works of the ancient engravers of the Italian School; accompanied by a critical catalog. . . .* London. W. Nicol, Cleveland-Row.

Demeulenaere-Douyère, Christiane. 2009. "Le Mexique s'expose à Paris: Xochicalco, Léon Méhédin et l'exposition universelle de 1867." *Histoire(s) de l'Amérique latine* 3.

———. 2010. *Exotiques Expositions . . . Les Expositions Universelles et les Cultures Extra-Européennes France, 1855–1937*. Paris: Somogy Éditions d'Art, Archives Nationales.

Derbec, Etienne. 1964. *A French Journalist in the California Gold Rush: The Letters of Etienne Derbec*. Edited by A. P. Nasatir. Georgetown, California: Talisman Press.

Desmond, Laurence Gustave and Phyllis Mauch Messenger. 1988. *A Dream of Maya: Augustus and Alice Le Plongeon in Nineteenth-Century Yucatan*. Albuquerque: University of New Mexico Press.

Díaz del Castillo, Bernal. 1956. *The Discovery and Conquest of Mexico 1517–1521*. New York: Farrar, Straus and Cudahy.

Digby, Adrian. 1936. "Comments on the Morphological Comparison of Two Crystal Skulls." *Man: A Monthly Record of Anthropological Science* 36: 107–9.

Doutrelaine, Louis T. 1867a. "La Pierre de Tlanepantla." In *Archives de la Commission Scientifique du Mexique*, vol. 3, 11–20. Paris: Imprimerie Impériale.

______. 1867b. "Un Manuscrit Mexicain de la Collection Boban." In *Archives de la Commission Scientifique du Mexique*, vol. 3, 120–133. Paris: Imprimerie Impériale.

Dumoutier, Gustave. 1882. *Les Stations du l'Homme Préhistorique sur les Plateaux du Grand-Morin (Seine-et-Marne)*. Paris: E. Boban.

Durán, Diego. 1994. *The History of the Indies of New Spain*. Translated, annotated, and with an introduction by Doris Heyden. Norman: University of Oklahoma Press.

Edison, Paul N. 1999. "Latinizing America: the French Scientific Study of Mexico 1830–1930." PhD dissertation. New York: Columbia University.

Emery, Elizabeth and Laura Morowitz. 2004. "From the living room to the museum and back again: The collection and display of medieval art in the fin de siècle." *Journal of the History of Collections* 16(2): 285–309.

Eudel, Paul. 1887. *Le Truquage, les contrefaçons dévoilées*. Paris: E. Dentu.

______. 1907. *Trucs et truqueurs*. Paris: Librairie Moliére

Evans, Susan Toby and David L. Webster, eds. 2001. *Archaeology of Ancient Mexico and Central America: An Encyclopedia*. New York: Garland Publishing.

Evans, Susan Toby. 2010. *Ancient Mexican Art at Dumbarton Oaks*. Washington, DC: Dumbarton Oaks.

Fauvet-Berthelot, Marie-France, Leonardo López Luján, and Susana Guimarães. 2007. "Six personnages en quête d'objets: histoire de la collection archéologique de la Real Expedición Anticuaria en Nouvelle Espagne." *Gradhiva: Revue d'Anthropologie et de Muséologie* 6: 104–26.

Feest, Christian. 1990. "Vienna's Mexican Treasures: Aztec, Mixtec, and Tarascan Works from the 16th Century Austrian Collections." *Archiv für Völkerkunde* 44: 1–66.

Fernández, Miguel Angel. 1988. *Historia de los Museos de México*. Mexico City: Banamex.

"For Huge Fortune A Claim Refused." 1935. *Evening Post* 120(79): 4.

Foshag, William F. 1953. "A Visit to Idar-Oberstein." *Gems and Gemology* 2(11): 339–42.

______. 1957. "Mineralogical Studies on Guatemalan Jade." *Smithsonian Miscellaneous Collections* 135(5): 1–60.

Foucrier, Annick. 2005. "The French and the Pacific World, 17th–19th centuries." In *The Pacific World Lands: Peoples and History of the Pacific 1500–1900*, 17–30. Hampshire: Ashgate.

Franck, Maximilien. 1831. *Bulletin de la Société de Géographie* 93(January): 116–26.

Frémont, Jessie Benton. [1878] 1960. *A Year of American Travel: Narrative of Personal Experience*. San Francisco: San Francisco Book Club of California.

Galvan Rivera, D. Mariano. 1987. *Colección de las Efemérides publicadas en el Calendario Del Mas Antiguo Galvan desde su fundación hasta el Año de 1987*. Mexico City: Antigua Libreria de Murguia. S.A.

Gann, Thomas. 1997. *Mystery Cities of the Maya*. Kempton, IL: Adventures Unlimited Press.

García Icazbalceta, Joaquin. 1881. *Don Fray Juan de Zumárraga*. Mexico City: Antigua Libreria de Andrade y Morales.

Génin, Auguste. 1910. *Notes sur le Mexique*. Mexico City: Imprenta Lacaud.

______. 1933. *Les Français au Mexique du XVI Siècle à Nos Jours*. Paris: Nouvelles Editions Argo.

Gibson-Wood, Carol. 1997. "Classification and Value in a Seventeenth-Century Museum: William Courten's Collection." *Journal of the History of Collections* 9(1): 61–77.

Glass, John. 1975a. "A Census of Native Middle American Pictorial Manuscripts," In *Handbook of Middle American Indians, Guide to Ethnohistorical Sources*, part 3, vol. 14, 81–252. Austin: University of Texas Press.

______. 1975b. "Annotated References." In *Handbook of Middle American Indians, Guide to Ethnohistorical Sources*, part 4, vol. 15, 537–734. Austin: University of Texas Press.

Gutfleish B., and J. Menzhausen. 1989. "How a Kunstkammer Should Be Formed." *Journal of the History of Collections* 1: 11.

Hall, James. 1996. *Hall's Dictionary of Subjects and Symbols in Art*. London: John Murray.

Hammond, Norman. 1978. "Crystal Skull to Cuello." In *Brukdown: The Magazine of Belize* 8: 4–5, 30.

Hamy, E. T. 1883. "Mémoires Originaux—Note sur une Inscription Chronographique de la fin de la période Aztéque, appartenant au Musée du Trocadéro." *Revue D'Ethnographie* 2: 198–02.

______. 1884. *Anthropologie du Mexique in Recherches Zoologiques pour servir a l'histoire de la Faune de l'Amerique Central et du Mexique*. 1st Part. Paris: M. Milne Edwards.

______. 1897a. "Note sur une figurine Yucatèque de la Collection Boban-Pinart au Musée d'Ethnographie du Trocadéro." *Journal de la Société des Américanistes de Paris* 2: 105–8.

______. 1897b. *Galerie Américaine du Musée d'ethnographie du Trocadéro: choix de pièces archéologiques et ethnographiques*. Paris: Ernest Leroux.

Hannan, Caryn. 2008. *Connecticut Biographical Dictionary*. Hamburg, MI: State History Publications.

Harvey, Joy. 1997. *"Almost a Man of Genius": Clémence Royer, Feminism, and Nineteenth-Century Science*. New Brunswick: Rutgers University Press.

Hassig, Ross. 1992. *War and Society in Ancient Mesoamerica*. Berkeley: University of California Press.

Heizer, Robert F., and Alan F. Almquist. 1971. *The Other Californians: Prejudice and Discrimination under Spain, Mexico, and the United States to 1920*. Berkeley: University of California Press.

Hicks, Dan. 2013. "Characterizing the World Archaeology Collections of the Pitt Rivers Museum." In *World Archaeology at the Pitt Rivers Museum*, eds. Dan Hicks and Alice Stevenson, 1–15. Oxford: Archaeopress.

Holmes, William Henry. 1884. "Evidences of the Antiquity of Man on the Site of the City of Mexico." *Transactions of the Anthropological Society of Washington* 3: 68–81.

______. 1885. "The Monoliths of San Juan Teotihuacan Mexico." *The American Journal of Archaeology and of the History of the Fine Arts* 1(4): 361–71.

______. 1886. "The Trade in Spurious Mexican Antiquities." *Science* 7(159): 170–72.

______. 1889. "On some spurious Mexican antiquities and their relation to ancient art" *Annual Report of the Smithsonian Institution* 1: 319–34.

Horne, Alistair. 2006. *La Belle France: A Short History*. New York: Vintage Books.

______. 2007. *The Fall of Paris: The Siege and Commune 1870–71*. New York: Penguin.

Hudson, Travis, and Craig Bates. 2015. *Treasures from Native California*. Edited by Thomas Blackburn and John R. Johnson. London and New York: Routledge.

Jenkins, Ian. 2003. "Ideas of Antiquity: Classical and Other Ancient Civilizations in the Age of Enlightenment." In *Enlightenment: Discovering the World in the Eighteenth Century*, ed. Kim Sloan, 168–77. London: British Museum Press.

Jover, Manuel. 2010. "L'ultime triomphe des vanités." *Connaissance des Arts* 679 (February): 36–43.

Jubinal, Achille. 1846. *La Armería real ou collection des principals pièces de la Galerie d'Armes Anciennes de Madrid*. Supplement. Paris: Dessins de M. Gaspard Sensi.

Kandell, Jonathan. 1988. *La Capital: The Biography of Mexico City*. New York: Random House.

Keen, Benjamin. 1971. *The Aztec Image in Western Thought*. New Brunswick: Rutgers University Press.

Kingsborough, Edward King Viscount. 1831. *Antiquities of Mexico*, vols. 1–5. London: A. Aglio.

Knapton, Ernest John. 1971. *France: An Interpretive History*. New York: Scribner.

Kohlstedt, Sally Gregory. 1980. "Henry A. Ward: the merchant naturalist and American museum development." *Journal of the Society for the Bibliography of Natural History* 9(4): 647–61.

Kunz, George Frederick. 1887. "Two Remarkable Mexican Antiquities." *The Studio. A journal devoted to the Fine Arts* August.

———. 1890. *Gems and Precious Stones in the United States, Canada and Mexico.* New York: The Scientific Publishing Co.

Kunz, George Frederick, and Charles Hugh Stevenson. 1908. *The Book of the Pearl.* New York: The Century Company.

Kunz, George Frederick, and Marie Beynon Ray. 1927. "American Travels of a Gem Collector." Reprinted in *The Saturday Evening Post*, 10 December.

Lartet, Édouard and Henry Christy. 1864. "Caverne du Périgord." *Extraits de la Revue Archéologique ou Recueil de Documents et de Mémoires.* Paris: Didier.

Leavitt, George A. 1886a. *The Boban Collection; Part the First: Antiquities, Curios and Coins.* New York: Geo A. Leavitt.

———. 1886b. *The Boban Collection; Part the Second: Valuable Books and Manuscripts.* New York: Geo A. Leavitt.

———. 1887. *The Boban Collection of Antiquities, Curiosities, Manuscripts, etc. Part II.* New York: Geo A. Leavitt.

Le Goff, Armelle and Nadia Prévost Urkidi. 2009. *Commission de exploration scientifique du Mexique* (1862–1893). Paris: Archives Nationales.

———, eds. 2011. *Homme de Guerre, Homme de Science? Le Colonel Doutrelaine au Mexique. Edition critique de ses dépêches (1864–1867).* Collection de Documents Inédits sur l'histoire de France, Section d'Histoire Contemporaine et du Temps present, 55. Paris: Édition du Comité des travaux historique et scientifique.

León y Gama, Antonio de. 1792. *Descripción histórica y cronológica de las dos piedras.* Mexico City: Impr. de Don F. de Zúñiga y Ontiveros.

Lombardo de Ruiz, Sonia. 1994. *El pasado prehispánico en la cultura nacional: memoria hemerográfica, 1877–1911.* México, DF: Instituto Nacional de Antropología e Historia.

Longpérier, Adrien de. 1850. *Notice des monuments exposés dans la salle des antiquités américaines (Mexique et Pérou), au musée du Louvre.* Paris: Vinchon.

López Luján, Leonardo. 2009. "'El adiós y triste queja del gran Calendario Azteca:' El incesante peregrinar de la Piedra del Sol." *Arqueología Mexicana* 91: 78–83.

———. 2015. *El capitán Guillermo Dupaix y su álbum arqueológico de 1794.* Mexico City: Ediciones del Museo Nacional de Antropología. Instituto Nacional de Antropología e Historia.

López Luján, Leonardo, and Marie-France Fauvet-Berthelot. 2005. *Aztèques—La collection de sculptures du Musée du quai Branly.* Lavaur: Société de l'imprimerie Artistique.

Lothrop, Samuel K., William. F. Foshag, and Joy Mahler. 1957. *Robert Woods Bliss Collection of Pre-Columbian Art.* London: Phaidon Press.

Madier de Montjau, Édouard. 1875. "Homélies sur les Évangiles en Langue Nahuatl." In *Archives de la Société Américaine de France* 2(1): 269–75. Paris: Leroux.

Maillefert, Eugenio. 1992. *Directorio del Comercio del Imperio Mexicano para el año de 1867.* Facsimile Ed. Mexico City: Instituto Dr. José María Luis Mora.

Marroqui, José María. 1969. *La Ciudad de Mexico*, vol. 2. México: Jesús Medina.

Matos Moctezuma, Eduardo. 1990. "Imperial Tenochtitlan." In *Mexico: Splendors of Thirty Centuries.* New York: Metropolitan Museum of Art.

Maurer, M. A., and R. Vaufrey. 1929. "Louis Capitan 1854–1929." *Journal de la Société des Américanistes* 21(2): 402–9.

Mauriès, Patrick. 2002. *Cabinets of Curiosities.* London: Thames and Hudson.

Mayer, Brantz. 1847. *Mexico as It Was and as It Is.* Philadelphia: G. B. Zieber & Co.

Mazaroff, Stanley. 2010. *Henry Walters and Bernard Berenson, Collector and Connoisseur*. Baltimore: The Johns Hopkins University Press.

McAllen, M. M. 2014. *Maximilian and Carlota: Europe's Last Empire in Mexico*. San Antonio: Trinity University Press.

McAndrew, John. 1965. *The Open-Air Churches of Sixteenth-Century Mexico*. Cambridge, MA: Harvard University Press.

McLendon, Sally. 2001. "California feather blankets: objects of wealth and status in two nineteenth-century worlds." In *Studies in American Indian Art: A Memorial Tribute to Norman Feder*, ed. Christian Feest, 132–61. ERNAS Monograph 2. Vienna: European Review of Native American Studies.

McPhee, Peter. 1992. *A Social History of France, 1780–1880*. London: Routledge.

Melgar y Serrano, José María. 1871. "Estudio sobre la antigüedad y el origen de la cabeza colossal de tipo etiópico que existe en Hueyapan en el canton de los Tuxtlas." *Boletín de la Sociedad Mexicana de Geografía y Estadística*, época 2, III: 104–9.

Merriman, John. 2014. *Massacre: The Life and Death of the Paris Commune*. New York: Basic Books.

Miller, Mary, and Simon Martin. 2004. *Courtly Art of the Ancient Maya*. San Francisco: Thames and Hudson.

Mission Scientifique. 1878. *Notice sur le Muséum ethnographique des missions scientifiques rédigée par chacun des missionnaires scientifiques sur les objets qu'il a rapportés*. Paris: Palais de l'Industrie.

Morant, G. M. 1936. "A Morphological Comparison of Two Crystal Skulls." *Man: A Monthly Record of Anthropological Science* 36: 105–7.

Morley, Grace. 1968. *Pre-Columbian Art, Collection given by Mrs. Alice and Mr. Nasli Heeramaneck*. National Museum, New Delhi: Caxton Press.

Morrison, Allen. 2003. "The Tramways of Mexico." Retrieved 8 August 2018 from http://www.tramz.com/mx/tto.html.

Mortillet, Adrien de. 1908. "Eugène Boban." *Revue Mensuelle Illustrée d'Archéologie et d'Anthropologie* 6: 188.

Mortillet, Gabriel de and Amédée Caix de Saint-Aymour, eds. 1872. "Collection d'antiquités mexicaines de M. Boban." *Indicateur de L'archéologue et du Collectionneur* 3: 174–77.

Moses, Claire Goldberg. 1984. *French Feminism in the Nineteenth Century*. Albany: State University of New York Press.

Museo Nacional de Antropología. 1992. *Catálogo del Archivo Histórico (1831–1936)*, vol. 1. Mexico City: Instituto Nacional de Antropología.

Nasatir, Abraham P. 1945. *French Activities in California*. Stanford: Stanford University Press.

Newmark, Harris. 1916. *Sixty Years in Southern California 1853–1913*. New York: Knickerbocker Press.

Nuttall, Zelia. 1910. "The Island of Sacrificios." *American Anthropologist* 12(New Series).

Orrin, G. W., Benito Nichols, and E. W. Orrin. 1886. *Guide to the Aztec Fair: Mexico Past and Present*. Mexico City: Orrin Bros. and Nichols.

Pagden, Anthony, and J. H. Elliott. 1986. *Letters from Mexico: Hernán Cortés*. New Haven: Yale University Press.

Parmenter, Ross. 1966. *Explorer, Linguist, and Ethnologist, A Descriptive Bibliography of the Published Works of Alphonse Louis Pinart, with Notes on His Life*. Los Angeles: Southwest Museum.

Pasztory, Esther. 1982. "Three Aztec Masks of the God Xipe." In *Falsifications and Misreconstructions of Pre-Columbian Art*, ed. Elizabeth P. Benson and Elizabeth H. Boone, 77–105. Washington, DC: Dumbarton Oaks.

Paz, Ireneo. 1895. *Leyendas Historicas escritas por Ireneo Paz; Segunda Serie, Leyenda Primera. Antonio Rojas*. Mexico City: Lit. y Encuadernacion de Ireneo Paz.

______. 1997. *Algunas campañas. Tomo I*. Mexico: Fondo de Cultura Económica.

Pérez Siller, Javier, and David Skerritt. 2010. *México Francia: Memoria de una sensibilidad común Siglos XIX–XX*, vol. 3–4. Mexico: Editorial EON.

Pinart, Alphonse L. 1883. *Catalog de livres rares et précieux Manuscrits et Imprimés* . . . Paris: Vve Adolphe Labitte.

Podgorny, Irina. 2008. "Portable antiquities: transportation, ruins, and communication in 19th century archaeology." *Historia ciencia saude-Manguinhos* 15(3): 577–95.

Price, Roger. 1972. *The Second French Republic: A Social History*. Ithaca: Cornell University Press.

______. 2004. *People and Politics in France 1848–1870*. Cambridge: Cambridge University Press.

Prost, Antoine. 1968. *Histoire de l'enseignement en France*. Paris: A. Colin.

Rau, Charles. 1879. "The Palenque Tablet in the United States National Museum" In *Smithsonian Institution Contributions to Knowledge*, 331, 1–76. Washington, DC: Smithsonian Institution.

Reichlen, Henry, and Robert F. Heizer. 1963. "The Scientific Expedition of Léon de Cessac to California, 1877–1879." In *The French and the Pacific World, 17th—19th Centuries*. Hampshire: Ashgate.

Reville, Albert. 1898. *Antiquités mexicaines. Les aventures d'une collection*. Rennes: F. Simon Impr.

Revue Scientifique de la France et de l'Etranger. 1878. *Les Missions Scientifiques: Muséum ethnographique du Palais de l 'industrie*. Paris: Librairie Germer Baillière.

Riviale, Pascal. 1999. "La Science en Marche au Pas Cadencé: les Recherches Archéologiques et Anthropologiques durant l'Intervention Française au Mexique (1862–1867)." *Journal de la Société des Américanistes* 85: 307–41.

______. 2001. "Boban ou les Aventures d'un Antiquaire au Pays des Américanistes." *Journal de la Société des Américanistes* 87: 351–62.

______. 2011. "Postface: Le colonel Doutrelaine, la Commission scientifique et les collections mexicaines." In *Homme de Guerre, Homme de Science? Le Colonel Doutrelaine au Mexique, Edition critique de ses Dépeches (1864–1867)*, eds. Armelle Le Goff and Nadia Prévost Urkidi. Collection de Documents Inédits sur l'histoire de France, Section d'Histoire Contemporaine et du Temps Present, 55: 453–58. Paris: Édition du Comité des travaux historique et scientifique.

Robertson, William Spence. 1940. "The Tripartite Treaty of London." *The Hispanic American Historical Review* 20(2): 167–189.

Rose, Timothy R., and Jane MacLaren Walsh. 2016. "The Stone Faces of Teotihuacan: Insights into Their Use, Manufacture and Sources" *Journal of Archaeological Science: Reports* 1–14. http://dx.doi.org/10.1016/j.jasrep.2016.06.057.

Rosny, Léon de. 1889. "Exposition Universelle." *Journal officiel de la République française* 29(Novembre 1889): 5938–40.

Russell, John. 1989. *Paris*. New York: Harry N. Abrams.

Rutsch, Mechthild. 2004. "Natural History, National Museum and Anthropology in Mexico." *Perspectivas Latinoamericanas* 1: 89–122.

Sabatini, Rafael. 1900. *The Life of Cesare Borgia*. New York: Brentanos.

Saint-Martin, Vivien. 1867. *L'Année Géographique*. Paris: Librairie de L. Hachette.

Sala, George Augustus. 1868. *Notes and Sketches of the Paris Exhibition*. London: Tinsley Brothers.

Sax, Margaret, J. M. Walsh, I. C. Freestone, A. H. Rankin, and N. D. Meeks. 2008. "The origin of two purportedly pre-Columbian Mexican quartz crystal skulls." *The Journal of Archaeological Science* 2751–60. http://dx.doi.org/10.1016/j.jasrep.2008.05.007.

Sax, Margaret, and Nigel Meeks. 2009. "The manufacture of a small crystal skull purported to be from ancient Mexico." *The British Museum Technical Research Bulletin* 3: 47–55.

Schávelzon, Daniel. 1994. "La arqueología del imperialismo: la invasión francesa a México (1864–1867)." *Mesoamérica*, cuaderno 28: 321–35.

Schwarz, Shirley J. 1996. *Greek Vases in the National Museum of Natural History, Smithsonian Institution, Washington, DC*. Rome: L'Erma di Bretschneider.

Sellen, Adam T. 2015. *The Orphans of the Muse*. Mérida: Universidad Nacional Autónoma de México.

Shapiro, Ann-Louise. 1985. *Housing the Poor of Paris, 1850–1902*. Madison: University of Wisconsin Press.

SI (Smithsonian Institution). 1869. *Annual Report of the Board of Regents of the Smithsonian Institution . . . for the year 1868*. Washington, DC: Government Printing Office.

Siméon, Rémi. 1977. *Diccionario de la Lengua Nahuatl o Mexicana*. Mexico: Siglo Veintiuno.

Simmonds, Peter Lund. 1858. *The Dictionary of Trade Products*. London: Routledge.

Simpson, Colin. 1986. *Artful Partners: Bernard Berenson and Joseph Duveen*. New York: Macmillan Publishing Co.

Solís, Felipe. 2009. *Teotihuacan Cité des Dieux*. Paris: Somogy Editions D'art.

Sotheby & Co. 1943. Catalogue of valuable Chinese Porcelain. London: Sotheby & Co.

Stephens, John L. 1841. *Incidents of Travel in Central America, Chiapas, and Yucatan*, vol. 1. New York: Harper & Bros.

St. John, Percy B. 1848. *The French Revolution of 1848: The Three Days of February*. New York: Putnam.

Tait, Hugh. 1992. "Reinhold Vasters: goldsmith, restorer and prolific faker." In *Why Fakes Matter*, ed. Mark Jones. London: British Museum Press.

Taladoire, Eric, and Jane MacLaren Walsh. 2014. "José María Melgar y Serrano. Viajero, coleccionista o saqueador?" *Arqueología Mexicana*, 129: 81–85.

Tissandier, Gaston. 1884. "Un Guerrier Aztèque de l'armée de Montézuma a l'époque de la conquète Espagnole (1521)." *La Nature* 25(601): 23–24.

______. 1889. "Les Antiquités Mexicaines a L'Exposition Universelle de 1889." *La Nature*: 119–20.

Tovar de Teresa, Guillermo. 1992. *La Ciudad de los Palacios: crónica de un patrimonio perdido, vols I & II*. Mexico City: Fundación Cultural Televisa, A.C.

Traugott, Mark. 1988. "Interdependencies in Global Crises: France and England in the Mid-Nineteenth Century." In *Global Crises and Social Movements*, ed. E. Burke. Boulder: Westview Press.

______.1993. *The French Worker: Autobiographies from the Early Industrial Era*. Berkeley: University of California Press.

Vanderwood, Paul J. 1992. *Disorder and Progress: Bandits, Police and Mexican Development*. Wilmington: Scholarly Resources.

Van Meer, Ron. 2005. "Philipp Joseph Becker: A German Businessman and Collector in 19th-Century Mexico": *Baessler-Archiv Band* 53: 27–41.

Verneau, Dr. R. 1888a. "Le Tatouage et la peinture corporelle: Les Pintaderas" *La Nature* 783: 58–62.

______. 1888b. "Un Tintinnabulum Bouddhique trouvé au Pérou." *La Nature* 795: 495–6.

______. 1889. "Le Papyrus Egyptien, La Tapa Océanienne et le Papier des Anciens Mexicains." *La Nature*: 811: 43–44.

______. 1908. "Nécrologie – Eugène Boban." *l'Anthropologie* 19: 369–70.

Walsh, Jane MacLaren. 1997. "Crystal Skulls and Other Problems." In *Exhibiting Dilemmas: Issues of Representation at the Smithsonian*, eds. Amy Henderson and Adrienne L. Kaeppler, 116–37. Washington, DC: Smithsonian Institution Press.

______. 2002. "Collections as Currency." In *Anthropology, History, and American Indians: Essays in Honor of William Curtis Sturtevant*, Smithsonian Contributions to Anthropology, vol. 44, eds. William L. Merrill and Ives Goddard, 201–09. Washington, DC: Smithsonian Institution Press.

______. 2004. "La Vasija Obsidiana de Texcoco." *Arqueología Mexicana* 12(70): 66–67.

______. 2006. "Falsificando la Historia: Los falsos objetos prehispánicos." *Arqueología Mexicana* 14(82): 20–25.

______. 2008a. "The Dumbarton Oaks Tlazolteotl: Looking Beneath the Surface." *Journal de la Société des Américanistes* 94(1): 7–43.

______. 2008b. "Legend of the Crystal Skulls." *Archaeology* 61(3): 36–41.

______. 2010a. "Skull of Doom." *Apollo*, February 42–47.

______. 2010b. "Retrato de una colección—El Museo Nacional en 1865." *Arqueología Mexicana* 17(102): 78–83.

Walsh, Jane MacLaren, and David R. Hunt. 2013. "The Fourth Skull: A Tale of Authenticity and Fraud." *The Appendix* 1(2). http://theappendix.net/issues/2013/4/the-fourth-skull-a-tale-of-authenticity-and-fraud.

Walsh, Jane MacLaren, and Timothy R. Rose. 2014. "Máscaras Teotihuacanas; Una tipología preliminar." *Arqueología Mexicana* 21(126): 78–85.

Washburne, E. B. 1886. *Recollections of a Minister to France 1869–1877, vols. I & II*. New York: Scribner.

Williams, Elizabeth A. 1985a. "Anthropological Institutions in Nineteenth-Century France." *ISIS* 76(3): 331–348.

______. 1985b. "Art and Artifact at the Trocadero." In *Objects and Others*, ed. George W. Stocking, Jr., 146–66. Madison: University of Wisconsin Press.

Wilson, David M. 2002. *The British Museum—A History*. London: The British Museum Press.

Wilson, Thomas. 1890. "Anthropology Congresses, National and International, held in Paris during, and a part of, The French Exposition of 1889." *The American Naturalist* 24(278): 197–200.

______. 1896. "Prehistoric Art; or The Origin of Art as Manifested in the Works of Prehistoric Man." In *Report of the US National Museum*. Washington, DC: Smithsonian Institution.

Wright, Gordon. 1987. *France in Modern Times*. New York and London: W.W. Norton.

Zaremba, Charles W. 1888. *The Merchants' and Tourists' Guide to Mexico*. Chicago: Althrop Publishing House.

INDEX

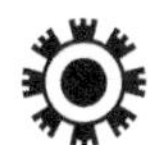